2006

2007

2008

2009

2010

2011

2012

2013

2014

2015

2016

**图书在版编目（CIP）数据**

爱我中华 护我长城 ：2006-2016 / 中国文化遗产研究院编．-- 北京 ：文物出版社，2017.10

ISBN 978-7-5010-4830-4

Ⅰ．①爱… Ⅱ．①中… Ⅲ．①长城－文物保护－中国 Ⅳ．① K928.77

中国版本图书馆 CIP 数据核字（2016）第 281105 号

# 爱我中华 护我长城

## 长城保护 2006—2016

中国文化遗产研究院 编

责任编辑：张小舟

书籍设计：特木热

责任印制：梁秋卉

出版发行：文物出版社

社 址：北京市东直门内北小街 2 号楼

邮 编：100007

网 址：http://www.wenwu.com

邮 箱：web@wenwu.com

经 销：新华书店

印 刷：北京金彩印刷有限公司

开 本：889mm × 1194mm 1/16

印 张：22.5

版 次：2017 年 10 月第 1 版

印 次：2017 年 10 月第 1 次印刷

书 号：ISBN 978-7-5010-4830-4

定 价：360.00 元

# 爱我中华 护我长城
## 长城保护 2006—2016

Love China · Protect the Great Wall
Conservation of the Great Wall
2006-2016

中国文化遗产研究院 编
CHINESE ACADEMY OF CULTURAL HERITAGE

文物出版社

# 目录

# Table of Contents

# 序

长城是中华民族的精神象征，是我国现存体量最大、分布最广的文化遗产，以其上下两千年、纵横数万里的时空跨度，成为人类历史上宏伟壮丽的建筑奇迹和无与伦比的文化景观。做好长城保护，对于展示中华民族灿烂文明，坚定文化自信，弘扬社会主义核心价值观，促进经济社会发展，具有十分重要的意义。

党中央、国务院历来重视长城保护。新中国成立伊始即开展长城调查与保护工作。1961 年起，一批长城重要点段被陆续公布为全国重点文物保护单位。1984 年，邓小平同志号召“爱我中华，修我长城”，推动了长城保护工作全面展开。1987 年，长城被联合国教科文组织列入《世界遗产名录》。2006 年，国务院颁布《长城保护条例》，进一步明确了各级政府和有关部门的法定职责。

党的十八大以来，习近平总书记对长城保护做出重要指示，国务院召开专题会议研究长城保护工作。长城沿线各级党委、政府始终把长城作为文化遗产保护工作的重中之重，积极开展法规体系建设、资源调查认定、保护维修、执法督察等工作，社会各界积极参与。

2014 年，“长城保护工程”结束，经过十年的努力，长城保护工作取得很大进展，一方面，基本摸清了长城的“家底”，另一方面，长城保护管理工作的被动局面也开始得到扭转，长城保护状况明显改善，长城保护社会效应不断彰显，长城精神得到传承弘扬，“政府主导，社会参与”的长城保护新局面逐渐形成。

为回顾、总结过去十年“长城保护工程”的成功经验，进一步厘清当前长城保护工作面临的机遇与挑战。值此《长城保护条例》颁布施行十周年之际，受国家文物局委托，中国文化遗产研究院以“长城保护工程”十年总结评估和《长城保护条例》实施情况执法专项督察成果为基础，组织编写了本报告。报告总结了中国

# Preface

The Great Wall is Chinese people's spiritual symbol. It is the most magnificent and widely spread cultural heritage of China. Existing over 2,000 years in time and stretching over thousands of kilometers on the globe, the Great Wall is the most spectacular architectural wonder and unparalleled historical and cultural landscape in human history. A sound conservation of the Great Wall has a great significance on displaying of the splendid civilization of the Chinese people, strengthening cultural confidence, carrying forward the core socialist values and boosting economic and social developments.

The Central Committee of the CPC and the State Council have always attached great importance to the conservation of the Great Wall. Right after the founding of the People's Republic of China, the Great Wall survey and conservation works were under way. Since 1961, a number of important sections of the Great Wall have been named the state priority protected sites. In 1984, comrade Deng Xiaoping called for people to "Love China, and repair the Great Wall", which boosted a comprehensive conservation of the Great Wall. In 1987, the Great Wall was listed on the UNESCO World Heritage list. In 2006, the State Council issued the *Regulation on the Conservation of Great Wall,* which further defined the legal duties of the governments at all levels and relevant departments.

Since the 18th National Congress of the communist Party, general secretary Xi Jinping has made important instructions on the conservation of the Great Wall. The State Council held special meetings studying the conservation of the Great Wall. The Chinese government always set the conservation of the Great Wall a top priority in cultural heritage conservation. Besides proactively building a legal framework, it also conducts resource survey and identification, conservation and restoration, law enforcement supervision works. All social circles joined the initiative as well.

In 2014, after 10-year hard work, the basic condition of the Great Wall was surveyed and the conservation efforts were put on the right track. The situation of the Great Wall conservation has been improved greatly and the social benefits of the conservation efforts were widened. The "Great Wall Spirit" was carried forward. With social participation, a government led conservation drive has been gradually formed.

In order to review and summarize the successful experiences of the Great Wall conservation Project in the past ten years and pinpoint the opportunities and challenges facing the conservation efforts, the Chinese Academy of Cultural

政府长城保护管理近年的全面工作情况，从中国长城资源概况、长城保护管理体制建设、长城保护维修工程、长城科学研究、长城旅游与宣传教育、长城保护管理工作的挑战与展望等六个方面展开，通过翔实、直观的数据，尽可能向社会呈现过去十年“长城保护工作”的全貌，汇报长城保护管理工作进展。

报告由我院长城保护研究室（原中国文化遗产研究院“长城保护工程”项目管理小组）的李大伟、刘文艳、许慧君、张依萌四位年轻同志共同完成。这四位同志平均年龄只有 36 岁，但几乎都是从参加工作开始，就投身长城保护研究事业。为了报告的编写，他们在长城沿线开展了大量实地调研工作，同时搜集、查阅了大量资料，付出了巨大的心血，最终完成了这部内容丰富，数据翔实，同时具有较高学术性和可读性的报告。这是我国第一部面向公众、针对长城保护管理工作开展的系统评估报告。由于长城体量巨大，研究成果汗牛充栋，庞杂的数据来源分散，本报告的内容难免存在缺漏和不完善之处，但毋庸置疑，这是一次从长城保护管理工作和公众宣传教育的角度开展应用性研究的有益尝试。

长城保护，需要全社会的参与。我们希望社会公众通过本报告，不但能够了解长城保护管理十年工作的成就，也能够理解这项工作的意义，并且有意愿力所能及地参与到这项艰难而伟大的工作中来，通过全社会的努力，促进长城保护管理工作不断取得新的进步。

中国文化遗产研究院院长　柴晓明

2017 年 7 月

Heritage, authorized by the State Administration of Cultural Heritage, compiled this report right before the 10th anniversary of the issuance of the *Regulations on the Conservation of Great Wall*. The report is based on the 10-year Great Wall conservation Project evaluation and the special supervision of the Regulation on the conservation of Great Wall. The report summarizes the Chinese government's full Great Wall conservation efforts in recent years. The report covers six aspects: the Great Wall resources, Great Wall conservation management system building, Great Wall restoration projects, Great Wall scientific research, Great Wall tourism, promotion and education and challenges and outlook of Great Wall conservation and management efforts. With detailed and clear data, the report is aimed to show all aspects of the conservation of the Great Wall in the past 10 years and progress made on conservation and management works.

The report was completed by four young comrades: Li Dawei, Liu Wenyan, Xu Huijun and Zhang Yimeng, who are from the Great Wall Conservation Research Office (formerly known as the project management group of the Great Wall Conservation Project) of the Chinese Academy of Cultural Heritage. With an average age of only 36, almost all of them have dedicated their career to the research of the Great Wall conservation. For the compiling of the report, they made great efforts on field research along the Great Wall as well as leafing through the massive data. As a result of their unselfish dedication, the report is not only full of rich datum, but also has high academic value and readability. This is the first ever public and systematic evaluation report on the Great Wall conservation and management works in China. Due to the Great Wall's magnificent physical presence and rather huge and scattered old research datum, this report may have its own imperfectness and omissions. Without doubt, this report is a pioneering practical research on the Great Wall's conservation and management as well as public promotion and education.

The conservation of the Great Wall requires the participation of the whole society. We hope that through the report, the public could learn these achievements of the Great Wall conservation and management in the past 10 years and understand the significance of the work. We hope the whole society could be inspired to join the great and difficult efforts to improve the conservation and management of the Great Wall in a united way.

Chai Xiaoming

Director of Chinese Academy of Cultural Heritage

July, 2017

# 前言

长城在我国具有崇高的政治地位和象征意义，是具有特殊意义的文化遗产，不仅在于它的宏伟和庞大，更在于在国人心目中的地位，长城保护也因此受到超乎寻常的关注和重视。长城有 2000 余年的修建史，作为文物得到认知和保护也有百年历史。但真正作为文物保护开始于中华人民共和国成立后，并延续近 70 年。长城保护实践得益于国家行动的推动，以三次国家顶层设计和推动的保护行动为基础，可划分为三个主要阶段。

20 世纪 50 年代，在中央人民政府政务院下发《关于保护古文物建筑的指示》的背景下，国家提出修复长城的建议，并最终选择了八达岭、居庸关、山海关三处进行修缮。从 1952 年开始到 1958 年先后对这几处长城的墙体、关城、关楼等进行了修缮和加固，并对游人开放。这是我国首次开展的长城文物保护工程，具有里程碑式意义。

郑振铎先生在 1957 年第一届全国人民代表大会第四次会议上总结了八年以来的古建筑保护工作，指出“在精打细算、不浪费、不铺张的方针下，八年来基本上保护了古代重要的寺庙、宫殿、城墙、桥梁、石阙、砖塔、木塔等。像长城、山西五台寺的唐代建筑……等等，不仅予以坚决的保护，妥善的保存，而且加以必要的修缮”。表明此时长城已经成为文物保护的重要组成部分。从 1961 年—2013 年，长城陆续被公布为 29 处全国重点文物保护单位。

20 世纪 80 年代，中央要求采取行动制止和纠正破坏长城的行为，由国务院组织了五批调查人员去各省市调查长城状况。随后 1979 年和 1983 年分别在呼和浩特和河北滦平县召开了两次全国长城保护座谈会，理清了长城保护思路，明确了保护目标和方法，极大促进和推动了长城保护工作。

1984 年 7 月，新闻媒体发起了“爱我中华，修我长城”的社会募捐活动。习仲勋和邓小平同志先后为这次活动题词，1987 年长城被列入《世界遗产名录》，长城受到更多的关注，这都促使 20 世纪 80、90 年

# Foreword

The Great Wall has a high political status and is a symbol of China. It is a cultural heritage carrying a special meaning to the Chinese people. Due to its magnificent presence and being favored by the Chinese people, conservation for the Great Wall attracts extraordinary attention. The Great Wall was built in over 2,000 years. It has been recognized as cultural relic for about 100 years. The real conservation started after the birth of the People's Republic of China and lasted nearly 70 years. The conservation of the Great Wall benefited from the national efforts. Based on the national top-level design and boost, the conservation efforts could be divided into three major phases.

The Central People's Government issued the instructions on the conservation of ancient architectures in 1950s. Badaling, Juyong Pass and Shanhai Pass sections of the Great Wall were chosen to be restored with the state's advice on repair of the Great Wall. From 1952 through 1958, the walls, passes and pass towers of the three sections were repaired, fortified and opened to tourists. As the first cultural relic conservation for the Great Wall, the project is a milestone.

In 1957, at the fourth conference of the 1st National People's Congress, Mr. Zheng Zhenduo summarized the conservation of ancient buildings in eight years. With the principle of cost-efficiency, the important ancient architectures including temples, palaces, city walls, bridges, stone statue, brick and wooden towers were basically protected. The architectures of the Tang Dynasty including the Great Wall and Shanxi's Wutai Temple were protected, preserved with necessary restorations. This indicates the Great Wall has become an important part of the cultural relics conservation since then. From 1961 through 2013, a total of 29 sections of the Great Wall had become State Priority Protected Sites by 2013.

In1980s, the central government requested to take actions to stop people from damaging the Great Wall. The State Council sent five teams to investigate these conditions of the Great Wall. Two national conventions on the conservation of the Great Wall were held in Hohhot and Hebei's Luanping County in 1979 and 1983, respectively. A consensus was reached on the conservation of the Great Wall with clear methods and targets, which greatly boosted the conservation of the Great Wall.

In July 1984, the press launched the public donation project under the slogan of "Love China, Repair the Great Wall". Both Xi Zhongxun and Deng Xiaoping wrote inscriptions for raising donations. The Great Wall was included on the World Heritage List in 1987, which drew more attention on the Great Wall. These efforts caused peaks of conservation works for the Great Wall in 1980s and 1990s. During the peak time, massive walls and Pass cities were restored including Shanhai Pass's Laolongtou, Jiaoshan, Huangyaguan, Hushan, Juyong Pass, Jiumenkou and Jiayu

代出现了长城保护高潮。在这场长城保护运动中，大量长城墙体、关城等，如山海关的老龙头、角山长城、黄崖关长城、虎山长城、居庸关长城、九门口、嘉峪关等都进行了大规模的修缮和复建，现在都已成为著名的旅游开放区。与此同时，随着 1982 年《文物保护法》颁布实施和《威尼斯宪章》等国际保护理念的引入，司马台长城以原状保护为主的修缮工程在当时以复建为主导的长城保护浪潮中独树一帜，也开启了长城原状保护的时代，具有标志性意义。在具体施工过程中，采取“原状保护”做法，尽可能保留长城遗迹遗存，得到了国内外专家的好评。

进入 21 世纪，随着长城沿线经济开发活动增加，人为损毁趋势也不断加剧。中央领导同志批示“要加强长城保护”。2003 年国务院七部委联合下发了《关于进一步加强长城保护管理的通知》，明确规定要加强对长城保护维修工作的管理，坚决杜绝“保护性”“建设性”破坏事件的发生。国家文物局报国务院批准，实施了《长城保护工程（2005—2014 年）总体工作方案》，明确提出“争取用较短的时间摸清长城家底、建立健全相关法规制度、理顺管理体制，在统一规划的指导下，科学安排长城保护维修、合理利用等工作，并依法加强监管，从根本上遏制对长城的破坏，为长城保护工作的良性发展打下坚实基础”的目的。从此开始了长达十年的“长城保护工程”。2006 年《长城保护条例》颁布实施，这是我国首次针对单一文物类型制定的专项保护法规，对长城保护起到了重要作用。

设立国家级长城组织协调和研究机构是近十年长城保护工作能够取得很大成绩的重要保证。2005 年国务院批准实施《长城保护工程（2005—2014 年）总体工作方案》，为有效开展长城保护工程，根据《关于成立“长城保护工程”领导小组和项目管理小组的通知》（文物保函〔2006〕601 号），国家文物局成立“长城保护工程”领导小组，负责研究解决长城保护中的重大问题，确定长城保护的指导原则和工作方针，决策重大事项。领导小组下设办公室，负责组织各有关部门实施长城保护工程，部署各项具体工作，指导和督促落实工作方案。办公室在中国文物研究所（现中国文化遗产研究院）设立“长

Pass, which have become renowned tourist attractions. With the *Law of the People's Republic of China on the Conservation of Cultural Relics* issued and implemented in 1982 and the introduction of the *Venice Charter*, Simatai section was repaired with the spirit of the *Venice Charter*: preserve and reveal the aesthetic and historic value of the monument, which was contrary to the past modern restorations of the Great Wall and opened a new era for the conservation of the Great Wall. The landmark project with a maximum conservation of the aesthetic and historic value of the monument was praised by both domestic and foreign experts.

At the beginning of the 21st century, with the economic development along the Great Wall, the man-made damage was increasing. The central government leaders requested to strengthen the conservation for the Great Wall. In 2003, the seven ministries of the State Council jointly issued the "notice on further strengthening conservation and management of the Great Wall", which clearly pointed out the need to strengthen management of the conservation efforts in order to avoid any damage under the name of "Conservation" and "construction". With the authorization from the State Council, the State Administration of Cultural Heritage implemented the *Master Plan on the Great Wall Conservation Project (2005—2014)*. The aim of the Plan is to conduct a thorough survey of the Great Wall in shortest time possible, build and improve the legal framework for the conservation of the Great Wall, streamline the management system, coordinate the restorations and utilization with a unified guidance, strengthen supervision under the law and fundamentally contain the damage to the Great Wall. With a sound groundwork of the plan, a 10-year systematic conservation project for the Great Wall was started.

*Regulation on the Conservation of Great Wall* was issued in 2006. This is China's first regulation designated for a single cultural relic, which plays a key role in the conservation for the Great Wall.

The establishment of the national level coordination and research institution is an important guarantee for the huge progress made on conservation of the Great Wall in the past 10 years. In 2005, the *Master Plan on the Great Wall Conservation Project (2005—2014)* was approved for implementation by the State Council, in order to carry out the Great Wall Conservation Projects, and in accordance with the *Notice on Establishing the Leading Team and Project Management Team for Great Wall Conservation Project(W.W.B.H[2006]601),* the State Administration of Cultural Heritage formed the Great Wall Conservation Project leading taskforce. The leading taskforce is in charge of solving major issues related to the conservation of the Great Wall and its principles and guidelines. The leading taskforce has a special office, which is responsible for organizing the related entities to carry out conservation projects, allocating specific works and supervising the implementation of the programs.

城保护工程”项目管理小组，由中国文物研究所（现中国文化遗产研究院）有关人员组成，负责具体组织实施领导小组办公室部署的“长城保护工程”的有关工作。

2007 年，长城资源调查工作启动。根据国家文物局、国家测绘局《关于联合成立国家长城资源调查工作机构的通知》（文物保发〔2007〕20 号），国家文物局和国家测绘局决定联合成立国家长城资源调查工作机构，同时在中国文物研究所（现中国文化遗产研究院）设长城资源调查项目工作组，负责日常工作。

2014 年之后，虽然“长城保护工程”已经结束，但长城保护管理工作更为繁重，为了持续地、更好地开展长城保护和研究工作，长城项目组延续至今，2017 年名称调整为长城保护研究室。由编制内业务人员 4 名，长期聘用专业人员 1 名组成。十年来，这个团队在国家文物局领导下，依托于文研院这个既有科研也有技术实施综合能力的平台，开展了长城保护与研究、专业评估与咨询、信息化与数据平台建设等多方面的工作，初步建立了一个规模不大，但较为精干的长城保护研究专业团队。

2006—2016 年的十年间，在国家文物局和各级人民政府的努力下，十年耕耘，十年努力，长城保护工作投入巨大，成效斐然。组织了首次全国范围内的长城资源调查，第一次明确了长城的走向、精确长度和防御系统的构成情况，并制作了迄今最准确、最完整的长城分布图。随后开展的长城资源认定，明确了长城遗产的构成和属性，奠定了长城保护管理的法定基础。

长城法规建设与管理日益完善。不断加强长城保护专项法规建设，逐步建立起以《中华人民共和国文物保护法》和《长城保护条例》为主体，相关法律法规、规范性文件以及各级地方性法规为补充的法律法规体系，建立了以文物保护单位为核心，统一要求、分级负责、属地管理的长城保护管理体制。

长城保护维修实践与理念更加科学合理。坚持“科学规划、原状保护”的原则，以文物本体抢险加固、消除安全隐患为长城保护的首要任务，组织实施了一批长城保护维修工程，有效维护了长城的真实性、完整性和历史风貌。

The office has a project management team at the Chinese Academy of Cultural Heritage, which is formerly known as the Chinese Cultural Relics Research Institute. The team is responsible for carrying out the works designated by the leading taskforce.

In 2007, the survey on the Great Wall resources was started. The State Administration of Cultural Heritage and the State Administration of Surveying, Mapping and Geoinformation jointly form the Great Wall resources survey institution with a team established at the Chinese Academy of Cultural Heritage, which is responsible for the daily works, in accordance with the Notice on Jointly Establishing National Great Wall Resource Surveying Operation Mechanism (W.W.B.F.[2007]20).

Though the Great Wall conservation Project was finished in 2014, the conservation and management of the Great Wall became more arduous. In order to continue to conduct the conservation and research works for the Great Wall. It is renamed the Great Wall conservation Research Office in 2017. The office has four designated posts and one hired specialist. Under the leadership of the State Administration of Cultural Heritage and developing on the Chinese Academy of Cultural Heritage scientific and technological platform, the team has become an elite specialized force on the research of the conservation of the Great Wall. It conducts research on conservation of the Great Wall, specialized evaluation and consulting, and informationization and data platform development.

From 2006 through 2016, with great efforts from the State Administration of Cultural Heritage and all levels of governments, the first nationwide survey on the Great Wall resources was conducted. The geographical trend of the Great Wall, its exact length and defensive system were defined for the first time. The most accurate and complete map to date for the Great Wall was made. The identification of the Great Wall resources made clear of the composition and property of the Great Wall cultural heritage, which laid the legal foundation for the conservation and management of the Great Wall.

The legislation works and management of the Great Wall have been improving constantly. *Law of the People's Republic of China on the Conservation of Cultural Relics and Regulation on the Conservation of Great Wall* are the major legal framework for conservation of the Great Wall. There are also other laws, regulations and local regulations supporting the conservation of the Great Wall. The Great Wall conservation management system is cultural relic conservation unit-centered with responsibility shared by different levels of governments and managements by respective local authorities as well as with the same request.

The conservation practices and principles for the Great Wall have become more scientific and reasonable. The conservation efforts stick to the "Scientific planning, natural conservation" principle. Emergent reinforcing and eliminating potential safety hazard are the primary tasks of the conservation of the

长城研究为保护提供了重要支撑。长城保护技术、大型遗产管理策略、地理信息技术等研究日益受到重视。长城资源调查报告陆续出版，长城考古逐渐兴起，长城建筑与军事聚落空间信息研究成果丰硕、高新技术手段在长城保护与监测上的研究应用日益增多。

长城旅游与宣传为长城保护注入了新的活力。长城旅游成为当地经济社会发展的支柱产业，有力扩大了公共文化供给，改善了长城沿线生态环境，推动了区域经济增长及国家扶贫攻坚战略的实施。与此同时，长城成为世界了解古代中国与现代中国的金色名片。

过去十年，经过不懈努力，长城保护工作取得了较大成绩，但与长城本身的特殊地位相比，在新形势下，长城保护管理工作面临着一系列的挑战。

长城具有身份多重、本体与环境多样、保存状况和保护理念复杂的特点。保存至今的长城大多已坍塌或损毁，甚至地面建筑已经消失。因此长城保护常常被政府所忽视，对长城保护的重要性认识不足，责任落实不到位。个别地方保护修复缺少有针对性的科学方案，施工管理过于粗放，质量不高，对长城本体和风貌造成影响。现代人为破坏加剧。制约长城保护的诸多困难与问题尚未得到有效解决，保护形势依然不尽如人意。加强长城保护必须本着对历史负责，对人民负责的态度，进一步完善政策措施，加强科学统筹，加大保护力度，落实政府责任，依法严格保护，促进社会参与，弘扬长城精神，充分发挥长城在传承和弘扬中华优秀传统文化中的独特作用。

中国文化遗产研究院<br>2017 年 7 月

Great Wall. A series of restoration projects were conducted. The Great Wall's authenticity, integrity and historical values are effectively maintained.

The research provides a strong support to the conservation of the Great Wall. People pay more and more attention to the conservation technologies, management strategies for major cultural heritages and geographic information technology. With the publication of the Great Wall resource survey reports, rising archaeological studies and rich achievements on study of the Great Wall and related military settlements, the new methods applied on the conservation and monitor of the Great Wall are on the rise.

Tourism and promotion revitalized the conservation of the Great Wall. The Great Wall tourism has become a pillar industry for the local economy, which has greatly improved the local cultural scene, improved the ecological environment along the Great Wall, boosted the regional economic growth and supported the national poverty alleviation strategy. The Great Wall, with ancient and modern connections, has become China's golden business card to the world.

In the past ten years, with continued efforts, great achievements have been made in the conservation of the Great Wall. Due to its special status and the new situation, the conservation and management of the Great Wall still face a series of challenges.

The Great Wall has multiple identities with diverse conditions and environments at different sections. The conservation and conservation concepts for different sections are rather complex. Most of the Great Wall have collapsed or are destroyed. Some ground structures even disappeared. The Great Wall's conservation is often neglected by government. The importance of the conservation of the Great Wall is not well understood and the responsibility is not in place. There is a lack of targeted scientific solutions for the restorations of some sections. The low-quality restoration management affected the Great Wall and its local scenes badly, which deteriorates the situation of the Great Wall. Many difficulties and problems facing the conservation of the Great Wall have not been effectively solved and conservation efforts are still unsatisfactory.

Strengthening the conservation of the Great Wall must adopt the attitude of being responsible for both history and the people. We must further improve policies, strengthen scientific planning, make greater Conservation efforts, fulfill government responsibility, carry out stricter supervision, raise social awareness and carry forward the "Great Wall Spirit". We need to work together to fully realize the Great Wall's unique role in inheriting and carrying forward the outstanding traditional Chinese culture.

Chinese Academy of Cultural Heritage

July, 2017

【摘要】

长城资源调查与研究工作是长城保护、管理等各项工作的基础。1952 年起，国家对居庸关、八达岭、山海关等长城重要点段陆续开展了调查和保护工作。1956 年起实施的首次全国文物普查中，北京、河北、甘肃、宁夏（1957 年设区）等地将明长城作为调查重点。1979 ~ 1984 年，结合第二次全国文物普查，各地对重要区域的春秋战国长城、秦汉长城、明长城和金界壕等遗存进行调查，出版了《中国长城遗迹调查报告集》，对我国长城资源有了进一步认识。2005 年，国家实施《长城保护工程（2005-2014）总体工作方案》，国家文物局开展了为期十年的国家长城保护项目。根据“方案”的部署，开展长城资源调查，摸清长城“家底”成为首要任务。2006 年，国家文物局组织长城沿线各地开展了中华人民共和国成立以来最为全面、系统的长城资源调查工作。多年来，国内相关科研机构、社会团体和民间组织以及相关专业人士也开展了多种形式的长城调查、勘测和研究工作。

# 第一章
# 长城调查与资源概况

## Chapter 1
## Great Wall Survey and Resource Summary

[Abstract]

The resource survey and research work are the foundation of the conservation and management of the Great Wall. Since 1952, survey and conservation works have been conducted on Juyong Pass, Badaling and Shanhai Pass sections of the Great Wall. During the first nationwide survey on cultural relics starting 1956, Beijing, Hebei, Gansu and Ningxia (established in 1957) put focus on the Ming Dynasty Great Wall. During the second nationwide survey on cultural relics from 1979 through 1984, the Great Wall built in the time of Spring and Autumn period, Warring States, Qin, Han and Ming dynasties and the moat built by Jin Dynasty were surveyed. The following "Survey Report on China Great Wall Relics" let people learn more about the Great Wall. Based on the "Master Plan on the Great Wall Conservation Project (2005—2014)" issued in 2005, the State Administration of Cultural Heritage launched a 10-year national conservation project for the Great Wall. The resource survey on the Great Wall became the No. 1 task according to the plan. In 2006, The State Administration of Cultural Heritage organized the local authorities to conduct the most thorough and systematic resource survey on the Great Wall since the founding of the People's Republic of China. The domestic related scientific research institutions, social organizations, non-governmental organizations and related professionals also conducted multiple surveys and research works on the Great Wall.

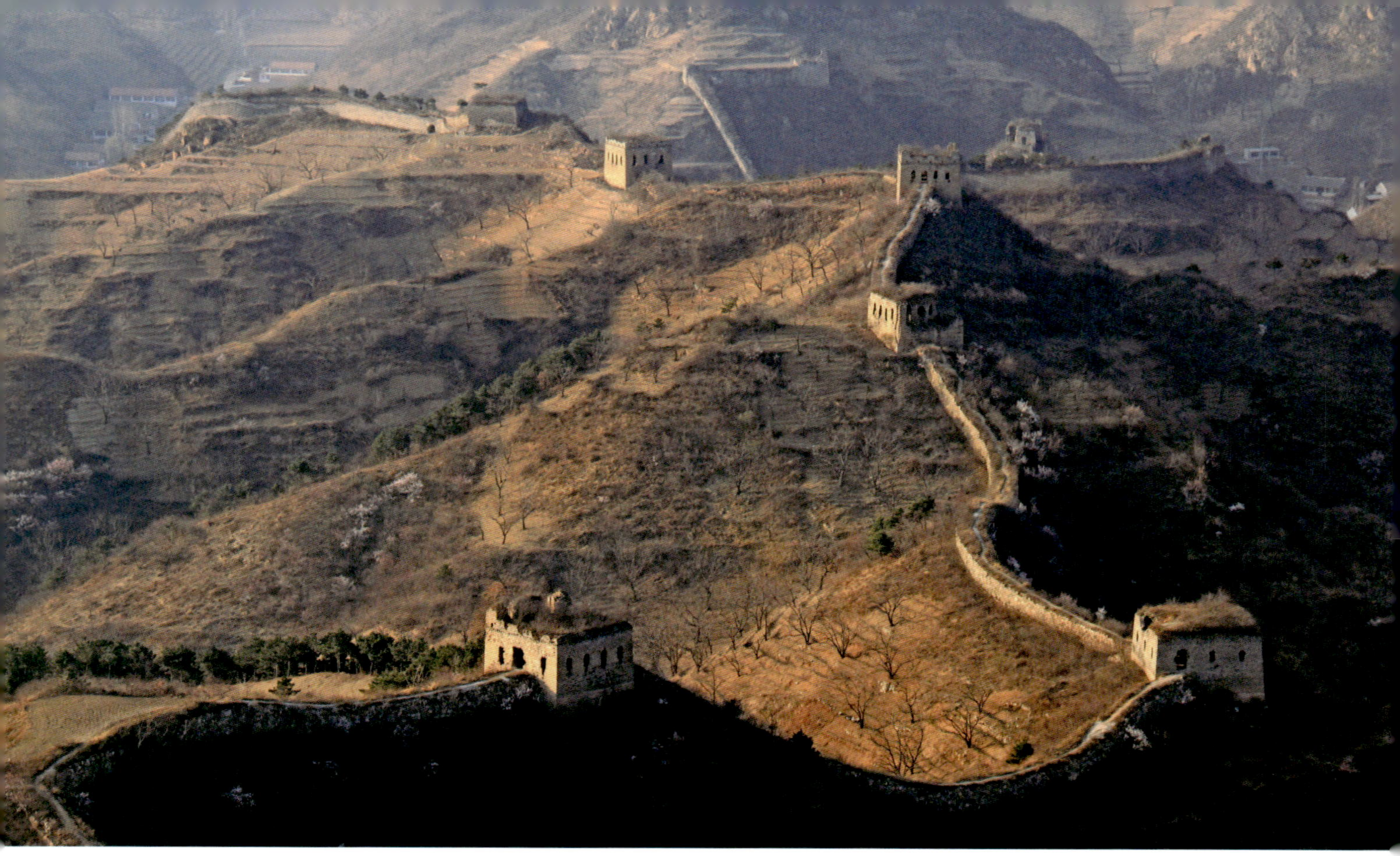

河北迁西榆木岭南岗明长城（严欣强 拍摄）

The section of the Great Wall of the Ming Dynasty at Nangang, Yumuling, Qianxi, Hebei (Photo by Yan Xinqiang)

## 第一节 长城资源调查与认定

※ 摸清家底——全面、系统地调查

※ 依法认定——明确法律保护身份

进入 21 世纪，长城保护面临日益严重的威胁，国家文物局报国务院批准，实施了《长城保护工程（2005—2014 年）总体工作方案》（以下简称《方案》），总体目标是："争取用较短的时间摸清长城家底、建立健全相关法规制度、理顺管理体制，在统一规划的指导下，科学安排长城保护维修、合理利用等工作，并依法加强监管，从根本上遏制对长城的破坏，为长城保护管理工作的良性发展打下坚实基础。"[1]《方案》共设置了九项任务，具体包括：

1、开展长城资源调查，建立长城文物记录档案；

2、编制《长城保护总体规划》，划定保护范围和建设控制地带；

[1] 国家文物局：《关于启动长城保护工程的通知》（文物保发〔2006〕8 号）。

# Section 1 Great Wall Resource Survey and Identification

- Complete and systematic survey
- Legal conservation identity confirmation

In 21st century, to meet the challenge of serious threats facing the conservation of the Great Wall, authorized by the State Council, the State Administration of Cultural Heritage carried out the *Master Plan on the Great Wall Conservation Project (2005—2014)*(hereafter referred to as *Plan*). The general aim was: get a whole picture of the Great Wall resource in shortest time possible, build a sound legal framework, streamline the management system, efficiently plan and arrange restoration works, reasonably commercialize, legally strengthen supervision in order to stop any further damage to the Great Wall and lay a solid foundation for the sound development of the conservation and management works[1]. The *Plan* set nine tasks:

1. Conduct survey on Great Wall resource; keep a record of the Great Wall cultural relics;

2. Make *Master plan of Great Wall Conservation,* set reservations and construction-free zones;

3. Make *Management Regulations on Great Wall Conservation,* set legal framework;

4. Streamline Great Wall conservation and management mechanism, clarify Great Wall conservation responsibility;

5. Raise public awareness on Great Wall conservation;

[1] State Administration of Cultural Heritage *Notice on Initiating the Great Wall Conservation Project* (W.W.B.F[2006]8)

3、制定《长城保护管理条例》，建立健全配套法规；

4、理顺长城保护管理体制，明确长城保护责任；

5、深入开展长城保护宣传教育工作；

6、加强长城保护科学研究，完成“长城及其保护管理研究”课题；

7、科学制定长城保护修缮计划，完成重点地段维修方案编制和重点部位抢救工程；

8、依法加强监管，严惩对长城的破坏行为；

9、增加对长城保护工作的经费投入。

《长城保护条例》（以下简称《条例》）第九条规定：“长城所在地省、自治区、直辖市人民政府应当对本行政区域内的长城进行调查；对认为属于长城的段落，应当报国务院文物主管部门认定，并自认定之日起1年内依法核定公布为省级文物保护单位。”

根据《方案》部署和《条例》的要求，国家文物局统一组织开展了长城资源调查与认定工作。通过长城资源调查与认定，从国家层面，确认长城的身份和构成，明确了保护责任和法律地位，为切实实施长城保护和管理奠定坚实基础。这是第一次由国家主导的、在全国范围内开展的、最为全面、系统的长城调查工作，调查范围覆盖了东经30.5°至75.2°，北纬32.5°至50.3°，高程海拔0米至3400米，调查所涉及的我国陆地领土面积超过4万平方千米。

## 一、长城资源调查

### （一）资源调查前期准备

长城分布范围广、保存现状复杂、调查难度大，如此大规模的专项文物调查与认定工作，在全世界范围内都没有先例。为了保证调查工作质量，国家文物局组织长城沿线各级文物行政部门和专业机构从2006年春开始，进行了近一年的前期准备。

#### 1、组建机构，建立有效工作方式

长城资源调查由国家文物局统一组织实施。考虑到长城调查

6. Strengthen Great Wall conservation scientific research, finish research on "Great Wall and its conservation and management";

7. Make scientific Great Wall conservation and restoration plan, finish emergent restoration plans for important sections and parts;

8. Strengthen supervision in accordance with law, severely punish the responsible party for damage to Great Wall;

9. Increase funds for Great Wall conservation.

Clause 9 of the *Regulation on the Conservation of Great Wall (the Regulation)*: The provinces, autonomous regions and municipalities are responsible for conducting survey on the Great Wall sections located in their respective domains and submit the self-confirmed sections to the State Council for recognition. The recognized section will be listed as provincial cultural heritage within one year after the recognition.

According to the *Plan* and the *Regulation,* the State Administration of Cultural Heritage organized the Great Wall resource survey and identification. The Great Wall's identity and sections were confirmed from the national level. The conservation responsibility and legal status were clarified. All of the efforts laid a solid foundation for the conservation and management of the Great Wall. This is the first nationwide, state-run, most complete and systematic survey on the Great Wall, which covers an area of over 40,000 square kilometer. The surveyed area is 30.5 to 75.2 degrees east longitude and 32.5 to 50.3 degrees north latitude with altitude from 0 to 3,400 meters.

## I. Great Wall Resource Survey

### (I) Preliminary works

The Great Wall's magnificent physical presence and complicated conditions posed a great challenge to the survey. There is no precedent on such large-scale survey and identification of a cultural relic worldwide. To ensure a quality survey, the State Administration of Cultural Heritage organized the local administrations and specialized institutions to make the year-long preliminary works since spring of 2006.

#### 1. Organize institution and build efficient working methods

The State Administration of Cultural Heritage led the Great Wall survey works. The State Administration of Cultural Heritage and the State Administration of Surveying, Mapping and Geoinformation jointly formed the Great Wall resources survey institution in 2006. The related leaders from the two units took the leading posts at the joint institution. They are responsible

图 1-1
国家文物局与国家测绘局签署长城资源调查合作协议（国家文物局 提供）

Fig. 1-1
State Administration of Cultural Heritage and State Administration of Surveying, Mapping and Geoinformation sign cooperation agreement on Great Wall resource survey (photo by State Administration of Cultural Heritage)

的技术需求，由国家文物局牵头，与国家测绘局联合组建了国家长城资源调查工作机构。2006 年，国家文物局和国家测绘局签署合作协议，联合组成了“国家长城资源调查领导小组”，由两局分管领导担任组长，相关司室负责人担任副组长，负责长城资源调查的组织、协调及重大问题的决策，统筹安排国家层面的数据整合、建档、建库，以及协调编制长城资源调查报告。

同时，在中国文化遗产研究院（原中国文物研究所）设“长城资源调查工作项目组”（后文简称“长城资源调查项目组”），负责日常工作的开展与协调。长城沿线各省（自治区、直辖市）文物行政部门也分别建立了相应的调查领导机构，形成了国家级与省级两级负责、文物与测绘跨部门协作的工作模式。（图 1-1）

长城沿线各相关省（自治区、直辖市）分别成立长城资源调查领导小组，负责组织协调文物部门和测绘部门共同开展本区域内的长城资源调查工作。河北省成立了由文物和测绘部门联合组成的“长城资源调查小组”，并在省文物局和测绘局分别设立了“长城资源调查工作领导小组”和“长城资源测量工作领导小组”；山西省建立了省级的“长城资源调查工作领导组”；辽宁、北京、天津、内蒙古、陕西、宁夏、甘肃、青海等省（自治区、直辖市）

for the survey's organization, coordination, important decision making, related national data bank building and coordination on compiling of the survey report.

At the same time, the Great Wall resource survey team was established at the Chinese Academy of Cultural Heritage (formerly known as the Chinese Cultural Relics Research Institute), which is responsible for the daily works. The related local cultural relics administrations also built corresponding survey organizations working closely with the national level survey organization. (Fig. 1-1)

The related local governments of provincial (Municipal or autonomous region) level respectively built the Great Wall resource survey taskforce coordinating the local cultural heritage administrations and surveying and mapping units to jointly conduct local surveys. Hebei province built the joint Great Wall resource survey team between cultural heritage and surveying and mapping units. The provincial cultural heritage administration and surveying and mapping bureau set up the Great Wall resource survey taskforce and the Great Wall resource surveying and mapping taskforce, respectively. Shanxi province set up the provincial Great Wall resource survey taskforce. Other provinces and municipalities including Liaoning, Beijing, Tianjin, Inner Mongolia, Shanxi, Ningxia, Gansu and Qinghai set up respective Great Wall resource survey taskforce. Tianjin also set up a team with experts to lead the survey works. The cultural heritage units are responsible for the field works of surveying, taking measurements, collecting data and recording. The surveying and mapping units are responsible for providing basic geographic information and technological support.

### 2. Establish standard work methods and technological requirements

The establishment of the standard work methods and technological requirements is a must for coping with the huge workload and massive workforce. The Great Wall resource survey team established a series of work standards covering survey area, survey object, and survey element and survey procedures.

After repeated study and revision, the State Administration of Cultural Heritage made the general conservation plan and working procedures. It organized the writing of 32 related standards and management systems including the Great Wall resource survey management system and survey data management system. The standards and management systems mainly cover: survey scope, object, content, method, procedure and safeguard measures; duties of different levels of survey institutions; basic principle, working method, information security and personnel safety guarantee; survey data storage facility and equipment requirement, survey data sorting, backup, transfer and centralization as well as survey data utilization and management safety

建立了“长城资源调查领导小组”并下设办公室；此外，天津市还设立了专家组，在技术上指导调查工作。文物部门的主要任务是开展田野调查，对长城资源进行现场勘查、考古测量，做好信息采集和登录工作。测绘部门的主要任务是为长城资源调查提供基础地理信息与技术支持。

2、建章立制，制定基础技术标准规范

针对长城调查工作量大面广、参与单位和人员众多的特点，必须要建立统一的技术规范和规章制度。在调查的技术准备方面，长城资源调查项目组制定各类技术标准，从调查区域、调查对象、调查要素、调查工作流程等方面对调查工作进行明确界定。

经过反复研究论证与修改完善，国家文物局制定了总体方案和工作规程，组织编制了长城资源调查管理办法、调查资料管理制度等 32 项相关技术标准规范与管理制度，主要内容包括：调查的范围、对象、内容、方法、工作流程、保障措施；各级长城调查机构的职责，调查工作的基本原则、工作方法、信息安全和人身安全保障；调查资料保管场地和设施要求及调查资料的整理、备份，移交、汇总等调查资料使用、管理中确保安全的措施；以及长城资源调查名称使用规范、文物编码规则、保存程度评价标准、调查档案归档立卷要求、调查报告体例格式、基础地理信息与专题要素数据生产外业和内业技术规定、基础地理信息和专题要素数据技术规定等等。（图 1-2）

2007 年调查初期，国家文物局确定北京、天津、河北、山西、内蒙、辽宁、黑龙江、山东、河南、陕西、甘肃、宁夏、新疆等 13 个省（自治区、直辖市）为调查区域。青海、湖北、吉林三省于全国调查启动后主动申请加入调查，并被纳入调查范围。

长城资源调查以县级行政区域为调查和统计单元，同一省区内交界处的调查任务划分，通过本省长城资源调查机构的协调，全部得到了解决；跨省（自治区、直辖市）的长城资源调查工作原则上由相关省份均担或由相关省份协商解决，并报长城资源调查项目办公室备案。

图 1-2
长城资源调查工作的部分规范与标准（中国文化遗产研究院 提供）

Fig. 1-2
Codes and standards of Great Wall resource survey (photo by Chinese Academy of Cultural Heritage)

measures. The Great Wall resource survey naming, cultural relic encoding rules, preservation status evaluation, survey filing, survey report format, technological requirements on basic geographic information and special data as well as its "indoors" and "outdoors" collection regulations are also covered by the set standards.

At the beginning of the survey in 2007, the State Administration of Cultural Heritage set survey areas in Beijing, Tianjin, Hebei, Shanxi, Inner Mongolia, Liaoning, Heilongjiang, Shandong, Henan, Shaanxi, Gansu, Ningxia and Xinjiang. Qinghai, Hubei and Jilin applied to join the survey works after the survey started and were included in the survey areas.

The Great Wall resource survey takes the county-level administrative region as basic survey and statistical unit. The provincial survey institution is responsible for coordinating the survey works in the overlapping areas within the province. The corresponding provinces (autonomous regions and municipalities) are responsible for coordinating the survey works in their respective overlapping areas, which is subject to report to the leading Great Wall survey taskforce.

### 3. Carry out pilot work and lay the foundation for survey works

In 2007, the State Administration of Cultural Heritage chose Hebei's Qinhuangdao and Gansu's Shandan County, two representative places, to conduct pilot survey works in order to build work procedures, codes and standards, which

3、开展试点，奠定调查工作基础

2007年，国家文物局选择比较有代表性的河北省秦皇岛市、甘肃省山丹县，率先开展了长城资源调查试点工作，旨在通过对合作方式、调查方法、步骤，技术路线，调查工作的组织管理等进行试点，建立工作程序，制定标准、规范和工作制度，使之具有可操作性和适用性，形成具体方案，为开展全国长城调查工作提供参考，为全面实施长城资源调查做好准备。

秦皇岛市域内长城是东部地区明代包砖城墙的代表，而山丹县则是西北地区汉、明两代夯土城墙的代表。两地的试点工作，有效检验并完善了相关技术标准规范与管理制度，也形成了比较成熟的田野调查方法，进一步磨合了文物、测绘部门的合作模式，积累了丰富的工作经验，为制定全国长城资源调查标准规范提供了直接参考。

4、开展人员培训，组建调查队伍

为确保全国调查工作在实施过程中标准统一，质量过硬，国家及省级文物部门分别开展了培训工作，培训内容涉及文物、测绘知识和长城资源调查相关技术标准规范与管理制度等内容。2007年，国家文物局组织了长城资源调查培训班，培训调查工作的技术骨干和管理人员。来自北京市、天津市、河北省、山西省、内蒙古自治区、辽宁省、黑龙江省、山东省、河南省、陕西省、甘肃省、宁夏回族自治区、新疆维吾尔自治区等13个省（自治区、直辖市）长城资源调查工作机构的127名文物、测绘部门的专业技术人员参加了培训。

省级培训由各省的长城资源调查机构负责，对本辖区参加调查、测量的专业人员进行全员培训，共培训专业人员1001人。

以参训人员为骨干力量，各省（自治区、直辖市）根据本地区长城分布的具体情况和工作需求，从文物、测绘行业的各级行政部门、专业机构以及各地高等院校抽调专业技术人员，组建长城资源调查队，并任命了调查总领队，负责具体实施长城资源调查、外业调绘、内业测量等工作。

paved way for the nationwide survey on the Great Wall resources.

Qinhuangdao section of the Great Wall is the typical Ming Dynasty brick walls in East China and the Shandan section of the Great Wall is the typical Han and Ming Dynasties rammed earth walls in Northwest China. The pilot survey works at the two areas effectively tested and improved the technology standards and management system. The mature field survey methods gained from the pilot works and rich work experiences from the sharpened coordination between cultural heritage and surveying and mapping units provide direct examples to the making of the nationwide survey standards.

4. Start personnel training for building survey teams

To ensure unified standards and quality works in nationwide survey, the national and provincial cultural heritage administrations launched respective training programs. The training programs covered cultural relics and surveying and mapping knowledge, related technology standards and management system. In 2007, the 127 technological personnel from cultural heritage and surveying and mapping units of Beijing, Tianjin, Hebei, Shanxi, Inner Mongolia, Liaoning, Heilongjiang, Shandong, Henan, Shaanxi, Gansu, Ningxia Hui Autonomous Region and Xinjiang Uygur Autonomous Region took part in the Great Wall resource survey training program conducted by the State Administration of Cultural Heritage. The program trained the key technological personnel and management staff for the survey.

A total of 1,001 specialists were trained in the provincial training programs, which was organized by the provincial survey institutions.

According to respective conditions and needs, the provinces (autonomous regions and municipalities) built the survey teams with the trainees as backbone as well as transferring specialists from cultural heritage and surveying and mapping units, specialized institutions and universities. The appointed general captain was responsible for running the survey works including field surveying and mapping and office measuring.

The provinces (autonomous regions and municipalities) built the survey teams with provincial cultural heritage unit as organizers and other levels of administrations as supporters. Beijing adopted the other way with its districts and counties and built their respective survey teams. A total of 1,295 technical personnel from 361 specialized institutions joined the 142 Great Wall survey teams, (Table 1-1, fig. 1-3, 1-4)

图 1-3
长城资源调查培训班学员现场考察学习（青海省长城资源调查队 提供）

Fig. 1-3
Great Wall resource survey training class trainees' field class (Photo by Qinghai Great Wall resource survey team)

组队方式上，各省（自治区、直辖市）普遍采取了由省级文物行政主管部门直接组队，相关地级市、县（区）配合的模式；北京市则采取了由各区（县）分别组队的方式。此次长城资源调查共组建 142 个调查队，来自全国 361 个专业机构的专业技术人员总数达到 1295 人。（表 1-1，图 1-3、1-4）

图 1-4
专家现场讲解电子全占仪使用方法（河北省长城资源调查队 提供）

Fig. 1-4
Expert lectures on Electronic Total Station (Photo by Hebei Great Wall resource survey team)

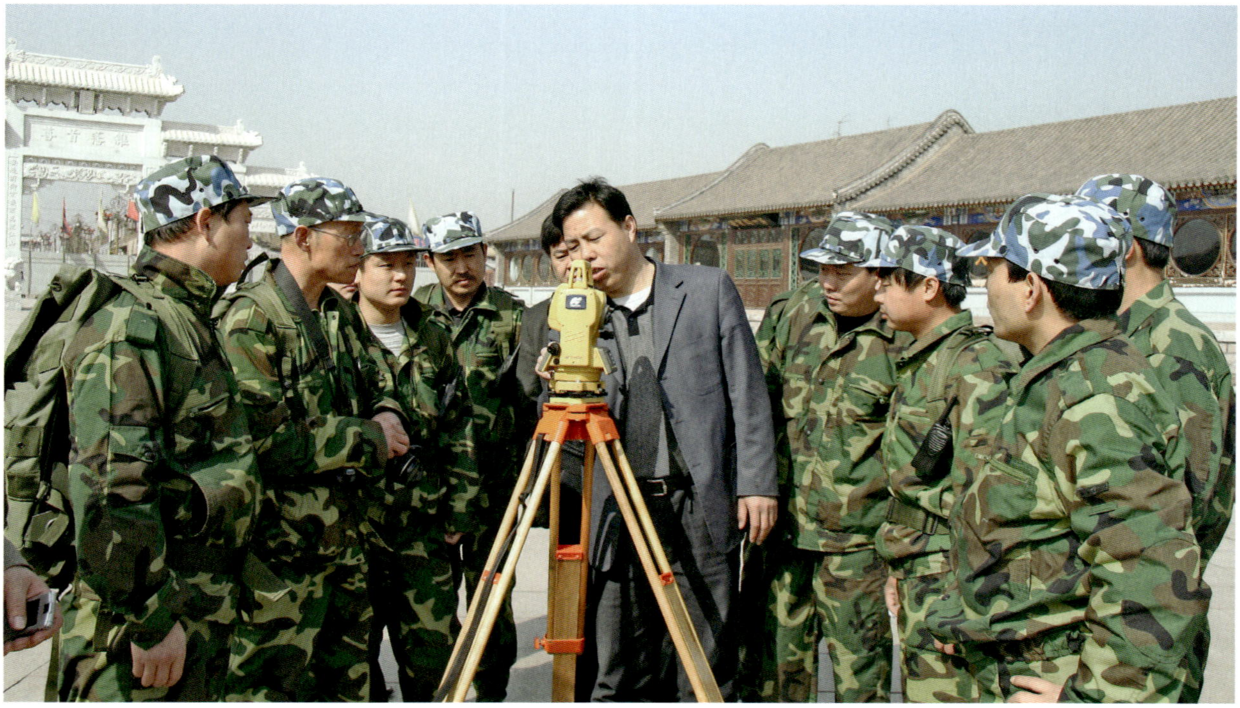

**表 1-1：各省（自治区、直辖市）长城资源调查队组成情况统计表**

Table 1-1: Survey personnel of provinces (autonomous regions and municipalities)

| 省份<br>Name | 长城资源调查队数量<br>Number of Great Wall survey team | 长城资源调查队员人数<br>Number of Great Wall survey personnel |
|---|---|---|
| 北京 / Beijing | 10 | 94 |
| 天津 / Tianjin | 3 | 21 |
| 河北 / Hebei | 16 | 120 |
| 山西 / Shanxi | 8 | 70 |
| 内蒙古 / Inner Mongolia | 28 | 212 |
| 辽宁 / Liaoning | 8 | 60 |
| 吉林 / Jilin | 4 | 42 |
| 黑龙江 / Heilongjiang | 4 | 27 |
| 山东 / Shandong | 2 | 31 |
| 河南 / Henan | 3 | 52 |
| 陕西 / Shaanxi | 14 | 92 |
| 甘肃 / Gansu | 17 | 135 |
| 青海 / Qinghai | 4 | 26 |
| 宁夏 / Ningxia | 5 | 39 |
| 新疆 / Xinjiang | 14 | 254 |
| 合计 / Total | 142 | 1295 |

图 1-5
部分长城资源调查装备（河北省长城资源调查队 提供）

Fig. 1-5
Great Wall survey equipment (Photo by Hebei Great Wall resource survey team)

5、配备调查装备，保障调查工作开展

长城多位于环境恶劣、地势险要、交通不便的地方。因此，长城调查工作不但非常辛苦，同时也存在一定的危险性。为保证野外调查工作的开展，国家文物局安排专项补助资金，为各省（自治区、直辖市）调查队配备了电脑、硬盘、绘图仪、测距仪、全站仪、手持 GPS、数码照相机、数码录像机、对讲机等考古调查、测绘所需的专业技术设备；各地还购买了越野车、登山鞋、帐篷等野外工作必需品；出于安全考虑，还为每个野外调查队员购买了人身意外保险，并配备了安全绳等安全设备。（图 1-5）

（二）资源调查方法与过程

长城资源调查以县级行政区域作为调查统计单元，采取文物、测绘专业人员联合组队模式。文物部门的主要任务是负责长城资源调查的前期研究，并采用田野考古工作方法进行属性研判、现场记录、考古测量、资料整理及建立记录档案，测绘部门的主要任务则是为长城资源调查提供基础地理信息与技术支持。在“文物定性、测绘定量”这一分工原则指导下，文物与测绘专业人员进行了密切协作，确保了现场记录、测绘成果的科学、精准。

5. Equipment guarantee a successful survey

Most sections of the Great Wall are located in harsh environment with steep terrain and inconvenient traffic conditions. Therefore, the Great Wall survey works are not only difficult but also dangerous. To ensure a smooth field survey, the State Administration of Cultural Heritage used special subsidy fund to buy computers, hard drives, range finders, total stations, handheld GPS, digital cameras, digital video recorders, walkie talkies for the survey teams. The off-road vehicles, boots, tents and other field work necessities are also purchased for the survey teams. All field survey team members are covered with personal accident policies as well as equipped with safety equipment including safety ropes. (Fig. 1-5)

**(II) Resource survey method and process**

The Great Wall resource survey takes county as basic survey and statistics unit. The survey team is jointly formed by cultural heritage and surveying and mapping units staff. The cultural heritage staffs are responsible for preliminary study and field archaeological works including identification, record keeping, measuring, data sorting and filing. The surveying and mapping staff are responsible for providing basic geographical information and technical support. Under the work principle of "identification by cultural heritage staff, measuring by surveying and mapping staff", they worked closely to ensure the accurateness of on-site records and surveying and mapping results.

To clarify the survey scope, the State Administration of Cultural Heritage organized experts to conduct research and argumentation on the subject. According to experts' opinions and for the purpose of cultural heritage survey, research and conservation, the Great Wall built respectively in Spring and Autumn period, Warring States period, Qin, Han and Ming dynasties and other related historical sites were included in the survey. A total of 445 counties of 16 provinces (autonomous regions and municipalities) are covered by the survey. The scope of the unprecedented survey far exceeded the scope of the Great Wall listed on the World Heritage List and the list of national key cultural relic conservation units.(table 1-2)

The nationwide survey on the Great Wall resources was started in May, 2007. The field works were completed in December 2010. The 1,295 specialists covered hundreds of thousands of kilometers in over three years. They successfully conducted field survey on each and every facility and related site of the Great Wall with detailed measuring and data recording. (Fig. 1-6.1-7)

## 表 1-2：长城资源分布省份一览表

| | |
|---|---|
| 参加长城资源调查的省份 | 北京市、天津市、河北省、山西省、内蒙古自治区、辽宁省、吉林省、黑龙江省、山东省、河南省、湖北省、陕西省、甘肃省、青海省、宁夏回族自治区、新疆维吾尔自治区 |
| 经过专家评估确定暂不参加长城资源调查的省份 | 江西省、湖南省、四川省、贵州省、云南省 |

为了明确调查范围，国家文物局专门组织专家对调查范围和内容进行了反复研究、论证，根据专家意见，并出于文化遗产调查、研究和保护的目的，将春秋战国长城、秦汉长城、明长城，以及中国境内其他与长城相关的历史遗迹或具备长城特征的线性文化遗产均作为调查对象，调查范围涉及 16 个省（自治区、直辖市）的 445 个区县。就调查的内容、深度和广度而言，此次长城资源调查的规模远远超过了《世界遗产名录》和全国重点文物保护单位名单中“长城”的规模。（表 1-2）

2007 年 5 月，全国长城资源调查正式开始，至 2010 年 12 月野外工作全部结束。1295 名专业技术人员在 3 年多的时间里，行程数十万公里，对中国境内所有的长城及相关遗存，进行了全覆盖式的系统的实地踏查，对长城每一段墙体、每一处设施和遗迹都进行了详细的调查、记录与测量，圆满完成了野外调查任务。（图 1-6、1-7）

图 1-6.1、1-6.2
长城资源调查队员跋山涉水（甘肃省长城资源调查队 提供）

Fig. 1-6.1 1-6.2
Great Wall resource survey team members in field work (Photo by Gansu Great Wall resource survey team)

图 1-7
长城资源调查现场研究（辽宁省长城资源调查队 提供）

Fig. 1-7
Great Wall resource survey field research (Photo by Liaoning Great Wall resource survey team)

The Great Wall resource surrey was divided into two phases covering the Ming Dynasty Great Wall and sections built in Qin and Han dynasties and other times, respectively, The survey on the Ming Dynasty Great Wall was started in Beijing, Tianjin, Hebei, Shanxi, Inner Mongolia, Liaoning, Shaanxi, Gansu, Qinghai, and Ningxia in May, 2007. The survey covered 202 counties and was completed in December 2008. The field survey was conducted on the Ming Dynasty Great Wall and areas within 1 kilometers of each side of the wall.

Table 1-2: Great Wall survey included or not

| | |
|---|---|
| Provinces included in this survey | Beijing, Tianjin, Hebei, Shanxi, Inner Mongolia, Liaoning, Jilin, Heilongjiang, Shandong, Henan, Hubei, Shaanxi, Gansu, Qinghai, Ningxia, Xinjiang |
| With experts recommendation, provinces not included in this survey | Jiangxi, Hunan, Sichuan, Guizhou, Yunnan |

长城资源调查分为明长城资源调查和秦汉及其他时代长城资源调查两个阶段进行，其中：

明长城资源调查自 2007 年 5 月起，在北京市、天津市、河北省、山西省、内蒙古自治区、辽宁省、陕西省、甘肃省、青海省、宁夏回族自治区等 10 个省（自治区、直辖市）202 个县（市、区）展开。至 2008 年 12 月，全部完成了明长城墙体及两侧各 1 千米范围内各类长城资源的田野调查工作。

秦汉及其他时代长城资源调查自 2009 年起，在北京市、河北省、山西省、内蒙古自治区、辽宁省、吉林省、黑龙江省、山东省、河南省、湖北省、陕西省、甘肃省、青海省、宁夏回族自治区、新疆维吾尔自治区等 15 个省（自治区、直辖市）381 个县（市、区）展开。至 2010 年 12 月，全部完成秦汉及其他时代长城墙体及两侧各 5 千米范围内各类长城资源的田野调查工作。

调查期间，国家文物局委托长城资源调查项目组先后组织专家开展了 50 余次现场工作指导，重点解决长城资源调查工作中出现的关键问题，在遗存的定性与断代、文物与测绘专业协调、跨地区和跨调查队协调等方面提供了技术指导。各省（自治区、直辖市）文物行政部门长城资源调查机构组织各地专家，对各调查队工作进行不定期检查、指导。

各省（自治区、直辖市）完成田野调查工作后，由省级文物行政部门组织各调查队汇总本省（自治区、直辖市）调查资料。资料汇总完成后，先后组织省级、国家级两级检查验收工作。按照《长城资源调查资料检查验收技术规定》，检查验收工作分室内、现场两部分进行。室内验收主要对各省（自治区、直辖市）提交的纸质调查登记表进行数据检查。现场验收，是指选取具有代表性的长城遗迹点，赴现场确认调查资料是否客观反映长城遗存现状。其中，对于部分调查数据量大的省份按照不低于 10% 的比例进行抽查。对于吉林、河南等调查量相对小的省（自治区、直辖市），则对调查资料全部进行了验收。（图 1-8、1-9）

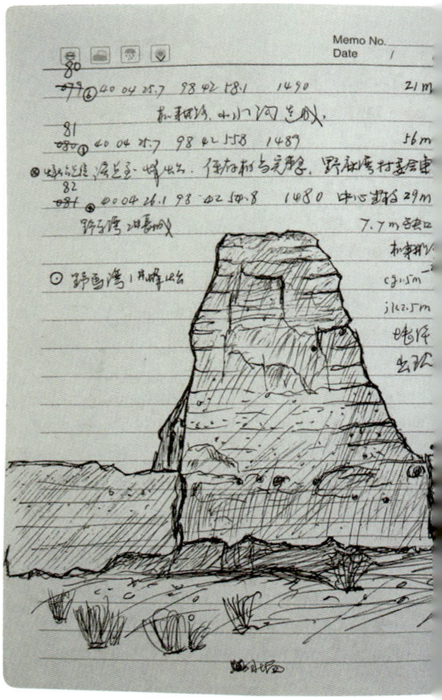


图 1-8
调查队员的现场笔记（甘肃省长城资源调查队 提供）

Fig. 1-8
survey field data (Photo by Gansu Great Wall resource survey team)

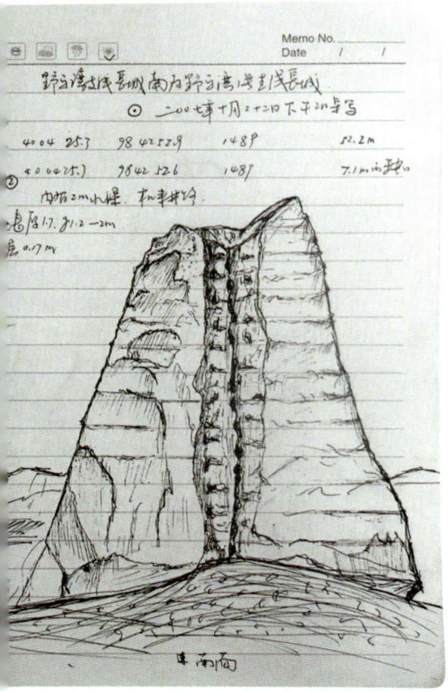


The survey on the Great Wall built in Qin and Han dynasties and the other times was started in 2009 and completed in Dec, 2010. The survey covered 381 counties of Beijing, Hebei, Shanxi, Inner Mongolia, Liaoning, Jilin, Heilongjiang, Shandong, Henan, Hubei, Shaanxi, Gansu, Qinghai, Ningxia and Xinjiang. The field survey was conducted on the Great Wall built in Qin and Han dynasties and the other times and areas within 5 kilometers of each side of the wall.

During the survey, the State Administration of Cultural Heritage authorized the Great Wall resource survey team to organize experts giving over 50 times of on-site instructions, which focused on the key issues of identification and dating, coordination between cultural heritage and surveying and mapping specialists and coordination between overlapping areas and survey teams of different regions. The provincial survey institutions organized experts to give occasional inspection and instruction to the survey teams.

After the field work was complete, the provincial cultural heritage administration was responsible for the collection of the survey data accumulated in the province. The national and provincial data inspections would be conducted respectively. According to the "Technical Guidelines on Acceptance of Great Wall Resource Data survey", the indoors and field inspections would be conducted respectively. The indoors inspection mainly put focus on the data of the submitted paper works. The field inspection would chose representative Great Wall section and double check the related data. To the rather huge amount of data submitted by the provinces, over 10% data were double checked. All of Jilin and Henan's data were double checked due to their rather small amount of data. (Fig.1-8,1-9)

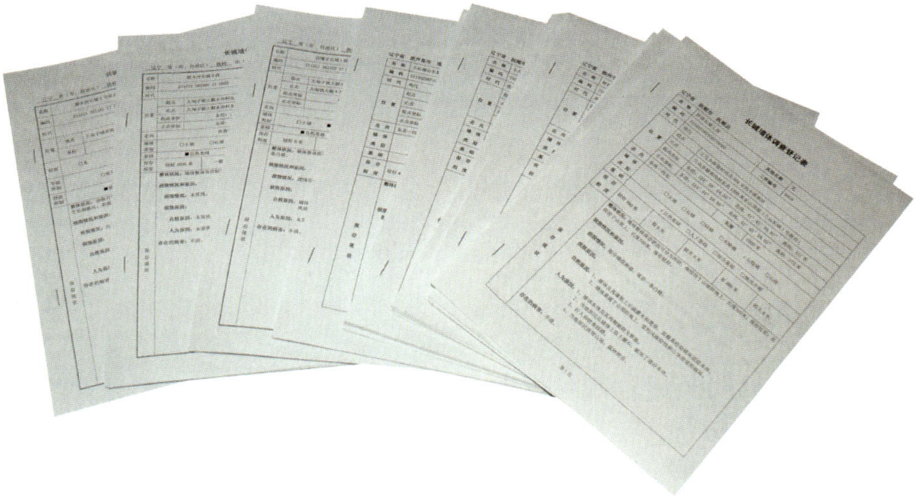

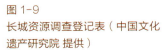

图 1-9
长城资源调查登记表（中国文化遗产研究院 提供）

Fig. 1-9
Great Wall resource survey form (photo by Chinese Academy of Cultural Heritage)

为确保长城资源调查成果精准、可靠，国家文物局推动空间信息技术广泛应用于长城资源调查。调查前期，根据历史文献和研究成果，在遥感影像资料上进行先期研判。田野调查中，使用卫星定位、红外测距仪等设备精确定位长城遗存，并对重要遗存进行三维扫描建模和测绘制图。室内量测阶段，采用遥感影像解译、数字摄影测量方法对长城遗存、基础设施以及地形地貌等基础地理数据进行识别和测量，并使用 ArcGIS 等软件进行加工处理，制作高分辨率长城数字正射影像、数字高程模型和数字线划图，绘制完成长城资源分布图，获取了误差不超过 4‰的长城长度数据。

此次长城资源调查，获取了大量文字、照片、录像以及测绘数据等第一手资料。共形成各类登记表格 46111 张，其中墙体登记表 10371 份，界壕 / 壕堑登记表 1607 份，敌台 8497 份，马面 8877 份，其他墙上单体建筑 70 份，关堡 2611 张，烽火台 11964 份，其他遗址遗迹 428 份，采（征）集文物登记表 1004 份。照片册页 196588 份，图纸册页 20606 份，录像 31070 份，拓片、摹本 596 份。 田野调查数据总量 3112.2GB，测绘数据 890GB，对长城长度、分布、时代、保护管理状况、自然与人文环境等有了系统、全面记录。

## 二、长城资源认定

长城资源调查工作结束后，2011 年国家文物局即依法启动长城资源认定工作。长城资源认定经历集中认定和后续补充认定两个阶段。长城资源认定明确了长城遗产的时代、分布、构成、性质、数量，奠定了长城保护管理法律基础，并形成了长城资源调查认定数据库。

To ensure the reliability of Great Wall resource survey data, the State Administration of Cultural Heritage boosted application of the special information technology in the survey. At first phase of the survey, the remote sensing image data acquired according to the historical and research papers was studied. In the field survey, satellite positioning and infrared rangefinder are used to precisely locate the remains of the Great Wall. The 3D scan modeling, surveying and mapping were used on the important remains of the Great Wall. In the office measuring phase, remote sensing data interpretation and digital photogrammetry were used to identify and measure the basic geographical data of the Great Wall, its infrastructure and the related terrain. Using the ArcGIS software, the high resolution digital elevation model and digital line graphics were made to draw the distribution map of the Great Wall resources. The Great Wall's length data error was less than 4‰.

The Great Wall resource survey acquired a huge amount of firsthand data including text, photos, videos and surveying and mapping data. A total of 46,111 forms including 10,371 forms of walls are filled. There are also 1, 607 trench forms, 8, 497 watchtower forms, 8,877 bastion forms, 70 other wall-top single structure forms, 2,611 pass and fortress forms, 11,964 beacon tower forms, 428 other remains forms, 1,004 cultural relic forms. A total of 196,588 pages of photos, 20,606 pages of drawings, 31,070 videos and 596 rubbings and copies are made. The total field survey data is 3,112.2GB and surveying and mapping data is 890GB. The systematic and full record of the Great Wall covers its length, distribution, dating, conservation and management situation, natural and humane environments.

## II. Great Wall Resource Identification

After the completion of the resource survey works, the State Administration of Cultural Heritage started the identification works for the Great Wall resources in 2011. The two stages of the Great Wall resources identification are centralized identification and supplementary identification. The identification of the Great Wall resources defined the Great Wall's dating, distribution, composition, nature and quantity, which laid the legal foundation for the conservation and management of the Great Wall and formed a database of the Great Wall resources.

（一）范围与过程

根据国家文物局《关于开展长城认定工作的通知》（文物保函〔2011〕1159号），长城资源认定对象为："已公布为全国重点文物保护单位或省级文物保护单位，并在长城资源调查中登记的墙体、关堡、关隘、烽火台、敌楼等各类长城遗产；在长城资源调查中已登记，但尚未公布为全国重点文物保护单位或省级文物保护单位的长城遗产。"[2]前者直接认定为长城，后者则由各省（自治区、直辖市）文物行政部门提出认定申请，由国家文物局组织专家进行评审后酌情批复。

认定过程主要包括初审、专家评审、批复认定等三个环节。初审阶段主要由专业机构就各省（自治区、直辖市）提交认定申请材料进行初步审核，并就出现的问题和疑义与各省级文物行政部门进行沟通，请其修改、完善。专家评审阶段，国家文物局组织国内考古、历史地理以及长城研究领域的权威专家、学者对各省（自治区、直辖市）提交并经过专业机构审核、完善的长城认定资料和相关结论进行了反复论证，并与各省（区、市）文物行政部门进行了多次核实确认。国家文物局根据专家审核结论于2012年5月至6月间，向15个省（自治区、直辖市）文物行政部门下发批复文件，确认长城认定结论。

2012年6月5日，国家文物局在居庸关举办了发布活动，向社会发布了我国各时代长城的分布、数量等基本信息和认定结论。（图1-10）

（二）内容与结论

长城资源认定的主要内容包括性质和时代。长城的性质，是长期以来学术界争论的焦点之一。主要观点认为，长城主要用于对外防御，属于古代政权之间以及古代政权与北方游牧民族之间的军事防御体系。有一些朝代或政权对前代留下的长城进行了整修和沿用，但使用功能转化为内部守卫或进行地区间的交通封锁、税卡等，不再具有对外防御功能。此外，还有一些长城资源，文献中没有明确记载，现场调查时也无法确定其时代和功能。经过专家慎重研究，本次长城资源认定工作，最终将明长城、秦汉等早期长城的墙体、壕堑、关、

[2] 国家文物局：《国家文物局关于开展长城认定工作的通知》（文保函〔1159〕号），2011年6月7日。

图 1-10
“长城长，中华情”长城资源认定成果发布会现场，北京居庸关，2012（中国文化遗产研究院 提供）

Fig. 1-10
"Great Wall, Chinese soul "Great Wall resource data launch ceremony at Juyong Pass, Beijing (Photo by Chinese Academy of Cultural Heritage)

**(I) Scope and process**

According to the "*Notice on Carrying out the Identification of Great Wall* (W.W.B.H.[2011]1159)"of the State Administration of Cultural Heritage, the targets identified as Great wall resources are: "the Great Wall heritages that have been launched as the state or provincial priority protected Sites, and were also registered in this survey including passes and fortresses, beacon towers and watchtowers; and the Greer Wall heritages that have been registered in this survey but yet were not launched as the state or provincial priority protected Sites [2]". The former will be identified as Great Wall, while the later need to be applied by provincial (autonomous regions and municipal) cultural heritage department and subject to the identification of State Administration of Cultural Heritage.

The identification process includes three phases: preliminary examination, expert review and final approval. The specialized institutions are responsible for the preliminary examinations. They will communicate with the provincial cultural heritage administrations to solve the problems and questions found in the submitted materials. During the expert review phase, the State Administration of Cultural Heritage organizes the renowned experts from archeology, historical geography and Great Wall research fields to thoroughly review the materials. The State Administration of Cultural Heritage gave the 15 provinces (autonomous regions and municipalities) identification certificates of Great Wall resources from May through June 2012.

On June 5, 2012, the State Administration of Cultural Heritage held a ceremony at Juyong Pass to release the identification information of the Great Wall including the distribution and quantity and other basic information of different times. (Fig. 1-10)

[2] State Administration of Cultural Heritage: *Notice on Carrying out the Identification of Great Wall* (W.B.H.1159) June 7, 2011.

堡以及附属的敌台、马面、烽火台等认定为长城，将其他具备长城特征的线性文化遗产纳入《长城保护条例》的保护范围，而没有认定湖北省境内的相关历史遗迹以及清代或清代以后新建的城墙、烽火台等。

在时代方面，明确的考古与文献证据是主要的认定标准。考古学的方法，即通过长城遗迹的地层叠压关系，以及对地层和墙体中包含遗物的特征来综合判定长城的修建、使用和废弃时代。长城资源认定工作将我国境内的长城划分为春秋战国（调查中登记的春秋、战国各诸侯国）、秦汉（调查中登记的秦、西汉、东汉）、南北朝（调查中登记的北魏、东魏、西魏、北齐、北周等时代）、隋、唐、五代、宋、辽、金、西夏（根据考古研究成果新增加的时代类型）、明和时代不明等 12 个不同时代类型，涉及长城资源类别包括“墙体”“界壕/壕堑”“单体建筑”“关堡”“相关遗存”五大类。对于部分无法证明时代的长城资源，出于文物保护管理工作的需要，经过专家反复研究、商讨，将河北、甘肃两省少部分时代不明但长城特征属性比较明确的历史遗迹认定为长城。

通过此次长城资源调查，全面、细致、准确地掌握了我国长城资源的规模、分布、构成、走向、时代，以及保护管理现状、人文与自然环境等方面的基本情况，对长城资源构成、属性等问题进行了深入研究、探讨，形成了较为一致的理解和认识，圆满完成国务院所确定的“摸清长城家底”，全面准确掌握长城现存状况的目标。

## 专栏：考古研究的基本方法与长城断代依据缺乏的原因

考古学有两个基本方法，一个叫“地层学”，一个是“类型学”。“地层学”是指，在未扰动的情况下，时代晚的地层叠压在时代早的地层上；而上一层包含的遗物，比下一层中的遗物年代要晚；“类型学”则是说，古人遗留下的物品，可以分为不同的类型，同类的东西，形态变化存在一定的规律，通过研究这种规律，可以判断器物的时代相对早晚关系。

将地层学和类型学用在长城调查上，可以通过判断城墙里面的包含物的时代，来圈定城墙的时代区间。

然而长城一般修建在边疆地区，地层关系很简单，城墙里面的包含物很少，尤其是石砌和包砖的城墙里，几乎找不到能够判断时代的东西。而文献上的记载，要通过实物来证明，才有说服力。因此，长城时代的判断就变得十分困难。

### (II) Content and conclusion

The main contents of the Great Wall resources identification are its nature and dating. The nature of the Great Wall has been one of the focuses of academic debate for a long time. The main point of view is that the Great Wall is mainly used for defense system, which was used by the ancient regimes to keep out the nomads from the north. Some later regimes restored sections of the Great Wall and used them as internal security posts and regional checkpoints without defensive functions. Some of the suspected Great Wall resources have no historical record and could not be confirmed on its function and dating. After experts' careful study, the Ming dynasty Great Wall, Qin and Han dynasties' Great Wall, trenches, passes, fortresses, watchtowers, bastions and beacon towers are confirmed as the Great Wall resources. The other lineal or serial cultural heritages with the Great Wall characteristics are also protected by *Regulation on the Conservation of Great Wall*. The related historical sites in Hubei and the walls and beacon towers built in Qing dynasty and thereafter are not confirmed as the Great Wall resources.

Clear archaeological and documentary evidence is the main criterion for cultural relic's dating. The method of archaeology is to judge the Great Wall remains' layers and characteristics of the respective relics contained in order to identify its building, using and abandoning times. The Great Wall resource identification clarifies the Great Wall was built in 12 different times: Spring and Autumn and Warring States period, Qin and Han dynasties, Northern and Southern dynasties, Sui, Tang, Five Dynasties, Song, Liao, Jin, Western Xia and Ming dynasties as well as the unidentified time. The Great Wall resources fall into five categories: wall, trench, individual building, pass and fortress, related remain. The experts, after careful study and discussion, decided to confirm the Great Wall resources in Hebei and Gansu, which dating could not be identified, as parts of the Great Wall in order to protect the small amount of historical remains with clear Great Wall characteristics.

Through the resource survey, people gained a full, detailed and accurate knowledge of the Great Wall. The Great Wall's scale, distribution, composition, trend and dating as well as conservation and management situation, natural and humane environments are clarified. Through intensive study on its composition and nature, the survey teams reached consensus and successfully completed the State Council's assignment of getting a whole and clear picture of the Great Wall.

### Column:Basic methods of archaeology and reason for lack of evidence on dating of the Great Wall

Archaeology has two basic methods, one is called stratigraphy, and the other is typology. According to stratigraphy, without disturbance, the upper layer is usually at a later time than the layer down below and the relics contained in the upper layer also belong to a later time than the relics contained in the layer down below. According to typology, the ancient relics can be divided into different types. The same type of relics has similar morphological changes. People can identify the date of relics through study of such laws.

By applying stratigraphy and typology to the survey of the Great Wall, people can identify the dating of the walls by studying the times of the objects contained in the walls.

Most sections of the Great Wall were built in the frontier regions. The stratigraphic relationship is very simple. There are few objects in the walls, especially the stone and brick walls. The historical records could be convincing only with proofs of relics. Therefore, it is very difficult for dating on such Great Wall sections.

# 第二节 历代长城资源概况

※ 总长度——21196.18 千米
※ 资源数量——43721 段 / 座 / 处遗存
※ 修建时代——春秋战国、秦汉、南北朝、隋、唐、五代、宋、辽、金、西夏、明，超过 2450 年
※ 分布范围——15 个省（自治区、直辖市），97 个地级市，404 个县（区）

## 一、长城的长度

根据 2012 年 6 月 5 日国家文物局公布的长城资源认定数据，现存中国长城资源，分布于北京市、天津市、河北省、山西省、内蒙古自治区、辽宁省、吉林省、黑龙江省、山东省、河南省、陕西省、甘肃省、青海省、宁夏回族自治区、新疆维吾尔自治区等 15 个省（自治区、直辖市）、97 个设区市（州、盟）、404 个县（区、旗），各类长城资源遗存总数 43721 处（座 / 段），其中墙体 10051 段，壕堑 / 界壕 1764 段，单体建筑 29510 座，关、堡 2211 座，其他遗存 185 处。墙壕遗存总长度 21196.18 千米。通过与国家测绘地理信息部门的通力合作，采用科学测绘方法准确获取明长城墙体的总长度为 8851.8 千米。（图 1-11）此外，南北朝时期、春秋战国、秦汉、宋辽金西夏时期长城墙体的总长度均超过 1000 千米。（图 1-12）

## Section 2 Great Wall resources in different times

- ※ Total length: 21,196.18km
- ※ Resource numbers: 43,721 remains
- ※ Building times: Spring and Autumn period, Warring States, Qin and Han dynasties, Northern and Southern dynasties, Sui, Tang, Five Dynasties, Song, Liao, Jin, Western Xia and Ming dynasties (over 2,450 years)
- ※ Distribution areas: 15 provinces (autonomous regions and municipalities), 97 prefecture-level cities, 404 counties

### I. Length of Great Wall

According to the statistics released by the State Administration of Cultural Heritage on June 5, 2012, the Great Wall resources are distributed in 15 provinces (autonomous regions and municipalities), 97 prefecture-level cities, and 404 counties in Beijing, Tianjin, Hebei, Shanxi, Inner Mongolia, Liaoning, Jilin, Heilongjiang, Shandong, Henan, Shaanxi, Gansu, Qinghai, Ningxia and Xinjiang. There are 43,721 remains including 10,051 sections of walls, 1,764 trenches, 29,510 single structures, 2,211 passes and fortresses and 185 other remains. The walls and trenches are 21,196.18km long. With the help from the geographic information department of the State Administration of Surveying, Mapping and Geoinformation, the length of the Ming dynasty Great Wall is identified as 8,851.8km. (Fig. 1-11), All the Great Wall sections built in Spring and Autumn period, Warring States, Qin and Han dynasties, Northern and Southern dynasties, Song, Liao, Jin and Western Xia dynasties are longer than 1,000km. (Fig. 1-12).

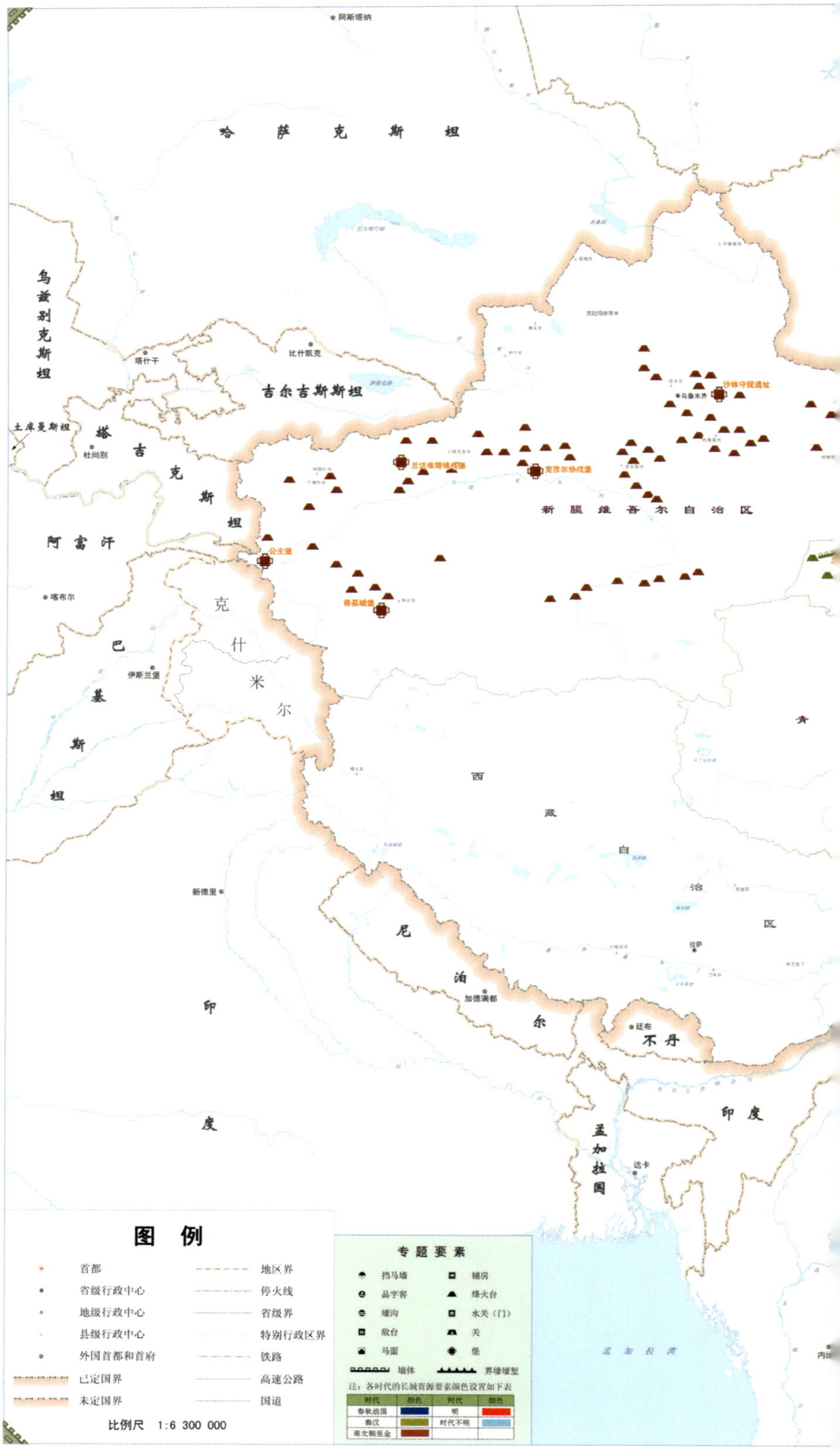


图 1-11
全国历代长城资源分布示意图
（国家基础地理信息中心 提供）

Fig. 1-11
Distribution of Great Wall resources in different times (Photo by State Basic Geographic Information Center)

罗 斯
蒙 古
乌兰巴托
黑 龙 江 省
吉 林 省
辽 宁 省
内 蒙 古 自 治 区
北 京 市
天 津 市
河 北 省
山 西 省
陕 西 省
甘 肃 省
宁 夏 回 族 自 治 区
山 东 省
河 南 省
江 苏 省
安 徽 省
上海市
湖 北 省
四 川 省
重 庆 市
浙 江 省
湖 南 省
江 西 省
福 建 省
贵 州 省
云 南 省
广 西 壮 族 自 治 区
广 东 省
海 南 省
台 湾 省
台湾岛
海南岛
香港特别行政区
澳门特别行政区
东沙群岛
朝 鲜
平壤
韩 国
首尔
日 本
东京
北海道岛
本州岛
四国岛
九州岛
日 本 海
东 海
南 海
太 平 洋
菲 律 宾
越 南
河内
老 挝
万象
柬 埔 寨
山海关
南海诸岛
1:11 000 000

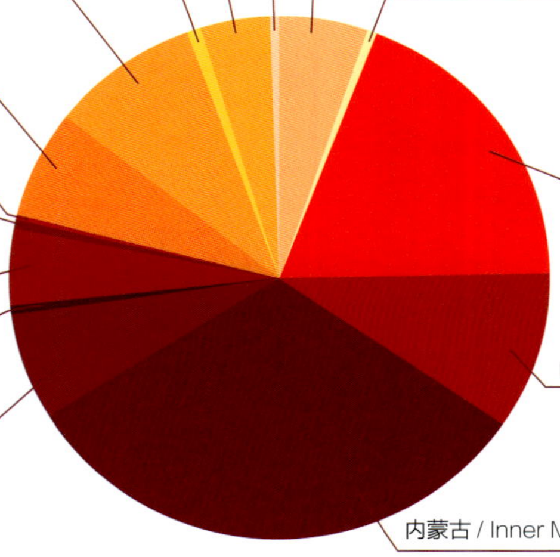

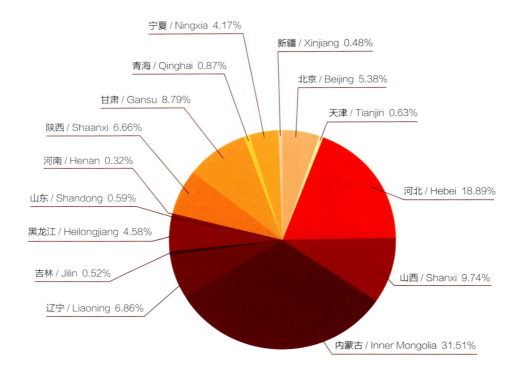


图 1-12
长城资源点段数量分省比例统计示意图 [3]

Fig. 1-12
Great Wall resources distributed by provinces [3]

## 二、长城的时代

根据历史与考古研究材料，“长城”一词最早的记录出现于公元前 5 世纪。近年整理出版的《清华大学藏战国竹简》[4] 中的《系年》篇有这样的记载：“晋敬公立十又一年（前 441 年）……齐人焉始为长城于济，自南山属之北海。”据此，长城的修建史至少可以上溯 2450 余年。现存最早的长城遗迹，也修建于春秋战国时代。至今在我国的辽宁、河北、山东、内蒙古、河南、陕西、山西、甘肃等地还能看到齐、楚、燕、赵、魏、秦、中山等战国时期诸侯国修建的长城遗迹。秦始皇统一六国后，命大将蒙恬“北筑长城”，将战国时期燕、赵、秦三国在北部边境修建的用于防御北方游牧民族的长城连接起来，东起辽东，西至临洮，总长度超过了一万华里，形成我国历史上最早的“万里长城”。

[3] 图片来源：国家文物局：《中国长城保护报告》，2016 年 11 月。

[4] 清华大学出土文献研究与保护中心编，李学勤主编：《清华大学藏战国竹简（贰）》，186 页，上海文艺出版集团、中西书局，2010 年。

[5] 曹婉如等：《中国古代地图集（战国—元）》，62 页，文物出版社，1990 年。

## II. Era of Great Wall

According to history and archeology research papers, the word "Great Wall" first appeared in 5th century BC. It was recorded in the book "Xi Nian" of "Tsinghua University collected Warring States bamboo slips I" [4] :"The people of Qi started building the Great Wall in 441 BC. The Great Wall started in the areas of Jinan's Pingyin and Changqing of today, continued along the ancient Ji river and ended at the shores of Bohai Sea." This record shows the building of the Great Wall could date back more than 2,450 years. The most ancient Great Wall remain was built in the Spring and Autumn period and Warring States. The Great Wall remains, built by Qi, Chu, Yan,

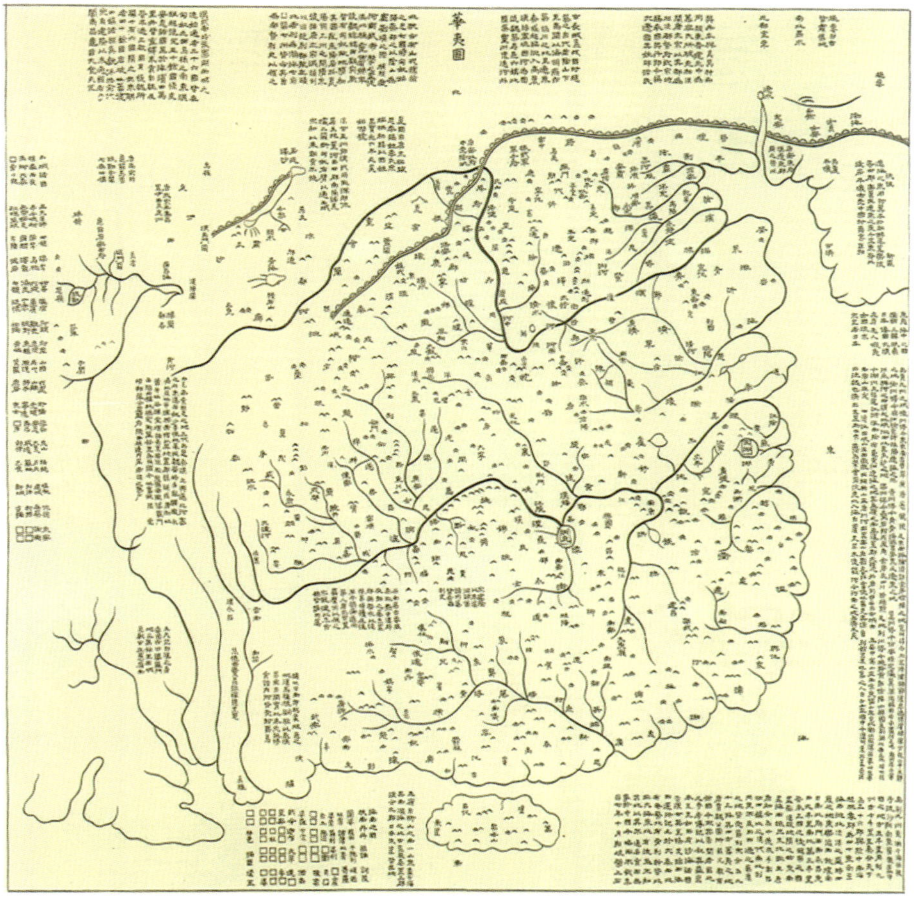


图 1-13
最早绘制长城的舆图——宋代《华夷图》[5]

Fig. 1-13
earliest Great Wall map - "Hua Yi Tu" of Song dynasty [5]

[3] Sources of the Photo: State Administration of Cultural Heritage: *The Report of Conservation of the Chinese Great Wall*. November 2016.

[4] Compiled by Tsinghua University Research and Conservation Center for unearthed Documents, Ed: Li Xueqin *Tsinghua University collected Warring States bamboo slips II* Shanghai Literature and Art Publishing House, and Zhongxi Book Company, 2010, P186

[5] Cao Wanru et al. *Chinese ancient maps: Warring States - Yuan dynasty*", published by Cultural Relics Publishing House in 1990, P62

从那时起，直至明代，很多中原王朝和地方政权都曾修筑过长城。比如：汉代的版图在汉武帝时期扩展到西域，汉朝的长城也从临洮延长到河西走廊的西端，春风不度的“玉门关”就是这时修建的。汉政府还在西域地区（今新疆维吾尔自治区）修建了数量众多的烽火台，它们也都是汉朝长城防御体系的组成部分。汉朝长城也成为中国古代延绵长度最长的长城。20 世纪初至 90 年代，考古工作者在甘肃、新疆、内蒙古等地汉代长城遗址中陆续发掘到数万枚简牍，简牍的内容主要是长城沿线的军事和社会生活档案记录，其中对当时长城分布也作了非常详细的记录；西晋时，西域地区的汉代烽火台得到了修补和沿用；隋、唐、明等朝代均修建过长城。

明长城是中国长城的精华，也是中国历史上最后一条系统修建的“万里长城”。今天我们见到的山海关、八达岭、嘉峪关长城等，均修建于明朝。明清时期关于修筑长城的官方和民间文献记录浩如烟海，有《皇明九边考》、《四镇三关志》、《山西宣大三镇通志》等专门的长城志书，也有《练兵实纪》等记录长城修建情况的文集、私人笔记，以及地方志。这些都是明长城研究的珍贵史料。（图 1-14）

除中原王朝外，南北朝时期的北魏、北齐等政权，隋唐时期的一些东北地方政权，以及与北宋同时代的西夏、辽、金政权等，也都修建了具备长城特征的线性防御设施。

以考古工作为基本依据，结合文献记载，国家最终认定中国境内现存长城包括了春秋战国、秦汉、南北朝、隋、唐、五代、宋、辽、金、西夏、明等 11 个主要时代，此外还有少量长城时代不明。按照分省统计，河北省、山西省、内蒙古自治区长城的时代数量最多，达到 6 个时代；其次为辽宁省和宁夏回族自治区（5 个时代）；陕西省和甘肃省（4 个时代）；吉林省（3 个时代）；北京市、黑龙江省和新疆维吾尔自治区（2 个时代）。而河南省和山东省仅有春秋战国时代长城分布；天津市和青海省境内则仅有明长城分布。（表 1-3，图 1-15）

---

［6］〔明〕李辅等修，高凤楼、许麟英撰：《全辽志》，上海书店出版社，1994 年。

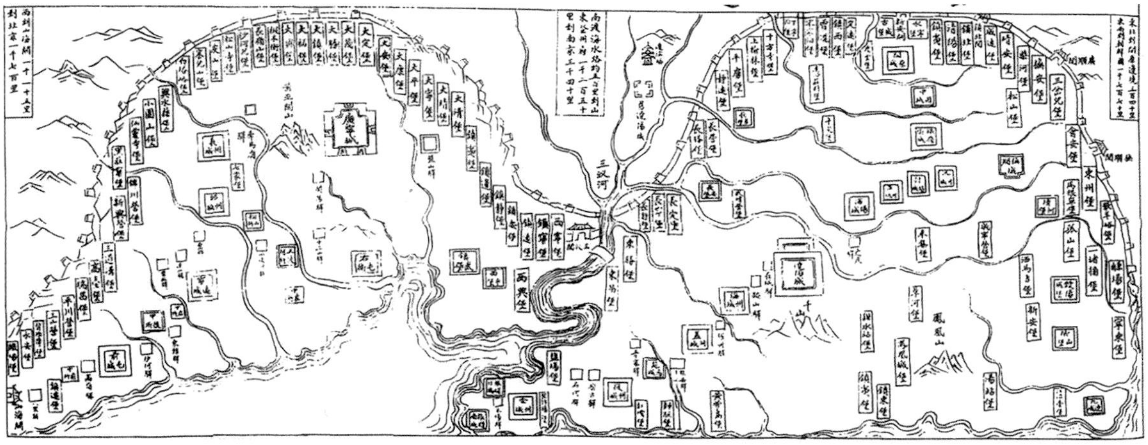

图 1-14
明代志书《全辽志》中的辽东（今辽宁地区）长城图[6]

Fig. 1-14
Map of Great Wall in Liaodong found in book "*The General History of the Liao Dynasty*" of Ming dynasty[6]

Zhao, Wei, Qin and Zhongshan of the Warring States, still could be seen in Liaoning, Hebei, Shandong, Inner Mongolia, Henan, Shaanxi, Shanxi and Gansu today. After conquering the six states, Qinshihuang ordered General Meng Tian to build the "Great Wall" to keep the northern nomads out. He linked the existing "Great Walls" built by Yan, Zhao and Qin. The finished "Great Wall" started at the Liaodong in eastern region and ended at Lintao in the western region. With total length exceeding 10,000 Li, it became the first "10,000 Li Great Wall" in history.

Between Qinshihuang era and Ming dynasty, many kingdoms in Central Plain area and the local regimes also built their own "Great Walls". With its expansion to the Western Regions in Martial Emperor Era, Han dynasty extended the Great Wall to the west end of Hexi Corridor. Yumenguan, mentioned in a famous poem, was built then. A great number of beacon towers were built in Western Regions (today's Xinjiang Uygur Autonomous Region) during Han dynasty. They are part of the defensive system of Han dynasty. The Great Wall reached its peak in length in Han dynasty. Between the beginning of the 20$^{th}$ century and 1990s, archeologist found tens of thousands of bamboo slips at the Han dynasty Great Wall remains in Gansu, Xinjiang and Inner Mongolia. The bamboo slips mainly recorded the military and civil lives along the Great Wall. The distribution of the Great Wall was also detailed in the records. The Western Jin dynasty continued to use the beacon towers, built by Han dynasty, in Western Regions. Sui, Tang and Ming dynasties continued to build the Great Wall.

[6] (Ming Dynasty) Edited by Li Fu et al, written by Gao Fenglou and Xu Linying: *The General History of the Liao Dynasty*, Shanghai, Shanghai Bookstore Publishing House, 1994

**表 1-3：长城资源时代数量分省统计表**

Table 1-3: Building times of Great Wall by provinces

| 政区 Administrative Region | 春秋战国 Spring and Autumn, Warring States | 秦汉 Qin, Han | 南北朝 Southern and Northern States | 隋 Sui | 唐 Tang | 五代 Five Dynasties | 宋、辽、金、西夏 Song, Liao, Jin, Western Xia | 明 Ming | 时代数量 Dynasty Number |
|---|---|---|---|---|---|---|---|---|---|
| 北京市 Beijing | × | × | ○ | × | × | × | × | ○ | 2 |
| 天津市 Tianjin | × | × | × | × | × | × | × | ○ | 1 |
| 河北省 Hebei | ○ | ○ | ○ | × | ○ | × | ○ | ○ | 6 |
| 山西省 Shanxi | ○ | ○ | ○ | ○ | × | ○ | × | ○ | 6 |
| 内蒙古自治区 Inner Mongolia | ○ | ○ | ○ | ○ | × | × | ○ | ○ | 6 |
| 辽宁省 Liaoning | ○ | ○ | ○ | × | × | × | ○ | ○ | 5 |
| 吉林省 Jilin | × | ○ | × | × | ○ | × | ○ | × | 3 |
| 黑龙江省 Heilongjiang | × | × | × | × | ○ | × | ○ | × | 2 |
| 山东省 Shandong | ○ | × | × | × | × | × | × | × | 1 |
| 河南省 Henan | ○ | × | × | × | × | × | × | × | 1 |
| 陕西省 Shaanxi | ○ | × | ○ | ○ | × | × | × | ○ | 4 |
| 甘肃省 Gansu | ○ | ○ | × | × | ○ | × | × | ○ | 4 |
| 青海省 Qinghai | × | × | × | × | × | × | × | ○ | 1 |
| 宁夏回族自治区 Ningxia | ○ | ○ | × | ○ | × | × | ○ | ○ | 5 |
| 新疆维吾尔自治区 Xinjiang | × | ○ | × | × | ○ | × | ○ | × | 3 |

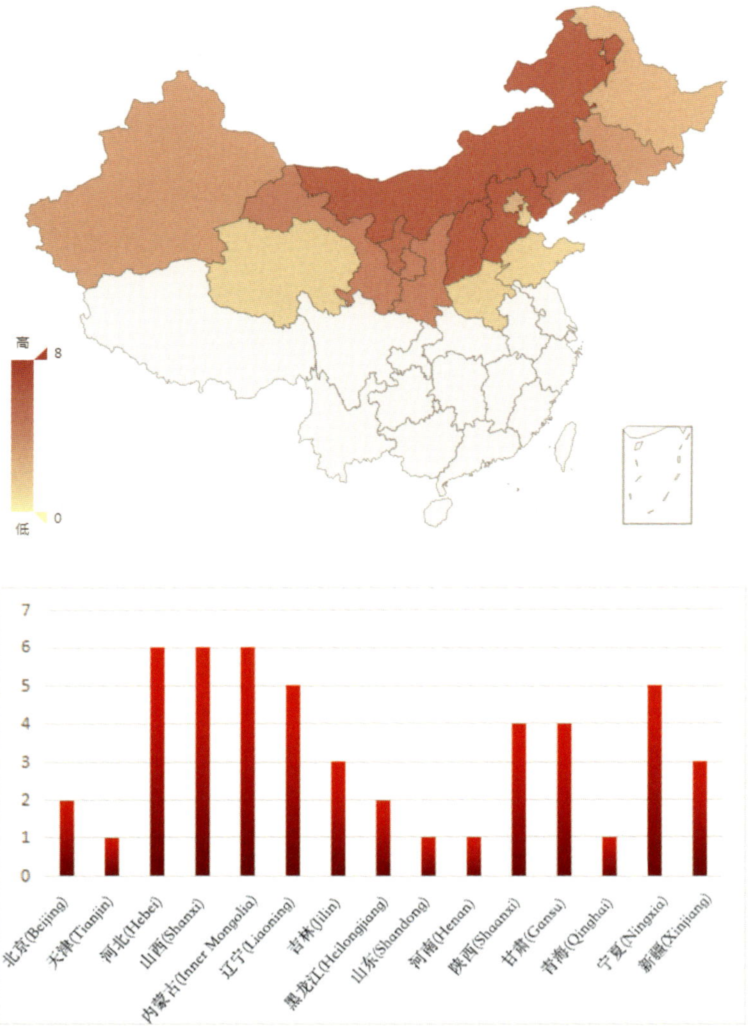


图 1-15
长城资源时代数量分省统计图

Fig. 1-15
Building times of Great Wall by provinces

The Ming dynasty Great Wall is the best part of the Great Wall. It is also the last systematically built"10,000 li Great Wall". All the renowned Shanhai Pass, Badaling and Jiayu Pass were built in Ming dynasty. There are lots of Ming and Qing dynasties' official and folk records on the building of the Great Wall. The "Huang Ming Jiu Bian Kao", "Si Zhen San Guan Zhi" "Shanxi Xuanda San Zhen Tong Zhi" are local history books, which are dedicated on the Great Wall. The private papers like the "Troop Training Journal" also covered the building of the Great Wall. Both of the local history books and the private papers are precious historical records for studying the Ming dynasty Great Wall.

## 三、长城的构成

### （一）基本构成

长城是世界上体量最大、蔚为壮观的历史文化遗产，同时也是由多种遗存及其所处自然环境共同构成的、具有独特审美价值的、文化景观特征突出的文化遗产。针对上述特点，长城作为综合的防御体系，包括了构成长城防御体系的各类设施，以及与防御体系相关的其他设施；还包括了体现长城防御、修筑理念的自然与人文环境等。（图 1-16）

长城防御体系由连续、不封闭的高墙为主体，并与关隘、城堡、敌台、烽燧等设施紧密结合的长达数百至数千公里的军事防御工程。

其中，墙体是长城防线设施中最主要的部分，它直接承担着阻挡游牧骑兵突袭的重任。明代墙体之上，普遍增筑马面和敌台。关堡，是长城防御体系中守御和屯兵的中心。关，从功能上来说，肩负着指挥中枢的作用，关内一般设有军事长官，是决策的发出地，起到总揽大局的作用。一般来说，关的建设依托于墙体，是出入长城的通道。堡，则是军队驻扎的场所，又被称为城障、障城、镇城、障塞、城堡、寨、戍堡、边堡、军堡、屯堡、民堡等，一般与墙体不发生直接关联。烽火台也称烽燧、墩台、烽堠、烟墩、狼烟台、狼烟墩，其功能主要是通过台顶点燃的烟火，起到传递信息的作用。除此之外，明长城防御体系中还有挡马墙、品字窖、壕沟、火池、烟灶等 5 种与报警、阻敌有关的其他防御设施。

与长城防御体系相关的还有砖瓦窑、采石场、居住址等生产生活设施，碑碣、刻石等文化设施，驿站等交通设施，这些也作为重要的长城资源纳入了此次调查。

图 1-16
长城的遗产构成

Fig. 1-16
Composition of Great Wall resources

Besides the kingdoms in Central Plains region, Northern Wei and Northern Qi of the Northern and Southern Dynasties, some local powers in Northeast China in the period of Sui and Tang dynasties and Western Xia, Liao and Jin regimes in the period of Northern Song also built the Great Wall like defensive walls.

Based on the archeology findings and historical papers, the state authority finally confirmed the Great Wall was mainly built in Spring and Autumn period, Warring States, Qin and Han dynasties, Northern and Southern dynasties, Sui, Tang, Five Dynasties, Song, Liao, Jin, Western Xia and Ming dynasties. There are a few Great Wall remains, whose date could not be identified yet. The Great Wall sections in Hebei, Shanxi and Inner Mongolia were built in six dynasties, Liaoning and Ningxia's in five dynasties, Shaanxi and Gansu's in four dynasties, Jilin's in three dynasties, Beijing, Heilongjiang and Xinjiang's in two dynasties. Henan and Shandong's Great Wall sections were only built in the Spring and Autumn period and Warring States time. Tianjin and Qinghai only have Ming dynasty Great Wall. (Table 1-3, Fig. 1-15)

## III. Composition of Great Wall

### (I) Basic composition

The Great Wall is the world's most magnificent and spectacular cultural heritage. Its multi-feature remains, blended with its natural surroundings, have unique aesthetic value and are cultural tourist attractions. The Great Wall's basic parts include the defensive walls and its supporting facilities as well as the natural and humane environments. (Fig. 1-16)

The Great Wall defensive system consists the consistent and unclosed high walls and the supporting passes, fortresses, bastions and beacon towers. The closely linked defensive system is often between hundreds and thousands of kilometers.

The walls are the main parts, which directly block the ambush from the nomad troopers. The bastions and watchtowers are widely added on the Ming dynasty Great Wall. The passes and fortresses are centers for defense and stationing troops. The pass is military commanding center, where the local military leader stations. Usually the pass is built with the wall forming the

## （二）设施构成

长城防御设施由墙体、敌楼、壕堑、关隘、城堡以及烽火台等相关历史遗存组成。其中：长城墙体按照材质可分为土墙、石墙、砖墙、木障墙等。除此之外，还包括山险墙、山险、河险及界壕 / 壕堑等特殊类型墙体。山险、河险等自然险形成的墙体，即在一些地势险峻的地方，无须建造人工墙体，而是直接利用自然天险进行防御，与人工墙体共同构成防线。“自然险”的长度超过 2000 千米，可以占到总长度的约 13%。（图 1-17）山险墙，即对自然山体或沟谷进行人工修葺或铲削形成的墙体。界壕 / 壕堑，即古人在草原、荒漠地区有时会采取向下挖掘深壕、筑土为墙的方式构筑的长城，这些壕与城墙首尾相连或并行，共同构成防线。（图 1-18、1-19、1-20）据统计，全国历代长城中的界壕 / 壕堑类遗存的总长度约 4800 千米，占到总长度的 22.8%。

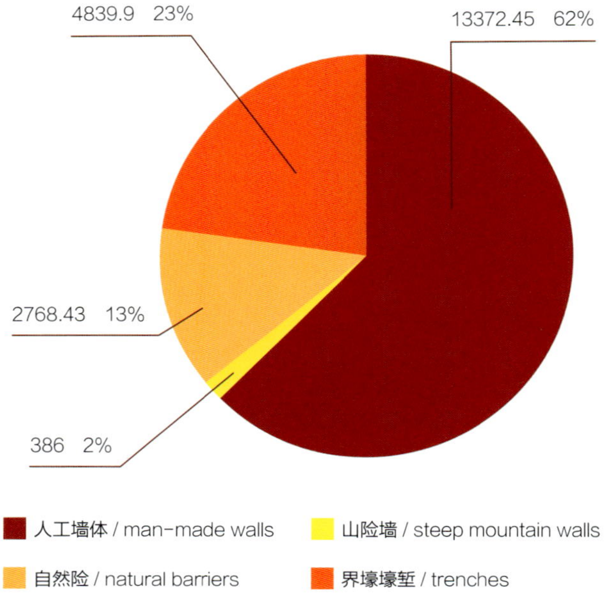


图 1-17
长城人工墙体与自然险长度统计饼状图

Fig. 1-17
Pie chart of Great Wall's man-made walls and natural barriers

图 1-18
宁夏回族自治区青铜峡市境内的夯土长城（张依萌 拍摄）

Fig. 1-18
Rammed earth walls in Qingtongxia, Ningxia (Photo by Zhang Yimeng)

图 1-19
黑龙江省齐齐哈尔市金界壕（张依萌 拍摄）

Fig. 1-19
Trenches of Jin at Qiqihar, Heilongjiang (Photo by Zhang Yimeng)

图 1-20
辽宁鼓山长城 5 段山险墙（辽宁省长城资源调查队 拍摄）

Fig. 1-20
Five sections of mountain walls at Gushan, Liaoning (Photo by Liaoning Great Wall resource survey team)

gate of the wall. Fortress is the center for stationing troops. It is not connected with the wall. It is also called "Chengzhang", "Zhangcheng", "Zhencheng", "Zhangsai", "Chengbao", "Zhai", "Shubao", "Bianbao", "Junbao", "Tunbao" and "Minbao". Beacon tower is also called "Fengsui", "Duntai", "Fenghou", "Yandun", "Langyantai" and "Langyandun". The beacon fire lit on the top of the beacon tower is used to send signals. The Great Wall defensive system also includes horse-blocking wall, horse trap, trench, fire pool and smoke stove, which are used for alarming and containing enemies.

The brick kilns, quarries and residential sites are related to the Great Wall defense system. The related cultural relics like steles and engraved stones and transportation facility like courier stations are also included in this survey.

### (II) Composition of facilities

The Great Wall defense facilities include walls, watchtowers, trenches, passes, fortress and beacon towers.

There are clay, stone, brick and wooden barrier walls. The natural walls include mountain, river and trench. The natural barriers like steep mountains and rivers are smartly fit into the man-made walls. Such natural barriers are over 2,000 km, which is about 13% of the Great Wall's total length. (Fig. 1-17) Some parts of the mountains and valleys are fixed to become natural walls. The trenches are dug at the grassland and desert areas. They are linked to the walls

长城的单体建筑包括敌台、马面、烽火台、城楼等。敌台，也称敌楼，是指跨墙体而建，突出于城墙的高台建筑，用于住兵、储藏兵器和作为战斗堡垒使用。（图 1-21）马面，即突出于城墙外侧，与城墙同高的台子，为了增加防守面，消除防守死角而建，同时也能起到加固城墙的作用。（图 1-22）烽火台，指长城沿线用于点燃烟火传递重要信息的高台，是长城防御体系的重要组成部分，一般独立于墙体而建，分布在沿墙体、通向长城的重要道路或河流，控制碍口的制高点等。（图 1-23）

图 1-21
河北省保定市涞源县插箭岭长城 5 号敌台
（河北省长城资源调查队 拍摄）

Fig. 1-21
No. 5 watchtower of Chajianling Great Wall at Laiyuan county of Baoding, Hebei (Photo by Hebei Great Wall resource survey team)

图 1-22
山西省朔州市朔城区墙体与马面
（山西省长城资源调查队 拍摄）

Fig. 1-22
Walls and bastions at Shuozhou, Shanxi
(Photo by Shanxi Great Wall resource survey team)

to form a consistent defense line. (Fig.1-18,1-19,1-20) The total length of the trenches is about 4,800 km, which is 22.8% of the Great Wall's total length.

The Great Wall's single buildings include watchtowers, bastions, beacon towers and gate towers. Watchtower is built on the top of the wall. It is used for accommodating soldiers, storing weapons and battle fortress. (Fig. 1-21)Bastion is built to add the defense space and eliminate dead angle. With the same height of the wall, the bastion is built overhanging the wall top. It also reinforces the wall. (Fig. 1-22)Beacon towers are built to send signals with beacon, which is an import part of the Great Wall defense system. The beacon towers are usually built off the walls and at commanding elevations (Fig. 1-23).

图 1-23
甘肃省金塔县汉代烽火台（张依萌 拍摄）

Fig. 1-23
Han dynasty beacon tower at Jinta county of Gansu Province (Photo by Zhang Yimeng)

关堡，即关隘和城堡。关隘，一般依托墙体而建，把守重要的通道口。（图 1-24）城堡，则多位分布在墙体内侧数公里范围之内，用于驻军，指挥和支援长城作战。（图 1-25）

除了墙、壕、单体、关堡之外，长城的构成元素还包括很多其他设施和结构，例如挡马墙、壕沟、品字窖等。挡马墙，即墙体主线外侧的矮墙，用于减缓敌方骑兵的进攻速度。壕沟，即城墙的护城壕。品字窖，又称陷马坑，也就是陷阱。此外，还有依附于墙体或与墙体相连的附属设施或结构，如女墙、障墙、箭窗、射孔等协助防守的设施，墙体上的各类排水设施，驻军的铺舍、登城的暗门、梯道、马道，以及长城跨越河道时建筑的供水流通过的水门等等。（图 1-26）

图 1-24
北京市昌平居庸关（北京市长城资源调查队 拍摄）

Fig. 1-24
Juyong Pass at Changping, Beijing (Photo by Beijing Great Wall resource survey team)

图 1-25
甘肃省金塔县汉长城——东大湾城堡（李国民 拍摄）

Fig. 1-25
Dongdawan fortress of Han dynasty Great Wall at Jinta county of Gansu Province (Photo by Li Guomin)

图 1-26
宁夏明长城的一座"品字窖"（宁夏回族自治区长城资源调查队 拍摄）

Fig. 1-26
Horse trap of Ming dynasty Great Wall in Ningxia (Photo by Ningxia Great Wall resource survey team)

The pass is usually built with the wall controlling import road. (Fig. 1-24) The fortress is located within several kilometers of the wall. It is for stationing troops and commanders. They are supposed to support the battles of the troops stationed on the walls. (Fig. 1-25)

Besides walls, trenches, passes and fortresses, the Great Wall also includes many other facilities and structures like horse-blocking wall and horse traps. The horse-blocking wall is the small walls built outside the main walls. They are built to slow down the charging speed of the cavalries.. The trenches are dug to protect the walls. There are also horse traps dug outside the walls. The parapet walls, barrier walls, arrow-shooting windows and shooting holes, built on the walls or connected to the walls, are part of the defense system. There are also drainage system incorporated in the walls as well as barracks, trapdoors, stairways and horse paths. The water gates are built when the Great Wall crosses rivers.

### (III)Numbers of Great Wall

The Great Wall resources of Qin and Han dynasties: the Great Wall of Spring and Autumn period and Warring States are mainly located in Hebei, Shanxi, Inner Mongolia, Liaoning, Shandong, Henan, Shaanxi, Gansu and Ningxia. There are 1,795 sections of walls and trenches, 1,367 single buildings, 160 passes and fortresses, 33 related remains, which total length is 3,080.14 km. Most of them are built with stones and rammed earth. Qin dynasty linked the defensive walls of Yan, Zhao and Qin, which is over 10,000 li long. Han dynasty Great Wall starts at Liaodong in the east and ends at Yumeng Pass of Guansu in

## （三）数量构成

秦汉及早期长城资源概况。春秋战国长城主要分布区域包括河北、山西、内蒙古、辽宁、山东、河南、陕西、甘肃、宁夏等省（自治区）。现存墙壕 1795 段，单体建筑 1367 座，关、堡 160 座，相关遗存 33 处，长度 3080.14 千米。多以土石或夯土构筑为主。秦代将燕、赵、秦三国的北部长城连为一体，“延袤万余里”[7]。汉代长城东起辽东，西至甘肃玉门关，总体呈东西走向，主要分布区域包括河北、山西、内蒙古、辽宁、甘肃、宁夏等省（自治区）。秦汉长城现存墙壕 2143 段，单体建筑 2575 座，关、堡 271 座，相关遗存 10 处，长度 3680.26 千米。玉门关以西至新疆维吾尔自治区阿克苏市，连绵分布有汉代烽火台遗迹。秦汉长城以土筑、石砌为主，甘肃西部等地以芦苇、红柳、梭梭木夹砂构筑方式较常见，烽火台除黄土夯筑外，还有土坯或土块砌筑等做法。

明长城资源概况。明长城资源保存相对完整、形制类型丰富，主要分布区域包括北京、天津、河北、山西、内蒙古、辽宁、陕西、甘肃、青海、宁夏 10 个省（自治区、直辖市）。其主线东起辽宁虎山，西至甘肃嘉峪关，在河北、山西、辽宁、陕西、甘肃、宁夏等地还出现多处分支。现存墙壕 5209 段，单体建筑 17449 座，关、堡 1272 座，相关遗存 142 处，长度 8851.8 千米。东部地区明长城以石砌包砖、夯土包砖或石砌为主，西部地区则多为夯土构筑。

其他时代长城资源概况。历史上北魏、北齐、隋、唐、五代、宋 / 西夏 / 辽等时代均不同程度修筑过长城，或在局部地区新建了具备长城特征的防御体系，在选址、形制、建造技术等方面都对后期长城的修筑产生了影响。现存墙壕 1276 段，单体建筑 454 座，关、堡 119 座。此外，金代在今黑龙江省甘南县，经内蒙古东部、河北北部至内蒙古自治区四子王旗一线，修筑了以壕沟为防御工程主体的界壕体系，称之为“金界壕”。现存墙壕 1392 段，单体建筑 7665 座，关、堡 389 座，长度 4010.48 千米。

[7]〔汉〕司马迁：《史记·蒙恬列传》，第 2566 页，中华书局，1963 年。

the east. It is mainly located in Hebei, Shanxi, Inner Mongolia, Liaoning, Gansu and Ningxia. Today's Qin and Han dynasties Great Wall has 2,143 sections of walls and trenches, 2,575 single buildings, 271 passes and fortresses and 10 related remains, which total length is 3,680.26 km. There are Han dynasty beacon towers dotted between west of Yumeng Pass and Aksu of Xinjiang. The Qin and Han dynasties Great Wall are mainly built with earth and stones. It is common to use reed, rose willow and sacsaoul wood mixed with sand in the building of the Great Wall in western Gansu. The beacon towers are built with tamped loess or sun-dried mud bricks.

The Ming dynasty Great Wall, in various shapes and structures, is in relatively good condition. It is mainly located in Beijing, Tianjin, Hebei, Shanxi, Inner Mongolia, Liaoning, Shaanxi, Gansu, Qinghai and Ningxia. Its eastern end is at Hushan of Liaoning and western end is at Jiayu Pass of Gansu. There are also some of its branches in Hebei, Shanxi, Liaoning, Shaanxi, Gansu and Ningxia. It has 5,209 sections of walls and trenches, 17,449 single buildings, 1,272 passes and fortresses and 142 related remains, which total length is 8,851.8 km. The eastern part of it is mainly built with stone bricks, tamped earth bricks and stones. The western part of its is mainly built with tamped earth.

The Great Wall resources of other dynasties: Northern Wei, Northern Qi, Sui, Tang, Five Dynasties, Song, Western Xia and Liao also built parts of the Great Wall. The location choices, shapes and structures and building technologies influenced the building of the Great Wall in later times. There are 1,276 sections of walls and trenches, 454 single buildings and 119 passes and fortresses. The "Jin border trenches" started in Gannan county of Heilongjiang winding through eastern Inner Mongolia and northern Hebei and ended at Siziwang Banner of Inner Mongolia. There are 1,392 sections of walls and trenches, 7,665 single buildings, 389 passes and fortresses, which total length is 4,010.48 km.

## IV. Building of Great Wall

The Great Wall is 21,000 km long including 13,700 km man-made walls and 4,800 km trenches. The ancient people applied the local materials and technologies in building the Great Wall. The walls are mainly built with tamped earth and stone bricks.

[7] (Han) Sima Qian: *Historical Records·The biography of Meng Tian* P2566, Zhonghua Book Company, 1963

## 四、长城的营造

在21000余千米的长城墙体中，有13700余千米为人工墙体，4800余千米为人工挖掘的界壕或壕堑。古人在修建长城的时候，考虑到技术和成本的问题，一般会采取因地制宜的方式选择建材。一般情况下，采用黄土夯筑或石块砌筑的方式来建造墙体。

夯土建筑是中国一项很古老的建筑技术，至迟在距今6000年前的新石器时代，中国的先人们就开始用夯土来建造房屋和城墙。[8]在我国的西北地区，包括山西、内蒙古、陕西、甘肃、青海、宁夏、新疆等省境内的长城，绝大部分使用夯土建造的。在全国范围内来说，历代长城中，夯土墙体长度最长，超过6000千米，占人工墙体总长度的约45.5%。

在北京、天津、河北、山西、内蒙古、辽宁、山东、河南、陕西等省市，由于石材丰富，石砌墙体比较普遍。有些石砌墙体由整齐的条石或尺寸相当的石块砌筑，并用白灰进行勾缝，有的则用毛石或石片直接垒砌，称为“毛石干垒”或“干插边”。全国现存的石砌墙体大约占总长度的四分之一。

此外，还有将近四分之一由特殊材质或工艺建造的墙体，比如甘肃等地位于沙漠、戈壁地区的汉代长城，会使用沙土和芦苇、红柳、梭梭木等植物分层构筑，称为“芦苇夹砂”或“红柳夹砂”，现在还能在西北地区看到这种类型的汉代长城，有的保存至今仍有一人多高。还有一些烽火台，会用土坯或“垡子”垒砌。“垡子”其实就是由河床或沼泽湿地中切出的淤泥块。现在这些烽火台仍然挺立在西北大地上。能够用最简单的材料建造出坚固的军事防御工程，这正是长城的伟大之处。（图1-27、1-28）

而我们最为熟悉的八达岭、山海关、嘉峪关等包砖墙体，大都分布在东部地区，或一些重要的关隘附近，约有总长度仅377.26千米，仅占长城总长度的约1.8%。

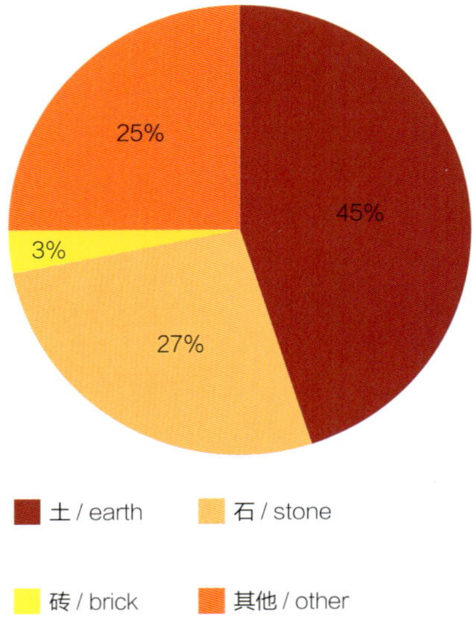


图1-28
长城人工墙体材质长度统计图（单位：千米）

Fig. 1-28
Pie chart of Great Wall's building materials (Unit: km)

[8] 参见张石玉、赵新萍、桥梁：《郑州西山仰韶时代城址的发掘》，《文物》1999年7期。

图 1-27
现存长城的各种材质（张依萌 拍摄）
a 土墙
b 石墙
c 砖墙
d 红柳、梭梭木夹砂

Fig. 1-27
Great Wall's different materials (Photo by Zhang Yimeng)
a. tamped earth wall
b. stone wall
c. brick wall
d. special(sand mixed rose willow and sacsaoul wood

The ancient Chinese started using the tamped earth to build houses and city walls at least in the New Stone Age era, which is 6,000 years ago.[8] Most of the Great Wall in northwest China including Shanxi, Inner Mongolia, Shaanxi, Gansu, Qinghai, Ningxia and Xinjiang, are built with tamped earth. The Great Wall sections, built with tamped earth, are the longest exceeding 6,000 km. It accounts for about 45.5% of the man-made walls.

The stones are rich in Beijing, Tianjin, Hebei, Shanxi, Inner Mongolia, Liaoning, Shandong, Henan and Shaanxi. So the stone walls are popular in such areas. Some stone walls are built with stone bars or stone bricks. The lime is applied to fill the cracks between the stones. Some walls are directly made with raw stones. The stone walls account for one fourth of the total length of the Great Wall.

Besides, about one fourth of the Great Wall was built with special material and technology. The Han dynasty Great Wall, located at desert and gobi areas of Gansu, was built with sand mixed reed, rose willow and sacsaoul wood, which is very solid. Such walls still could be seen today. Some are one man's high. Some beacon towers are built with sun-dried mud bricks or "Fa Zi", which is silt piece. Such beacon towers are still standing in northwest China. The Great Wall, a strong military defense system, is built with simplest materials, which contributed the greatness of the Great Wall. (Fig. 1-27, 1-28).

The most familiar sections including Badaling, Shanhai Pass and Jiayu Pass, built with bricks, are located at the strategic locations in east China, which length is about 377.26 km accounting for about 1.8% of the Great Wall's total length.

[8] Reference: Zhang Yushi, Zhao Xinping and Qiao Liang, "Unearthing of Yangshao cities at Xishan, Zhengzhou","Cultural Relics",1999-7-15.

# 第三节 长城的功能与价值

※ 长城的功能——坚固防线、地理标识、沟通桥梁
※ 长城的价值——历史见证、科技集成、文学灵感、生活家园、国家象征、人类遗产

长城是中华文明的伟大成就，是中华民族先民在 2400 余年的漫长历史中，在险恶的自然环境和较低的生产力条件下，创造的伟大人类工程奇迹；长城是数量巨大、类型丰富、分布范围宽广的各类遗存与其所处自然环境共同构成的、具有突出普遍价值和独特文化景观特征的文化遗产。在我国各个历史时期，长城发挥着保卫国家长治久安、维护人民生活稳定、保障多元文明交流的重要作用。20 世纪以来，长城成为中华民族精神的象征，也是中国和中华民族形象的代表，在世界范围内具有广泛的影响力。

长城历经成百上千年自然环境变化与社会时代变迁，各类遗存蕴含着丰富的历史信息，包括“材料、工艺、设计及其环境和它所反映的历史、文化、社会等相关信息”。[9] 长城“在历史深化过程中形成的包括各个时代特征、具有价值的物质遗存都

[9] 国际古迹遗址理事会中国国家委员会：《2015 中国文物古迹保护准则》，10 页。

## Section 3 Function and Value of Great Wall

※ Function: strong defense line, geographic landmark, communication bridge
※ Value: historic witness, technology showpiece, literary inspiration, living home, national symbol, human heritage

The Great Wall is a great achievement of the Chinese civilization. It is a great human engineering miracle, which was made by the ancient Chinese against the hazardous natural conditions and low productivity in over 2,400 years. The Great Wall cultural heritage, with magnificent physical presence, rich structure types and wide distribution as well as blended with natural environment, has outstanding universal value and unique cultural landscape features. The Great Wall played a key role in protecting national security, maintaining people's peaceful life and guaranteeing multicultural exchanges in different historical times. It has become the spiritual symbol of the Chinese people since the 20$^{th}$ century. It is also the image representative of both China and Chinese people. It enjoys a widespread influence worldwide.

The Great Wall has existed for over thousands of years withstanding environmental evolution and social changes. Its resources contain rich historical information. Its material, craftsmanship, design and environment reflect the historical, cultural and social information.[9] The Great Wall's historical features

[9] Chinese National Committee for the International Council on Monuments and Sites: *Principles for the Conservation of Heritage Site in China 2015, P10*

应得到尊重”，[10]保有敬畏之心。保护长城，要实现“对其价值、价值载体及其环境等体现文物古迹价值的各个要素的完整保护”。[11]保护长城的根本目的不是要重现长城当年的辉煌，而是要真实、完整、客观地保存长城承载的历史信息，保护其古朴和沧桑感，传承和发扬它在历史、艺术、科学等方面无与伦比的价值。

## 一、长城的功能

### 1、坚固防线

作为军事防御工程而存在的长城，是战争的产物。在不同历史时期，长城修建的目的、建造能力、长城的功能与防御对象不尽相同。例如，在北方游牧民族活动比较频繁的时期，战国秦、赵、燕在北部地区修筑的长城，主要是防御戎、楼烦、林胡、东胡等游牧民族；秦、汉、明等统一王朝以及其间北魏、东魏、北齐、北周、隋、辽、西夏、金北方地区各政权也广泛修筑长城，以防御匈奴、柔然、突厥、蒙古等游牧民族的侵扰。冷兵器时代，长城坚固的防御体系不但有效地阻滞了草原民族对中原的侵扰，其宏大的建筑形态更对长城以北的民族和政权产生了战略威慑力，为保卫国家长治久安发挥了不可替代的重要作用。

### 2、边界标识

长城修筑的地理位置，基本限定了东亚大陆农耕民族同游牧、渔猎民族两种不同政治、经济形态和生活方式的分布区域。“边界”和“内外”的概念因此而清晰起来。《汉书·西域传》谓“秦始皇攘却戎狄，筑长城，界中国”；《后汉书·乌桓鲜卑列传》云：“天设山河，秦筑长城……所以别内外，异殊俗也。”长城的修筑，拓展了“中国”的地理和政治概念。

---

[10] 国际古迹遗址理事会中国国家委员会:《2015中国文物古迹保护准则》，10页。

[11] 国际古迹遗址理事会中国国家委员会:《2015中国文物古迹保护准则》，10页。。

and valuable cultural relics should all be respected.[10] In conservation of the Great Wall, people should have respect to it at first. Its value, cultural relics and related environment all need to be protected as a whole.[11] The purpose of conservation of the Great Wall is not to revitalize its old glory, but to truly, fully and objectively conserve its historical information and presence and carry forward its unique historical, artistic and scientific values.

## I. Function of Great Wall

### 1. Strong defense line

The Great Wall, as a military defense project, is the product of war. In different historical periods, the purpose, building capacity, function and target of the Great Wall are different. In Warring States period, Qin, Zhao and Yan built defensive walls in the north to contain nomadic regimes of Rong, Loufan, Linhu and Donghu. Qin, Han and Ming dynasties and northern regimes: Northern Wei, Eastern Wei, Northern Qi, Northern Zhou, Sui, Liao, Western Xia and Jin also built massive defensive walls in order to contain nomadic people of Hun, ROEN, Turks and Mongolia. In cold weapon era, the solid Great Wall defense system effectively kept the nomads from invading the Central Plains. Its magnificent structure posed a strategic deterrence to the northern regimes. It played a key role in safeguarding the national security.

### 2. Border landmark

With its geographical location, the Great Wall sets apart the farming people with hunting and fishing nomads as well as their respective political, economical and living ways in East Asian continent. The concept of "boundary" and "inside and outside the Great Wall" is clear.... According to “The Western Regions Annals, the Book of Han”, Qinshihuang built the Great Wall to contain nomadic people of Rong and Di, which set boundaries for China. According to “The Wu Huan and Xian Bei Annals, the Book of Later Han”, the mountains, rivers and the Qin dynasty Great Wall set apart the inside and outside peoples as well as their respective living styles. The building of the Great Wall enriches China's geographical and political concepts.

---

[10] Chinese National Committee for the International Council on Monuments and Sites: *Principles for the Conservation of Heritage Site in China 2015. P10*

[11] Chinese National Committee for the International Council on Monuments and Sites: *Principles for the Conservation of Heritage Site in China 2015. P10*

3、发展保障

长城在发挥军事防御功能的同时，有效地调整了农耕与游牧经济的关系，削弱了战争对社会经济的负面影响。长城一方面阻挡了草原骑兵对农业生产的侵扰和破坏；另一方面，长城也限定了农耕文明的边界，避免了农耕民族对草原的不当开发，农业生产方式对草原经济、生态与文化的破坏。长城两侧的文明因此都能够在较为和平、安宁的环境中得到持续发展。

4、文明桥梁

长城并没有真正阻断民族、经济与文化的交流，而是为二者的交流和相互补充提供了场所和边界，起着调解两种经济方式和民族关系、促进文明之间和平交往的作用。特别是位于交通道口、山口等处的关、堡还为不同地区人群贸易、交流提供了庇护，成为重要的贸易市场和物资供求、集散基地，客观上有利于长城沿线游牧、农耕民族对话交流、民族团结和文化融合，形成农耕民族与游牧、渔猎民族既内外有别，又“你中有我、我中有你”的关系。

此外，汉武帝时期，丝绸之路贯通之后，汉、唐等古代政权在西域地区修筑了大量烽燧、驿站、屯堡等设施，也在客观上保障了丝绸之路的畅通与往来使节、客商和贸易的安全。

## 二、长城的价值

### （一）历史价值

1、历史见证

长城是中国历史上一系列重大事件的物质见证。春秋战国时期，列国长城的修筑，见证了中原各地人口与资源关系的变化，从地广人稀到因争夺资源而进行战争；秦筑“万里长城”，见证了中国从分裂走向统一；河西汉塞与西域汉唐烽燧的修筑，见证了汉武帝“断匈奴右臂”的战略、汉与匈奴势力的消长与丝绸之路的开拓；金界壕的开挖见证了蒙古的崛起；明长城见证了古代中原文明走向保守和衰落；20 世纪 30 年代“长城抗战”，长城见证了中华儿女抵御外敌的不屈精神。

3. Guarantee for development

Besides its military function, the Great Wall also plays a man-made barrier role in separating the farming and fishing and hunting economies. It weakens the negative impact brought by war on economy. The Great Wall not only blocks the nomadic troopers' intrusion and destruction on farming but also sets boundary for the farming civilization, which avoids farming's improper development in grasslands. Thus both civilizations inside and outside the Great Wall enjoy sustainable developments in a relatively peaceful and harmonious environment.

4. Bridge of civilizations

The Great Wall did not really end economic and cultural exchanges between different peoples. On the contrary, it provided a venue for the exchanges. It blended the two different economies and relations between different nationalities as well as boosting peaceful exchange between different civilizations. The passes and fortresses located at key transportation spots provided "markets" for trades and exchanges. Some even became important regional markets, Objectively, the Great Wall boosted the exchanges between the farming people and the fishing and hunting people. The national unity and cultural integration were boosted as a result.

Moreover, the Silk Road came into existence during the Martial Emperor period. Both Han and Tang built massive beacon towers, military outposts and courier stations in Western Regions, which played important roles in safeguarding the Silk Road trade and the safety of diplomats and businessmen.

## II. Value of Great Wall

### 1. Historical value of Great Wall

(1) Witness of history

The Great Wall is the witness of a series of important historical events. The building of the Great Wall in Spring and Autumn period and Warring States, witnessed the changes of population and resources and the related wars. The Qin dynasty Great Wall witnessed the unification of then China. The Han passes in Hexi region and beacons built by Han and Tang dynasties in Western Regions witnessed Martial Emperor's strategy of "cutting Hun's right arm" and the expansion of the Silk Road. The "Jin border trenches" witnessed the rise of Mongolia. The Ming dynasty Great Wall witnessed the fall of the civilization of Central Plains. The "Battle of Great Wall" in 1930s showed the Chinese people's unbeatable spirit.

2、科技集成

长城，作为延绵数万公里、层级丰富、构成复杂的庞大建筑体系，其建筑和维护需要先进的测绘技术、建筑技术和科学管理体系加以支撑。长城各时代、各地区遗存丰富，全面记录着2400多年来各类、各地区建筑技术不断发展演变的过程。

军事科学方面。长城的修筑经历了多个历史阶段，从春秋战国时期各诸侯国在各自边界修建“列燧”或“列城”并逐步通过墙体将它们联结形成区域性连续防线，到秦统一后将北方各诸侯国的长城连为一体，再到汉代逐步发展形成完备的军事防御体系和网络，体现了积极防御的军事思想，也见证了古代中国军事防御工程不断发展、完善的过程。

长城的管理由国家统一组织实施。从汉代的“都尉—候官—部—隧”，到明代的“镇—路—关堡—墩台”军事管理体系，从《塞上烽火品约》到明代的烽火燃放制度，长城的管理采用了分段、分级原则，这种管理模式不仅权责明晰，同时能够高效准确地传递敌情信息，支撑了长城维护与战争的需要，对于当代军事管理科学有重要的参考作用。

此外，明长城敌台的建设，巧妙地将火药的应用与长城建筑结合在一起，见证了冷兵器时代到热兵器时代的过渡。

地理科学方面。至秦始皇时期，长城修筑技术形成“因地形，用险制塞”[12]重要原则。在修筑中注意充分利用自然山险、水险，并根据地形地貌灵活选择尺度、形制和做法，有效控制工程整体规模，降低管理维护成本。长城的防御节点通常选址在重要道口、山口等往来必经之地和山海交界等处，形成既便于交通，又有利于防守的布局。这些规划经验和做法在当时世界范围内都具有较为先进的水平，并对其后两千余年里历朝历代长城及其他军事防御工程的勘探、选址和建设产生了直接影响。

建筑技术方面。长城建筑类型丰富，包括墙体、单体建筑、关堡等多种形制，以及砖、石、土、木等多种材料和工艺。作为国家统一组织实施的军事防御工程，在修筑长城过程中汇集了大量各地工匠，集中体现了我国古代各地区建筑技术的发展水平。此外，长城所在地多属山地、戈壁、

[12] 〔汉〕司马迁：《史记·蒙恬列传》，中华书局，1963年，第2565页。

(2). Technology integration

The magnificent Great Wall winding over 20,000 km is a multi-layer complicated construction miracle. Its construction and maintenance need advanced surveying and construction technologies as well as scientific management system. The Great Wall cultural relics and remains keep the record of the technological evolution in over 2,400 years.

Military Science

The building of the Great Wall was continued in different times. The kingdoms of Spring and Autumn period and Warring State built fortresses at frontiers and linked them gradually, which formed the regional defense lines. Qin dynasty linked all the separate defense lines together. The Great Wall became a sound military defense system in Han dynasty. The Great Wall showed the military concept of proactive defense and witnessed the improvement and evolution of the ancient Chinese military project.

The management of the Great Wall was organized by the state. The command chain of Han dynasty is "Duwei-Houguan-Bu-Sui" and Ming dynasty's is "Zhen-Lu-Guanpu-Duntai". The "Sai Shang Feng Huo Pin Yue" and Ming dynasty's beacon rules show the management of the Great Wall defense system is by both sections and levels, which guarantees a efficient alarming system. The management system meets the needs of war and the Great Wall's maintenance, which is an important reference to modern military management science.

The watchtowers of the Ming dynasty Great Wall smartly combined the use of gunpowder with the Great Wall, which witnessed the transition of cold weapon era to hot weapon era.

Geographical science

The important principle of "using natural barriers for building passes" [12] is widely applied in Qinshihuang era. The natural barriers like steep mountains and rivers were fully used with application of flexible designs and methods in building key defensive posts. The key Great Wall defensive posts were often located at important road or mountain and river crossings, which have both convenient transportation and defensive advantage. The principle and application were at advanced levels worldwide. They directly influenced the design and building of the Great Wall and other defense projects in the next 2,000 years.

[12] (Han) Sima Qian: *Historical Records·The biography of Meng Tian* P2565, Zhonghua Book Company, 1963.

沙漠、草原等交通不畅、地形复杂的险恶之地，施工及后期管理维护难度大，各地在实施修筑长城过程中，往往就地取材、因地制宜地采用砖石混筑、土石混筑、土木混筑、夯土版筑等多种做法，使得各类长城建筑成为各地同类建筑形制的典型代表。

3、文学灵感

长城建筑形象高大雄伟，空间尺度延袤壮阔，与崇山峻岭、草原荒漠、河流湖泊共同形成伟大的文化景观，具有独特的美学特征，成为充满诗意的文化形象与符号，以及古今中外无数文学、艺术作品的重要元素。一生从未到过中国的奥地利著名作家弗兰兹・卡夫卡写下了《中国长城修建时》。在国内，至迟在汉代，已有文学作品将长城作为表现题材，表达民间疾苦、边塞生活的萧肃、体现家国情怀。其中，“边塞诗”作为古代诗歌的一种重要形式，与长城密切相关。“男儿宁当格斗死，何能怫郁筑长城”“秦时明月汉时关、万里长征人未还”“塞上长城空自许，镜中衰鬓已先斑”等均是耳熟能详、脍炙人口的名句。

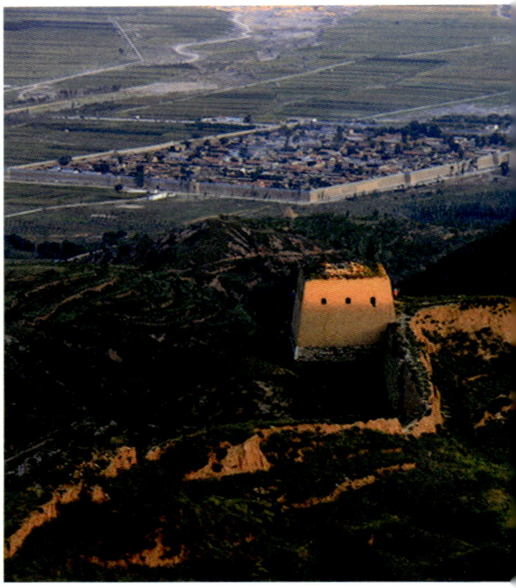

图 1-29
作为现代人生活家园的山西省山阴县明长城旧广武堡（严欣强 拍摄）

Fig. 1-29
Ming dynasty Great Wall's Jiuguangwu fortress, modern people's living home at Shanyin county of Shanxi (photo by Yan Xinqiang)

## （二）现实价值

1、生活家园

在防御功能日益衰退后，长城沿线许多关口、城堡逐渐发展成为重要的城镇，如明长城九边十三镇的镇城，包括广宁（今辽宁省北镇市）、东宁（今辽宁省辽阳市）、山海关（今秦皇岛市山海关区）、三屯营（今河北省迁西县三屯营镇）、昌平（今北京市昌平区）、宣化（今河北省张家口市宣化区）、正定（今石家庄市正定县）、保定（今河北省保定市）、大同（今山西省大同市）、偏关（今山西省偏关县城）、宁武（今山西省宁武县城）、绥德（今陕西省绥德县）、榆林（今陕西省榆林市）、宁夏（今宁夏回族自治区银川市）、固原（今宁夏回族自治区固原市）、甘州（今甘肃省张掖市）等，以及数量庞大的城堡，绝大部分发展成为现代城镇或村庄，至今仍然有大量人口居住其中，与当代人的生活融为一体。保护长城，就是保护我们的生活家园。（图 1-29、1-30）

Building technologies

The Great Wall is rich in architectural types, which include walls, single buildings, passes and other forms. Multiple technologies and materials including brick, stone, earth and wood are used. As a national defense project, the craftsmen from each and every part of the state took part in the building of the Great Wall, which showcases the technological levels of the ancient people. Due to most sections of the Great Wall were located at remote mountain areas, Gobi, desert and grasslands, the building and maintenance were very difficult. People often applied the local materials and technologies in the building of the Great Wall. The brick stone wall, earth stone wall, earth wood wall and rammed earth wall are typical examples of the same type walls of different regions.

(3).Literary inspiration

The magnificent Great Wall, naturally blended with mountains, grasslands, desert, rivers and lakes, is a great cultural landscape, which has unique aesthetic characteristics. The Great Wall has become poetic cultural image and symbol. It became important elements in the Chinese and foreign literary and artistic works at all times. The famous Austrian writer Franz Kafka, who never came to China, wrote the book "The Great Wall of China". The Great Wall appears in the Chinese literature works as early as Han dynasty. The works show average people's hard life, bleak life at frontiers and nationalism. The frontier poems, an important part of ancient poetry, are closely related to the Great Wall. Many famous poems mention the Great Wall.

**2. Practical Value**

(1). Living home

With its defensive function fading, many Great Wall's passes and fortresses developed into important towns. The frontier fortresses of Ming dynasty Great Wall have developed into today's towns and cities. They are Guangning (Beizheng city of Liaoning), Dongning (Liaoyang city of Liaoning), Shanhai Pass(Shanhaiguan District of Qinhuangdao), Santunying (Santunying town of Qianxi, Hebei), Changping (Changping district of Beijing),Xuanhua (Xuanhua district of Zhangjiakou, Hebei), Zhengding (Zhengding district of Shijiazhuang), Baoding(Baoding city of Hebei), Datong (Datong city of Shanxi), Pianguan (Pianguan county of Shanxi),Ningwu (Ningwu county of Shanxi), Suide (Suide county of Shanxi), Yulin (Yulin city of Shanxi), Ningxia (Yinchuan city of Ningxia),Guyuan (Guyuan city of Ningxia)and Guanzhou (Zhangye city of Gansu). A great number of fortresses have become today's towns and villages. A large population still lives in them. Protecting the Great Wall is actually protecting their living homes.

图 1-30
作为城镇中心的明长城宣府镇城（今张家口市宣化区）（张依萌 拍摄）

Fig. 1-30
Ming dynasty Great Wall's Xuanfuzhen fortress, Xuanhua district of Zhangjiakou city (Photo by Zhang Yiming)

## 2、国家象征

孙中山先生撰写的《建国方略》有专门的段落对长城的概念及其与中华民族的关系进行论述，并称长城为“世界独一之奇观”。[13]

1933 年 3 月至 5 月，时国民政府指挥国民革命军在长城的义院口、冷口、喜峰口、古北口、罗文峪、界岭口等地发起了抗击侵华日军进攻的战役，史称“长城抗战”。这是“九一八”事变后我国军队在华北进行的第一次较大规模的抗击日本侵略者的战役。“长城抗战”表现了中国广大爱国官兵为反抗侵略而具有的高尚的抗战热情和顽强的抵御能力。此后，1937 年 9 月中旬，八路军第 115 师在师长林彪、副师长聂荣臻指挥下在长城平型关地区集结待机，伏击日军辎重队，打破了日军不可战胜的神话，

[13] 孙中山：《建国方略》，第 40 页，辽宁人民出版社，1994 年。

(2).National symbol

Mr. Sun Yat-sen contributed a whole paragraph on the Great Wall and its relationship with the Chinese people in his famous book "*The International Development of China*". He says the Great Wall is the world's unique wonder.[13]

From March through May 1933, then Chinese government led the National Revolutionary Army to fight against the Japanese invader at the Great Wall's Yiyuankou, Lengkou, Xifengkou, Gubeikou, Luowenyu and Jielingkou. This battle is known as "Battle of Great Wall", wihich was the first large-scale battle against Japanese invaders in North China after the "918 incident". The "Battle of Great Wall" showed the noble passion for fighting against Japanese invader and tenacious resistance of the Chinese army. In mid-September 1937, commander Lin Biao and vice commander Nie Rongzhen led the 115th Division of the 8th Route Army successfully ambushed the Japanese supply convoy, which ended the myth of "Invincible Japanese troops" and boosted the Chinese people's morale in fight against Japanese aggression. It is a heavy blow to the Japanese

图 1-31
2015 年抗战胜利日大阅兵现场的长城花坛
（图片来源：新华网）

Fig. 1-31
The Great Wall flower bed at 2015 China Victory Day parade (Photo by Xinhua Net)

[13] Sun Yat-sen: *The International Development of China*, P40, Liaoning People's Publishing House, 1994

河北涞源隋家庄明长城（黄东辉 拍摄）

The section of the Great Wall of the Ming Dynasty at SuiJiaZhuang, Laiyuan, Hebei (Photo by Huang DongHui)

高涨了全国人民的反侵略志气，打击了日军的侵略气焰，震动全国，意义深远。（图 1-31）

长城作为中国军民抗击日本侵略者的重要战场，使长城与民族兴亡、国家兴衰联系在一起，成为鼓舞全国人民奋勇抗敌的精神支柱和坚韧不屈的民族精神象征。《义勇军进行曲》的歌词——“把我们的血肉筑成我们新的长城”，就是在这一形势下写成并广为流传的。中华人民共和国成立之后，随着《义勇军进行曲》成为国歌，使长城作为中华民族的形象象征，在国家层面得到了正式确认。

在长城象征意义得到不断深化和强调的同时，长城的形象也逐渐走入中国百姓日常生活，人们自觉或不自觉的通过多种方式宣传和利用长城。在世界范围内，作为中国知名度最高的文化遗产之一，长城是世界了解中国的重要窗口，多国政要、社会名流登高长城。此外，1991 年北京亚运会以长城形象为会徽形象，2008 年北京奥运会、2010 年广州亚运会等重大体育赛事在长城上点燃火炬，见证了中国体育事业腾飞和民族伟大复兴。

invader. The victory shocked the whole country and carried a far-reaching significance.

The Great Wall became an important battle ground for the Chinese army and people to fight against the Japanese invader. Then the Great Wall has connected to the rise and fall of the country and its prosperity. It has become a spiritual pillar and a tenacious symbol of the national spirit. The song "March of the Volunteers" became popular since then. "With our flesh and blood, let us build a new Great Wall!" is part of the lyrics. It became the national anthem of the People's Republic of China. The Great Wall is recognized by the state as the Chinese people's symbol.

With its symbolic significance being continuously deepened and emphasized, the image of the Great Wall has become popular in people's daily lives. People promote and apply the image of Great Wall in multiple ways consciously or unconsciously. The Great Wall is one of China's most famous cultural heritages on the world stage. The Great Wall is an important window for the world to understand China. The foreign political figures and celebrities visit the Great Wall. - In 1991, the Beijing Asian Games emblem used the Great Wall image. The major sports games including the 2008 Beijing Olympic Games and the 2010 Guangzhou Asian Games held the torch-lighting ceremonies on the Great Wall. The Great Wall witnessed the Chinese people's revitalization in sports field and the great rejuvenation of the nation.

### (3). Heritage of the Mankind

The Great Wall was included on the UNESCO *World Heritage List* in 1987. The World Heritage Committee wrote on the Great Wall's unique value: The Great Wall reflects collision and exchanges between agricultural civilizations and nomadic civilizations in ancient China. It provides significant physical evidence of the far-sighted political strategic thinking and mighty military and national defense forces of central empires in ancient China, and is an outstanding example of the superb military architecture, technology and art of ancient China. It embodies unparalleled significance as the national symbol for safeguarding the security of the country and its people.

According to the *Operational Guidelines for the implementation of the World Heritage Convention,* one cultural heritage must first have outstanding universal value to be enlisted on the World Heritage List. The World Heritage Committee thinks the Great Wall meet five criteria :(i),(ii), (iii),(iv) and (vi) have the outstanding universal value. (Table 1-4)The World Heritage Committee describes the Great Wall's outstanding universal value as:

## 专栏：古人对长城的认知

在现存的古文献中，古人对长城的评价与今人的观点并不相同。从东汉至三国时期陈琳的《饮马长城窟行》到清朝康熙皇帝的长城诗句，体现出对修筑长城劳民伤财的反感、控诉甚至轻蔑，又或者如唐代诗人王昌龄的《出塞》，描述了边城的苍凉与孤寂。

另一方面，古人又认为长城是"中华"或者"华夏"概念中必不可少的内容。唐朝人贾耽于贞元十七年（801年）绘制了《海内华夷图》，宋代将其稍加改动，并镌刻在石碑上。这幅图最重要的之处，就是描绘出了长城范围和位置。此后历代绘制的中国疆域地图中，长城几乎成了必不可少的要素，直至当代，依然如此。（图1-13）。

大约在十七世纪，长城的防御意义逐渐淡去，此时伴随文艺复兴而起的启蒙运动正席卷欧洲大陆。西方来华传教士和启蒙思想家们对中国文化的好奇与日俱增。在当时的欧洲，中国呈现出了几乎完美的形象，他们根据有限的知识和无限的想象，将中国描绘成了柏拉图的"理想国"，并将这个想象的中国作为打破欧洲宗教桎梏的工具和社会变革的标杆。在这个过程中，他们重新认识了长城，将它定义为一项伟大的工程。

比利时传教士南怀仁（1623-1688年）曾说过："世界七大奇迹加在一起，也比不过（长城）这项工程，欧洲人当中流传的有关它的所有传说，都与我的亲眼所见相去甚远。"[14]在狄德罗、大朗贝尔等人编纂的《百科全书》（第一版）第三卷的"中国"条目[15]和第十卷的"城墙"条目[16]下，也提到了中国长达数百法里的长城，并认为它是比埃及金字塔更雄伟、壮观。而伏尔泰在《风俗论》第一章"古代的中国；中国的军事力量；中国的法律、风俗和科学"[17]中则写到：长城"就其用途及规模来说，这是超过埃及金字塔的伟大建筑。"西方人对长城和中国的超现实想象，直至20世纪上半叶还一直存在。

[14] Ferdinand Verbiest,Voyages de L'Empereur de la Chine dans la Tartarie［...］(Paris:Estienne Michallet, 1685),p:51-54.

[15] "CHINE, (la) Géog. grand empire d'Asie, borné au nord par la Tartarie, dont elle est séparée par une muraille de quatre cents lieues ; à l'orient par la mer ; à l'occident par des hautes montagnes & des deserts ; & au midi par l'Océan, les royaumes de Tunquin, de Lao, & de la Cochinchine.", Denis Diderot, Encyclopédie ou Dictionnaire Rraisonné des Sciences, des Arts et des Métiers.Paris:Briasson etc,1751-1772, Tome 3CHINE, p. 339.

[16] "MURAILLE DE LA CHINE, (Architect. ancienne.) fortification de l'empire Chinois, monument supérieur par son immensité aux pyramides d'Egypte, quoique ce rempart n'ait pas empêché les Tartares Mantcheoux de subjuguer la Chine. Cette grande muraille, qui séparoit & défendoit la Chine des Tartares, bâtie 137 ans avant l'ere chrétienne, subsiste encore dans un contour de 500 lieues, s'éleve sur des montagnes, descend dans des précipices, & a presque par-tout 20 de nos piés de largeur, sur plus de trente de hauteur. (D. J.)", Denis Diderot, Encyclopédie ou Dictionnaire Rraisonné des Sciences, des Arts et des Métiers.Paris:Briasson etc,1751-1772, Tome 10MURAILLE, p. 866.

[17] "La grande muraille qui séparait et défendait la Chine des Tartares, bâtie cent trente-sept ans avant notre ère, subsiste encore dans un contour de cinq cents lieues, s'élève sur des montagnes, descend dans des précipices, ayant presque partout vingt de nos pieds de largeur, sur plus de trente de hauteur : monument supérieur aux pyramides d'Égypte, par son utilité comme par son immensité.",Voltaire, Essai sur les mœurs et l'esprit des nations, Chapitre IDE LA CHINE, DE SON ANTIQUITÉ, DE SES FORCES, DE SES LOIS,DE SES USAGES, ET DE SES SCIENCES, .

## Column: Ancient people's knowledge of the Great Wall

According to the historical papers, some ancient people had bad feelings toward the Great Wall. Both Chen Lin, lived through Eastern Han and Three Kingdoms and Emperor Kangxi of Qing dynasty expressed their antipathy, accusation and even contempt toward the building of the Great Wall for its harassing people and wasting money. The Tang Dynasty poet Wang Changling described the coldness and loneliness of the frontier life along the Great Wall in his poem "On the Frontier."

On the other side, the ancient people think the Great Wall is an inalienable part of the concept of "Zhong Hua" or "Huan Xia", which are Chinese nation. Jia Dan of Tang dynasty drew the nation's map in 801. The stone "Map of the Han People and Minorities of the Song Dynasty" is slightly different from Jia Dan's map. Most importantly, the Great Wall was recorded on the map. Since then, the Great Wall has become an important part of all the maps till today. (Fig. 1-13).

Around 17th century, the defensive significance of the Great Wall faded away. The Renaissance movement was sweeping Europe. The foreign missionaries and Enlightenment thinkers were increasingly curious about the Chinese culture. In Europe, China was almost perfect. Based on their limited knowledge and wild imagination, the Europeans portrayed China as Platon's "ideal country" and used imagined Chinese as a tool to break religious shackles and benchmark for social changes. In this process, they re-understood the Great Wall defining it as a great project.

The Belgian missionary Ferdinand Verbiest (1623-1688) once said that the world's seven wonders combined was still dwarfed by the Great Wall and all the European legends about Great Wall were not even close to what he saw [14]. The entry of "China" [15] in Vol. 3 and the entry of "Wall" [16] in Vol. 10 in the first edition of the *Encyclopedia* compiled by Denis Diderot and Jean le Rond d'Alembert, mentioned twice the Great Wall and thought it was more magnificent than Egypt's pyramids. Voltaire writes in the first chapter of his book "Essai sur les Mœurs et l'Esprit des Nations": Ancient China: Chinese military forces; Chinese laws, Costumes and Science [17] that speaking on its function and scale, the Great Wall dwarfs Egypt's pyramids. The western people's surreal imagination of the Great Wall and China existed until the first half of the 20th Century.

[14] Ferdinand Verbiest,*Voyages de L'Empereur de la Chine dans la Tartarie* [...] (Paris:Estienne Michallet, 1685), p:51-54.

[15] "CHINE, (la) Géog. grand empire d'Asie, borné au nord par la Tartarie, dont elle est séparée par une muraille de quatre cents lieues ; à l'orient par la mer ; à l'occident par des hautes montagnes & des deserts ; & au midi par l'Océan, les royaumes de Tunquin, de Lao, & de la Cochinchine.", Denis Diderot, *Encyclopédie ou Dictionnaire Rraisonné des Sciences, des Arts et des Métiers*. Paris:Briasson etc,1751-1772, Tome 3CHINE, p. 339.

[16] "MURAILLE DE LA CHINE, (Architect. ancienne.) fortification de l'empire Chinois, monument supérieur par son immensité aux pyramides d'Egypte, quoique ce rempart n'ait pas empêché les Tartares Mantcheoux de subjuguer la Chine. Cette grande muraille, qui séparoit & défendoit la Chine des Tartares, bâtie 137 ans avant l'ere chrétienne, subsiste encore dans un contour de 500 lieues, s'éleve sur des montagnes, descend dans des précipices, & a presque par-tout 20 de nos piés de largeur, sur plus de trente de hauteur. (D. J.)", Denis Diderot, *Encyclopédie ou Dictionnaire Rraisonné des Sciences, des Arts et des Métiers*. Paris:Briasson etc,1751-1772, Tome 10MURAILLE, p. 866.

[17] "La grande muraille qui séparait et défendait la Chine des Tartares, bâtie cent trente-sept ans avant notre ère, subsiste encore dans un contour de cinq cents lieues, s'élève sur des montagnes, descend dans des précipices, ayant presque partout vingt de nos pieds de largeur, sur plus de trente de hauteur : monument supérieur aux pyramides d'Égypte, par son utilité comme par son immensité.",Voltaire, Essai sur les mœurs et l'esprit des nations, Chapitre IDE LA CHINE, DE SON ANTIQUITÉ, DE SES FORCES, DE SES LOIS,DE SES USAGES, ET DE SES SCIENCES, .

3、人类遗产

1987 年，长城正式列入联合国家教科文组织《世界遗产名录》。世界遗产委员会对长城价值的阐释为：“长城反映了中国古代农耕文明和游牧文明的相互碰撞与交流，是古代中国中原帝国远大的政治战略思想、以及强大的军事、国防力量的重要物证，是中国古代高超的军事建筑建造技术和建筑艺术水平的杰出范例，在中国历史上有着保护国家和民族安全的无以伦比的象征意义。”

根据《实施保护世界自然与文化遗产公约的操作指南》要求，一项文化遗产要想列入世界遗产名录，首先要具有“突出的普遍价值（Outstanding Universal Value）”。世界遗产委员会认为，长城符合其中的 (i) 、(ii) 、(iii) 、(iv) 、(vi) 五条标准（表 1-4），具备突出的普遍价值。世界遗产委员会将长城的突出普遍价值描述为：

明长城是绝对的杰作，不仅因为它体现的军事战略思想，也是完美建筑。作为从月球上能看到的唯一人工建造物[18]，长城分布于辽阔的大陆上，是建筑融入景观的完美范例。

春秋时期[19]，中国人运用建造理念和空间组织模式，在北部边境修筑了防御工程，修筑长城而进行的人口迁移使民俗文化得以传播。

保存在甘肃修筑于西汉时期的夯土墙和明代令人赞叹和闻名于世的包砖城墙同样是中国古代文明的独特见证。

这个复杂的文化遗产是军事建筑群的突出、独特范例，它在 2000 年中服务于单一的战略用途，同时它的建造史表明了防御技术的持续发展和对政治背景变化的适应性。

长城在中国历史上有着无以伦比的象征意义。它防御了外来入侵，也是从外族蛮夷习俗中保留自己的文化。同时，其修造过程的艰难困苦，成为了许多中国古代文学中的重要题材。”[20]

具有“真实性（authenticity）”与“完整性（integrity）”也是世界遗产的价值判断标准。长城世界遗产的真实性概括为：“长城的现有遗存真实

[18] 我们从月球上并不能看到长城，这一说法源于西方人的夸张想象，大约诞生于 20 世纪初。参见 William Edgar Geil: The Great Wall of China, New York; Sturgis and Walton, 1909.p17.

[19] 根据文献记载，长城的始建可能早到春秋时期，目前已发现的长城遗迹最早为战国时期。

[20] 本节未注释的引文出处：世界遗产第二轮定期报告 The Great Wall (Section II)，2012 年。

The Great Wall was continuously built from the 3rd century BC to the 17th century AD on the northern border of the country as the great military defence project of successive Chinese Empires, with a total length of more than 20,000 kilometers. The Great Wall begins in the east at Shanhaiguan in Hebei province and ends at Jiayuguan in Gansu province to the west. Its main body consists of walls, horse tracks, watch towers, and shelters on the wall, and includes fortresses and passes along the Wall.

The Great Wall reflects collision and exchanges between agricultural civilizations and nomadic civilizations in ancient China. It provides significant physical evidence of the far-sighted political strategic thinking and mighty military and national defence forces of central empires in ancient China, and is an outstanding example of the superb military architecture, technology and art of ancient China. It embodies unparalleled significance as the national symbol for safeguarding the security of the country and its people.

Criterion (i): The Great Wall of the Ming is, not only because of the ambitious character of the undertaking but also the perfection of its construction, an absolute masterpiece. The only work built by human hands on this planet that can be seen from the moon[18], the Wall constitutes, on the vast scale of a continent, a perfect example of architecture integrated into the landscape.

Criterion (ii): During the Chunqiu period[19], the Chinese imposed their models of construction and organization of space in building the defence works along the northern frontier. The spread of Sinicism was accentuated by the population transfers necessitated by the Great Wall.

Criterion (iii): That the Great Wall bear exceptional testimony to the civilizations of ancient China is illustrated as much by the rammed-earth sections of fortifications dating from the Western Han that are conserved in the Gansu province as by the admirable and universally acclaimed masonry of the Ming period.

Criterion (iv): This complex and diachronic cultural property is an outstanding and unique example of a military architectural ensemble which served a single strategic purpose for 2000 years, but whose construction history illustrates successive advances in defence techniques and adaptation to changing political contexts.

Criterion (vi): The Great Wall has an incomparable symbolic significance in the history of China. Its purpose was to protect China from outside aggression, but also to preserve its culture from the customs of foreign barbarians. Because its construction implied suffering, it is one of the essential references in Chinese literature, being found in works like the "Soldier's Ballad" of Tch'en Lin (c. 200 A.D.) or the poems of Tu Fu (712-770) and the popular novels of the Ming period [20].

Integrity

The Great Wall integrally preserves all the material and spiritual elements and historical and cultural information that carry its outstanding universal value. The complete route of the Great Wall over 20,000 kilometers, as well as elements constructed in different historical periods which

[18] The view appeared in the early 20th century and originated from the exaggerative imagination of the western people. In fact, the Great Wall is not visible from the moon. Refer to William Edgar Geil: The Great Wall of China, New York: Sturgis and Walton, 1909. P17

[19] According to records in literature, the construction of the Great Wall possibly started in the Spring and Autumn Period and the earliest site of the Great Wall discovered so far orginated from the Warring States Period.

[20] Source of the quotation: The second round periodic reporting of World Heritage: the Great Wall (Section II) 2012

## 表 1-4：长城的“突出普遍价值”描述

| 世界文化遗产遴选标准[21] | 世界遗产委员会对长城的价值评价[22] |
|---|---|
| (I) 人类创造性的智慧的杰作 | 明长城是绝对的杰作，不仅因为它体现的军事战略思想，也是完美建筑。作为从月球上能看到的唯一人工建造物，长城分布于辽阔的大陆上，是建筑融入景观的完美范例。 |
| (II) 一段时间内或文化期内在建筑或技术、艺术、城镇规划或景观设计中一项人类价值的重要转变 | 春秋时期，中国人运用建造理念和空间组织模式，在北部边境修筑了防御工程，修筑长城而进行的人口迁移使民俗文化得以传播。 |
| (III) 反映一项独有或至少特别的现存或已经消失的文化传统或文明 | 保存在甘肃修筑于西汉时期的夯土墙和明代令人赞叹和闻名于世的砖砌城墙同样是中国古代文明的独特见证。 |
| (IV) 是描绘出人类历史上一个重大时期的建筑物、建筑风格、科技组合或景观的范例 | 这个复杂的文化遗产是军事建筑群的突出、独特范例，它在 2000 年中服务于单一的战略用途，同时它的建造史表明了防御技术的持续发展和对政治背景变化的适应性。 |
| (VI) 直接或明显地与具有突出普遍重要意义的事件、生活传统、信仰、文学艺术作品相关 | 长城在中国历史上有着无以伦比的象征意义。它防御了外来入侵，也是从外族蛮夷习俗中保留自己的文化。同时，其修造过程的艰难困苦，成为了许多中国古代文学中的重要题材。 |

保持了其原有的位置、材料、形式、工艺、结构。组成长城防御体系的各相关要素仍保持原有的布局构成，长城与地形地势的完美结合、其蜿蜒于大地上的景观特征、以及其中体现的军事理念都得以真实地保存。”

长城世界遗产的完整性概括为：“长城完整地保存了承载其突出普遍价值的全部物质、精神要素、以及历史文化信息。长城约 2 万千米的整体线路、以及历代修建的、组成其复杂防御体系的墙体、城堡、关隘、烽火台等各要素完整地保存至今，完整保存了不同时期、不同地域长城修建的工程做法，长城在中华民族中无以伦比的国家、文化象征意义传承至今。”

[21] 联合国教育、科学及文化组织 保护世界文化与自然遗产的政府间委员会：实施《世界遗产公约》操作指南［R］11 页 . 巴黎，2015 年。

[22] 长城世界遗产第二轮定期报告 Periodic Reporting: The Great Wall ( Section II )，2012.p1.

table 1-4: Description of Great Wall's "Outstanding Universal Value"

| World Heritage selection criterion[21] | World Heritage Committee's evaluation on Great Wall[22] |
|---|---|
| (I)to represent a masterpiece of human creative genius; | The Great Wall of the Ming is, not only because of the ambitious character of the undertaking but also the perfection of its construction, an absolute masterpiece. The only work built by human hands on this planet that can be seen from the moon, the Wall constitutes, on the vast scale of a continent, a perfect example of architecture integrated into the landscape. |
| (II)to exhibit an important interchange of human values, over a span of time or within a cultural area of the world, on developments in architecture or technology, monumental arts, town-planning or landscape design | During the Chunqiu period, the Chinese imposed their models of construction and organization of space in building the defense works along the northern frontier. The spread of Sinicism was accentuated by the population transfers necessitated by the Great Wall. |
| (III)to bear a unique or at least exceptional testimony to a cultural tradition or to a civilization which is living or which has disappeared; | That the Great Wall bear exceptional testimony to the civilizations of ancient China is illustrated as much by the rammed-earth sections of fortifications dating from the Western Han that are conserved in the Gansu province as by the admirable and universally acclaimed masonry of the Ming period. |
| (IV)to be an outstanding example of a type of building, architectural or technological ensemble or landscape which illustrates (a) significant stage(s) in human history | This complex and diachronic cultural property is an outstanding and unique example of a military architectural ensemble which served a single strategic purpose for 2000 years, but whose construction history illustrates successive advances in defense techniques and adaptation to changing political contexts. |
| (VI)to be directly or tangibly associated with events or living traditions, with ideas, or with beliefs, with artistic and literary works of outstanding universal significance. | The Great Wall has an incomparable symbolic significance in the history of China. Its purpose was to protect China from outside aggression, but also to preserve its culture from the customs of foreign barbarians. Because its construction implied suffering, it is one of the essential references in Chinese literature. |

constitute the complicated defence system of the property, including walls, fortresses, passes and beacon towers, have been preserved to the present day. The building methods of the Great Wall in different times and places have been integrally maintained, while the unparalleled national and cultural significance of the Great Wall to China is still recognised today. The visual integrity of the Wall at Badaling has been impacted negatively by construction of tourist facilities and a cable car.

Authenticity

The existing elements of the Great Wall retain their original location, material, form, technology and structure. The original layout and composition of various constituents of the Great Wall defence system are maintained, while the perfect integration of the Great Wall with the topography, to form a meandering landscape feature, and the military concepts it embodies have all been authentically preserved. The authenticity of the setting of the Great Wall is vulnerable to construction of inappropriate tourism facilities.

[21] UNESCO Intergovernmental Committee for the Conservation of the World Cultural and Natural Heritage: Operational Guidelines for the implementation of the World Heritage Convention [R] Paris 2015 P11

[22] The second round periodic reporting: the Great Wall (Section II) 2012 P1

【摘要】

1987年长城被联合国教科文组织列入《世界遗产名录》以来，中国政府始终坚持认真履行《保护世界文化和自然遗产公约》，不断加强长城保护专项法规建设，逐步建立起以《中华人民共和国文物保护法》和《长城保护条例》为主体，相关法律法规、规范性文件以及各级地方性法规为补充的法律法规体系，实施了以文物保护单位为核心，统一要求、分级负责、属地管理的长城保护管理体制。国家文物局负责指导长城保护宏观管理工作，协调、解决长城保护中的重大问题，监督、检查长城沿线各地实施长城保护工作；县级以上地方人民政府及其相关部门，依法承担相应的长城保护管理责任，具体实施长城日常管理、保养维护、执法巡查、保护工程实施等工作。长城保护管理体制在实践中不断完善，最大限度地保护了长城的价值、真实性和完整性，为大型文化遗产的保护管理积累了有益的中国经验。

# 第二章
# 长城立法与管理体制

## Chapter 2
## Great Wall Lawmaking and Management System

[Abstract]

Since the Great Wall was enlisted by UNESCO on the *World Heritage List* in 1987, the Chinese government has consistently fulfilled its obligations in accordance with the "Convention on the Conservation of the world cultural and natural heritage". It kept strengthening the legal framework for Conservation of the Great Wall. It gradually established a legal framework, with the *Law of t he People's Republic of China on the Conservation of Cultural Relics* and the Regulation on the Conservation of Great Wall as core, which was supplemented by the relevant laws and regulations, normative documents and local laws and regulations. The Great Wall Conservation and management system is cultural heritage Conservation unit centered with principles of unified requirements, classified responsibilities and territorial management. The State Administration of Cultural Heritage is responsible for the macro management, coordination and solving the major problems found in the Great Wall Conservation works as well as supervising and inspecting the Conservation works at local levels. The local people's governments (above county level) and their relevant departments, in accordance with the law, bear the corresponding responsibility for the Conservation and management of the Great Wall. They carry out the routine management, maintenance, inspection and implementation of the Conservation works for the Great Wall. The Great Wall Conservation and management system is improving in practice, which is a guarantee for maximally protecting the value, authenticity and integrity of the Great Wall. It has accumulated Chinese experience for the Conservation and management of large cultural heritages.

宁夏青铜峡明长城（张依萌 拍摄）

The section of the Great Wall of the Ming Dynasty in Qingtongxia, Ningxia (Photo by Zhang Yimeng)

## 第一节　长城保护法律法规体系

- 相关法律——文物保护法及实施条例
- 行政法规——《长城保护条例》
- 部门规章——世界文化遗产管理
- 规范性文件——“四有”工作、保护工程管理、执法巡查、保护员管理、保护规划编制
- 国际文件——世界遗产公约、威尼斯宪章、奈良真实性文件

目前，我国已经建立起由《中华人民共和国文物保护法》《中华人民共和国文物保护法实施条例》等法律法规，《考古发掘管理办法》《文物保护工程管理办法》等部门规章，《全国重点文物保护单位保护规划编制要求》《文物保护工程监理资质管理办法（试行）》《文物保护工程施工资质管理办法（试行）》《文物保护工程勘查设计资质管理办法（试行）》《文物保护单位执法巡查办法》《国家文物局文物安全案件督察督办管理规定（试行）》《文物违法行为举报管理办法（试行）》《全国重点文物

# Section 1 Great Wall conservation laws and regulations system

- laws - Law of the People's Republic of China on the Conservation of Cultural Relics and regulations for implementation
- Administrative regulations - *Regulation on the conservation of Great Wall*
- Department regulations - World heritage management
- Regulative documents: "conservation scope, conservation sign, files and file-keeping institution"("Four basic works"), conservation project management, inspection, conservation personnel management, conservation planning
- International documents - "Convention for the Conservation of the Cultural and Natural World Heritage", "Venice Charter ", "The Nara Document on Authenticity"

China has passed the *"Law of the People's Republic of China on the Conservation of Cultural Relics"* and "Implementing Regulations of Law of the PRC on the Conservation of Cultural Relics". The *"Measures for the Administration of Archaeological Excavations", "Measures for the Administration of Cultural Relics Conservation Projects", "Requirements for The Preparation of Conservation Plans for National Key Cultural Relic Conservation Units", "Administrative Measures for the Supervision of Cultural Relics Conservation Projects* (trial)", *"Measures for the Administration of the Construction Qualification Of Cultural Relics Conservation Projects* (trial)", *"Measures for the Administration of the Quality of Exploration and Design of Cultural Relics Conservation Projects* (trial)",*"Measures For The Law Enforcement And Inspection Of Cultural Relics Conservation Units"*, "National Security Supervision Bureau Of Cultural Heritage Case Management Regulations (Trial)", "Cultural Relics Report Illegal Management Measures (Trial)", *"Work Rules on the Recording of State Priority Protected Sites Record,"* and *"Criterion of National Key Cultural Relics Conservation Special Subsidy Fund Management"* are all part of the cultural relics legal system. The

保护单位记录档案工作规范》《国家重点文物保护专项补助资金管理办法》等规范性文件所构成的我国文物保护法律法规体系，以及以《中国文物古迹保护准则》及其案例阐释为代表的行业规范性文件，为长城的依法保护奠定了坚实基础。

作为世界文化遗产的长城点段，保护管理工作受到《保护世界自然与文化遗产公约》及其操作指南、《威尼斯宪章》《奈良真实性文件》《西安宣言》等国际公约、宪章等文件的指导和约束。为加强世界文化遗产保护，国务院办公厅转发了文化部、建设部、文物局、发展改革委、财政部、国土资源部、林业局、旅游局、宗教局等 9 部门《关于加强我国世界文化遗产保护管理工作的意见》；文化部出台了《世界文化遗产保护管理办法》；国家文物局先后制定了《世界文化遗产专家咨询管理办法》《世界文化遗产监测巡视管理办法》等规范性文件，规范和推动了世界文化遗产保护工作。这些国际公约、宪章及相关文件为长城保护工作提供了科学指导。

针对长城特点和保护需求，2006 年 10 月 11 日，国务院正式颁布长城专项保护法规——《长城保护条例》（以下简称《条例》），并于当年 12 月 1 日起正式施行。《条例》明确了各级政府和相关部门长城保护的法定职责，确定了长城认定、保护、管理、利用等基本制度，这是国务院首次就单项文化遗产保护制定专门性法规，为长城保护管理提供了具有针对性的法规依据。国家文物局在开展长城保护管理过程中，针对各地工作中出现的主要问题和实际需要，组织中国文化遗产研究院等专业机构陆续编制并颁布实施了《长城保护维修工作指导意见》《长城“四有”工作指导意见》《长城保护员管理办法》和《长城执法巡查管理办法》等规范性文件，对《条例》的相关内容进行了细化和落实。（表 2-1）

"guidelines for the conservation of cultural relics and historical sites in China" and its listed cases are the industry standards. All the laws and regulations lay a solid foundation for lawfully protect the Great Wall.

As World Cultural Heritage, the Great Wall's conservation and management are also guided and restricted by the *Convention Concerning the Conservation of the World Cultural* and *Natural Heritage and the Operational Guidelines for the Implementation of the World Heritage Convention,* the *Venice Charter,* the *Nara Document on Authenticity* and *The Xi'an Declaration on the Conservation of the Setting of Heritage Structures, Sites and Areas.* In order to strengthen the conservation of world cultural heritage, the State Council forwarded the "Opinions on strengthening the conservation and management of world cultural heritages in China" to the Ministry of Construction, Ministry of Culture, Cultural Relics Bureau, Development and Reform Commission, Ministry of Finance, Ministry of Land and Resources, Forestry bureau, Tourism Bureau, Bureau of Religious Affairs. The Ministry of Culture issued the "conservation and management measures on world cultural heritages" and the State Administration of Cultural Heritage issued the "world cultural heritage expert consultation management measures", "world cultural heritage monitoring and inspection management measures", which standardized and promoted the world cultural heritage conservation works. The international conventions, charters and related documents give scientific guidance to the conservation of the Great Wall.

According to the features of the Great Wall and conservation needs, on October 11, 2006, the State Council officially announced the *Regulation on the Conservation of Great Wall* and formally implemented it on December 1 of the same year. The "Regulations" clarified all levels of government and relevant departments' responsibilities on conservation of the Great Wall, the Great Wall identification, conservation, management and utilization. This is the first state regulation issued for the conservation of a individual cultural heritage. In order to solve the major issues and meet the actual needs in the local conservation works, the State Administration of Cultural Heritage organized the China Academy of Cultural Heritage and other professional institutions wrote the *Guidance on Conservation and Maintenance Work of the Great Wall, Work Constructive Opinion for Great Wall "Four Basic Works"", Measures for the Management of Inspection personnel of the Great Wall and Measures for the Management of Inspection of the Great Wall, which detailed the state's Regulation on the Conservation of Great Wall* and helped its implementation. (Table 2-1)

**表 2-1：国家级长城保护相关重要专门法规与规范性文件一览表**

| 序号 | 文件名称 | 发文号 | 实施时间 | 文件类型 |
|---|---|---|---|---|
| 1 | 长城保护条例 | 中华人民共和国国务院令第 476 号 | 2006 年 12 月 1 日 | 行政法规 |
| 2 | 长城保护维修工作指导意见 | 文物保发〔2014〕4 号 | 2014 年 2 月 10 日 | 规范性文件 |
| 3 | 长城“四有”工作指导意见 | | | |
| 4 | 长城执法巡查管理办法 | 文物督发〔2016〕1 号 | 2016 年 1 月 25 日 | |
| 5 | 长城保护员管理办法 | 文物督发〔2016〕2 号 | | |

此外，结合长城资源调查、认定、量测及数据整合、数据库建设等工作，还制定了行业标准《长城资源要素分类、代码与图式》（WW/T 0029-2008），以及一系列规范性、指导性文件，包括《长城资源调查名称使用规范》《长城资源调查文物编码规则》《长城资源保存程度评价标准》，以及长城基础地理信息与专题要素数据生产外业技术规定、长城基础地理信息与专题要素数据生产内业技术规定、长城基础地理信息与专题要素数据技术规定、长城资源调查数据整合技术规定、长城测量与资源系统建设总体技术规定等。

In addition, in order to benefit the Great Wall resource survey, identification, surveying and mapping as well as data integration, database building, the industry standards like the "classification, code and schema of the Great Wall resource elements (WW/T 0029-2008)", "name usage rules in Great Wall resource survey" and a series of regulatory and guidance documents are made. The "Great Wall resource survey relics encoding rules", "evaluation criteria for Great Wall resource preservation degree", and the rules on Great Wall basic geographic information and field work technology for thematic elements production, Great Wall resources survey data integration technology and general technical regulations for Great Wall measurement and resource system building are also made.

Table 2-1: The state-level regulations and documents on conservation of Great Wall

| Order | Name | Issuance No. | Issuance date | Document type |
|---|---|---|---|---|
| 1 | Regulation on the Conservation of Great Wall | No. 476 Order of the State Council | December 1, 2006 | Administrative regulations |
| 2 | Guidance on conservation and maintenance work of the Great Wall | W. W. B. F (2014) No. 4 | Feb. 10, 2014 | Normative document |
| 3 | Work Constructive Opinion for Great Wall "Four Basic Works" | | | |
| 4 | Measures for the management of inspection of the Great Wall | W.W.D.F (2016) No. 1 | Jan. 25, 2016 | |
| 5 | Measures for the management of inspection personnel of the Great Wall | W.W.D.F (2016) No. 2 | | |

长城沿线各省（自治区、直辖市）人民政府根据地方的实际情况，制定了实施细则或专门法规。自 20 世纪 90 年代起，长城沿线部分地区就已经开展了地方性的长城保护立法工作。近年来，各省（自治区、直辖市）和市县级政府也结合实际制定了地方性法规或政府规章。其中，北京市人民政府在 2003 年颁布了《北京市长城保护管理办法》（北京市人民政府令〔2003〕第 126 号），成为我国第一部省级层面长城保护的地方性法规。此外，河北、山西、内蒙古 3 省（自治区）还出台长城保护相关政策文件。甘肃省人民代表大会常委会在 2010 年修订的《甘肃省文物保护条例》中新增专门的长城保护内容。2016 年，河北省人民政府颁布了《河北省长城保护办法》（河北省人民政府令〔2016〕6 号）。近期，山东、甘肃、青海等省也已启动了长城保护地方性法规的立法工作。

此外，长城沿线部分市（州、盟）、县（市、区）等也制定了一系列长城保护法律文件，包括辽宁省葫芦岛市 2002 年制定的《葫芦岛市九门口长城保护管理规定》，北京市平谷区 2004 年制定的《平谷区长城保护管理规定》，甘肃省武威市 2009 年制定的《武威市凉州区长城保护管理办法》，山丹县 2009 年制定的《山丹县长城保护管理办法》，酒泉市 2013 年制定的《玉门关遗址保护管理办法》，内蒙古自治区伊金霍洛旗 2007 年制定的《伊金霍洛旗秦国长城遗址保护管理暂行办法》，黑龙江省牡丹江市 2012 年制定的《牡丹江边墙保护管理办法》等。

以 2006 年《长城保护条例》颁布为标志，我国长城保护已初步建立了较为完善的国家—省—市—县—遗产地多级长城保护法律法规及规范体系，长城专项法规建设正进入快车道。

All provinces (People's government of autonomous regions and municipalities) along the the Great Wall have made detailed rules or regulations in accordance with the actual conditions of the local areas. Since 1990s, some of the local governments have made conservation legislation. In recent years, the provinces (autonomous regions, municipalities) and the municipal and county governments have also formulated local regulations or government conservation regulations in accordance with the actual situation.

Among them, the Beijing Municipal People's Government issued the "Beijing Great Wall conservation and management measures" (Beijing Municipal People's government order No. 126 of 2003), which is China's first provincial-level regulations on the Great Wall conservation. In addition, the 3 provinces (autonomous region) of Hebei, Shanxi and Inner Mongolia have issued relevant policies on the conservation of the Great Wall. In 2010, the Standing Committee of the Gansu Provincial People's Congress added the *Regulation on the conservation of the Great Wall* to the cultural relics conservation regulations of the province. In 2016, the People's Government of Hebei province issued the "Hebei Great Wall conservation measures"(Order No. 6 of 2016 of the People's Government of Hebei province). Recently, Shandong, Gansu, Qinghai and other provinces have started legislation works on the conservation of the Great Wall.

In addition, some of the cities (prefectures, leagues), counties (county-level cities, districts) along the Great Wall also issued a series of legal documents on the conservation of the Great Wall. Huludao, a city of Liaoning, issued the "Huludao Jiumenkou Great Wall conservation and management regulations" in 2002. In 2004, Beijing's district of Pinggu issued the "Pinggu Great Wall conservation and management regulations". Gansu's city of Wuwei issued the "Liangzhou District Great Wall conservation and management measures" in 2009. Shandan county issued the "Shandan Great Wall conservation and management measures" in 2009, Jiuquan city issued the "Yumen Pass remains conservation and management measures "in 2013. The Inner Mongolia Autonomous Region's Ejin Horo Banner issued the "Ejin Horo Banner Qin dynasty Great Wall remains conservation and management tentative measures" in 2007. Heilongjiang's city Mudanjiang issued the "Mudanjiang historical walls conservation and management measures" in 2012.

With the issuance of the *Regulation on the Conservation of Great Wall* in 2006, the conservation of the Great Wall in China has formed a relatively sound multi-level legal system with national, provincial, municipal, county and local regulations in place. With the strengthening of the conservation of the Great Wall in whole society, the building of the Great Wall's legal system is entering the fast lane.

## 专栏：与长城保护管理相关的重要国际文件

1、《保护世界自然与文化遗产公约》：

1972年10月17日至11月21日，联合国教科文组织在巴黎举行的第十七届大会上通过，1975年正式生效。旨在维护、增进和传播文化遗产知识，应对全球文化和自然遗产受到的日益严重的破坏威胁，对各国文化遗产保护加以科学指导和援助，“为集体保护具有突出的普遍价值的文化和自然遗产建立一个根据现代科学方法制定的永久性的有效制度”。公约明确了世界遗产的定义、价值、组织机构、保护管理原则等内容，明确了世界遗产申报制度。迄今已有178个国家或地区加入该公约。中国于1985年11月22日成为缔约国。

2、《威尼斯宪章》：

1964年5月31日，从事历史文物建筑工作的建筑师和技术人员国际会议第二次会议在威尼斯通过的决议，故简称“威尼斯宪章”。宪章肯定了历史文物建筑的重要价值和作用，把它看作是人类“共同的遗产”，认为“为子孙后代而妥善地保护它们是我们的责任。我们必须不走样地把它们的信息传下去。”宪章明确了历史文物建筑的概念、保护原则、方法、技术标准等内容，特别强调了文物建筑及其环境的完整性。

3、《奈良真实性文件》：

1994年11月1至6日，由日本政府文化事务部与联合国教科文组织、国际文化财产保护与修复研究中心（ICCROM）及国际古迹遗址理事会（ICOMOS）共同在奈良举办的“与世界遗产公约相关的奈良真实性会议”起草，最终版本由奈良会议总协调人Raymond Lemaire先生和Herb Stovel先生编辑。

《奈良真实性文件》以《威尼斯宪章》的精神为基础，突出强调了“文化多样性和遗产多样性”，关于所谓“真实性”，提出了“出于对所有文化的尊重，必须在相关文化背景之下来对遗产项目加以考虑和评判”，为处于弱势地位的亚洲文化遗产保护工作进行了有力支持。

4、《西安宣言》：

2005年10月17日至21日，在中国西安召开的国际古迹遗址理事会第15届大会通过。宣言强调了“周边环境”是体现古建筑、古遗址和历史区域真实性的一部分，需要通过建立缓冲区加以保护。将环境对于遗产和古迹的重要性提升到一个新的高度。同时不仅仅提出对历史环境深入的认识和观点，还进一步提出了解决问题和实施的对策、途径和方法。具有较高的指导性和实践意义。

5、《考古遗产保护与管理宪章》：

国际古迹遗址理事会全体大会第九届会议于1990年10月在瑞士洛桑通过。宪章规定了有关考古遗产管理不同方面的原则，其中包括公共当局和立法者的责任，有关遗产的勘察、勘测、发掘、档案记录、研究、维护、保护、保存、重建、信息资料、展览以及对外开放与公众利用等的专业操作程序规则以及考古遗产保护所涉及的专家之资格等，提出了对考古遗产的保护不能仅仅依靠适用考古学方法，它需要较广泛的专业和科学知识与技能基础。

## Column:Great Wall conservation and management related international documents

1. *Convention concerning the Conservation of the World Cultural and Natural Heritage:*

The UNESCO held its 17th conference in Paris Oct. 17-Nov. 21, 1972 . The "Convention for the Conservation of the Cultural and Natural World Heritage" was passed at the conference. The Convention concerning the Conservation of the World Cultural and Natural Heritage entered into force in 1975.

The efforts are aimed at preserving and boosting the promotion of cultural heritage knowledge, combating the ever increasing damage to global cultural and natural heritages and giving scientific guidance and support to nations on their conservation of cultural heritages. It is also aimed at building a scientific and permanent system on collectively protecting the cultural and natural heritages with outstanding universal values.

The convention clarifies the definition of the world heritage as well as its value, organization, conservation and management principles. The world heritage declaration system has also been defined. A total of 178 countries have acceded the convention. China acceded the convention on Nov. 22, 1985.

2. *Venice Charter:*

The Venice Charter for the Conservation and Restoration of Monuments and Sites was drawn up by a group of conservation professionals at the Second International Congress of Architects and Specialists of Historic Buildings in Venice on May 31, 1964. The Charter confirms the important value and function of the historical buildings. The concept of historic monuments and sites was interpreted as the common heritage, therefore safeguarding them for the future generations with authenticity was defined as the common responsibility. The Charter defines the concept of historic buildings, conservation principles, methods and technology standards. It emphasizes on the conservation of the historical buildings and their environments as a whole.

3. *The Nara Document on Authenticity:*

Nov. 1-6, 1994, the cultural affairs department of Japanese government, UNESCO, ICCROM and ICOMOS jointly held the conference in Nara. The Nara Document on Authenticity was drafted at the conference. The general coordinators of the conference, Raymond Lemaire and Herb Stovel edited the draft. The Nara Document on Authenticity is based on the Venice Charter's spirit, emphasized on the cultural diversity and heritage diversity. On authenticity, the Document says due to respect on all cultures, the evaluation on heritage projects must take the related cultural background into consideration, which gives strong support to the relatively weak conservation of the Asian cultural heritages.

4. *The Xi'an Declaration on the Conservation of the Setting of Heritage Structures, Sites and Areas:*

The 15th General Assembly of ICOMOS was held in Xi'an Oct. 17-21, 2005. The "Xi'an Declaration on the Conservation of the Setting of Heritage Structures, Sites and Areas" was passed at the assembly. The Declaration emphasizes the surrounding environment is part of the authenticity of historical buildings, remains and areas. It is needed to build buffer zones to protect the surrounding environments. The Declaration uplifts environment's importance to heritages and historical sites to a new level. It not only raises deep understanding and new concept on historical environments, but also gives solutions, methods and ways to the problems, which has higher instructive and practical significance.

5. *Charter for the Conservation and Management of the Archaeological Heritage:*

The Charter for the Conservation and Management of the Archaeological Heritage was passed by the International Committee for the Management of Archaeological Heritage (ICAHM) at its 9th General Assembly in Lausanne in Oct, 1990. The Charter sets rules on principles on heritage management including government and lawmakers' responsibilities, surveying, unearthing, file keeping, researching, maintenance, conservation, conservation, restoration, data, exhibition and related procedures as well as expert qualifications.

The Charter recognizes that conservation of heritages cannot be based upon the application of archaeological techniques alone. It also requires a wider basis of professional and scientific knowledge and skills.

# 第二节 长城保护管理队伍建设

- 长城管理机构——国家、地方各级文物行政管理部门与日常管理机构
- 长城专业机构——研究与咨询机构、技术队伍
- 长城保护员——各地聘请沿线居民协助文物部门开展长城巡查维护
- 长城民间社团——凝聚社会力量、引导公众参与长城保护

长城保护管理，遵循我国以各级文物保护单位为基础，分级负责、属地管理的文物管理体制。与此同时，作为特殊类型的文物，长城保护管理较之普通文物保护单位，又具有独特性。我国长城保护管理结合自身国情，依托文物保护单位的法定保护体系和世界文化遗产管理制度，在建立起具有中国特色的大型线性遗产管理体制机制方面进行了一系列有益探索。

## 一、管理机构

长城保护管理已经建立起由国务院文物行政部门、地方人民政府及文物行政部门、长城所在地保护管理机构组成的多级管理体制。其中，国家文物局作为国务院文物行政部门，主管全国文物保护工作，负责协调、解决长城保护中的重大问题，组织编制长城保护总体工作方案、国家级保护规划，研究制定相关法规、规范和指导性文件，监督、检查长城沿线各地实施长城保护、管理、维修、展示、利用等工作。

## Section 2 Great Wall conservation and management team setup

- Great Wall management agency—national, local cultural relic administrative departments at all levels and daily management organization
- Great Wall special agency—residents along Great Wall employed all regions to assist cultural relic department in conducting Great Wall patrol and maintenance
- Great Wall supervisors—residents along Great Wall are employed by each region to assist cultural heritage departments in carrying out Great Wall inspection and maintenance
- Voluntary associations of Great Wall—cohesion of social power, guide public engagement of Great Wall conservation

Great Wall conservation and management abides by cultural relic management system of our country, based on cultural relic conservation sites at all levels, graded responsibility, localization management. At the same time, cultural relic with special type, Great Wall conservation and management has uniqueness compared with common cultural relic conservation sites. Great Wall conservation and management of our country carries out a series of beneficial exploration in the aspect of establishing large-scale linear heritage management system with Chinese characteristics, based on cultural relic conservation sites' legal conservation system and world cultural heritage management system.

### I. Conservation Management Team Governing Body

Great Wall conservation and management has established multiple management system comprising cultural heritage administrative departments of the State Council, local people's governments and cultural heritage administrative departments, conservation and management agencies where Great Wall section

长城所在地县级以上人民政府及其文物主管部门依照有关法律法规的规定，负责本行政区域内的长城保护管理，具体实施长城日常管理、保养维护、执法巡查、保护工程实施等工作。长城段落为行政区域边界的，其毗邻的县级以上地方人民政府通过定期召开由相关部门参加的联席会议，研究解决长城保护中的重大问题。

截止2016年10月，长城沿线15个省（区、市）、97个设区市、404个县共有直接参与长城保护的文物行政部门、专业机构、单位523个。其中，省级文物行政部门15个，地市级部门、专业机构、单位97个，县级411个，长城所在地专门保护管理机构43个。上述各类长城保护管理机构共计485个，工作人员4573人。

## 二、专业队伍

近年来，中国文化遗产研究院、中国文物信息咨询中心、中国古迹遗址保护协会、中国世界文化遗产专家委员会等专业机构、团体等也参与了长城保护相关技术咨询、指导工作。

在长城保护工程实施过程中，一大批具有学术水平、研究能力和技术水平的高校、相关科研院所、企业等参与了长城保护相关专业咨询工作。在长城保护勘察设计、施工队伍中，已经改变了过去由文物行业专业技术单位独自支撑的局面，其他行业的事业单位、高校、企业纷纷进入到文物保护行业，纷纷获得了文物保护工程勘察设计资质和文物保护工程施工资质。目前，长城保护工作各环节都出现了具有各自背景、技术专长的队伍。他们的参与一定程度上缓解了文物保护专业技术力量不足的问题。据统计，2005-2014年间，[23]参与长城保护工作的专业机构共140家。从各单位的背景来看，其中40家为文物行业专业技术单位，

[23] 本报告中所引用的长城保护管理业务数据，有一些是来自于全国各省、市、县文物部门向“长城资源保护管理信息系统”在线提交的“长城保护工程（2005-2014年）”实施期间的数据，2015、2016年的数据在本报告出版之时仍在组织填报和审核，为尽量保证数据的客观和来源统一，报告中的部分数据统计以2005-2014年为区间，特此说明。

locates, among which State Administration of Cultural Heritage as cultural heritage administrative departments of the State Council, is in charge of national cultural heritage conservation work, coordinating and settling major issues of Great Wall conservation, organizing and compiling Great Wall conservation overall working scheme, conservation planning at national level, studying and formulating relevant laws and regulations and guidance documents, supervising, checking Great Wall conservation, management, maintenance, display, using and other works conducted by regions along Great Wall.

Local people's government above the county level and cultural heritage competent department where Great Wall locates as per relevant provisions of laws and regulations take charge of Great Wall conservation and management within its administrative region, concretely conducting Great Wall daily management, maintenance, law enforcement and patrol, conservation engineering execution and etc.. Where Great Wall section is located at administrative region boundaries, local people's government above the county level adjacent to it shall regularly convene joint conference participated by related departments to research the solution to major issues of Great Wall conservation.

By the end of October 2016, 523 cultural heritage administrative departments, special agencies of Great Wall conservation directly from 15 provinces (zones, cities), 97 prefecture-level cities, 404 counties engaged in it, including 15 cultural heritage administrative departments at the province level, 97 departments, special agencies, units at prefecture level, 911 departs at the county level, 43 special conservation and management agencies where Great Wall locates. The above mentioned various kinds of Great Wall conservation and management agencies totals 485 with 4573 staff.

## II. Specialized Team

In recent years, some specialized agencies, organizations, such as Chinese Academy of Cultural Heritage, China Cultural Heritage Information and Consulting Center, China Cultural Relics Conservation Association, Committee of Experts of Chinese World Cultural Heritage and etc. also engage in technology consulting, guidance works related to Great Wall conservation.

包括勘察设计单位10家，施工单位17家，施工监理单位13家；另外的100家为高校和其他行业的专业技术单位，包括勘查设计单位17家，施工单位55家，监理单位27家。这些不同专业背景、不同技术专长的勘察设计、施工、监理队伍参与到长城保护工程，为长城保护带来了新鲜的血液，壮大了长城研究保护的技术队伍力量。

## 三、保护员制度

长城分布地域广，且大多处于人迹罕至和经济欠发达地区，其保护难度超过了任何其他文物保护单位。从长期实践经验来看，完全依靠政府、文物部门的现有力量对其进行全线实时监控和管理难度极高，必须调动全社会力量关注并积极参与长城保护，才能全面扭转长城保护不利局面。

在这方面，国家文物局鼓励各地探索在长城沿线居民中聘请保护员的方式，让他们担负起定期巡查、及时发现和反映问题、向当地群众宣传长城保护等责任。长城沿线附近很多居民长期生活、工作于此，聘请他们作为长城保护员既可以够弥补文物工作人员不足，保护管理覆盖不及时的问题，又能调动和发挥长城沿线居民认识、宣传、保护长城的积极性。

2016年2月，国家文物局出台了《长城保护员管理办法》。在2016年6月，中国文化遗产日河北承德主场城市活动开幕式上，国家文物局正式向12位长城保护员代表颁发工作证书，使得原来的业余长城保护志愿者有了正式的身份，明确了责任地段，队伍更加正规化。截止2016年10月，全国长城保护员人数达到4650人。国家文物局已陆续开展长城保护员培训、装备配备等工作，并将尽可能给予更大的支持，发挥他们的积极性和重要作用。

During the project implementation process of Great Wall conservation, a large batch of colleges and universities, related scientific research institutions, enterprises with academic level, research capacity and technology level participate in relevant professional consulting works of Great Wall conservation. As for Great Wall conservation survey and design service, construction team, the situation solely supported by specialized technology units of cultural heritage industry has been altered, public institutions, colleges and universities, enterprises from other industries have engaged in cultural heritage conservation industry one after another, which have the qualification for cultural heritage conservation engineering surveying and design and qualification for cultural heritage conservation engineering construction in succession. At present, each link of Great Wall conservation has built its own background, technical expertise team. Their participation relieves the issue of specialized technical force scarce for cultural heritage to certain extent. According to the statistics, from 2005 to 2014[23], 140 specialized agencies participated in Great Wall conservation work. From the aspect of individual background, 40 specialized technical units in cultural heritage industry, including 10 survey and design units, 17 construction units, 13 construction supervising units; the rest are colleges and universities and specialized technical units from other industries, including 17 survey and design units, 55 construction units, 27 supervising units. Participation of survey and design, construction, supervising teams with different professional backgrounds, different technical expertise in Great Wall Conservation Project injects fresh blood to Great Wall research, develops technology team force of Great Wall research and conservation.

## III. Supervisor System

The distribution area of Great Wall is expansive and most of areas located at secluded and underdeveloped regions, its conservation difficulty is in excess of any other cultural heritage conservation sites. From the point of long-term practical experience, it is infeasible that conducting total line real time monitoring and management solely depended on government, existing force from cultural heritage departments. Only mobilizing all forces from the whole society to concern and actively participate in Great Wall conservation, the adverse situation of Great Wall conservation could be totally reversed.

[23] The business data of Great Wall conservation and management quoted in the report, some data is from "Great Wall conservation works (2005-2014)" online submitted by national cultural heritage departments of provinces, cities, counties to "Great Wall resources conservation and management information system" during the implementation period. The data in 2015, 2016 is organized to fill in and check when publishing the report, in order to guarantee the objectiveness and uniform sources of data as far as possible, some data statistics in the report are adopted that in the 2005-2014, hereby certify.

2015 年下半年，为统一开展长城保护员的核实、审查工作，国家文物局委托中国文化遗产研究院对长城沿线 15 省（市、自治区）的长城保护员做了核实和更正，完成了 3000 多名长城保护员信息的备案。（图 2-1、2-2，表 2-2）

近年来，长城保护员中涌现出了一批优秀代表。如北京市的梅景田同志长期坚持每个月踏查长城三四次。当发现有护林员在长城边上悄悄建房子时，他和村干部进行了坚决的制止；为了阻止游客攀爬长城，他用镰刀在山林中开辟出一条“旅游专线”；因为阻止游人在长城上私刻乱画，他曾被六七个年轻人围攻。不管在保护长城过程中有多大的困难，都没能阻止梅景田保护长城的热情。2007 年梅景田被国家文物局授予“文物保护特别奖”、2008 年被评为“全国优秀长城保护员”。再如甘肃省的姜有玉同志，1986 年被县文物主管部门正式聘任为长城保护员，并颁发了证书，长期以来，他自始至终默默无闻守护长城，坚持定期巡查长城，制止并报告破坏长城行为，到长城周边群众居住集中的丰城堡村、开发区、郭泉村等进行广泛宣传。

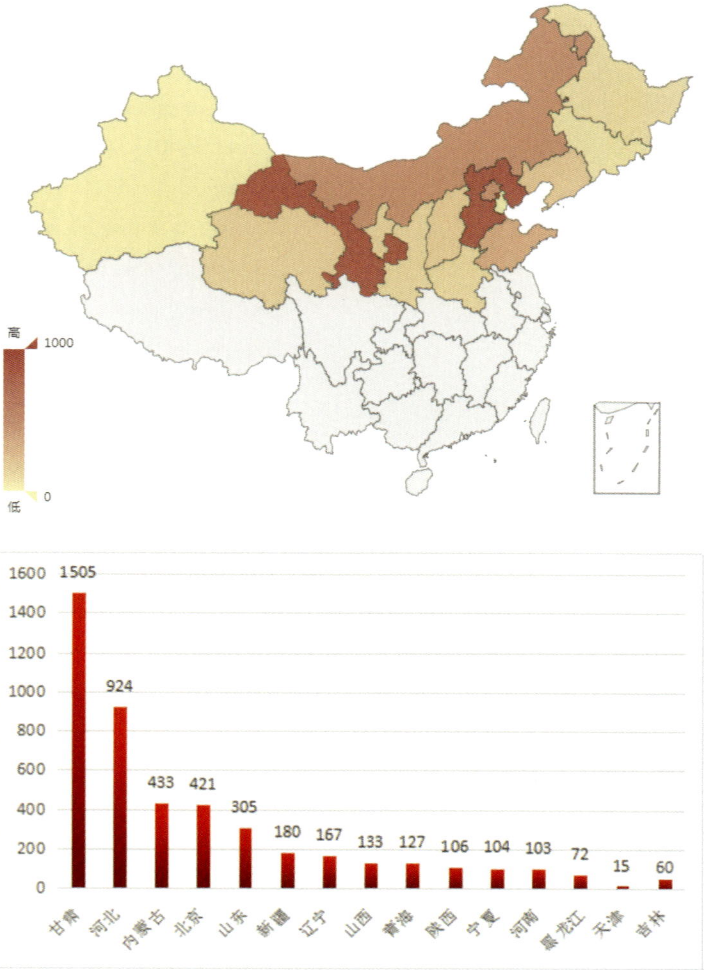


图 2-1
全国长城保护员人数分省统计图

Fig. 2-1
Statistical chart on distribution number of persons in charge of protecting Great Wall in involved province

图 2-2
正在巡查长城的保护员（张依萌 拍摄）

Fig. 2-2
Person in charge of Great Wall Conservation is at patrol (photo by Zhang Yimeng)

In this respect, State Administration of Cultural Heritage encourages involved regions to explore the way of employing supervisors along Great Wall, assume responsibilities of patrol at regular intervals, timely find and reflecting issues, publicize Great Wall conservation and etc. Because many residents along Great Wall live and work here long-term, employing these persons as supervisors of Great Wall not only makes up scarce number of staff and involved area under conservation and management not timely but also mobilizes and plays positive enthusiasm from residents along Great Wall knowing, publicizing and protecting Great Wall.

In February 2016, State Administration of Cultural Heritage issued *Measures for the Management of Inspection Personnel of the Great Wall,* in June 2016, at the opening ceremony of Heibei Chengde host city activity on the Chinese cultural heritage day, State Administration of Cultural Heritage officially awarded employee's card to 12 supervisors for Great Wall, thus, the original amateur volunteers of Great Wall conservation gained their new identifications. It specified corresponding zone for person to undertake the responsibility, team got more and more normalization. By the end of October 2016, the number of supervisors for Great Wall reached 4650. State Administration of Cultural Heritage has carried out works of Great Wall supervisors training, equipment and outfits and etc. one after the other, to give utmost support as far as possible, to play their positivity and important roles.

In the second half year of 2015, in order to carry out the work of Great Wall supervisor verified and reviewed, State Administration of Cultural Heritage authorized Chinese Academy of Cultural Heritage to conduct verification and

## 表 2-2：各省（自治区、直辖市）长城保护员设置和管理情况

Table 2-2: Establishment and management situation of persons in charge of protecting Great Wall of involved provinces (autonomous regions, municipalities directly under the Central Government)

| 省份<br>Province | 已聘请长城保护员数量（名）<br>Quantities of employed persons in charge of Great Wall Conservation (number) |
|---|---|
| 北京 / Beijing | 421 |
| 陕西 / Shaanxi | 106 |
| 甘肃 / Gansu | 1505 |
| 青海 / Qinghai | 127 |
| 宁夏 / Ningxia | 104 |
| 山西 / Shanxi | 133 |
| 内蒙古 / Inner Mongolia | 433 |
| 黑龙江 / Heilongjiang | 72 |
| 天津 / Tianjin | 15 |
| 新疆 / Xinjiang | 180 |
| 山东 / Shandong | 305 |
| 河北 / Hebei | 924 |
| 吉林 / Jilin | 60 |
| 辽宁 / Liaoning | 167 |
| 河南 / Henan | 103 |
| 合计 / Sub-total | 4650 |

数据来源：国家文物局：长城执法专项督查总结报告，2016 年，内部资料。

review on Great Wall supervisors from 15 provinces, cities and autonomous regions along Great Wall. And the Great Wall supervisors' information has been completely put on records. (Table 2-2 Fig 2-1, 2-2)

For the past few years, a batch of excellent representatives from Great Wall supervisors spring up. For example, comrade Mei Jingtian from Beijing sticks to inspect Great Wall on the spot for several times for a long run. When he found some forest ranger privately built house along Great Wall, village cadres and he would resolutely prohibit; in order to avoid tourists climbing Great Wall, he opened up a path of "travelling special line" in the forest with his sickle; he was ever besieged by several young people, because h prevented tourists from doing private painting and arbitrary doodle on Great Wall. No matter what difficulties he encounters during the process of protecting Great Wall, Mei Jingtian keeps his enthusiasm in protecting Great Wall. In 2007, Mei Jingtian was awarded "cultural heritage conservation special award" by State Administration of Cultural Heritage, in 2008, he was awarded as "national excellent Great Wall supervisors". Another example is Jiang Yutong from Gansu Province, in 1986, he was duly employed as Great Wall supervisor by county cultural heritage competent department, issued the certificate. For a long period, he guards Great Wall from beginning to end unknown to public and adheres to inspect Great Wall at regular intervals, prevents and reports actions of damaging Great Wall, conducts expansive publicity to residential concentration areas of Great Wall, such as Fengchengbao Village, Development Zone, Guoquan Village and etc..

Liang Qingli, a generation after the 80s, lives at Yumuling Village, Qianxi County, every three to four days, he would go home from the county where he works driving car for 40 minutes to inspect Great Wall. Every time, he goes to the mountain at four o' clock before dawn, goes downhill at 8 o' clock in the morning. Young Liang is also a amateur commentator, often publicizes Great Wall knowledge to villagers and tour pals attracted to a scenic spot. His bedroom is filled with flags, calligraphy works presented by tour pals passed, newspapers and interview report on him by TV station. Under his influence, many young people begin to be interested in Great Wall and jointly engage in it. Young Liang and his friends together go to Great Wall to collect trash, when they find some bricks collapsed sometimes, they would simply assemble and place it on the appropriate place. Except for protecting Great Wall, he also engages in some public benefit activities within his power. With his appeal, some warm-hearted people donate to families in financial or material difficulties in Yumuling, improving their lives.

家住迁西县榆木岭村的 80 后长城保护员梁庆立，每隔三四天，就要从他在县城打工的地方驱车 40 分钟回家一趟，巡视长城一次。每次都是凌晨四点上山，早上 8 点下山。小梁同时还是业余讲解员，经常向村民和慕名而来的驴友们宣传长城知识。他的卧室挂满了爬山经过此地的驴友送给他的旗帜、书法作品，还有报纸和电视台对他的采访报道。在他的影响下，村里很多年轻人也开始对长城感兴趣，并且开始和他一起并肩战斗。小梁和他的朋友们一起上长城捡垃圾，有时见到塌落的砖石，也做一做简单的垒砌。除了保护长城，他也做一些力所能及的公益活动，在他的呼吁下，一些他接触过的爱心人士也对榆木岭村困难户进行捐助，改善他们的生活。

这些优秀的长城保护员代表用他们的实际行动，为宣传和保护长城做出了贡献，引起了良好的社会反响。

## 四、社会力量

长城是中华民族伟大民族的精神象征和形象代表，长城保护的社会基础好、社会参与度高。1987 年，习仲勋、黄华、马文瑞、王光英、杨静仁、何鲁丽等共同发起成立了“中国长城学会”。长城沿线部分省（自治区、直辖市）也相继成立了长城保护、研究相关社会组织。近年来，“长城保护志愿服务总队”“长城小站”“国际长城之友协会”等长城保护社会团体、志愿者组织蓬勃发展，成为新时期参与长城保护的生力军，在凝聚社会力量、引导公众参与长城保护方面发挥了重要作用。

据不完全统计，我国现有经过正式注册的长城相关社会团体、志愿者组织近 30 个，此外还有大量由长城爱好者自发组成的非正式团体、活动群、兴趣小组等。受“长城保护工程”实施的影响，2006 年之后，长城相关社会团体、志愿者组织更关注并通过建言献策、亲身参与、宣传教育等方式参与长城保护工作。很多新成立的社会团体、志愿者组织在名称中加入了“保护”二字，这也从一个侧面反映出当前长城相关社会团体、志愿者组织发展的时代特点。

These excellent representatives of Great Wall supervisors contribute to publicity and conservation of Great Wall by their practical actions, which give rise to favorable social response.

## IV. Social Force

Great Wall is the spirit symbol image representative of Chinese great nations and Great Wall conservation has solid social foundation and high degree of social participation. In 1987, Xi Zhongxun, Huang Hua, Ma Wenrui, Wang Guangying, Yang Jingren, He Luli and others jointly sponsored and established "Great Wall Society of China". Some provinces (autonomous regions and municipalities direct under the Central Government) have established social organizations related to Great Wall conservation, research in succession. For the past few years, Great Wall conservation social organizations, voluntary organizations such as "Great Wall conservation voluntary service corps", "Great Wall Station", "international friends of the Great Wall" are prosperous, becoming fresh troops engaging in Great Wall conservation in new era, playing a crucial role in uniting social strength, guiding public to participating in Great Wall conservation.

According to the incomplete statistics, there are nearly 30 social organizations, voluntary organizations related to Great Wall by official register, besides, a large number of informal groups, activity groups, hobby teams and etc. were formed by Great Wall fans. After 2016, social organizations, voluntary organizations related to Great Wall concern more about Great Wall conservation by the way of offering advice and suggestions, personal involvement, publicity and education and other ways to participate in it. Many newly established social organizations and voluntary organizations add "conservation" into their name, which reflects the epochal characteristics of social organizations and voluntary organizations related to Great Wall from one side.

Among social organizations and voluntary organizations, the establishment of some organizations is directly related to Great Wall resource survey and affirmation work uniformly organized and conducted by the State. For example, Shanxi Culture Relics Bureau, China supported to establish Great Wall Conservation Research in Shanxi Province whose president is former Deputy Director of Shanxi People' Congress and branches are set up in regions along Great Wall whose principals are all leaders from local government and people's congress. These social organizations collect all kinds of social resources, gather a variety of social powers to positively devote themselves into Great Wall research, publicity and education works, conduct a series of content-rich activities in various forms, play an active part in popularization of Great Wall conservation knowledge and concept and awareness and promotion of management level of Great Wall conservation

各类社会团体、志愿者组织中，有一些团体的建立与国家统一组织实施的长城资源调查和认定工作开展直接相关。例如，山西省文物局支持成立了由山西省人大原副主任任会长的山西省长城保护研究会，并在长城沿线各地市设立分会，均由当地政府、人大领导任负责人。这些社团汇聚了多种社会资源、集合了各类社会力量积极投身长城研究、宣传与教育工作，开展了一系列形式多样、内容丰富的活动，对长城保护知识、理念和意识的普及，推动长城保护管理水平提升起到了积极作用。（表 2–3）

## 表 2-3：现有的主要长城民间团体一览表

Table 2-3: List of existing main Great Wall civil body

| 序号<br>Serial No. | 团体名称<br>Name of organization | 成立时间<br>Establishing time |
|---|---|---|
| 1 | 中国山海关长城研究会<br>Chinese Shanhai Pass Great Wall Research | 1984 |
| 2 | 中国老年历史研究会万里长城研究所<br>Chinese Geriatric History Research Society Great Wall Research Institution | 1986 |
| 3 | 中国长城学会<br>Great Wall Society of China | 1986.6 |
| 4 | 中国嘉峪关长城研究会<br>China Jiayu Pass Great Wall Research Institution | 1986.9 |
| 5 | 北京市西城区长城摄影协会<br>Photography Association in Xicheng District, Beijing | 1992.12 |
| 6 | 神木县长城协会<br>Great Wall Association in Shenmu County | 1994 |
| 7 | 辽宁省长城学会<br>Liaoning Great Wall Society | 1995 |
| 8 | 八达岭长城文化艺术协会<br>Badaling Great Wall Culture & Art Association | 1997 |
| 9 | 长城小站<br>Great Wall Station | 1999 |
| 10 | 中国长城博物馆学术研究委员会<br>China Great Wall Museum Academic Research Committee | 2000.4 |

| | | |
|---|---|---|
| 11 | 国际长城之友协会<br>International Friends of the Great Wall | 2001 |
| 12 | 中国文物学会长城研究委员会<br>Chinese society of Cultural Relics Great Wall Research Committee | 2001 |
| 13 | 内蒙古自治区长城学会<br>Inner Mongolia Great Wall Society | 建立时间不详<br>Establishing time unknown |
| 14 | 南召县楚长城研究会<br>Chu Great Wall Research Institution in Nanzhao County | 2001.6 |
| 15 | 中国长城博物馆长城研究委员会<br>China Great Wall Museum Great Wall Research Council | 2001.6 |
| 16 | 秦皇岛长城研究会<br>Qinhuangdao Great Wall Research Society | 建立时间不详<br>Establishing time unknown |
| 17 | 河西学院大学生宣传与保护长城协会<br>Academician Publicity and Conservation Great Wall Association of Hexi University, Gansu, China | 2006 |
| 18 | 山西省长城保护研究会<br>Great Wall Conservation Research in Shanxi Province | 2007.7 |
| 19 | 大同长城学会<br>Datong Great Wall Society | 2007.8.28 |
| 20 | 南阳市楚长城文化研究会<br>Chu Great Wall Culture Research in Nanyang City | 2008 |
| 21 | 朔州市长城保护研究会<br>Great Wall Conservation Research in Shuozhou City | 2009.6 |
| 22 | 忻州市长城学会<br>Xinzhou Great Wall Society | 2010.1.22 |
| 23 | 中国长城书画家协会<br>The China Great Wall Academy of Painting and Calligraphy | 2010.9 |
| 24 | 右玉县长城保护研究会<br>Great Wall Conservation Research in Shiyu County | 2010.11.3 |
| 25 | 平顶山楚长城研究会<br>Pingdingshan Chu Great Wall Research | 2011 |
| 26 | 嘉峪关市长城文化研究会<br>Great Wall Culture Research in Jiayu Pass | 2012.4 |
| 27 | 大同长城保护与发展研究中心<br>Datong Great Wall Conservation and Development Research Center | 2015.2 |

注：数据由报告编写者通过走访各地文物行政部门及中国长城学会、长城小站等获得。
Note: Data is obtained by report author interviewing administrative departments from place to place and Great Wall Society of China y, Great Wall l Station and etc.

# 第三节 长城日常保护管理工作

- 四有工作——公布各级文物保护单位 209 处
  85% 以上划定保护范围
  竖立各类保护标识近 80000 处
  半数以上建立文物记录档案
- 保护规划——完成 15 省（自治区、直辖市）省级规划、18 个重要点段规划编制，总体规划全面启动
- 长城执法——执法巡查 200 余次，督察督办案件 60 余起

## 一、开展执法与专项督察

长城沿线各级文物行政部门及依法被授权或受委托承担文物行政执法职能的机构（以下简称“执法机构”）对本行政区域内的长城文物本体安全及保护管理工作进行监督检查，对已经发生的文物安全案件进行督察、督办。2016 年《长城执法巡查办法》（后文简称《办法》）颁布实施，对长城专项执法、巡查工作做出了明确规定，突出了工作责任、工作机制和管理要求。《办法》第二条规定：“各级文物行政部门、文物执法机构，对本行政区域内各级文物保护单位进行的日常性检查工作”。开展长城执法巡查与安全督察，是长城保护各项法律法规得到执行、长城文物本体及周边景观得到切实保护的重要保证。

## Section 3 Daily Conservation and Management

- Four basic works - publish 209 cultural heritage conservation sites at all levels
  Demarcates more than 85% conservation scope
  Setup various kinds of conservation signs nearly 80000 sites
  Establish more than halves of cultural heritage log archives
- Conservation planning - accomplish planning at province level in 15 provinces (autonomous regions, municipalities direct under the Central Government)
  Planning and compilation of 18 major sections
  Overall launch general planning
- Great Wall law enforcement - conduct inspection for over 200 times by law enforcement, supervise and settle over 60 cases

### I. Law enforcement and special supervision

Cultural heritage administrative departments at all levels along Great Wall and agencies assuming cultural heritage administrative law enforcement function by authorization or entrustment (hereinafter referred to as "law enforcement agency") conduct supervision and check on Great Wall cultural heritage ontology safety and conservation and management work within the administrative region, superintend and handle cultural heritage safety cases occurred. In 2016, *Great Wall Law Enforcement Inspection Measures* (hereinafter referred to as *Measures*) was issued, which clearly specified special project for Great Wall law enforcement, inspection work and highlighted job responsibility, working mechanism and management requirements. Article II of *Measures* stipulates: "cultural heritage administrative departments at all levels and cultural heritage law enforcement agencies conduct daily inspection work on cultural heritage sites within its administrative region." Conducting Great Wall law enforcement inspection and safety supervision is the important guarantee for execution of all laws and regulations related to Great Wall conservation and practical conservation of Great Wall ontology and its surrounding landscape.

### （一）2016 国家文物局长城执法专项督察

为贯彻落实习近平总书记关于加强长城保护的重要指示，贯彻落实《国务院关于进一步加强文物工作的指导意见》和全国文物工作会议精神，2016 年 9 月至 10 月，国家文物局组织开展了首次“长城执法专项督察”，专项督察重点对照《长城保护条例》，全面检查长城沿线省级政府和文物行政部门履行长城保护法定职责情况，督促落实长城保护政府责任，完善长城保护基础工作，建立长城监管与执法常态化机制，严肃查处破坏长城本体及历史风貌的违法犯罪案件，得到了新闻媒体高度关注和社会各界广泛支持。督察范围覆盖长城沿线 15 个省份、 404 个县域。在专项督察结果基础上，形成督察报告，上报国务院，并通报长城沿线省级人民政府和省级文物行政管理机关。

此次“长城执法专项督察”突出量化考核。按照任务要求，中国文化遗产研究院承担编制工作方案和督察工作手册与评分细则，承办人员培训，参加现场督察，牵头完成分省报告和总报告的任务。中国文化遗产研究院将《文物保护法》《长城保护条例》等法律法规中对省级人民政府及其文物行政部门应履行的长城保护法定要求，量化编制为百分制的《长城执法专项督察对照检查表》，包括长城段落认定与公布、“四有”等基础工作、监管与执法常态化机制、政府保护责任落实等 4 个大项、13 个子项、36 个小项督察内容。工作方式上采取“国家文物局督察、省级自查、随机抽查相结合”，“案件督办、试点示范、社会监督相结合”，通过自上而下层级监督和基层工作的试点示范两方面强化工作实效。

长城沿线省级政府和文物主管部门高度重视，按时完成了自查任务。宁夏回族自治区副主席带队实地督察，黑龙江、辽宁、青海主管副省长就专项督察做出批示。各省文物主管部门自查长城沿线市（县、区）70 余个，山西、甘肃组织开展了省内交叉检查，北京、天津、河北在国家文物局指导下开展了长城执法联合巡查。各地切实进行自查自纠，普遍加强了长城保护标志和档

**(I) Special supervision for Great Wall law enforcement of State Administration of Cultural Heritage in 2016**

In order to implement the important indication of General Secretary Xi Jinping, carry out the Guidance on Further Strengthen Cultural Heritage Work by the State Council and spirit of national cultural heritage meeting, in September to October 2016, State Administration of Cultural Heritage organized and conducted "special project for Great Wall law enforcement" activity for the first time. In line with *Regulation on the Conservation of Great Wall*, special project for Great Wall law enforcement overall inspected the situation of governments at province level and cultural heritage administrative departments implementing legal responsibility for Great Wall conservation along Great Wall, supervised and urged to fulfill government responsibility for Great Wall conservation and perfect basic work of Great Wall conservation, established normalized mechanism of Great Wall supervision and law enforcement, sternly investigated and treated illegal criminal cases of damaging Great Wall ontology and historic feature, which drew highly attention from news media and expansive supports from all sectors of society. Supervision scope covers 15 provinces, 404 counties along Great Wall. On the basis of special supervision, it formed supervision report and reported to the State Council and notified it to people's government at province level and cultural administrative agencies at province level for general information.

The "Great Wall law enforcement special supervision" highlighted quantitative assessment. As per task requirements, Chinese Academy of Cultural Heritage undertook working scheme, supervising workbook and detial rules of scoring, presided over personnel training, participated in site supervision and took the lead to accomplish provincial report and general report. Chinese Academy of Cultural Heritage quantized Great Wall conservation legal requirements on provincial people's governments and cultural heritage administrative departments under laws and regulations such as *Law of the People's Republic of China on the Conservation of Cultural Relics, Regulation on the Conservation of Great Wall* and etc. to compile as centesimal *Comparison Check List of Great Wall Law Enforcement Special Supervision* inclusive of 4 major items, 13 sub-items and 36 minor items of supervision contents, such as, identifying and publish Great Wall section, basic works of "Four basic works" and etc., supervision and law enforcement normalized mechanism, government' conservation responsibility. Working mode adopted "combination of being supervised by State Administration of Cultural Heritage, self-examination of provincial level, random inspection", "combination of supervising and handling cases, pilot demonstration, social

案建设，甘肃在督察期间整体划定公布全省长城保护范围和建设控制地带，北京、山西、甘肃等省市对自查发现案件进行了重点督办。

2016 年 9 月 20 日至 9 月 30 日，国家文物局组织五个督察组，对长城沿线 15 个省（自治区、直辖市）长城保护管理情况进行了实地督察。根据要求，各督察组按照听取汇报、查阅资料、实地抽查、初步反馈等程序进行实地督察，分别查阅了各省（自治区、直辖市）涉及长城保护和管理方面的各项资料，实地抽查了 41 个县域的 104 处长城段落（表 2-4）。实地督察结束后，国家文物局汇总 15 个省份督察情况，形成专项报告上报国务院，有关内容向全国文物系统和全国文物安全部际联席会议成员单位通报，并向社会公布。

**表 2-4：实地督察概况统计表**

Table 2-4: Statistical table of on-site supervising survey

| 督察组<br>Inspectorate | 抽查县域<br>County under spot check | 长城段落数<br>Number of Great Wall sections | 督察建议<br>Supervising suggestion | 发现安全隐患<br>Potential risk found | 发现案件线索<br>Case clue found |
|---|---|---|---|---|---|
| 京津冀<br>Beijing – Tianjin - Hebei | 7 | 18 | 14 | 0 | 1 |
| 蒙陕宁<br>Inner Mongolia- Shaanxi - Ningxia | 14 | 17 | 16 | 3 | 7 |
| 甘青新<br>Gansu – Qinghai - Xinjiang | 6 | 30 | 12 | 2 | 4 |
| 晋鲁豫<br>Shanxi – Shandong - Henan | 8 | 28 | 14 | 1 | 4 |
| 辽吉黑<br>Liaoning – Jilin- Heilongjiang | 6 | 11 | 19 | 1 | 0 |
| 合计<br>Sub-total | 41 | 104 | 75 | 7 | 16 |

supervision", from two aspects of hierarchy supervision from top to bottom and pilot demonstration of grass-roots work to strengthen work effectiveness.

Governments at province level and cultural heritage competent departments along Great Wall paid high attention and accomplished self-examination task on time. Vice Chairman of Ningxia Hui Autonomous Region led a team to supervise on the spot, competent Vive Governor of Heilongjiang, Liaoning, Qinghai and others made written instructions on special supervision. Cultural heritage competent departments from each involved provinces conducted self-examination over 70 cities (counties, regions) along Great Wall, Shanxi, Gansu carried out cross check in the provinces, under guidance of State Administration of Cultural Heritage, Beijing, Tianjin, Hebei conducted joint inspection of Great Wall law enforcement. Each region feasibly conducted self-inspection and self-rectification, generally enhancing establishment of Great Wall conservation signs and archives, Gansu overall demarcated and published Great Wall conservation scope and construction control area in the province during the whole supervision period, Beijing, Shanxi, Gansu and other provinces and cities carried out supervision and settlement on cases found during the process of self-inspection by emphasis.

From September 20 to September 30 of 2016, State Administration of Cultural Heritage organized 5 supervision teams to conduct field supervision on management situation of Great Wall conservation from 15 provinces (autonomous regions, municipalities direct under the Central Government) along Great Wall. According to requirements, each supervision team carried out supervision on the spot in line with procedures of debriefing, looking up material, physical test and preliminary feedback and etc., respectively consulting each items materials involved Great Wall conservation and management from each province (autonomous region, municipality direct under the Central Government), physical tests on 104 Great Wall sections of 41 counties (Table 2-4). After the end of supervision on the spot, State Administration of Cultural Heritage summarized supervision situations from 15 provinces and formed special report to submit to the State Council, notified relevant contents to National Cultural Heritage System and meeting members units of National Cultural Heritage Safety Inter-ministry Joint Meeting for general information and publicized.

督察组根据《长城执法专项督察评分细则》的规定，对 4 大督察项，13 项督察项目，36 项评分细则进行了量化考核，按照百分制，统计出各省（自治区、直辖市）总得分和各分项得分。向省级文物主管部门反馈初步督察建议 75 条，发现安全隐患 7 起，发现案件线索 16 起。

从各省得分情况看，15 个省份的平均分为 78.42，有 7 个省份低于平均分。北京、甘肃 2 个省份得分在 90 分以上，得分分别为 92.5 分和 91 分，居前两位；宁夏、山西、河北、山东、黑龙江 5 个省份在 80 ～ 90 分数段；内蒙古、吉林、新疆、青海、陕西 5 个省份在 70 ～ 80 分数段，天津、河南、辽宁 3 个省份在 60 ～ 70 分数段。

关于 4 大督察项，根据得分统计情况来看，长城监管与执法常态化工作、长城段落认定与公布情况开展较好，分别占该项总分值的 80% 以上，而长城“四有”等基础工作总体情况一般，占该项总分值的 74.8%，政府保护责任落实情况得分最低，只占该项总分值的 51.6%，仅为总分值的 1/2 多一点。（表 2-5）

**表 2-5：督察类别得分情况统计表**

Table 2-5: Statistical table of supervising category scores situation

| 序号<br>Serial No. | 项目类别<br>Item category | 分项总分值<br>Total score of Subitems | 15 个省份总得分<br>Total scores from 15 provinces | 实际得分所占比例<br>Actual score's occupying proportion |
|---|---|---|---|---|
| 1 | 长城监管与执法常态化机制<br>Normalized mechanism of Great Wall supervision and law enforcement | 600 | 532.2 | 88.7% |
| 2 | 长城段落认定与公布<br>Identified and published Great Wall sections | 150 | 121.9 | 81.3% |
| 3 | 长城“四有”等基础工作<br>Basic works of Great Wall “Four basic works” and etc. | 525 | 392.1 | 74.7% |
| 4 | 政府保护责任<br>Government Conservation responsibilities | 225 | 115.6 | 51.3% |

宁夏青铜峡明长城（王云刚拍摄）

The section of the Great Wall of the Ming Dynasty in Qingtongxia, Ningxia (Photo by Wang Yungang)

Supervision team, according to the Provisions of Great Wall Law Enforcement Special Supervision Scoring Detailed Rules, conducted quantitative assessment on scoring detailed rules of 4 major supervision items, 13 supervision items, 36 items of scoring detailed rules, as per centesimal system, calculated out total scores and each itemized scores of each province (autonomous region, municipality direct under the Central Government), made 75 feedback suggestions to departments in charge of cultural heritage at province level, found 7 cases of potential safety hazards, found 16 case clues.

From the aspect of each province's scores, the average score of 15 provinces was 78.42, with 7 provinces' scores below the average scores. Scores of Beijing, Gansu are above e 90n, respectively scoring 92.5 and 91, ranked the first two places; 5 provinces of Ningxia, Shanxi, Hebei, Shandong, Heilongjiang, whose scores among the 80-90 score section; 5 provinces of Inner Mongolia, Jilin, Xinjiang, Qinghai, Shaanxi, whose scores among the 70-80 score section; 3 provinces of Tianjin, Henan, Liaoning, whose scores among the 60-70 score section.

As for 4 major supervision items, according to scoring statistical situation, Great Wall supervision and law enforcement normalization work and Great Wall section affirmation and publish situation go well, occupying over 80% of the total scores of the item, however, the general situation of basic work, such as Great Wall "Four basic works" is good, occupying 74.8% of the total scores, the lowest score is the implementation of government conservation responsibility, only occupying 51.6% of the total scores, only a little bit more 1/2 of the total scores. (Table 2-5)

关于 13 项督察项目，根据得分统计情况来看，长城案件查处和长城执法巡查工作开展情况最好，得分占该项总分值的 93% 以上。最差的项目是领导责任落实情况，只占该项总分值的 42.7%。设置长城保护机构和长城保护员、省级长城保护规划编制情况、核对公布公布省级以上文物保护单位的总体情况表现较好，得分占应得总分的占 80% 以上；长城监督管理、经费保障、建立长城档案和设置长城保护标志情况一般，实际得分占应得总分的 70% 以上；长城宣传普法得分占应得总分的 66.7%；保护范围、建设控制地带划定公布总体情况和责任追究落实情况较差，得分占总分值的 1/2 多一点。（图 2-3）

此次督察反映出省级人民政府日益重视长城保护工作，支持力度逐步加强。2015 年国务院召开长城保护座谈会后，11 个省级政府召开 19 次专题会议，研究长城保护工作。长城保护经费基本纳入省级财政预算，2016 年起天津、河北、内蒙古、吉林、宁夏省级财政设立长城保护专项经费，北京市近 3 年每年列支长城保护经费约 1.2 亿元，甘肃省筹措经费近 2000 万元完善长城四有工作，山西省级财政每年专项拨付长城保护员经费近 50 万元。甘肃省人民政府发布《甘肃省文物重大安全事故行政责任追究规定》，将长城损毁列为重大文物安全事故，北京、河北、陕西、河南等省（市）建立了长城保护奖励制度。

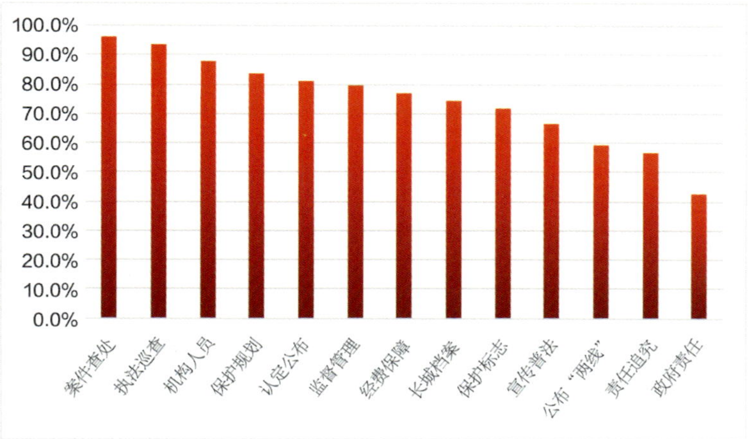


图 2-3
各督察项目总得分占该项分值比例示意图

Fig. 2-3
Schematic diagram on each supervision project's score proportion of total scores

As for 13 supervision items, according to the general scoring statistical situation, the implementation situations of Great Wall cases investigation and settlement and Great Wall law enforcement inspection are best, the scoring occupies over 93% of the total scores. The worst one if leader responsibility implementation, the scoring only occupies 42.7% of the total scores. The overall situations of setting up Great Wall conservation agency and Great Wall supervisors, Great Wall conservation planning at province level, check publishing cultural heritage sites above the province level are better, the scoring occupies over 80% of the deserved total scores. The situation of Great Wall supervision and management, expenditure guarantee, establishing Great Wall archives and setting up Great Wall conservation signs is good, the actual scoring occupies over 70% of the deserved total scores; the scoring of Great Wall publicity and popularized law occupy 66.7% of the total scores. The implementation of publishing general situations of conservation scope, construction control area demarcation are worse, the scoring occupies only a little bit more 1/2 of the total scores. (Fig 2-3)

The supervision reflects Great Wall conservation work gradually draws the attention from people's government at province level, supporting force is gradually strengthened. In 2015, after Great Wall conservation forum held by the State Council ended, 11 governments at province level held 19 special sessions, to research Great Wall conservation work. Great Wall conservation expenditure basically included into financial budget at province level, from 2016, Tianjin, Hebei, Inner Mongolia, Jilin, Ningxia provincial level financing have set up Great Wall conservation special expenditure. Beijing listed and expended Great Wall conservation expenditure for about RMB 120 million in recent 3 years; Gansu raised fund for nearly RMB 20 million to perfect Great Wall Four basic work; Shanxi provincial financing annually special appropriation for nearly RMB 500 thousand to persons in charge of Great Wall conservation. Gangu provincial government issued Rules of Administrative Responsibility Investigation on Cultural Relic Major Safety Accidents in Gansu Province, listing Great Wall damage as major cultural relic safety accident, Beijing, Hebei, Shaanxi, Henan and etc. established Great Wall conservation incentive system.

**(II) Situation of law enforcement agencies at all levels**

According to statistical situations from "Great Wall law enforcement special supervision" of State Administration of Cultural Heritage, 15 provinces (autonomous regions, municipalities directly under the Central Government) have established cultural relic law enforcement agency, including 504 local governments' cultural relic law enforcement agencies at all level undertaking Great Wall law enforcement responsibilities. From the aspect of agency type,

## （二）各级执法机构情况

根据国家文物局“长城执法专项督察”统计情况，长城沿线15个省（自治区、直辖市）均已建立了文物执法机构，其中各级地方政府文物执法机构中肩负长城文物执法职责的共计504个。从机构类型上看，长城沿线的区市、县（区）长城文物执法监督机构包括文化综合执法机构、文物督察执法机构、文管所/博物馆、文广新局/文物局、景区管理机构和长城专门监督执法机等6种类型，其中长城文物执法工作主要由各地文广新局/文物局、文化综合执法机构、文管所/博物馆、文物督察执法机构承担。（表2-6）

**表2-6：长城沿线15省长城执法机构分类数量统计表**

Table 2-6: Great Wall law enforcement agency category number statistical table of 15 provinces along Great Wall

| 省份 Province | 文化综合执法机构 Cultural integration law enforcement agency | 文物督察执法机构 Cultural relic supervision law enforcement agency | 文管所/博物馆 Cultural relic management institute/ museum | 文广新局/文物局 Department of Culture, Radio, Film, TV, Press and Publication/ cultural relic bureau | 景区管理机构 Management organ of scenic spot | 长城专门监督执法机构 Great Wall special supervision law enforcement organ | 合计 Total |
|---|---|---|---|---|---|---|---|
| 北京 Beijing | 1 | 6 | - | - | - | - | 7 |
| 天津 Tianjin | 1 | 1 | - | - | - | - | 2 |
| 河北 Hebei | 33 | 3 | 15 | 16 | 1 | - | 68 |
| 山西 Shanxi | 8 | 7 | 4 | 29 | - | - | 48 |
| 内蒙古 Inner Mongolia | 28 | 2 | 34 | 25 | - | - | 89 |
| 辽宁 Liaoning | 22 | 8 | 15 | 18 | - | 1 | 64 |
| 吉林 Jilin | 3 | - | 8 | 4 | - | - | 15 |

it totals 6 types, such as Great Wall cultural relic law enforcement supervision agencies at prefecture, county (district) level, inclusive of cultural integration law enforcement agency, cultural relic supervision law enforcement agency, cultural relic management institute /museum, department of Culture, radio, film, TV, press and publication / cultural relic bureau, management organ of scenic spot and Great Wall special supervision law enforcement organ and etc., wherein, Great Wall cultural relic law enforcement work is mainly undertaken by department of culture, radio, film, TV, Press and Publication, cultural relic bureau, cultural integration law enforcement agency, cultural relic supervising law enforcement agency, cultural relic management institute/ museum, cultural relic supervising law enforcement agency of involved regions. (Table 2-6)

| | | | | | | | |
|---|---|---|---|---|---|---|---|
| 黑龙江 Heilongjiang | 3 | - | 4 | 1 | - | - | 8 |
| 山东 Shandong | 7 | 1 | - | 17 | - | - | 25 |
| 河南 Henan | 8 | 4 | 2 | 5 | - | - | 19 |
| 陕西 Shaanxi | 7 | 8 | 2 | 4 | 1 | - | 22 |
| 甘肃 Gansu | 2 | - | 4 | 41 | - | - | 47 |
| 青海 Qinghai | 1 | - | 7 | 9 | - | - | 17 |
| 宁夏 Ningxia | 24 | - | - | - | - | - | 24 |
| 新疆 Xinjiang | 1 | - | 9 | 39 | - | - | 49 |
| 合计 Total | 149 | 40 | 104 | 208 | 2 | 1 | 504 |

（三）执法巡查工作情况

近年来，长城沿线各地持续开展执法巡查工作。根据各地填报信息，2005-2014年间，各地开展长城执法巡查共计233次。从统计结果来看，95次巡查中发现了问题，包括自然损毁、人为破坏、自然与人为双重破坏三类，其中自然损毁事件31起，人为破坏事件37起，自然与人为双重破坏事件20起。各地在执法巡查过程中对发现的问题进行了处理，其中立案查处5次，限期整改11次，申报维修项目22次，及时修补损毁之处7次，设立保护标志和围栏7次，采取抢险措施4次。

（四）文物安全案件督察情况

近年来，出现一些工程建设、生产生活活动破坏长城的违法案件。其中，2005-2014年间，各地发生人为因素导致的长城安全督查案件40起，涉及开矿、耕种、取土、建设工程、盗掘等多种人为破坏长城行为，因基础设施建设、长城沿线居民生产生活造成的文物安全案件数量最多，共25起，占总数的62.5%；其次是文物犯罪案件9起，占总数的22.5%；文物安全责任事故6起，占总数的15%。通过对案件处理结果的梳理，可以发现，文物犯罪案件都以刑事案件立案，并进行处理；文物安全责任事故都按照治安案件，进行了治安处罚；其他文物安全案件都进行了行政处罚。

2005-2014年间，8个省（自治区、直辖市）填报自然因素突发事件导致长城破坏的安全督查案件30起，基本都是由于强烈的气候现象造成的突发性事件，文物行政部门进行督促后做出处理。造成长城自然损毁的原因中，强降雨造成的水冲数量最多，有17处，占总数的56.7%；其次是雷击有9处，占总数的30%；风蚀有2次，强风造成的损毁有1次，自然坍塌1次。对于自然因素造成的损毁情况，文物行政部门采取了相应的抢险加固、设置防护设施等措施。

### (III) Working situation of law enforcement inspection

In recent years, regions along Great Wall continuously conduct law enforcement inspection work. According to the filling information of regions, from 2005 to 2014, it totaled 233 activities of Great Wall law enforcement and patrol conducted by all regions. From the statistical results, problems were found in 95 patrols, such as natural damage, man-made sabotage, five types of dual damages from natural defacement and man-made sabotage, including 31 natural damage events, 37 man-made sabotage events, 20 dual events caused by natural damage and man-made sabotage. The problems found during the patrol were settled by regions, including 5 cases on file and settlement, rectifications made within time limit for 11 times, reported maintenance items for 22 times, timely repair the damaged section for 7 times, setting up conservation sign and fence for 7 times, taking rescue measures for 4 times.

### (IV) Cultural relic safety supervision situation

In recent years, illegal cases of damaging Great Wall caused by engineering construction, production and living occur. Wherein, from 2005 to 2014, 40 Great Wall safety supervision cases caused by man-made factor, including various kinds of man-made damaging Great Wall actions, such as mining, cultivating, soil unloading, engineering construction, resurrect and etc., among which cultural relic safety cases caused by infrastructure construction, production and living activities of residents along Great Wall were most, totaling 25, taking up 62.5% of the total cases; following it, cultural relic criminal cases, totaling 9, taking up 22.5% of the total cases; 6 cases of cultural relic safety liability accidents, occupying 15% of the total cases; by clear up the cases' handling results, it easily to see, cultural relic criminal cases were put on record as criminal lawsuit to handle; cultural relic safety liability accidents were given security punishment as per public security cases; other cultural relic safety cases were given administrative punishment.

From 2005 to 2014, 30 Great Wall safety supervision cases were caused by natural factor filled and reported by 8 provinces (autonomous regions, municipalities direct under the Central Government), were emergency incidents basically caused by strong weather phenomena, cultural relic administrative departments made settlements after supervision. Among the reasons causing Great Wall natural damage, the most number of reasons was strong rainfall, totaling 17, occupying 56.7% of the total cases; followed by lightning strike, totaling 9, occupying 30 of the total cases; 2 cases of wind erosion, damage caused by fresh gale for 1 time, natural collapse for 1 time. As for damage situation caused by natural factor, cultural relic administrative department

针对上述情况，国家文物局和各省级文物主管部门（执法机构）加大了长城案件督办和查处力度。2014 年以来，国家文物局共督办、转办长城案件 23 件，其中有 2 件未按时回复，其余均得到及时办理；省级文物主管部门（执法机构）发现和上报长城违法案件 20 件，督办长城违法犯罪案件 38 件，办结 23 件，其中主动督办案件 20 件。有 13 个省（自治区、直辖市）文物行政部门与公安机关建立起了执法联动机制，移交涉嫌犯罪案件或联合执法案件数量 184 件。（表 2-7）

**表 2-7： 长城案件查处情况统计简表**

Table 2-7: Statistical abridged table of Great Wall case investigating and prosecuting situation

| 省份<br>Province | 国家文物局督办、转办的长城案件数量<br>Number of Great Wall cases supervised and transmitted to handle by State Administration of Cultural Heritage | 各省（自治区、直辖市）发现和上报长城违法犯罪案件数量<br>Number of Great Wall illegal cases found and reported by involved provinces (autonomous regions, municipalities directly under the Central Government) | 督办长城违法犯罪案件数量<br>Number of Great Wall illegal cases by supervised and handled | 已结案数量<br>Number of settled cases | 主动督办案件数量<br>Number of cases supervised and handled actively | 移交涉嫌犯罪案件或联合执法案件数量<br>Number of handed over suspected criminal cases and joint law enforcement cases |
|---|---|---|---|---|---|---|
| 北京<br>Beijing | 2 | 0 | 2 | 2 | 0 | 0 |
| 山西<br>Shanxi | 3 | 1 | 4 | 3 | 1 | 1 |
| 内蒙古<br>Inner Mongolia | 4 | 7 | 6 | 0 | 4 | 0 |
| 吉林<br>Jilin | 0 | 0 | 0 | 0 | 0 | 0 |
| 山东<br>Shandong | 0 | 0 | 0 | 0 | 0 | 0 |
| 陕西<br>Shaanxi | 2 | 1 | 5 | 5 | 3 | 0 |

adopts corresponding enforcement with an emergency, setting up conservation facilities and so on.

Based on such situation, State Administration of Cultural Heritage and cultural relic competent departments at province level (law enforcement agency) enhance Great Wall cases supervision and investigation force. Since 2014, State Administration of Cultural Heritage has settled 23 Great Wall cases by supervision, transferring to handle, among which 2 cases haven't been relied timely, the rest been replied timely; 20 Great Wall illegal cases founded and reported by cultural relic competent departments at province level (law enforcement agency), 38 Great Wall illegal criminal cases by supervision to handle, settled 23 cases, including 20 cases under active supervision for settlement. cultural relic administrative departments and public security organs from 13 provinces (autonomous regions, municipalities directly under the Central Government) established linkage mechanism of law enforcement, handed over 184 suspected criminal cases or joint law enforcement cases

| | | | | | | |
|---|---|---|---|---|---|---|
| 青海<br>Qinghai | 0 | 0 | 0 | 0 | 0 | 0 |
| 新疆<br>Xinjiang | 0 | 0 | 0 | 0 | 0 | 0 |
| 辽宁<br>Liaoning | 0 | 0 | 1 | 0 | 1 | 1 |
| 黑龙江<br>Heilongjiang | 1 | 1 | 0 | 0 | 0 | 0 |
| 河南<br>Henan | 1 | 2 | 2 | 1 | 1 | 1 |
| 甘肃<br>Gansu | 2 | 3 | 4 | 2 | 4 | 4 |
| 河北<br>Hebei | 6 | 4 | 9 | 7 | 3 | 2 |
| 宁夏<br>Ningxia | 2 | 1 | 3 | 1 | 1 | 0 |
| 天津<br>Tianjin | 0 | 0 | 2 | 2 | 2 | 0 |
| 合计<br>Subtotal | 23 | 20 | 38 | 23 | 20 | 9 |

### 专栏：长城文物执法典型案例
### ——秦汉长城呼和浩特市坡根底段破坏事件处理经过[24]

2009年9月15日，呼和浩特市科考矿业公司探矿工程队在新城区坡根底段秦汉长城上钻探金矿，对长约100米的长城墙体造成了严重破坏。

呼和浩特市文物事业管理处在接到举报后，于9月17日向公司下达了《责令限期改正通知书》，公司口头表示立即停工。但是，当10月9日和10月12日，自治区文物局、呼和浩特市文物事业管理处再次上山核查时，发现该公司并未停工，继续在长城上架井钻探，进一步扩大了破坏范围。该矿区先后五次被勒令停工，但《责令限期改正通知书》等文件对矿方来说只是一纸空文。

2009年10月27日，呼市公安局治安支队接到自治区公安厅移交的呼和浩特市科考矿业有限责任公司破坏秦汉长城的违法犯罪案件。

受理该案后，呼市警方立即成立了专案组。办案人员在了解基本案情、掌握相关证据后，对呼和浩特市科考矿业有限公司探矿项目负责人张某某、田某某依法实施了刑事拘留，并于2009年12月7日向呼市人民检察院提请逮捕。

## 二、加强“四有”基础工作

长城“四有”工作，即保护范围与建设控制地带划定、文物保护单位标志设立、文物保护单位记录档案和保护管理机构建设，是国家依法实施长城保护管理的基础，是长城文物执法的基础依据。国家文物局1991年发布了《全国重点文物保护单位保护范围、标志说明、记录档案和保管机构工作规范（试行）》（以下简称《国保四有规范》）；2003年发布了《全国重点文物保护单位记录档案工作规范（试行）》（文物保发〔2003〕93号）；2014年针对长城特点专门发布了《长城“四有”工作指导意见》（文物保发〔2014〕4号，以下简称《长城“四有”意见》）。上述规范性文件对长城各级文物保护单位的“四有”工作程序和实施方法都做了明确的规定和要求。2016年国家文物局“长城执法专项督察”对各地长城“四有”工作情况进行了一次全面检查。

[24] 根据中国广播网新闻报道整理（http://news.cnr.cn/gnxw/200912/t20091209_505735488.html）

### Special column: typical case of Great Wall cultural relic law enforcement—handling process of destructive incident on bottom segment of slop section of Great Wall of Qin and Han dynasties in Hohhot City [24]

On September 2009, prospection project team from Hohhot Scientific Investigation Mining Company drilled gold mine at bottom segment of slop section of Great Wall of Qin and Han dynasties, caused heavy damage to wall body of Great Wall, with the length of about 100 meters.

After receiving report, Hohhot Cultural Relic Management Bureau issued *Notice of Order to Make Correction within Time Limit* to the company on September 17, the company orally expressed it would knock off immediately. However, on October 9 and October 12, Administration of Cultural Heritage of Autonomous Region, Hohhot Cultural Relic Management Bureau found the company hadn't shut off, when they went to the mountain and inspected again. The company still drilled on Great Wall with well assembling and the damage range expanded further. Five orders had been issued on such mining to prohibit shut off in succession, but *Order to Make Correction within Time Limit* and other documents were just worthless pieces of papers to drilling party.

On October 27, 2009, detachment of Hohhot Public Security Bureau received the illegal criminal case of Hohhot Scientific Investigation Mining Company destroying Great Wall of Qin and Han dynasties submitted by Public Security Department of Autonomous Region.

After the acceptance of the case, Hohhot police immediately set up special investigating team. After personnel handling a case knew the basic case, mastered relevant proof, legally execute criminal detention to principals Zhang, Tian of Hohhot Scientific Investigation Mining Company. On December 7, 2009, it submitted arrest to people's procuratorate of Hohhot.

## II. Strengthen the "Four haves"

"Four haves" of Great Wall, is demarcation of conservation scope and construction control area, establishment of cultural relic conservation site' sign, establishment of cultural relic conservation site log archive and conservation and management organs, it is the foundation for our country to implement Great Wall conservation and management by law, is the important basis for Great Wall cultural relic law enforcement. In 1991, State Administration of Cultural Heritage issued *Job Specification on Norm, Sign Instruction, Log Archive, Conservation and Management Organization of Important Heritage Site under State Conservation(Trial)* (hereinafter referred to as *National Conservation Four Haves Norm*); in 2003, issued *Job Specification on Log Archive of Important Heritage Site under State Conservation (Trial)* (W. W B F (2003) No. 93); in 2014, *Work Constructive Opinion for Great Wall "Four Haves"* (W. W. B. F (2014) No. 4, hereinafter referred to as *Great Wall "Four Haves" Opinion*) was specially issued aiming at Great Wall characteristic. The

[24] Systemize it according to news report of Chinese Radio Network (http://news.cnr.cn/gnxw/200912/t20091209_505735488.html)

### （一）文物保护单位公布情况

文物保护单位公布与管理，是我国文物保护工作的一项基本制度，是长城“四有”工作开展的基础。1961 年我国首次公布全国重点文物保护单位，“万里长城——八达岭”“万里长城——嘉峪关”“万里长城——山海关”就名列其中。此后，国务院陆续将“金山岭长城”“玉门关及长城烽燧遗址”“魏长城遗址”、“固阳秦长城遗址”“万里长城——紫荆关”“万里长城——九门口”等长城重要点段长城陆续公布为全国重点文物保护单位。长城沿线各级人民政府也相继公布一大批省级及省级以下文物保护单位。2001 年之前，长城文物保护单位公布与管理主要以具体的点段为单元进行。

2001 年，长城保护管理工作进入新阶段。国务院在公布第五批全国重点文物保护单位过程中，首次将“长城”作为统一的文物保护单位名称进行了公布，为长城确定了整体保护的总体方向。此后，在第六批、第七批全国文物保护单位公布过程中，纳入国家最高层级进行保护管理的“长城”的点段不断扩展。截止 2016 年，已经有 9 个省的长城被整体纳入为全国重点文物保护单位“长城”。此外，依据《长城保护条例》的要求，长城各地也公布了一大批长城省级文物保护单位。

据统计，全国已公布各级长城文物保护单位 209 处，其中全国重点文物保护单位 29 处，省级文物保护单位 89 处，市县级文物保护单位 91 处，已经涵盖全国长城段落 37924 处，长度 17732.1 千米，烽火台 9970 座，关堡 1879 座，其他各类单体建筑 15586 座，相关遗存 166 处，占所有长城认定段落的 86.7% 以上。河北、内蒙古、黑龙江、山东、河南、甘肃、青海、宁夏等省（自治区）长城段落核定公布为省级以上文物保护单位比例达到 100%。北京市、辽宁省、吉林省、黑龙江省、山东省、河南省、青海省、宁夏回族自治区、新疆维吾尔自治区等 9 个省区已经将省级文物保护单位公布情况在省级人民政府或省级文物行政部门网站进行公示。其中，按照《长城保护条例》要求，在自认定之

above mentioned normative documents have clear regulations and requirements on "Four haves" working procedure and implementation methods of Great Wall cultural relic conservation sites at all levels. In 2016, State Administration of Cultural Heritage "Great Wall law enforcement special supervision" carried out an overall collection on working situations on Great Wall "Four haves" of involved regions.

### (I) The situation of publishing cultural relic conservation sites

Publishing and management of cultural relic conservation sites is the basic system for our country's cultural relic conservation work, the basis for conducting Great Wall "Four haves". In 1961, our country firstly published important heritage site under state conservation, such as "the Great Wall--Badaling", "the Great Wall—Jiayu Pass", "the Great Wall—Shanhai Pass" listed on it. Besides, the State Council identified Grecat Wall important sections, such as "Jinshanling Great Wall", "Yumen Pass and Great Wall beacon tower site", "Wei Great Wall site", "Guyang Qing Great Wall site", "the Great Wall--Zijingguan", "the Great Wall-- Jiumenkou" and etc. as important heritage sites under state conservation one after the other. People's governments at all levels along Great Wall published a large batch of cultural relic sites at province level and below province level one after the other. Before 2001, publishing and management of Great Wall cultural relic conservation sites were conducted as per specific section as unit.

In 2001, Great Wall conservation and management usher a new stage. The State Council, during the process of publishing the 5$^{th}$ batch of important heritage site under state conservation, firstly issued "Great Wall" as the uniform cultural relic conservation site name, confirming the general conservation direction for Great Wall. Hereafter, during the process of publishing the 6$^{th}$ batch, the 7$^{th}$ batch of national cultural relic conservation site, sections of "Great Wall" include into the national highest level for conservation and management are gradually expanded. Up to 2016, Great Wall located in 9 provinces has been totally included into "Great Wall" of important heritage site under state conservation. Besides, as per requirements of *Regulations on Great Wall Conservation*, regions along Great Wall have published a large batch of Great Wall provincial cultural relic conservation sites.

Statistically, 209 nationwide Great Wall cultural relic conservation sites issued to public, among which 29 key cultural relic conservation sites, 89 cultural relic conservation sites at province level, 91 cultural relic conservation sites at city and county level, covering 37924 sites of Great Wall sections with the length of 17732.1 kilometers, 9970 beacon towers, 1879 forts, other

日起 1 年内（即 2013 年 7 月前）公布为省级以上文物保护单位的长城段落有 25126 处，占所有长城认定段落的 57.3%。[25]（表 2-8、2-9、2-10）

2016 年国家文物局长城执法专项督察结束后，部分地区对长城“四有”工作进展不理想的问题进行了整改。2017 年 3 月 2 日，陕西省人民政府第四次常务会议决定，将陕西省内 42 处长城公布为省级文物保护单位，强调“保护为主、抢救第一、合理利用、加强管理”的方针，加大境内长城保护力度，妥善处理好文物保护与经济社会发展的关系。

### （二）保护范围与建设控制地带划定情况

国家文物局 2014 年印发了《长城“四有”工作指导意见》对长城保护范围和建设控制地带划定原则、空间方位等提出了指导性要求。

关于保护范围。《长城“四有”工作指导意见》要求以长城资源调查和认定工作为基础，开展充分的科学研究、评估和测绘，依据各类长城资源的价值和分布情况，以及保护管理工作的实际需要，科学划定长城保护范围。长城保护范围应划定在长城本体之外并保持一定的安全距离，保证长城相关遗址、遗迹得到完整保护。原则上，长城墙体（含界壕 / 壕堑）保护范围应以长城墙体及依附于墙体的敌台、马面、关堡和相关遗存应以墙基外缘为基线向两侧各扩不少于 50 米作为边界；独立于长城墙体之外的敌台、关堡、烽火台和相关遗存等保护范围应以单体建筑基础外缘为基线，四周各外扩不少于 50 米作为边界。对于构成复杂和环境复杂的长城段落，其保护范围可以划分为一般保护区和重点保护区。保护范围须在地图上明确标识边界范围，印制相应的图纸，并按第四章要求提供图形数据。

[25] 河北省 2013 年之前省级以上文物保护单位公布情况数据不清，未列入统计。

various kinds of individual buildings, 15586 sites, related 166 remaining, occupying more than 86.7% of identified Great Wall sections. The proportion of Great Wall sections identified to public as cultural relic sites above province level from Hebei, Inner Mongolia, Heilongjiang, Shandong, Henan, Gansu, Qinghai, Ningxia and other provinces (autonomous regions), reaches 100 %. 8 provinces such as Beijing, Liaoning Province, Jilin Province, Heilongjiang Province, Shandong Province, Henan Province, Qinghai Province, Ningxia Hui Autonomous Region, Xinjiang Uygur Autonomous Region and etc. has published situation of cultural relic conservation sites at province level on provincial government or provincial cultural relic administrative website. Wherein, as per requirements of Regulations on Great Wall Conservation, within 1 year after the identification date, 25126 Great Wall sections identified as cultural relic conservation sites at province level before July 2013, taking up 57.3% of all Great Wall identified sections [25]. (Table 2-8, 2-9, 2-10)

In 2016, after the accomplishment of Great Wall law enforcement special supervision by State Administration of Cultural Heritage, some regions conducted rectifications to undesirable issues of Great Wall "Four basic works" working progress. On March 2, 2017, the 4th executive meeting of The People's Government of Shaanxi Province decided to issue 42 Great Wall section within Shaanxi territory to public as cultural relic conservation sites at province level, strengthened the policy of "conservation oriented, rescue in the first place, rational utilization, strengthening management", enhanced Great Wall conservation force within its scope, duly handle the relationship between cultural relic conservation and economic and social development.

### (II) Conservation scope and construction control area's demarcation situation

State Administration of Cultural Heritage issued *Work Constructive Opinion for Great Wall "Four Haves"* and made constructive requirements to Great Wall conservation scope and construction control area's demarcation principle, spatial orientation and so on.

As for conservation scope, *Work Constructive Opinion for Great Wall "Four Haves"* demands taking Great Wall resources surveying and identification work as basis, fully conducting scientific research, evaluation and surveying

[25] The publishing situation of cultural heritage conservation sites at the province level in Hebei Province before the year of 2013 is unknown, not included into the statistics.

## 表 2-8：长城全国重点文物保护单位清单（截至 2013 年 3 月）

Table 2-8: List of important heritage sites under state Conservation of Great Wall

| 序号<br>Serial No. | 名称<br>Name | 时代<br>Times | 位置<br>Location | 批次<br>Batch No. | 公布时间<br>Publishing time |
|---|---|---|---|---|---|
| 1 | 万里长城 - 八达岭<br>Great Wall of China -Badaling | 明<br>Ming | 北京市延庆县<br>Yanqing County, Beijing | 第一批<br>The 1st batch | 1961.3 |
| 2 | 万里长城 - 山海关<br>Great Wall of China – Shanhai Pass | 明<br>Ming | 河北省秦皇岛市<br>Qinhuangdao City, Hebei Province | 第一批<br>The 1st batch | 1961.3 |
| 3 | 万里长城 - 嘉峪关<br>Great Wall of China –Jiayu Pass | 明<br>Ming | 甘肃省嘉峪关市<br>Jiayu Pass City, Gansu Province | 第一批<br>The 1st batch | 1961.3 |
| 4 | 金山岭长城<br>Jinshanling Great Wall | 明<br>Ming | 河北省滦平县<br>Luanping County, Hebei Province | 第三批<br>The 3rd batch | 1988.1 |
| 5 | 居延遗址（含黑城遗址）<br>Juyan Sites (including Heicheng Sites) | 汉<br>Han | 内蒙古自治区额济纳旗、甘肃省金塔县<br>Ejin Banner, Inner Mongolia Autonomous Region, Jinta County, Gansu Province | 第三批<br>The 3rd batch | 1988.1 |
| 6 | 兴城古城<br>Xingcheng | 明<br>Ming | 辽宁省兴城<br>Xingcheng, Liaoning Province | 第三批<br>The 3rd batch | 1988.1 |
| 7 | 玉门关及长城烽燧遗址（包括大方盘小方盘）<br>Yuman Pass and Great Wall beacon towers sites (including Yumen Pass and Hecangcheng) | 汉<br>Han | 甘肃省敦煌市<br>Dunhuang City, Gansu Province | 第三批<br>The 3rd batch | 1988.1 |
| 8 | 万里长城 - 紫荆关<br>Great Wall of China -zijingguan | 明<br>Ming | 河北省易县<br>Yixian County, Hebei Province | 第四批<br>The 4th batch | 1996.11 |
| 9 | 固阳秦长城遗址<br>Guying Qin Great Wall site | 秦<br>Qin | 内蒙古自治区固阳县<br>Guying County, Inner Mongolia Autonomous Region | 第四批<br>The 4th batch | 1996.11 |
| 10 | 万里长城 - 九门口<br>Great Wall of China-Jiumenkou | 明<br>Ming | 辽宁省绥中县、河北省抚宁县<br>Suizhong County, Liaoning Province; Funing County, Hebei Province | 第四批<br>The 4th batch | 1996.11 |
| 11 | 魏长城遗址<br>Wei Great Wall site | 战国<br>Warring States | 陕西省渭南市<br>Weinan City, Shaanxi Province | 第四批<br>The 4th batch | 1996.11 |
| 12 | 金界壕遗址<br>Jin Jiehao site | 金<br>Jin | 内蒙古自治区呼伦贝尔市、兴安盟、通辽市、赤峰市、乌兰察布盟、包头市，黑龙江省甘南县、龙江县、齐齐哈尔市<br>Hulunbeier City, Hinggan League, Tongliao City, Chifeng City, Wulancabu League, Baotou City, Inner Mongolia Autonomous Region; Gannan County, Longjiang County, Tsitsihar City, Heilongjiang Province | 第五批<br>The 5th batch | 2001.6 |
| 13 | 克孜尔尕哈烽燧<br>Keziergaha beacon tower | 汉<br>Han | 新疆维吾尔自治区于田县<br>Yutian County, Xinjiang Uygur Autonomous Region | 第五批<br>The 5th batch | 2001.6 |
| 14 | 孔雀河烽燧群<br>Kongquehe beacon towers group | 汉、晋<br>Han, Jin | 新疆维吾尔自治区尉犁县<br>Yuli County, Xinjiang Uygur Autonomous Region | 第五批<br>The 5th batch | 2001.6 |
| 15 | 米兰遗址<br>Milan site | 汉—唐<br>Han —Tang | 新疆维吾尔自治区若羌县<br>Ruoqian County, Xinjiang Uygur Autonomous Region | 第五批<br>The 5th batch | 2001.6 |

| | | | | | |
|---|---|---|---|---|---|
| 16 | 长城<br>Great Wall | 春秋至明<br>Spring and Autumn Period to Ming | 北京市、河北省、山西省、内蒙古自治区、陕西省、山东省、宁夏回族自治区、辽宁省<br>Beijing, Hebei Province, Shanxi Province, Inner Mongolia Autonomous Region, Shaanxi Province, Shandong Province, Ningxia Hui Autonomous Region, Liaoning Province | 第五批<br>The 5th batch | 2001.6 |
| | （1）长城－司马台段<br>(1) Great Wall – Simatai section | 明<br>Ming | 北京市密云县<br>Miyun County, Beijing | 第五批<br>The 5th batch | 2001.6 |
| | （2）乌龙沟长城<br>(2) Wulonggou Great Wall | 明<br>Ming | 河北省涞源县<br>Laiyuan County, Hebei Province | 第五批<br>The 5th batch | 2001.6 |
| | （3）长城—雁门关<br>(3) Great Wall—Yanmen Pass | 明<br>Ming | 山西省代县<br>Dai County, Shanxi Province | 第五批<br>The 5th batch | 2001.6 |
| | （4）齐长城遗址<br>(4) Qi Great Wall site | 战国<br>Warring States | 山东省长清县、济南市、章丘市、肥城市、泰安市、莱芜市、淄博市、沂源县、临朐县、安丘市、诸城市、沂水县、莒县、五莲县、胶南市、青岛市<br>Changing County, Jinan City, Zhangqiu City, Feicheng City, Tai'an City, Laiwu City, Zibo City, Yiyuan County, Linqu County, Anqiu City, Zhucheng City, Yishui County, Juxian County, Wulian County, Jiaonan City, Qingdao City | 第五批<br>The 5th batch | 2001.6 |
| | （5）秦国长城遗址<br>(5) Qin Great Wall site | 战国<br>Warring States | 内蒙古自治区伊金霍洛旗<br>Ejin Horo Banner, Inner Mongolia Autonomous Region | 第五批<br>The 5th batch | 2001.6 |
| | （6）长城—清水河段<br>(6) Great Wall—Qingshuihe section | 明<br>Ming | 内蒙古自治区清水河县<br>Qingshuihe County, Inner Mongolia Autonomous Region | 第五批<br>The 5th batch | 2001.6 |
| | （7）燕长城遗址<br>(7) Yan Great Wall site | 战国<br>Warring States | 辽宁省建平县<br>Jianping County, Liaoning Province | 第五批<br>The 5th batch | 2001.6 |
| | （8）镇北台<br>(8) Zhenbeitai | 明<br>Ming | 陕西省榆林市<br>Yulin City, Shaanxi Province | 第五批<br>The 5th batch | 2001.6 |
| | （9）宁夏回族自治区秦长城遗址<br>(9) Qin Great Wall site of Ningxia Hui Autonomous Region | 战国<br>Warring States | 宁夏回族自治区彭阳县、西吉县、固原县<br>Pengyang County, Xiji County, Guyuan County, Ningxia Hui Autonomous Region | 第五批<br>The 5th batch | 2001.6 |
| 17 | 万全右卫城<br>Wanquanyouhucheng | 明<br>Ming | 河北省万全县<br>Wanquan County, Hebei Province | 第六批<br>The 6th batch | 2006.5 |
| 18 | 中前所城<br>Zhongqiansuocheng | 明至清<br>Ming to Qing | 辽宁省绥中县<br>Suizhong County, Liaoning Province | 第六批<br>The 6th batch | 2001.6 |
| 19 | 榆林卫城<br>Weicheng, Yulin | 明至清<br>Ming to Qing | 陕西省榆林市<br>Yulin City, Shaanxi Province | 第六批<br>The 6th batch | 2006.5 |
| 20 | 麻扎塔格戍堡址<br>Mazhartage Maobao site | 唐<br>Tang | 新疆维吾尔自治区墨玉县<br>Moyu County, Xinjiang Uygur Autonomous Region | 第六批<br>The 6th batch | 2006.5 |
| 21 | 牡丹江边墙<br>Mudanjiang side wall | 唐至金<br>Tang to Jin | 黑龙江省牡丹江市、宁安市<br>Mudanjiang City, Ning'an City, Heilongjiang Province | 第六批<br>The 6th batch | 2006.5 |
| 22 | 金界壕遗址<br>Jin Jiehao site | 金<br>Jin | 河北省丰宁满族自治县<br>Fengning Manchu Autonomous County, Hebei Province | 第六批，归入第五批金界壕遗址<br>The 6th batch included into the 5th batch of Jin Jiehao site | 2006.5 |

| | | | | | |
|---|---|---|---|---|---|
| 23 | 长城<br>Great Wall | 战国至明<br>Warring States to Ming | 北京市、内蒙古自治区、辽宁省、河南省、甘肃省<br>Beijing, Inner Mongolia Autonomous Region, Liaoning Province, Henan Province, Gansu Province | 第六批，归入第五批长城<br>The 6th batch included into the 5th batch of Great Wall | 2006.5 |
| | （1）明长城遗址<br>(1) Ming Great Wall site | 明<br>Ming | 北京市密云县、怀柔县、平谷县、昌平区、门头沟区<br>Miyun County, Huairou County, Pinggu County, Changping District, Mentougou District of Beijing | 第六批<br>The 6th batch | 2006.5 |
| | （2）汉长城遗址<br>(2) Han Great Wall site | 汉<br>Han | 内蒙古自治区磴口县、乌拉特后旗、乌拉特中旗、乌拉特前旗<br>Dengkou County, Urat Rear Banner, Urat Middle Banner, Urat Front Banner of Inner Mongolia Autonomous Region | 第六批<br>The 6th batch | 2006.5 |
| | （3）汉长城遗址<br>(3) Han Great Wall site | 汉<br>Han | 辽宁省建平县<br>Jianping County, Liaoning Province | 第六批<br>The 6th batch | 2006.5 |
| | （4）明长城遗址<br>(4) Ming Great Wall site | 明<br>Ming | 辽宁省绥中县<br>Suizhong County, Liaoning Province | 第六批<br>The 6th batch | 2006.5 |
| | （5）魏长城遗址<br>(5) Wei Great Wall site | 战国<br>Warring States | 河南省新密市、荥阳市<br>Xinmi City, Xingyang City of Henan Province | 第六批<br>The 6th batch | 2006.5 |
| | （6）秦长城遗址<br>(6) Qin Great Wall site | 战国<br>Warring States | 甘肃省临洮县、渭源县、陇西县、通渭县、静宁县、镇原县、环县、华池县<br>Lintao County, Weiyuan County, Longxi County, Tongwei County, Jingning County, Zhenyuan County, Huan County, Huachi County of Gansu Province | 第六批<br>The 6th batch | 2006.5 |
| | （7）汉长城遗址<br>(7) Han Great Wall site | 汉代<br>Han Dynasty | 甘肃省敦煌市、安西县、玉门市、金塔县、酒泉市、高台县、临泽县、张掖市、山丹县、永昌县、武威市、民勤县、古浪县、天祝藏族自治县、永登县、景泰县<br>Dunhuang City, Anxi County, Yumen City, Jinta County, Jiuquan City, Gaotai County, Linze County, Zhangye City, Shandan County, Yongchang Couty, Wuwei City, Minqin County, Gulang County, Tianzhu Tibetan Autonomous County, Yongdeng County, Jingtai County | 第六批<br>The 6th batch | 2006.5 |
| | （8）明长城遗址<br>(8) Ming Great Wall site | 明代<br>Ming Dynasty | 甘肃省嘉峪关市、酒泉市、高台县、临泽县、张掖市、山丹县、永昌县、武威市、民勤县、古浪县、景泰县、靖远县、天祝藏族自治县、兰州市<br>Jiayu Pass City, Jiuquan City, Gaotai County, Linze County, Zhangye City, Shandan County, Yongchang County, Wuwei City, Minqin County, Gulang County, Jingtai County, Jingyuan County, Tianzhu Tibetan Autonomous County, Lanzhou City of Gansu Province | 第六批<br>The 6th batch | 2006.5 |
| 24 | 赤柏松古城址<br>Chibaisong city site | 西汉<br>Western Han Dynasty | 吉林省通化县<br>Tonghua County, Jilin Province | 第七批<br>The 7th batch | 2013.3 |
| 25 | 大营城址<br>Daying city site | 宋至明<br>Song to Ming | 宁夏回族自治区固原市原州区<br>Yuanzhou District, Guyuan City, Ningxia Hui Autonomous Region | 第七批<br>The 7th batch | 2013.3 |
| 26 | 兴武营城址<br>Xingwuying city site | 明<br>Ming | 宁夏回族自治区盐池县<br>Yanchi County of Ningxia Hui Autonomous Region | 第七批<br>The 7th batch | 2013.3 |
| 27 | 昌吉州境内烽燧群<br>Beacon group within Changji Prefecture territory | 唐至清<br>Tang to Qing | 新疆维吾尔自治区昌吉回族自治州<br>Changji Hui Prefecture of Xinjiang Uygur Autonomous Region | 第七批<br>The 7th batch | 2013.3 |
| 28 | 古代吐鲁番盆地军事防御遗址<br>Turpan Depression military defense site at ancient times | 唐至清<br>Tang to Qing | 新疆维吾尔自治区吐鲁番地区<br>Turpan area of Xinjiang Uygur Autonomous Region | 第七批<br>The 7th batch | 2013.3 |

| | | | | | |
|---|---|---|---|---|---|
| 29 | 哈密境内烽燧遗址<br>Beacon tower site within Kumul territory | 唐至清<br>Tang to Qing | 新疆维吾尔自治区哈密地区<br>Kumul Prefecture of Xinjiang Uygur Autonomous Region | 第七批<br>The 7th batch | 2013.3 |
| 30 | 张家口堡<br>Zhangjiakou castle | 汉、魏晋南北朝、唐、明、清<br>Han, Wei, Jin, Northern and Southern Dynasties, Tang, Ming | 河北省张家口<br>Zhangjiakou, Hebei Province | 第七批<br>The 7th batch | 2013.3 |
| 31 | 洗马林城墙<br>Ximalin city wall | 明至清<br>Ming to Qing | 河北省万全县<br>Wanquan County, Hebei Province | 第七批<br>The 7th batch | 2013.3 |
| 32 | 长城<br>Great Wall | 汉、魏晋南北朝、唐、明<br>Han, Wei, Jin, Northern and Southern Dynasties, Tang, Ming | 北京市、河北省、辽宁省、吉林、青海、宁夏回族自治区<br>Beijing, Hebei Province, Liaoning Province, Jilin, Qinghai, Ningxia Hui Autonomous Region | 第七批，归入第五批长城<br>The 7th batch, included into the 5th batch of Great Wall | 2013.3 |
| | （1）岔道城城墙<br>(1) Chadaocheng city wall | 明代<br>Ming Dynasty | 北京市延庆区<br>Yanqing District, Beijing | 第七批<br>The 7th batch | 2013.3 |
| | （2）喜峰口长城<br>(2) Xifengkou Great Wall | 明代<br>Ming Dynasty | 河北省宽城县<br>Kuancheng County, Hebei Province | 第七批<br>The 7th batch | 2013.3 |
| | （3）大境门长城<br>(3) Dajingmen Great Wall | 明代<br>Ming Dynasty | 河北省张家口市<br>Zhangjiakou City, Hebei Province | 第七批<br>The 7th batch | 2013.3 |
| | （4）浮图峪长城<br>(4) Futuyu Great Wall | 明代<br>Ming Dynasty | 河北省涞源县<br>Laiyuan County, Hebei Province | 第七批<br>The 7th batch | 2013.3 |
| | （5）宁静安长城<br>(5) Ningjing'an Great Wall | 明代<br>Ming Dynasty | 河北省涞源县<br>Laiyuan County, Hebei Province | 第七批<br>The 7th batch | 2013.3 |
| | （6）白石口长城<br>(6) Baishikou Great Wall | 明代<br>Ming Dynasty | 河北省涞源县<br>Laiyuan County, Hebei Province | 第七批<br>The 7th batch | 2013.3 |
| | （7）插箭岭长城<br>(7) Chajianling Great Wall | 明代<br>Ming Dynasty | 河北省涞源县<br>Laiyuan County, Hebei Province | 第七批<br>The 7th batch | 2013.3 |
| | （8）狼牙口长城<br>(8) Langyakou Great Wall | 明代<br>Ming Dynasty | 河北省涞源县<br>Laiyuan County, Hebei Province | 第七批<br>The 7th batch | 2013.3 |
| | （9）倒马关长城<br>(9) Daomaguan Great Wall | 明代<br>Ming Dynasty | 河北省唐县<br>Tang County, Hebei Province | 第七批<br>The 7th batch | 2013.3 |
| | （10）明长城虎山段遗址<br>(10) Ming Great Wall Hushan section site | 明代<br>Ming Dynasty | 辽宁省宽甸县<br>Kuandian County, Liaoning Province | 第七批<br>The 7th batch | 2013.3 |
| | （11）南树林子长城<br>(11) Nanshulinzi Great Wall | 明代<br>Ming Dynasty | 辽宁省义县<br>Yi County, Liaoning Province | 第七批<br>The 7th batch | 2013.3 |
| | （12）龟山长城<br>(12) Guishan Great Wall | 明代<br>Ming Dynasty | 辽宁省凌海市<br>Linghai City, Liaoning Province | 第七批<br>The 7th batch | 2013.3 |

| | | | | |
|---|---|---|---|---|
| (13)植股山段长城<br>(13) Zhigusan section of Great Wall | 明代<br>Ming Dynasty | 辽宁省葫芦岛市<br>Huludao City, Liaoning Province | 第七批<br>The 7th batch | 2013.3 |
| (14)小虹螺山段长城<br>(14) Small Hongluoshan section of Great Wall | 明代<br>Ming Dynasty | 辽宁省葫芦岛市<br>Huludao City, Liaoning Province | 第七批<br>The 7th batch | 2013.3 |
| (15)翠岩墩台<br>(15) Cuiyan abutment wall | 明代<br>Ming Dynasty | 辽宁省凌海市<br>Linghai City, Liaoning Province | 第七批<br>The 7th batch | 2013.3 |
| (16)刘家沟长城3号敌台<br>(16) Liujiagou Great Wall No. 3 enemy broadcasting station | 明代<br>Ming Dynasty | 辽宁省凌海市<br>Linghai City, Liaoning Province | 第七批<br>The 7th batch | 2013.3 |
| (17)台子沟长城3号敌台<br>(17) Taizigou Great Wall No. 3 enemy broadcasting station | 明代<br>Ming Dynasty | 辽宁省凌海市<br>Linghai City, Liaoning Province | 第七批<br>The 7th batch | 2013.3 |
| (18)江台山烽火台<br>(18) Gangtaishan beacon | 明代<br>Ming Dynasty | 辽宁省黑山县<br>Heishan County, Liaoning Province | 第七批<br>The 7th batch | 2013.3 |
| (19)二台子烽火台<br>(19) Ertaizi beacon | 明代<br>Ming Dynasty | 辽宁省黑山县<br>Heishan County, Liaoning Province | 第七批<br>The 7th batch | 2013.3 |
| (20)顺山堡烽火台<br>(20) Shuanshanbao beacon | 明代<br>Ming Dynasty | 辽宁省绥中县<br>Suizhong County, Liaoning Province | 第七批<br>The 7th batch | 2013.3 |
| (21)赫甸城城址<br>(21) Hediancheng city site | 明代<br>Ming Dynasty | 辽宁省宽甸县<br>Kuandian County, Liaoning Province | 第七批<br>The 7th batch | 2013.3 |
| (22)镇边堡城址<br>(22) Zhenbian fortress city site | 明代<br>Ming Dynasty | 辽宁省北宁市<br>Beining City, Liaoning Province | 第七批<br>The 7th batch | 2013.3 |
| (23)大茂堡<br>(23) Damaobao | 明代<br>Ming Dynasty | 辽宁省凌海市<br>Linghai City, Liaoning Province | 第七批<br>The 7th batch | 2013.3 |
| (24)通化县汉长城遗址<br>(24) Han Great Wall site of Tonghua County | 汉代<br>Han Dynasty | 辽宁省通化县<br>Tonghua County, Liaoning Province | 第七批<br>The 7th batch | 2013.3 |
| (25)唐代老边岗土墙<br>(25) Laobiangang cob wall of Tang Dynasty | 唐代<br>Tang Dynasty | 吉林省德惠市、农安县、公主岭市、梨树县、四平市<br>Dehui City, Nong'an County, Gongzhuling City, Lishu County, Siping City of Jilin Province | 第七批<br>The 7th batch | 2013.3 |
| (26)青海省明长城<br>(26) Ming Great Wall in Qinghai Province | 明代<br>Ming Dynasty | 青海省西宁市、大通县、湟中县、湟源县、民和县、乐都县、化隆县、贵德县、门源县<br>Xining City, Datong County, Huangzhong County, Huangyuan County, Minhe County, Ledu County, Hualong County, Guide County, Menyuan County of Qinghai Province | 第七批<br>The 7th batch | 2013.3 |
| (27)明长城—河东墙段、三关口段、姚滩段、大水沟段<br>(27) Ming Great Wall—Hedong wall section, Sanguankou section, Yaotan section, Dashuigou section | 明代<br>Ming Dynasty | 宁夏回族自治区兴庆区、灵武市、永宁县、盐池县、沙坡头区、平罗县<br>Xingqing District, Lingwu City, Yongning County, Yanchi County, Shapotou District, Pingluo County of Ningxia Hui Autonomous Region | 第七批<br>The 7th batch | 2013.3 |

**表 2-9：长城沿线各省（自治区、直辖市）文物保护单位公布情况统计简表**

Table 2-9: Publishing situation statistic table on cultural relic Conservation sites of involved provinces (autonomous regions, municipalities directly under the Central Government) along Great Wall

| 省份 Province | 截止 2016 年公布省级以上文物保护单位段落数（处）The number of published sections of cultural relic Conservation sites above the province level (site) by the end of 2016 | 截止 2016 年所占全省长城段落比例（%）The occupying proportion of the sections of Great Wall in the whole province by the end of 2016 (%) | 2013 年之前工作的省级以上文物保护单位数（处）Cultural relic Conservation sites above the province level playing its role before 2013 (site) | 2013 年之前所占全省长城段落比例（%）The occupying proportion of the sections of Great Wall in the whole province before 2013 (%) | 得分 Score（10 分） |
|---|---|---|---|---|---|
| 山东 Shandong | 243 | 100 | 243 | 100 | 10 |
| 河南 Henan | 141 | 100 | 141 | 100 | 10 |
| 甘肃 Gansu | 3842 | 99.7 | 3824 | 100 | 10 |
| 青海 Qinghai | 381 | 100 | 381 | 100 | 10 |
| 宁夏 Ningxia | 1829 | 100 | 1829 | 100 | 10 |
| 山西 Shanxi | 4266 | 100 | 4266 | 100 | 9.8 |
| 黑龙江 Heilongjiang | 2006 | 100 | 1753 | 87 | 9.6 |
| 北京 Beijing | 2328 | 98.8 | 2328 | 99.8 | 9.3 |
| 天津 Tianjin | 256 | 96.7 | 256 | 96.7 | 9.3 |
| 吉林 Jilin | 228 | 99 | 76 | 33 | 9 |
| 河北 Hebei | 8276 | 100 | 8276 | 100 | 8.6 |
| 内蒙古 Inner Mongolia | 13804 | 100 | 9744 | 70.6 | 7 |
| 新疆 Xinjiang | 97 | 45.8 | 97 | 45.8 | 4 |
| 辽宁 Liaoning | 120 | 4 | 94 | 3.1 | 2.8 |
| 陕西 Shaanxi | 105 | 3.6 | 94 | 3.2 | 2.5 |
| 合计 Total | 37922 | 86.6 | 33402 | 88.1% | 平均 Average 8.12 |

**表 2-10：长城各级文物保护单位包含长城资源统计简表**

Table 2-10: Statistical abridged table of Great Wall cultural relic Conservation sites at all levels inclusive of Great Wall resources

| 保护级别<br>Conservation level | 墙体（千米）<br>Wall body<br>(kilometer) | 烽火台（座）<br>Beacon tower<br>(stand) | 关堡（座）<br>Fort<br>(stand) | 其他单体建筑（座）<br>Other individual<br>buildings (stand) | 相关遗存（处）<br>Related remains<br>(site) |
|---|---|---|---|---|---|
| 全国重点文物保护单位<br>Important heritage sites under state Conservation | 10619.6 | 3316 | 879 | 11022 | 41 |
| 省级文物保护单位<br>Cultural relic Conservation sites at province level | 7064.1 | 6572 | 962 | 4434 | 125 |
| 市县级文物保护单位<br>Cultural relic Conservation sites at city and county level | 48.4 | 82 | 38 | 6 | 0 |
| 尚未核对公布为文物保护单位<br>Cultural relic Conservation sites hasn't been approved and identified | 3634.7 | 2280 | 343 | 1849 | 20 |
| 总数 Total | 21366.8 | 12250 | 2222 | 17311 | 186 |
| 公布为省级以上文物保护单位数量比例<br>The quantitative proportion of cultural relic Conservation sites published as above the province level | 82.80% | 80.70% | 82.90% | 89.30% | 87.20% |

## 专栏：我国的文物保护单位制度

文物保护单位制度是我国开展文物保护管理的基础。1961 年 3 月 4 日国务院发布的《文物保护管理暂行条例》是明确建立我国文物保护单位管理制度的早期文件。

1982 年颁布，2015 年最新修订的《中华人民共和国文物保护法》第十三条规定：

“国务院文物行政部门在省级、市、县级文物保护单位中，选择具有重大历史、艺术、科学价值的确定为全国重点文物保护单位，或者直接确定为全国重点文物保护单位，报国务院核定公布。

“省级文物保护单位，由省、自治区、直辖市人民政府核定公布，并报国务院备案。

“市级和县级文物保护单位，分别由设区的市、自治州和县级人民政府核定公布，并报省、自治区、直辖市人民政府备案。

“尚未核定公布为文物保护单位的不可移动文物，由县级人民政府文物行政部门予以登记并公布。”

自 1961 年至今，国务院已经陆续公布了七批，共 4296 处全国重点文物保护单位。

and mapping, as per value and distribution situations of various kinds of Great Wall resources and actual requirements of conservation and management works, demarcating Great Wall conservation scope scientifically. Great Wall conservation scope shall be demarcated outside Great Wall ontology maintaining a certain safe distance, guaranteeing the sites, relics related to Great Wall could be completely protected. In principle, the conservation scope of wall body (including Jin Jiehao or fosse) of Great Wall should take wall body of Great Wall and attached enemy broadcasting station, protruded section, fortress to wall body as boundary and relevant relics should take periphery of footing as baseline expanding at least 50 meters towards two sides as boundary; the conservation scope independent from wall body outside Great Wall, such as enemy broadcasting station, fortress, beacon towers and related relics and etc. should take periphery of individual building foundation as baseline, expanding at least 50 meters towards all around as boundary; 3. As for sections of Great Wall with complex composition and complex environment, its conservation scope may be divided as general conservation area and key conservation area. 4. Conservation scope must be clearly marked on the map with boundary scope, print the corresponding drawing and provide graphic data as per requirements of Chapter 4.

## Special column: Cultural relic conservation site system in our country

Cultural relic conservation site system is the foundation for our country to carry out cultural relic conservation and management. On March 4, 1961, Provisional Regulations on Cultural Relic Conservation and Management was early file for clearly establishing our country's cultural relic conservation site management system.

Article XIII under *Cultural Relic Conservation Law of the People's Republic of China* newly revised in 2015, issued in 1982, stipulates:

"Cultural Relic Administration Department of the State Council selects cultural relic conservation sites with significant historic, art, scientific value from cultural relic conservation sites at province, city and county level as important heritage sites under state conservation or directly confirms as important heritage sites under state conservation and report to the State Council for approval, then publish".

"Cultural relic conservation sites at the province level shall be approved and published by the people's government of province, autonomous region, municipalities directly under the Central Government and reported to the State Council for filing."

"Cultural relic conservation sites at the city and county level shall be respectively approved and published by the people's government of city, autonomous prefecture and county, and reported to the people's government of province, autonomous region, municipalities directly under the Central Government for filing."

"Immovable cultural heritage that hasn't been approved and identified as cultural relic conservation sites shall be registered and published by cultural relic administrative department of the people's government in county."

Since 1961 up to now, The State Council has published seven batches in succession, totaling 4296 important heritage sites under state conservation.

关于建设控制地带。《长城“四有”工作指导意见》要求长城建设控制地带应根据长城的周边环境风貌和景观视廊保护的实际需要划定。原则上，位于城市的长城建设控制地带应自长城保护范围边界外扩不少于 100 米作为边界；位于农村和郊野地区的长城建设控制地带应自长城保护范围边界外扩不少于 500 米作为边界。建设控制地带须在地图上明确标识边界范围，印制相应的图纸，并按第四章要求提供图形数据。

近年来，长城沿线各地在开展长城“四有”基础工作、日常管理及规划编制过程中，以《长城“四有”工作指导意见》为依据，并结合文物保护单位保护要求、地方保护管理实际需求、长城所在地的地形地貌等，陆续划定并公布了一大批长城文物保护单位的保护范围和建设控制地带。截止 2016 年 10 月，在全部 209 处长城文物保护单位中，共有 97 处开展了保护范围和建设控制地带的划定工作，涉及 216 个县，涵盖认定点段 18803 处，占所有长城段落的 42.9%。其中包括长城长度 10369.3 千米，烽火台 6446 座、关堡 1083 座、相关遗存 153 处。其中，北京市、河北省、吉林省、黑龙江省、甘肃省、宁夏回族自治区已经全部划定和公布本省（自治区、直辖市）行政区划范围内长城的保护范围和建设控制地带。

2016 年国家文物局“长城执法专项督察”结束后，根据国家文物局提出的整改要求，2016 年 11 月 8 日，山西省人民政府印发《关于公布山西省历代长城保护范围及建设控制地带的通知》（晋政函〔2016〕122 号），统一划定并公布了经过国家文物局认定的山西省历代长城保护范围及建设控制地带，并明确了相应的保护管理规定。陕西省在探索开展省级以上文物保护单位保护管理规划过程中，将全省各时代长城纳入管理规划编制范围，划定了长城保护范围和建设控制地带。目前，上述规划已经编制完成，并将于 2017 年内由陕西省人民政府公布实施。其他各省（自治区、直辖市）也结合正在实施的省级长城保护规划编制工作，推进各地长城保护范围与建设控制地带划定工作。

As for construction control area, *Work Constructive Opinion for Great Wall "Four Haves"* requires construction control area of Great Wall should be demarcated according to the actual demand of Great Wall's surrounding environmental feature and style and landscape visual corridor conservation. In principle, construction control area of Great Wall located in urban area, should take at least 100 meters outside the Great Wall conservation boundary as boundary; construction control area of Great Wall located in rural and suburb area, should take at least 500 meters outside the Great Wall conservation scope boundary as boundary. Construction control area should clearly signs boundary scope on the map, print corresponding drawing and provide graphic data as per requirements of Chapter 4.

In recent years, during the process of regions along Great Wall conducting Great Wall "Four haves", daily management and planning compilation, a large batch of cultural relics conservation sites' conservation scope and construction control area are successively demarcated and identified, based on *Work Constructive Opinion for Great Wall "Four Haves"*, by combining cultural relics conservation sites' requirements, local conservation and management's actual requirements, landform where Great Wall sections locate. By the end of October 2016, among totaling 209 Great Wall cultural relics conservation sites, 97 sites have been demarcated conservation scope and construction control area, involving 216 counties, covering identified 18803 sections taking up 42.9% of Great Wall sections. Wherein, Great Wall length is 10369.3 kilometers, 6446 beacon towers, 1083 forts, 153 related remains. Wherein, Beijing, Hebei Province, Jilin Province, Heilongjiang Province, Gansu Province, Ningxia Hui Autonomous Region have totally demarcated and issued Great Wall conservation scope and construction control area in its own province (autonomous region, municipality directly under the Central Government) under its administration region.

In 2016, after the accomplishment of "Great Wall law enforcement special supervision", as per the rectification requirement of State Administration of Cultural Heritage, on November 8, 2016, The People's Government of Shanxi Province issued *Notice on Publishing Great Wall Conservation Scope and Construction Control Area at all Ages in Shanxi Province* (J. Z. H (2016) No. 122), uniformly demarcated and published Great Wall conservation scope and construction control area at all Ages in Shanxi Province approved by State Administration of Cultural Heritage and specified the corresponding conservation and management provisions. During the process of exploring and conducting the conservation and management planning of cultural relic conservation site above province level from Shaanxi Province, it incorporated

### （三）保护标志设立情况

长城保护标识包括保护标志牌、保护界桩和保护说明牌三类。其中，保护单位标志牌按照全国重点文物保护单位有关规定执行。考虑到长城分布范围及所处位置特点，《长城“四有”工作指导意见》规定“长城沿线各县级行政区域内均应至少设立1块长城保护标志牌。对于同一县级行政区域内具有两条或两条以上独立走向或不同时代长城的情形，各长城线路或不同时代长城至少分别设立1块保护标志牌。”此外，《长城“四有”工作指导意见》还规定了保护界桩和保护说明牌两类保护标识。

根据长城执法专项督察统计情况，截止2016年10月，长城沿线各地共设立长城保护标志牌6516座，设置保护界桩72605根，设置保护说明牌743座。其中甘肃省保护标志牌数量占全国总数的59%，界桩数量占全国总数的74.5%；辽宁省、宁夏回族自治区、山东省、黑龙江省、内蒙古自治区、河北省等，也设置比较多。（表2-11）

### （四）文物记录档案编制情况

完整的文物记录档案是长城的基础档案资料。全国长城资源调查工作形成了完整、丰富、规范的调查资料，长城沿线43721处长城资源点段均有单独的记录，上述调查资料已经完成整理归档工作。目前，各地正陆续开展长城文物记录档案编制工作。据统计，截止2016年10月，已经建立长城记录档案539个，涵盖长城认定段落25154处，占总数的55.1%。[26]（表2-12）29处长城全国重点文物保护单位完成了全部长城文物记录档案编制工作。

[26] 河北省记录档案涵盖长城认定段落数无法提供相关数据，故未统计在内。

the whole province's Great Wall sections at all ages into management planning compilation scope and demarcated Great Wall conservation scope and construction control area. At present, the compilation of the above planning has been finished and shall be issued for implementation by the People's Government of Shaanxi Province in 2017. Other provinces (autonomous regions, municipalities directly under the Central Government) are promoting the corresponding demarcation work of Great Wall conservation scope and construction control area by combining provincial Great Wall conservation planning compilation under the implementation.

**(III) Conservation signs setup situation**

Great Wall conservation signs include three types of conservation signboard, conservation boundary marker and conservation instruction plate, among which conservation site signboard is executed as per related provisions of important heritage sites under state conservation, in consideration of Great Wall distribution scope and location features, *Work Constructive Opinion for Great Wall "Four Haves"* stipulates "at least 1 Great Wall signboard should be setup within administrative regions at county level along Great Wall. As for the situation where two lines or more than two lines of Great Wall with independent direction or different times within the same level of administrative region, each Great Wall lines or Great Wall at different times should at least separately setup I stand of conservation signboard." Moreover, *Work Constructive Opinion for Great Wall "Four Haves"* also stipulates two types of conservation signs as conservation boundary marker and conservation instruction plate.

According to Great Wall law enforcement special supervision statistics, by the end of October 2016, regions along Great Wall has set 6516 Great Wall conservation signal boards, set 72605 sticks of conservation boundary markers, set 743 stands of conservation instruction plates, among which conservation signal boards set in Gansu accounts for 59% of the total quantities in the country, with the quantities of boundary markers accounting for 74.5% of the total quantities in the country; Liaoning Province, Ningxia Hui Autonomous Region, Shandong Province, Heilongjiang Province, Inner Mongolia Autonomous Region, Hebei Province and etc. with relatively more signs.

**(IV) Cultural relic log archive compilation situation**

Intact cultural relic log archive is the basic archival data of Great Wall. National Great Wall resources surveying work has formed complete, abundant, normative surveying data with 43721 Great Wall resource sections along Great Wall separately logging, the above mentioned data has accomplished sort and file work. At present, various regions are conducting Great Wall recording

**表 2-11：各省（自治区、直辖市）长城保护标志设置情况**

Table 2-11: Great Wall Conservation sign setting situation ofinvolved provinces (autonomous regions, municipalities directly under the Central Government)

| 省份 Province | 设置保护标志牌数（座） Number of setup signboard (stand) | 设置保护界桩数量（根） Number of setup Conservation boundary marker (stick) | 设置保护说明牌数（座） Number of setup Conservation instruction plate (stand) |
|---|---|---|---|
| 北京 Beijing | 377 | 0 | 81 |
| 甘肃 Gansu | 3852 | 54098 | 0 |
| 宁夏 Ningxia | 387 | 6973 | 200 |
| 山西 Shanxi | 428 | 0 | 0 |
| 山东 Shandong | 18 | 1178 | 281 |
| 黑龙江 Heilongjiang | 74 | 949 | 74 |
| 新疆 Xinjiang | 99 | 91 | 0 |
| 内蒙古 Inner Mongolia | 561 | 726 | 200 |
| 河南 Henan | 43 | 228 | 0 |
| 辽宁 Liaoning | 46 | 8080 | 40 |
| 青海 Qinghai | 46 | 223 | 0 |
| 河北 Hebei | 426 | 0 | 0 |
| 天津 Tianjin | 11 | 0 | 0 |
| 吉林 Jilin | 3 | 0 | 3 |
| 陕西 Shaanxi | 145 | 59 | 145 |
| 合计 Total | 6516 | 72605 | 743 |

**表 2-12：各省（自治区、直辖市）长城记录档案建设情况**

Table 2-12: Establishment situation of Great Wall log file of involved provinces (autonomous regions, municipalities directly under the Central Government)

| 省份<br>Province | 已建立长城记录档案个数<br>Number of having established Great Wall log file | 涵盖长城认定段落数量（处）<br>Number of covering Great Wall identified section (location) | 所占长城认定段落比例（%）<br>Occupying proportion of Great Wall identified section (%) |
|---|---|---|---|
| 北京<br>Beijing | 380 | 2356 | 100 |
| 黑龙江<br>Heilongjiang | 5 | 2006 | 100 |
| 山东<br>Shandong | 1 | 260 | 100 |
| 甘肃<br>Gansu | 38 | 3843 | 100 |
| 青海<br>Qinghai | 12 | 381 | 100 |
| 宁夏<br>Ningxia | 19 | 1829 | 100 |
| 新疆<br>Xinjiang | 9 | 205 | 100 |
| 天津<br>Tianjin | 11 | 275 | 100 |
| 河北<br>Hebei | 14 | 454 | 5.49 |
| 山西<br>Shanxi | 1 | 2 | 0.004 |
| 辽宁<br>Liaoning | 9 | 83 | 2.8 |
| 吉林<br>Jilin | 5 | 76 | 33 |
| 陕西<br>Shaanxi | 29 | 34 | 0.1 |
| 内蒙古<br>Inner Mongolia | 6 | 13804 | 100 |
| 河南<br>Henan | 0 | 0 | 0 |
| 合计<br>Total | 539 | 25154 | 58.5 |

与此同时，国家文物局委托中国文化遗产研究院建立了“长城资源保护管理信息系统”，对长城资源调查和文物保护单位资料进行了全面数字化，并整合进入该系统，为长城信息化、精准化监测管理奠定了坚实基础。

（五）保护管理机构情况

《长城保护条例》第十五条规定：“长城所在地省、自治区、直辖市人民政府应当为本行政区域内的长城段落确定保护机构；长城段落有利用单位的，该利用单位可以确定为保护机构。”截止 2016 年 10 月，在文物保护“属地管理”的体制下，长城沿线所有省、市、县均有明确的文物行政管理机构负责长城保护管理，但专门保护管理机构数量很少。根据 2016 年国家文物局“长城执法专项督察”统计数据显示，长城沿线 15 个省份共设置或指定 485 个保护管理机构负责长城保护管理工作，其中 43 个为长城专门保护管机构，只占 0.9%。（表 2-13）

**表 2-13：各省（自治区、直辖市）长城保护管理机构设置情况**

Table 2-13: Setup situation of Great Wall Conservation and management of involved provinces (autonomous regions, municipalities directly under the Central Government)

| 省份<br>Province | 设置或指定保护机构数量<br>Numbers of setup or designated Conservation organizations | 长城专门保护管理专门机构数量<br>Number of special organizations on Great Wall special Conservation and management |
|---|---|---|
| 北京<br>Beijing | 17 | 17 |
| 天津<br>Tianjin | 4 | 1 |
| 河北<br>Hebei | 61 | 2 |
| 山西<br>Shanxi | 52 | 5 |
| 内蒙古<br>Inner Mongolia | 89 | 0 |
| 辽宁<br>Liaoning | 57 | 4 |

| | | |
|---|---|---|
| 吉林<br>Jilin | 11 | 0 |
| 黑龙江<br>Heilongjiang | 5 | 0 |
| 山东<br>Shandong | 19 | 0 |
| 河南<br>Henan | 13 | 1 |
| 陕西<br>Shaanxi | 29 | 10 |
| 甘肃<br>Gansu | 49 | 3 |
| 青海<br>Qinghai | 12 | 0 |
| 新疆<br>Xinjiang | 49 | 0 |
| 宁夏<br>Ningxia | 18 | 0 |
| 合计<br>Total | 485 | 43 |

archive compilation work in succession. Statistically, by the end of October 2016, 539 Great Wall recording archives has been establish, covering 25154 Great Wall identified sections, accounting for 55.1% [26] of the total. (Table 2-12) There are 29 Great Wall National heritage conservation sites have finished the whole heritage recording archives compilation work.

At the same time, Chinese Academy of Cultural Heritage is entrusted by State Administration of Cultural Heritage to establish "Great Wall conservation and management information system", totally digitize data survey on Great Wall and data of heritage conservation sites and integrate such data into the system, which builds a solid foundation for Great Wall informationized, precise monitoring management.

**(V) Situation of conservation and management organization**

Article XV of *Regulation on the Conservation of Great Wall* stipulates:

[26] Log archives covering Great Wall identified sections of Hebei Province fails to provide relevant data, hereof, not included into the statistics.

为加强遗产地能力建设，国家文物局每年举办世界文化遗产相关保护管理培训班，已有来自包括长城在内的各遗产地的700多名学员接受了系统的世界文化遗产保护培训，在提高遗产地保护人员的综合素质和管理能力方面发挥了重要作用。2016年7月，为贯彻落实国家领导人对长城保护管理工作的重要指示，推动各地按照统一的要求和标准进行长城的保护管理，国家文物局于2016年在宁夏银川举办了“长城保护管理培训班（第一期）”。中国文化遗产研究院受国家文物局委托，负责编制《长城保护员培训班培训方案》，制定培训计划、设计培训教学大纲储备师资等，参与设计了培训课程和教学内容，受国家文物局委托主持部分培训内容。来自全国50个地市的文物行政部门的长城保护管理负责人参加了培训，国家文物局、长城保护规划编制、工程实施、相关科研机构的领导和专家学者亲自向学员们授课，讲解长城保护管理理念、政策法规、工作案例，并由长城保护管理工作开展较好的基层单位代表介绍长城保护工作经验，有力促进了基层长城保护管理工作整体水平的提升。（图2-4）根据国家文物局的工作计划，此后将陆续开展针对各级文物行政部门、长城保护员的长城保护管理培训，并将这一工作逐渐制度化。

图2-4
长城保护管理培训班开班仪式
（张依萌 拍摄）

Fig. 2-4
Opening ceremony for training class of Great Wall Conservation and management (photo by Zhang Yimeng)

"Provinces, autonomous regions, municipalities direct under the Central Government where sections of Great Wall are located should establish conservation organization for the section of Great Wall within its administrative region scope". Where the using unit is located within the section of Great Wall, such using unit shall be deemed as conservation organization." By the end of October, 2016, under the system of cultural relic conservation following "localization administration", definite cultural relic administrative management organizations of the provinces, cities, counties along Great Wall, but the number of special conservation and management organization is scarce. According to the statistics from "Great Wall law enforcement special supervision" of State Administration of Cultural Heritage in 2016, totaling 485 sites of conservation and management organizations are in charge of Great Wall conservation and management set or designated from 15 provinces along Great Wall, only occupying 0.9%. (Table 2-13)

In order to enhance heritage site capacity building, State Administration of Cultural Heritage annually holds conservation and management training class related to world cultural heritage, and more than 700 trainees from heritage sites inclusive of Great Wall have accepted systematic world cultural heritage conservation training. It plays important role in improving the comprehensive quality and management capacity of person in charge of protecting heritage site. In July 2016, in order to implement the important indications from national leaders on Great Wall conservation and management works, promote authorities from each region to conduct Great Wall conservation and management as per uniform requirement and standard, State Administration of Cultural Heritage held "Great Wall conservation and management training class (the first phase)" in Yinchuan, Ningxia, 2016. Chinese Academy of Cultural Heritage authorized by State Administration of Cultural Heritage, is responsible for compiling *Training Class's Training Scheme on Person in Charge of Protecting Great Wall,* formulating training plan, designing training syllabus, reserving qualified teachers and etc., participating in designing training courses and teaching content, presiding over part of training contents entrusted by State Administration of Cultural Heritage. Persons who are in charge of Great Wall conservation and management from 50 prefectural and municipal heritage administrative departments around the country engage themselves in the training, and leaders and experts and scholars from State Administration of Cultural Heritage, Great Wall conservation planning and compilation, project implementation, relevant scientific and research organizations personally give lessons to trainees, explaining Great Wall conservation and management concept, policies and regulations, job cases, grass-roots units who obtain better achievements in Great Wall conservation and management works introduce Great Wall conservation's working experience. It powerfully promotes grass-roots Great Wall conservation and management work' overall level (Fig 2-4). As per the working plan of State Administration of Cultural Heritage, Great Wall conservation and management training aiming at heritage administrative departments, persons in charge of protecting Great Wall shall be successively conducted, and such job shall be gradually institutionalization.

## 三、开展“长城保护工程”总结评估，发布《中国长城保护报告》

长城保护工作历来受到党和国家的重视，进入21世纪，面对长城保护的严峻形势， 为落实中央指示精神，国家文物局报国务院批准，实施了《长城保护工程（2005—2014年）总体工作方案》（以下简称“长城保护工程”），“希望通过‘长城保护工程’的实施，扭转当前长城保护工作的被动局面”。2014年，“长城保护工程”结束，又值“十三五”规划编制启动，为全面总结实施十年工作进展，国家文物局委托中国文化遗产研究院开展“长城保护工程”总结验收与评估工作。

本次总结评估工作由国家文物局总体指导，委托中国文化遗产研究院组织实施，负责制定评估方案，委托国信司南（北京）地理信息技术有限公司依托长城信息系统开发评估数据采集软件。中国文化遗产研究院协调和指导长城沿线各级文物行政机构开展数据填报和自评估报告编写，组织专家现场检查验收，直接收集和整理国家文物局长城相关管理数据资料以及媒体相关长城的公开资料，汇总分析并撰写总结评估报告。长城沿线各省级文物行政管理部门负责组织本辖区有关市、县文物行政部门开展自检，填报相关数据并编制自评估报告。

评估内容以《长城保护条例》为依据，“长城保护工程”设定的任务为标准，形成十二项任务，包括：开展长城资源调查，建立长城文物记录档案；编制《长城保护总体规划》，划定保护范围和建设控制地带；制定《长城保护管理条例》，建立健全配套法规；理顺长城保护管理体制，明确长城保护责任；深入开展长城保护宣传教育工作；加强长城保护科学研究，完成“长城及其保护管理研究”课题；科学制定长城保护修缮计划，完成重点地段维修方案编制和重点部位抢救工程；依法加强监管，严惩对长城的破坏行为；增加对长城保护工作的经费投入；开展长城资源认定；公布省级以上文物保护单位；长城辟为参观游览区的应依法备案，并核定旅游容量指标。

## III. Evaluate "Great Wall Conservation Project", issue *China Great Wall Conservation Report*

Great Wall conservation work is constantly valued for Party and the county, entering the 21th century, in the face of severe condition of Great Wall conservation, in order to implement the central instruction spirit, State Administration of Cultural Heritage implemented the *Master Plan on the Great Wall Conservation Project (2005—2014)* (hereinafter refer to as "Great Wall Conservation Project") authorized by the State Council, "hoping to turn the passive situation of Great Wall conservation work around by implementation of 'Great Wall Conservation Project'". In 2004, "Great Wall Conservation Project" was completed, "the 13th Five-Year Plan" planning and compilation was launched by coincidence, Chinese Academy of Cultural Heritage was authorized by State Administration of Cultural Heritage to conduct summary and acceptance as well as assessment work.

The summary and assessment work was generally guided by State Administration of Cultural Heritage, it authorized Chinese Academy of Cultural Heritage to organize and carry out, formulate assessment scheme in charge, authorized Geo-compass (Beijing) Geographic Information Technology Co. to develop evaluation data acquisition software based on Great Wall information system. Chinese Academy of Cultural Heritage coordinated and guided heritage administrative organization at all levels along Great Wall to conduct data filing and self-assessment report compiling, organized experts to check and accept at site, directly collected and systemized State Administration of Cultural Heritage's Great Wall relevant management data material and media related Great Wall public data, analyzed from collected data and prepared summary and assessment report. Heritage administrative departments at provincial level along Great Wall are responsible for organizing related heritage administrative departments at city, prefecture level under its administration to carry out self-inspection, filling and reporting relevant data and compiling self-assessment report.

Assessment content was based on *Regulation on the Conservation of Great Wall,* took tasks set by "Great Wall Conservation Project" as criterion to form twelve tasks, including: to carry out Great Wall resources investigation, to build Great Wall heritage log file; to compile *Master plan of Great Wall conservation,* to designate conservation scope and construction control zone; to formulate *Management Regulations on Great Wall Conservation,* to establish and perfect corresponding regulations and laws, to disentangle Great Wall conservation and management system, to explicitly define Great Wall conservation responsibility; to carry out Great Wall conservation's publicity and education work in a deep-going way, to strengthen Great Wall conservation's scientific research, to complete "Great Wall and its conservation and management research"; to formulate Great Wall conservation and renovation plan in a scientific way, to finish major section's maintenance scheme compilation and key sites' rescue project; to legally enhance supervision, severely punish the sabotage to Great Wall, to increase the fund investment on Great Wall conservation work; to conduct Great Wall resources recognition; to public heritage conservation sites at county level; to put Great Wall section as tourist sightseeing on record by law, check and rectify tourism carrying capacity index.

By summarizing and assessing the implementation situation of twelve tasks during the ten years, it formed assessment report. It is the overall review and summary on our country's Great Wall

通过对这十二项任务在十年间的实施情况进行了总体评估，形成了评估报告。这是对我国长城保护十年工作的全面回顾和总结，在此基础上，国家文物局在《长城保护条例》实施十周年之际，发布了《中国长城保护报告》，从长城资源调查与研究、长城法规建设与管理、长城维修实践与理念、长城文化与时代价值、长城保护目标与行动等五大方面，分别总结和阐释了《长城保护条例》实施十周年以来，长城保护工程取得的成绩，并提出了行动目标。

中国政府首次就长城保护工作向社会发布了工作报告，对指导长城保护、回应社会关切、凝聚工作合力具有重要作用。

## 四、推进文物保护规划

长城保护规划是长城保护管理工作开展的重要依据。《长城保护条例》第十条规定："国家实行长城保护总体规划制度。国务院文物主管部门会同国务院有关部门，根据文物保护法的规定和长城保护的实际需要，制定长城保护总体规划，报国务院批准后组织实施。长城保护总体规划应当明确长城的保护标准和保护重点，分类确定保护措施，并确定禁止在保护范围内进行工程建设的长城段落。长城所在地县级以上地方人民政府制定本行政区域的国民经济和社会发展计划、土地利用总体规划和城乡规划，应当落实长城保护总体规划规定的保护措施。"。根据长城特点和保护管理需求，国家文物局制定了《长城保护总体规划编制导则》，明确了长城保护规划的对象、原则、目标和编制要求等。

### （一）保护规划对象

长城保护规划对象是经过长城资源调查并经国家文物局批复认定的分布在 15 个省、直辖市和自治区 404 个县市行政辖区内的全部长城资源，以及与长城直接关联的周边自然环境。

对于经过长城资源调查、其他文物普查调查或经过分析评估认为与长城存在关联，但未报或未经国家文物局认定的相关历史文化遗存、非物质文化遗产以及地理—文化特性，可考虑纳入长

conservation during the ten years, on this basis, on the tenth year of implementing *Regulation on the Conservation of Great Wall*, State Administration of Cultural Heritage issues China Great Wall Conservation Report, from five aspects, such as Great Wall resources survey and research, Great Wall laws and regulations construction, Great Wall maintenance practice and concept, Great Wall culture and times value, Great Wall conservation goal and action and etc., respectively summarizes and interprets the achievements obtained by Great Wall Conservation Project since the ten years' implementation of *Regulation on the Conservation of Great Wall*, puts forward the action objectives.

The government of China issues working report on Great Wall conservation work to the public for the first time, which plays vital function to guide Great Wall conservation, response the concern of the society, cohesion of working resultant force.

## Ⅳ. Promoting cultural relics conservation planning

Great Wall conservation planning is the significant basis for conducting Great Wall conservation and management work. Article X under Regulation *on the Conservation of Great Wall* stipulates: "The state implements Master plan system on Great Wall conservation. Heritage Competent Department of the State Council in company with relevant departments of the State Council, according to provisions of heritage conservation law and actual requirements of Great Wall conservation, formulates master plan of Great Wall conservation and organizes to carry out after being approved by the State Council. Master plan of Great Wall conservation should specify Great Wall's conservation standard and conservation focal points, confirm conservation measures by classification, designate the Great Wall section where engineering construction is prohibited to proceed within the conservation scope. Local people's government above the county level where Great Wall section locates should formulate national economic and social development plan, land using overall planning, urban and rural planning of its own administration area, implement the conservation measures stipulated under master plan of Great Wall conservation." According to the characteristic and conservation and management requirements of Great Wall, State Administration of Cultural Heritage formulates *Guideline on Master Plan and Compilation of Great wall Conservation,* specifies the object, principle, goal and compilation requirements and etc. of Great Wall conservation.

### (I) Conservation and planning object

Conservation object of Great Wall conservation and planning is entire Great Wall resources distributed in 15 provinces, municipalities direct under the Central Government, and autonomous regions, 404 counties' and cities' administrative areas, under Great Wall resources survey and identification of official reply from State Administration of Cultural Heritage and peripheral natural environment directly related to Great Wall.

As for historic and cultural relics, intangible cultural heritages and geo-cultural characteristics deemed as related to Great Wall, after Great Wall resources survey, other archaeological survey or analysis and evaluation, which haven't been reported or haven't been confirmed by State

城保护规划范围进行统筹考虑，并可视情况对其保护提出原则性要求。

（二）编制基本原则

编制长城保护规划要严格遵守“保护为主、抢救第一、合理利用、加强管理”的文物工作方针。依据《长城保护条例》“科学规划、原状保护”的理念，长城保护规划编制应当遵循以下基本原则：

1. 坚持价值导向、整体保护原则

长城拥有整体价值，并因建造年代、形制结构和所处地理－文化区域的不同而拥有多种价值特征。长城与所处区域的地形地貌之间，各类遗存功能与空间等方面存在内在的、体系性价值关联。构建长城保护规划体系必须坚持价值导向、整体保护原则，注重遗产价值体系的历时性与共时性，在各级规划中应明确辨析长城点段对遗产整体价值的支撑角度或自身特性，建立遗产局部与整体的关联，维护长城的整体性。

2. 坚持最小干预、原状保护原则

长城受到长期自然侵蚀、历代兴废、功能转变以及战争破坏影响，所呈现的以遗址形态为主的历史风貌及其所承载的各类遗迹遗痕，与众多历史事件直接关联，蕴含了丰富的历史信息，是长城价值的重要组成部分。各级规划制定规划目标、原则和措施时，必须坚持最小干预、原状保护原则，真实、完整地保护遗产的全部历史信息。

3. 坚持分级分类、因地制宜原则

长城遗存类型、形制、结构和材料丰富，保存状况差异甚大，各种价值承载要素自身及其与遗产价值整体的关联程度不尽相同；且长城分布区域的地理—文化背景变化丰富，地形地貌多样，生态条件 / 气候、社会经济 / 生业方式、民族文化等各种差异较大，单一规划措施难以应对各种不同的保护管理挑战，必须采取问题导向方针，分级分类、因地制宜地制定行之有效的、可操作的规划措施。

Administration of Cultural Heritage, may be taken into consideration to incorporate into Great Wall conservation and planning scope, to plan as a whole, and principle requirements should be put forwards for its conservation as the case may be.

### (II) Compiling basic principles

Compiling Great Wall protection and planning should strictly abide by the heritage working policy of "protection oriented, rescue in the first place, rational utilization, and strengthening management". In line with *Regulation on the Protection of Great Wall,* the concept of "scientific planning, protection for original state', Great Wall protection and planning compilation should comply with the following basic principles:

1 Stick to the principle of value guidance, overall protection

Great Wall has integral value, with various value characteristics due to the time of construction, construction style and diverse geographical and cultural regions. Great Wall has intrinsic, systematic value correlation with aspects, such as landform area where it locates, various remaining function and space. Establishing Great Wall protection and planning system must insist principle of value guidance, overall protection, emphasize on the diachronism and synchronism of heritage value system, clearly discriminate and analyze Great Wall section' supporting role to heritage's overall value or its own characteristics, build up the correlation between the partial and whole of heritage, maintain Great Wall's integrality.

2 Stick to the principle of minimum interference, protection for original status

Subject to long-term natural erosion, success and supersession from successive dynasties, functional shift and wars destructive influence, Great Wall's presented historic feature in the state of historic site and the loaded relic track, which is directly related to numerous historical events and implies abundant historical information, is an important part of Great Wall's value. When formulating planning target, principle and measurement, planning departments at all levels must stick to the principle of minimum interference, protection for original status, and truly and completely protect all historic information of heritage.

3 Stick to the principle of hierarchical classification, adaptation to local conditions

Great Wall has abundant remains type, form, structure and material, therefore, the disparities of conservation status is wide. The bearing element and its correlation degree with overall heritage's value differ from each other; geo-cultural background of area where Great Wall distributed changes frequently, diverse landform, discrepancies among ecological condition, weather, social economy, means of livelihood, national culture are great. So, sole planning measurement is unable to cope with various protection and management challenges, the issue oriented policy must be adopted herein, effective and practicable planning measurement is formulated by hierarchical classification, adaptation to local conditions.

4. 坚持突出重点、分期分批原则

长城属于超大型文化遗产，类型众多、保存环境多样、保护需求差异大、保护任务量极为繁重，规划编制须在整体保护目标下，坚持突出重点、分期分批的原则，并可针对保护管理压力的轻重缓急程度，采取优先行动计划，实事求是地制定分期计划，以分步骤推进的方式，提升保护管理规划措施实施的可行性和可操作性。

5. 坚持分段管理、加强协调原则

长城所处行政区域内的分布情况差异较大，跨越行政区域及两地共管现象普遍；长城保护管理涉及各级政府中的文物、文化、土地、生态、建设、规划等若干部门和诸多利益相关方，因此，规划措施必须依据属地管理的要求、按照分段管理原则制定。同时，在规划层面，考虑到长城作为线性文化遗产的特性，加强统筹协调，做好相关长城保护规划之间，以及与遗产地各类相关规划之间的衔接。

6. 坚持社会效益、合理利用原则

长城是人类文明发展史上具有重大启迪意义的文化遗产，对当代社会具有突出的教育意义，对遗产地经济、社会全面可持续发展也具有一定的促进作用。长城保护规划应本着合理、科学、适度的原则，在长城资源的合理利用方面以发挥遗产的社会效益为主，兼顾生态效益、文化效益、经济效益等。

（三）主要规划目标

从规划角度贯彻落实《长城保护条例》中关于“长城保护总体规划制度”的要求和“整体保护、分段管理”的规定，构建科学、合理、完整、可行的长城保护规划体系，制定可指导长城沿线各级政府和有关部门开展辖区内各类长城遗存保护、管理与利用的规范性文件，确定长城保护重点、保护措施和实施计划，明确实施保障，加强依法执行与程序管理，提升长城保护工作力度和实施效果。

4 Stick to the principle of highlight the key points, by stages and in groups

Great Wall is an ultra-large type of cultural heritage with large-scale of remains, numerous types, diverse conservation environments, wide differences of protection requirements, onerous protection task load, thereof, planning and compilation must stick to the principle of highlight the key points, by stages and in groups under the overall protection goal, adopt prior action plan as per the order of importance and emergency under the protection and management pressure, formulate staging plan as the case may be, to push the practicable and operational implementation of protection and management planning measurement by the way of step by step.

5 Stick to the principle of subsection management, strengthening coordination

A large difference among the distribution situations where Great Wall distributes within the administrative regions, it is common that Great Wall section is under multi-administrative regions and jointly administrated by two regions. Great Wall protection and management involves several departments and numerous interest related parties on cultural relic, culture, land, ecology, construction, planning and etc., therefore, the planning measures must be formulated in line with localization management requirements, subsection management principle. At the same time, at the planning level, taking the uniqueness of Great Wall linear cultural heritage into consideration, it should enhance overall plan and coordination, come off the links among relevant Great Wall protection and planning and various related planning on heritage site.

6 Stick to the principle of social benefit, rational utilization

Great Wall is a cultural heritage with significant enlightenment meaning in the human civilization development history. It has outstanding education meaning to contemporary society, has some positive effect on heritage site's comprehensive and sustainable economic and social development. Great Wall protection and planning should be in conformity with rational, scientific, moderate principle, in the respect of rational utilization of Great Wall resources, take social benefit of heritage as orientation, combine ecological benefits, cultural benefits, economic benefits and etc.

**(III) Main planning target**

From the point of planning, it should carry out the requirements of "Master plan of Great Wall conservation" under *Regulation on the Conservation ofGreat Walland* regulations of "overall conservation, subsection management", establish scientific, rational, integral, practicable Great Wall conservation and planning system, enact normative documents for guiding governments at all levels and relevant departments along Great Wall to conduct all kinds of Great Wall remains conservation, management and using within its own administrative regions, confirm Great Wall conservation key point, conservation measurement and implementation plan, specify implementing guarantee, enhance execution according to law and program management, promote Great Wall conservation work force and implementation effect.

（四）规划基本要求

1、保障长城的完整性

完整保护长城的各类价值载体 / 构成要素及其历史信息：长城本体包含了各个历史时期建造的人工的，或与自然地形结合而成的各种形式与材质的防御体系设施；长城各类相关历史文化遗存包括了与遗产价值密切关联的、分布相对独立的人工建造物；长城的非物质文化遗产包含了与长城的建造、维护等活动相关的各种传统建造技艺，长城的地理—文化特性等历史信息，包含了与长城缘起与沿用过程相关的各种地理、气候、生业、民族等多种文明要素与文化传统。

2、保护长城的真实性

真实保护长城的各类价值载体 / 构成要素及其历史信息：长城的真实性包括长城自然残损的历史风貌；长城的形制、结构、材质、工艺、位置、走向，以及长城本体上承载了各类历史文化信息的遗迹遗痕；长城环境的真实性包括历史地理的环境特色和防御性景观特性；长城背景环境的真实性包括了长城沿线地质地貌、地理气候、生态环境等的地理—文化特征，包含了生业方式、民族族群等人类生产生活活动的历史特性。

3、保持长城的延续性

持续保护长城各类价值载体 / 构成要素，使之世代传承：长城遗产的延续性主要体现在维护遗产各类本体保存的稳定性，以及减缓各种自然病害与灾变的销蚀作用、抵制人为建设活动的损毁现象；体现在长城所在地的生态环境保护与开发活动的合理控制，包括统筹协调遗产保护、生态保护、基本农田保护与遗产所在地的社会经济发展。

（五）编制工作进展

我国长城保护规划分为总体规划、省级规划和重要点段规划三个层次。自 2007 年起，长城沿线 15 省（自治区、直辖市）文物行政部门陆续启动了省级长城保护规划编制工作。截止 2016 年底，长城省级保护规划编制工作基本完成。按照工作安排，国

## (IV) Basic requirements of planning

1 Guarantee the integrity of Great Wall

Integrally protect Great Wall's various value carriers, components and historic information: Great Wall ontology contains defense system facilities of various forms and textures constructed by manpower or combining natural landform at each historic age; a variety of related historical culture of Great Wall incorporates artificial buildings closely related to heritage value, with relatively independent distribution; intangible cultural heritage of Great Wall contains historic information of various kinds of traditional construction technique, geo-cultural characteristics of Great Wall in correlation with Great Wall construction, maintenance and other activities, contains various kinds of civilized factor and cultural tradition, such as various geology, weather, means of livelihood, nationality related to the origin and following of Great Wall.

2 Protect authenticity of Great Wall

Truly protect Great Wall's various value carriers, components and historic information: authenticity of Great Wall contains historic feature caused by Great Wall natural damage; form, structure, texture, technology, location, direction of Great Wall and various kinds of historic culture information relic track carried by Great Wall ontology; authenticity of Great Wall environment contains environmental characteristics of historical geography and defensive landscape features; authenticity of Great Wall background environment contains landform, geography and weather, ecological environment and other geo-cultural characteristics along Great Wall, contains the historical traits, such as means of livelihood, nationality ethnic group and other human production and life activities.

3 Maintain the continuation of Great Wall

Continuously protect Great Wall's various value carriers, components, keep it being passed from generation to generation: the continuation of Great Wall heritage is mainly reflected in maintaining various heritage ontology conservations' stability, slowing down erosion caused by various natural diseases and catastrophes, boycotting damage phenomenon from man-made construction activities, including, overall plan and coordinate heritage conservation, ecology conservation, basic farmland conservation and the social and economic development where heritage locates.

## (V) Compiling working progress

Great Wall conservation in our country is divided into three levels. Since 2007, heritage administrative departments along Great Wall have successively launched provincial Great Wall conservation planning and compiling work. By the end of 2016, provincial conservation planning and compiling for Great Wall conservation has basically completed, in accordance with work scheduling, State Administration of Cultural Heritage entrusted special organization to launch compilation work for master plan of Great Wall conservation, and the project will be completed before the end of 2017. (Fig. 2-5,2-6,2-7)

家文物局同时委托专业机构启动了长城保护总体规划的编制工作，这项工作将于 2017 年底前完成。（图 2-5、2-6 、2-7）

此外，依据《中华人民共和国文物保护法》《长城保护条例》，全国重点文物保护单位的嘉峪关、玉门关、雁门关等 18 处长城重要点段，已经陆续编制了文物保护规划。同时，国家文物局也鼓励各地根据各地工作安排，循序渐进地开展长城重要点段保护、展示、环境整治等规划编制工作。国家文物局将持续对上述规划编制提供技术和经费支持。（表 2-14）

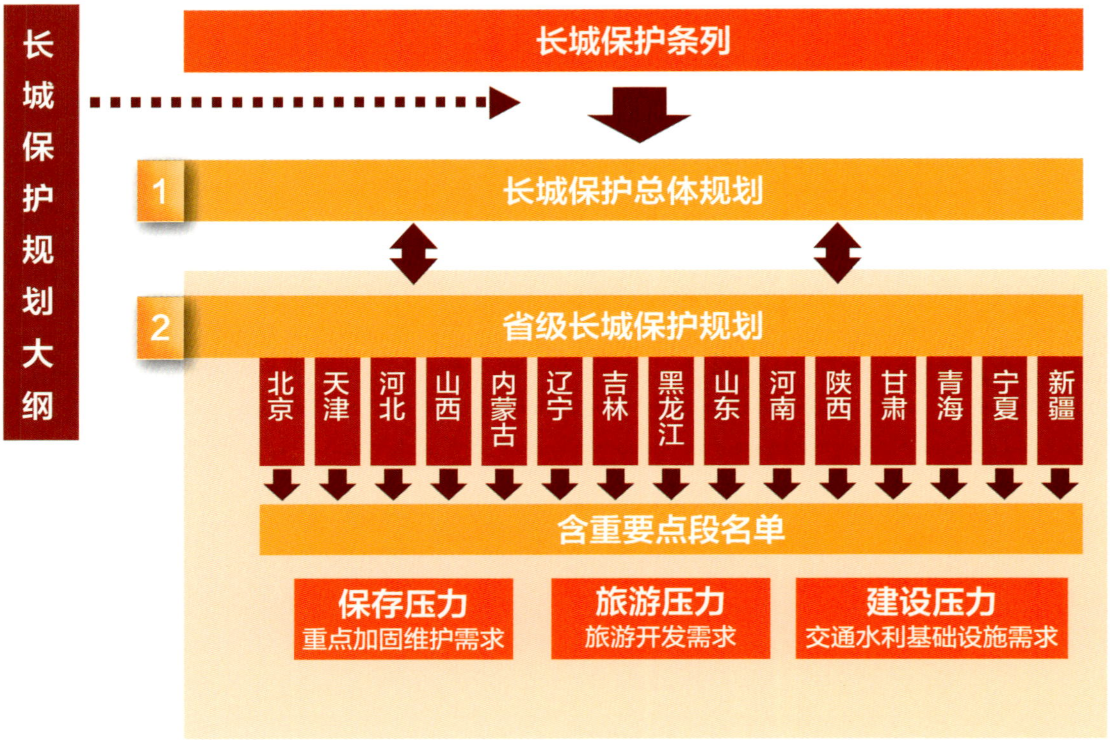


图 2-5
长城保护规划体系框架设计图

Fig. 2-5
Frame design drawing of planning system on Great Wall Conservation

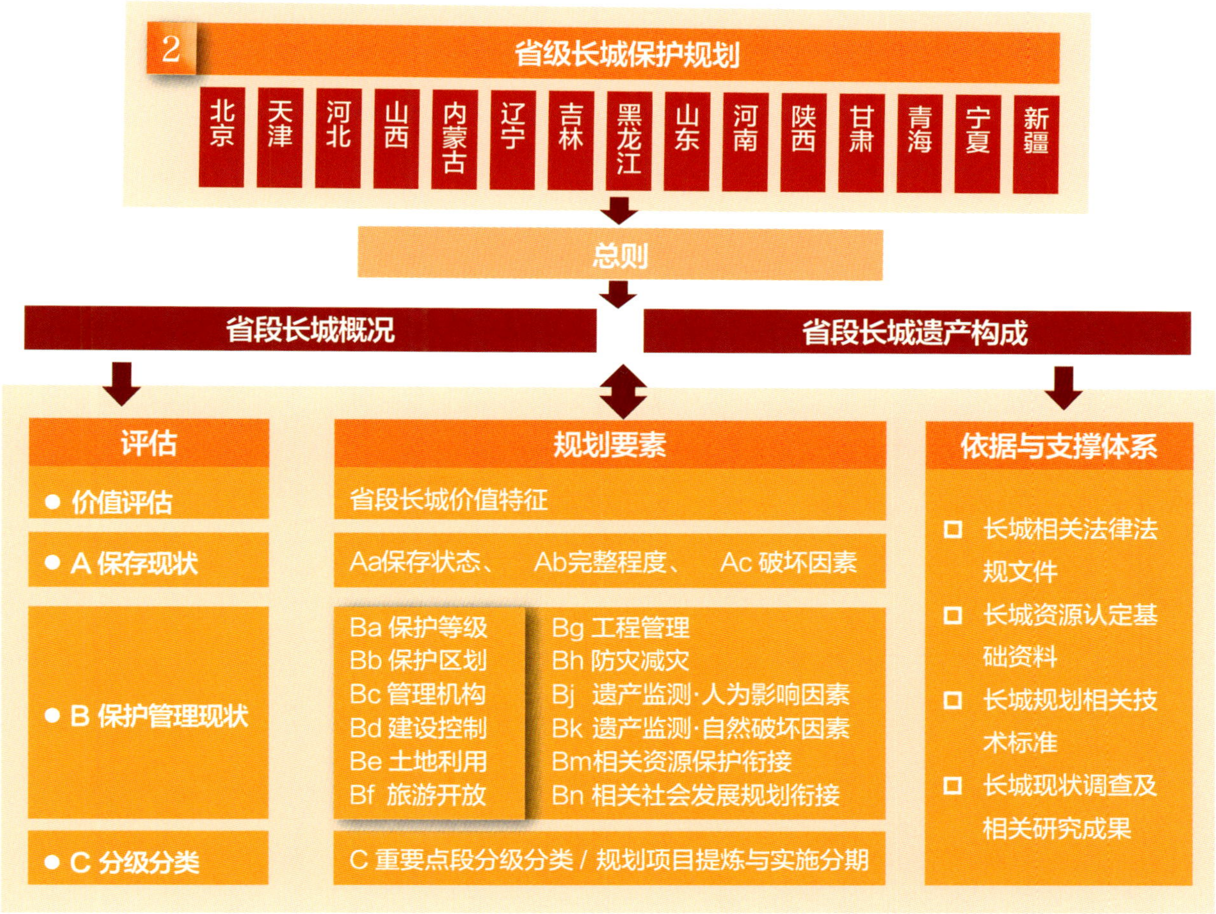


图 2-6
省级长城保护规划框架图

Fig. 2-6
Frame diagram on provincial Great Wall Conservation planning

Besides, in accordance with *Law of the People's Republic of China on the Conservation of Cultural Relics, Regulation on the Conservation of Great Wall,* 18 important sections of Great Wall, such as Jiayu Pass, Yumen Pass, Yanmen Pass and etc. issued as national key cultural relics conservation sites to the public were successively compiled the cultural relic conservation planning. In the meantime, State Administration of Cultural Heritage encourages authorities from place to place to progressively conduct conservation, display, environment renovation and other planning and compiling works as per the local concrete working arrangement. State Administration of Cultural Heritage continuously provides technology and financial support to the above mentioned planning and compiling. (Table 2-14)

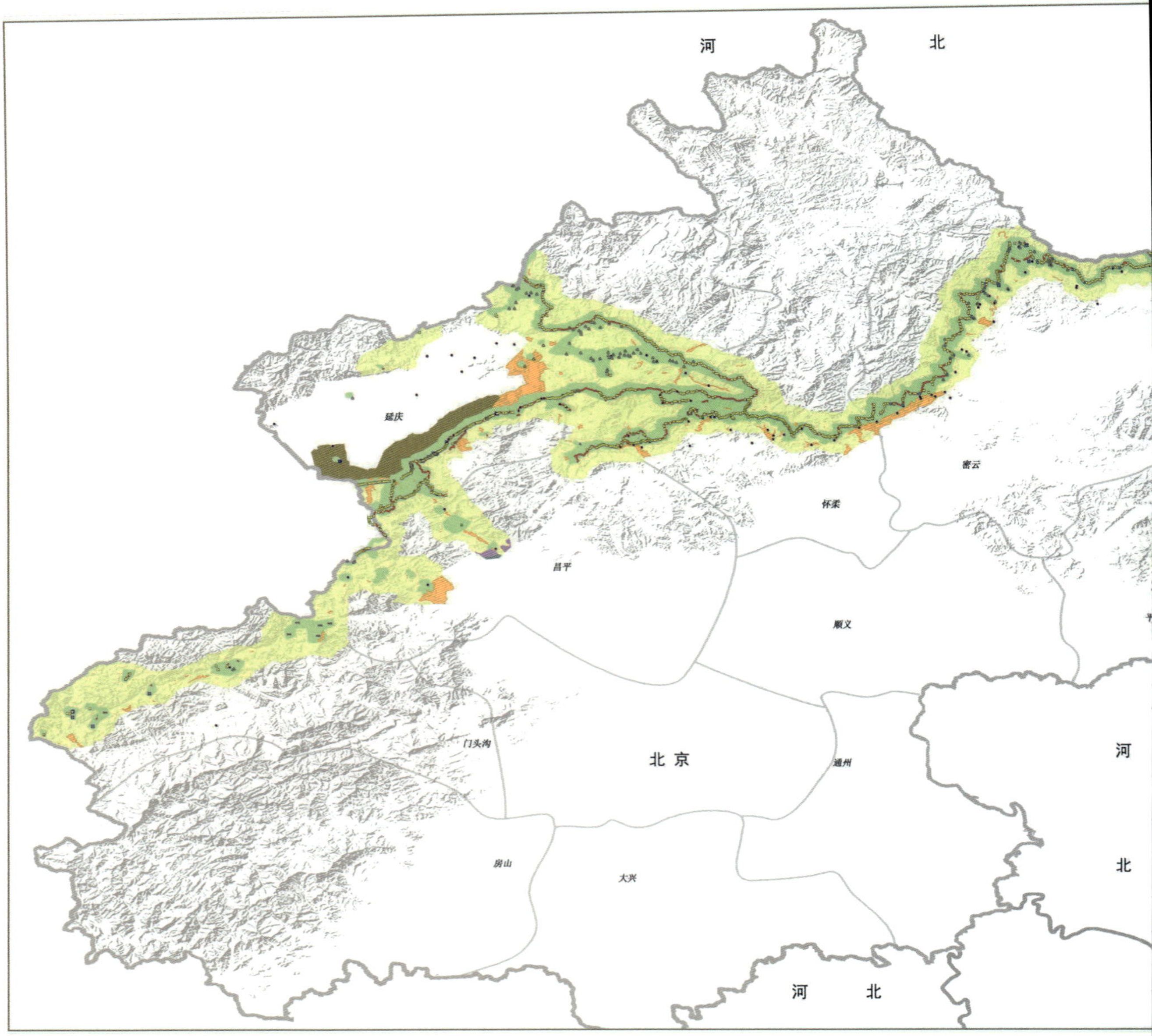


北京建工建筑设计研究院　北京建筑大学建筑遗产研究院

图 2-7.1
北京市长城总体保护规划图件——保护区划图

Fig. 2-7.1
Planning maps on Great Wall overall conservation in Beijing – conservation zoning plan

图 2-7.2
河北省明长城保护规划图件——长城分布图

Fig. 2-7.2
Planning maps on Great Wall conservation in Hebei Province – distribution drawing of Great Wall

图 2-7.3
内蒙古自治区长城保护规划图件——长城分布总图

Fig. 2-7.3
Planning maps on Great Wall conservation in Inner Mongolia Autonomous Region – general drawing on distribution of Great Wall

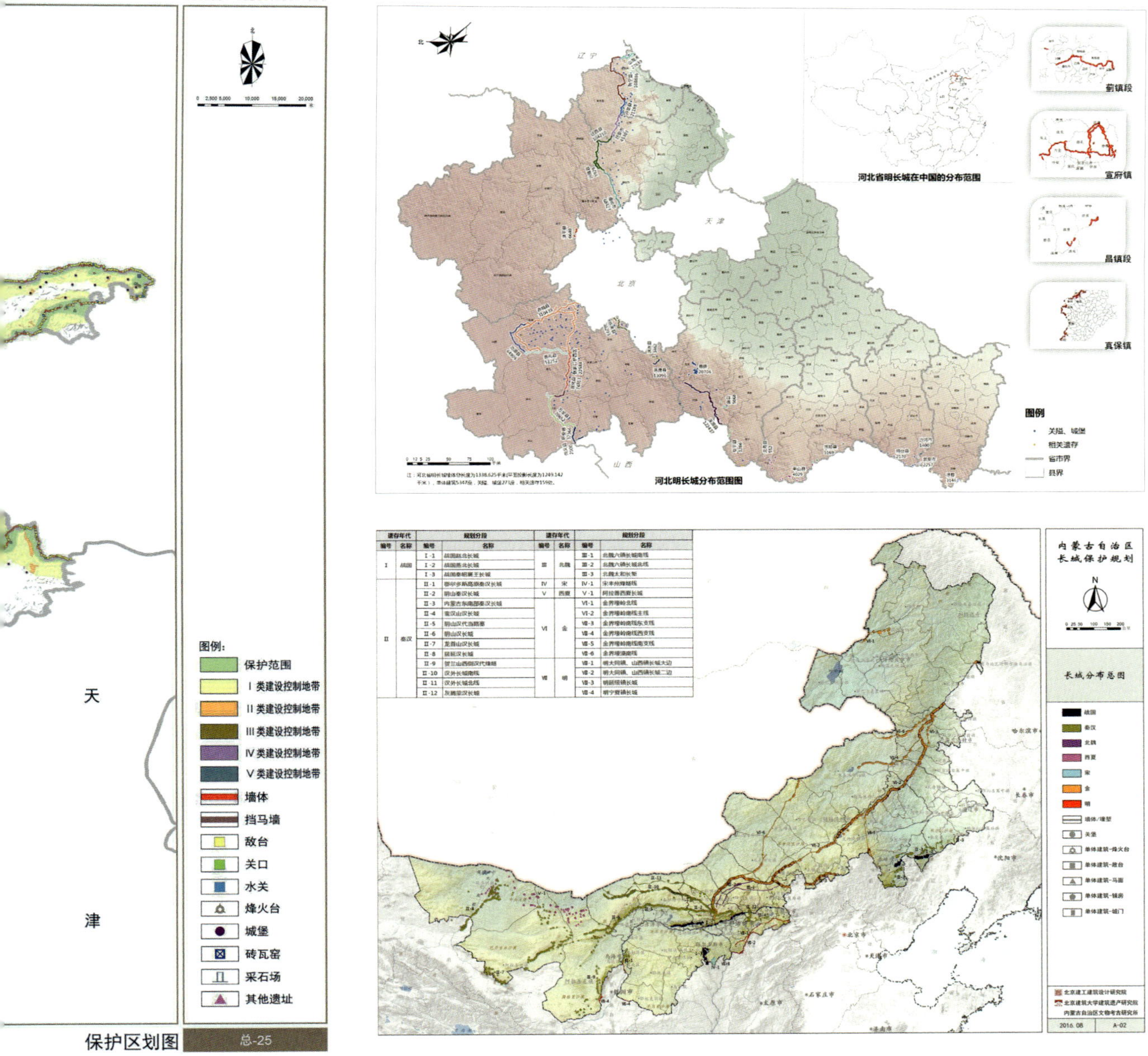


图 2-7
部分省（自治区、直辖市）长城保护规划图件

Fig. 2-7
Planning maps on Great Wall Conservation in parts of provinces (autonomous regions, municipalities direct under the Central Government)

## 表 2-14：各省（自治区、直辖市）长城保护规划编制情况

Table 2-14 Planning and compiling situation on Great Wall conservation of involved provinces (autonomous regions, municipalities direct under the Central Government)

| 省份<br>Province | 规划暂定名<br>Tentative name by planning | 编制单位<br>Compiling unit |
|---|---|---|
| 北京<br>Beijing | 北京市长城总体保护规划<br>Master Plan of Great Wall Conservation in Beijing | 北京建筑大学建筑遗产研究院<br>北京市城市规划设计研究院<br>Institute of Architecture Heritage of Beijing University of Civil Engineering and Architecture<br>Beijing Municipal Institute of City Planning & Design |
| 天津<br>Tianjin | 天津市明长城保护规划<br>Great Wall of the Ming Dynasty Conservation Plan in Tianjin | 天津大学建筑设计研究院<br>Tianjin University Research Institute of Architectural Design & Urban Planning |
| 河北<br>Hebei | 河北省明长城保护规划<br>Great Wall of the Ming Dynasty Conservation Plang in Hebei Province | 河北省古代建筑保护研究所<br>Hebei Institute of Preservation of Ancient Buildings |
| 山西<br>Shanxi | 山西省长城保护规划<br>Great Wall Conservation Plan in Shanxi Province | 山西省古建筑保护研究所<br>山西省古建筑设计有限公司<br>Shanxi Institute of Preservation of Ancient Buildings<br>Shanxi Ancient Buildings Design Co., Ltd. |
| 内蒙古<br>Inner Mongolia | 内蒙古自治区长城保护规划<br>Great Wall Conservation Plan in Inner Mongolia Autonomous Region | 北京建工建筑设计研究院、北京建筑大学建筑遗产研究院、内蒙古自治区文物考古研究所<br>Beijing Jiangong Architectural Design and Research Institute<br>Institute of Architecture Heritage of Beijing University of Civil Engineering and Architecture<br>Institute of Archaeology of Inner Mongolia |
| 辽宁<br>Liaoning | 辽宁省明长城保护规划<br>Great Wall of the Ming Dynasty Conservation Plan in Liaoning Province | 辽宁省文物保护中心、<br>哈尔滨工业大学城市规划设计研究院<br>Cultural Relic Preservation Center in Liaoning Province<br>Urban Planning and Design Institute of Harbin Institute of Technology |
| | 辽宁省早期长城保护总体规划（战国－辽）<br>Master Plan of Great Wall Conservation at early Stage in Liaoning Province (Warring States- Liao) | 中国文物信息咨询中心、东南大学建筑设计研究院有限公司、辽宁省文物保护中心<br>China Cultural Heritage Information and Consulting Center<br>Architecture Design Institution of Southeast University Co., Ltd.<br>Cultural Relic Preservation Center in Liaoning Province |
| 吉林<br>Jilin | 吉林省长城保护管理总体规划<br>Great Wall Conservation Overall Plan in Jilin Province | 中国中建设计集团有限公司 · 遗产保护研究中心<br>China State Construction Engineering Corporation Design Group Co., Ltd.<br>Heritage Conservation and Research Center |
| 黑龙江<br>Heilongjiang | 金界壕遗址（黑龙江段）文物保护规划<br>Jinjiehao Site (Heilongjiang section) Heritage Conservation Plan | 哈尔滨工业大学城市规划设计研究院<br>Urban Planning and Design Institute of Harbin Institute of Technology |
| | 牡丹江边墙文物保护规划<br>Mutankiang Side Wall Heritage Conservation Plan | 哈尔滨工业大学城市规划设计研究院<br>Urban Planning and Design Institute of Harbin Institute of Technology |

| | | |
|---|---|---|
| 山东<br>Shandong | 长城——齐长城遗址保护总体规划<br>Great Wall – the Great Wall of Qi Site Conservation Overall Plan | 山东省文物科技保护中心<br>Cultural Relic Sci-tech Preservation Center in Shandong Province |
| 河南<br>Henan | 河南省魏长城保护规划<br>Great Wall of Wei Site Conservation Planning in Henan Province | 郑州大学城市规划设计研究院有限公司<br>Institute of Architectural Design & Urban Planning of Zhengzhou University Co., Ltd. |
| 陕西<br>Shaanxi | 陕西段明长城保护总体规划<br>Master Plan of Great Wall of the Ming Dynasty Conservation in Shaanxi Province | 陕西省文化遗产研究院<br>陕西省文物局 · 西北大学文化遗产保护规划中心<br>Shaanxi Provincial Institute of Cultural Heritage<br>Cultural Relics Bureau of Shaanxi Province Northwest University Cultural Heritage Conservation Planning Center |
| | 陕西省魏长城遗址保护总体规划<br>Master Plan of Great Wall of Wei Site Conservation in Shaanxi Province | 陕西省文化遗产研究院、陕西省考古研究院<br>Shaanxi Provincial Institute of Cultural Heritage<br>Institute of Archaeology of Shaanxi Province |
| | 早期长城陕西段（战国秦、隋）保护规划<br>Shaanxi Section of Great Wall at Early Stage (Warring States, Qin, Sui Dynasty) Conservation Plan | 陕西省文化遗产研究院、陕西省考古研究院、国家测绘地理信息局第二地形测量队<br>Shaanxi Provincial Institute of Cultural Heritage<br>Institute of Archaeology of Shaanxi Province<br>The 2th Landform Surveying Team of National Administration of Surveying, Mapping and Geoinformation |
| 甘肃<br>Gansu | 甘肃省长城保护规划<br>Great Wall Conservation Plan in Gansu Province | 敦煌研究院、甘肃省文物保护维修研究所、兰州大学、西北大学、甘肃莫高窟文化遗产保护设计咨询有限公司、甘肃省基础地理信息中心<br>Dunhuang Academy<br>Research Institute of Cultural Heritage Conservation and Maintenance in Gansu Province<br>Lanzhou University<br>Northwest University<br>Gansu Mogao Caves Cultural Heritage Designing and Consulting Co., Ltd.<br>Gansu Basic geographic information Center |
| 青海<br>Qinghai | 青海省明长城保护总体规划<br>Master Plan of Great Wall of the Ming Dynasty in Qinghai Province | 兰州大学<br>Lanzhou University |
| 宁夏<br>Ningxia | 宁夏回族自治区长城总体保护规划大纲<br>Master Plan of Great Wall Brief in Ningxia Hui Autonomous Region | 北京建工建筑设计研究院、北京建筑大学建筑遗产研究院、宁夏回族自治区文物考古研究所<br>Beijing Jiangong Architectural Design and Research Institute<br>Institute of Architecture Heritage of Beijing University of Civil Engineering and Architecture<br>Ningxia Institute of Cultural Relics and Archeology |
| 新疆<br>Xinjiang | 新疆长城资源保护规划<br>Great Wall Resources Conservation Plan in Xinjiang | 新疆维吾尔自治区文物古迹保护中心<br>北京工业大学建筑勘察设计院<br>Conservation Center of Heritage Sites in Xinjiang Uygur Autonomous Region<br>Institute of Architectural Exploratory and Design, Beijing University of Technology |

【摘要】

长城是世界上体量最大、蔚为壮观的历史文化遗产，同时也是由多种遗存及其所处自然环境共同构成的具有独特审美价值的文化景观。保存至今的古老长城面临着多种自然病害和人为损坏的威胁，保护长城是一项刻不容缓的紧迫任务。我国政府高度重视长城保护工作，坚持“科学规划、原状保护”的原则，以文物本体抢险加固、消除安全隐患为长城保护的首要任务，组织实施了一批长城保护维修工程，有效维护了长城的真实性、完整性和自然历史风貌。

# 第三章
# 长城保护维修工作

# Chapter 3
# Conservation and Maintenance work of the Great Wall

[Abstract]

The Great Wall is the world's largest historical and cultural heritage object, and is a uniquely aesthetic cultural landscape consisting of varied remains and the natural environments in which they exist. The surviving ancient Great Wall is threatened by various kinds of natural and man-made damage, and the conservation of the Great Wall is urgent and pressing. Attaching great importance to the conservation of the Great Wall, the Chinese government, based on the principle of "scientific planning and as-is conservation" and giving priority to emergency strengthening of cultural heritage objects themselves and elimination of potential safety hazards, implemented an array of Great Wall Conservation and maintenance projects, effectively maintaining the authenticity, integrity and natural and historic features of the Great Wall.

河北涞源烟煤洞明长城（杜震欣 拍摄）

The section of the Great Wall of the Ming Dynasty at Yanmeidong, Laiyuan, Hebei (Photo by Du Zhenxin)

## 第一节 长城保护维修工程概况

- ※ 新中国最早的长城保护项目——1952 年修复八达岭长城
- ※ 2006 年以来的长城保护项目——218 项，400 千米余墙体，1400 余座单体建筑
- ※ 长城保护工程类别——抢险加固，保护修缮，保护设施，保养维护

1952-1954 年，在郭沫若“保护文物，修复长城，向游人开放”的提议下，国家文物局主持勘察、修缮了北京的八达岭长城。这是新中国第一项长城保护维修工程。改革开放之初，习仲勋、邓小平同志先后提出了“爱我中华，修我长城”的口号，一些具有重要价值的长城段落，以山海关、嘉峪关、居庸关、金山岭长城为代表的重要节点、段落陆续得到保护修缮。

虎山长城位于辽宁省丹东市宽甸满族自治县，是明长城的东端起点。20 世纪 80 年代初，丹东市文物部门在文物普查中发现虎山长城墙体及墙基，残损情况非常严重。1992 年 2 月，《虎山长城修复设计方案》获国家文物局批准实施，共维修、修复长城墙体 1250 米，城楼、烽火台、敌台、马面等 12 座，并修建了雕塑、栈道等配套设施后，向社会开放。

## Section 1 Overview of Great Wall Conservation and Maintenance Projects

※ The first Great Wall Conservation Project implemented after the founding of the People's Republic of China—restoration of the Badaling Great Wall in 1952
※ Great Wall Conservation Projects implemented since 2006—218 projects; walls totalling a length of 400 odd km; 1,400 odd single structures
※ Types of Great Wall Conservation Projects—emergency strengthening, conservation and maintenance, protective facilities, and maintenance

From 1952 through 1954, after Mr. Guo Moruo proposed "conserving cultural heritage, restoring the Great Wall and opening it to tourists", the State Administration of Cultural Heritage organised the investigation and repair of the Badaling Great Wall in Beijing. This was the first Great Wall conservation and maintenance project implemented after the founding of the People's Republic of China. Shortly after the inception of the reform and opening-up policy, Messrs. Xi Zhongxun and Deng Xiaoping proposed the slogan "Love China and Repair the Great Wall", and thereafter, some Great Wall sections of significant value, such as the Shanhai Pass, Jiayu Pass, Juyong Pass and Jinshanling sections, received conservation and maintenance one after another.

The Hushan Great Wall, located in Kuandian Man Autonomous County, Dandong City, Liaoning Province, is the eastern starting point of the Ming Great Wall. In the early 1980s, the cultural heritage authority of Dandong City found in an archaeological survey that the wall and footing of the Hushan Great Wall were severely damaged. In February 1992, *Design Plan for the Restoration of the Hushan Great Wall* was approved by the State Administration of Cultural Heritage, followed by repair and restoration of a 1,250 m long wall and 12 structures such as gate towers, beacon towers, watchtowers and battlements, and construction of sculptures, plank roads and other supporting facilities before the wall was opened to the public.

河北省秦皇岛市山海关区政府响应“爱我中华，修我长城”口号，统一规划山海关长城的保护修复工作，陆续维修、修复了入海石城、澄海楼、宁海城、孟姜女庙等景点，一并对外开放。据统计，自 1984 年 10 月至 1999 年底，山海关区共投入修复长城的经费计 4979 万元人民币，同期接待游客数量达到 5400 万人。[27]

居庸关长城位于北京市昌平区。自 1993 年始，十三陵特区办事处先后投资约 1 亿元，对居庸关长城进行保护修缮。至 1997 年，工程基本完工，总计维修、修复长城墙体 4142 米，敌楼、铺房、烽燧等建筑 28 座。（图 3-1）

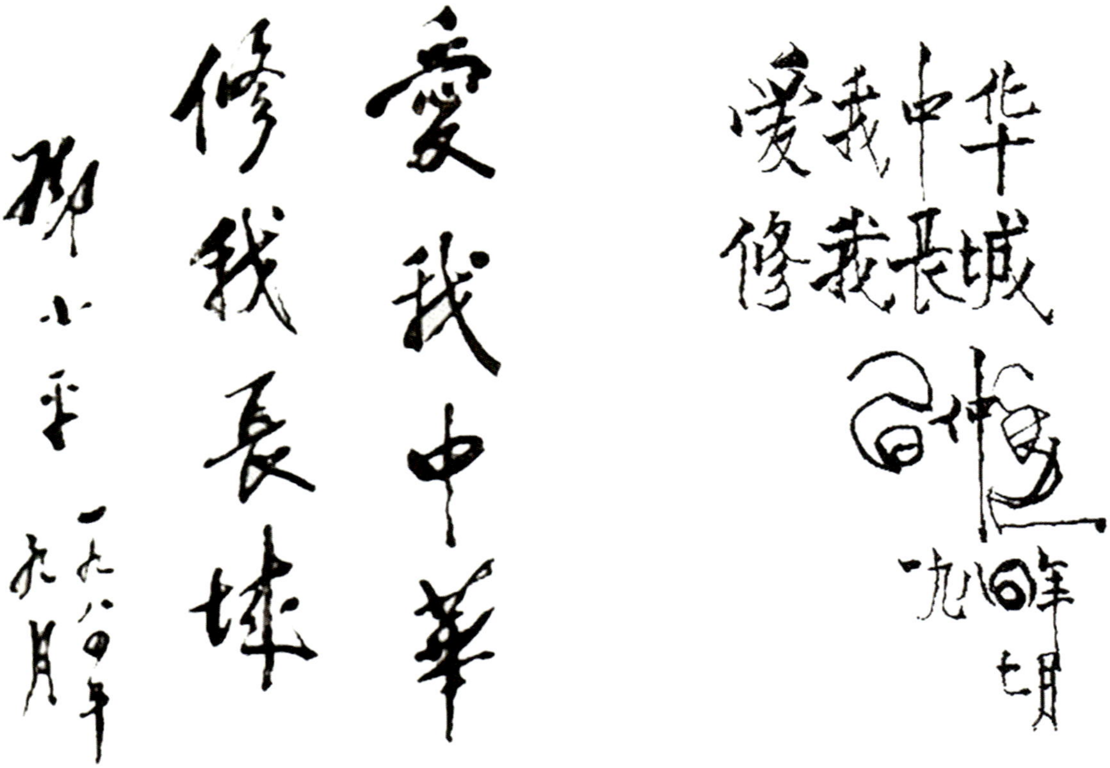


图 3-1
习仲勋、邓小平同志“爱我中华，修我长城”题词

Fig. 3-1
Inscriptions saying “Love China and Repair the Great Wall” by Xi Zhongxun and Deng Xiaoping

[27] 沈朝阳等：《秦皇岛长城》，方志出版社，2002 年。

In response to the slogan "Love China and Repair the Great Wall", the Shanhaiguan District Government of Qinhuangdao City, Hebei Province planned the conservation and restoration of the Shanhai Pass Great Wall, and successively repaired and restored the Estuary Stone City, the Chenghai Tower, the Ninghai City, the Temple of Lady Meng Jiang and other scenic spots, all of which were to the public. According to statistics, from October 1984 to the end of 1999, Shanhaiguan District spent a total of RMB 49.79 million restoring the Great Wall and received 54 million tourists [27].

The Juyong Pass Great Wall is located in Changping District, Beijing City. From 1993 on, the Office of the Shisanling Special Zone successively invested around RMB 100 million in the conservation and maintenance of the Juyong Pass Great Wall. In 1997, the project was largely completed, achieving repair and restoration of a 4,142 m long wall and 28 structures such as watchtowers, simply structured huts and beacon towers. (Fig. 3-1)

During the 35 years from 1952 to 1985, by using state and local government funds, Jiayu Pass City (formerly administered by Jiuquan County; the city was established in 1965) repaired the Jiayu Pass fort and surrounding Great Wall sections 18 times; restored the gate tower of Jiayu Pass, repaired the walls north and south of the fort, the Mansion of the Youji General, the wellhouse, the Temple of Lord Guan and other ancient architectural structures, repainted the fort, strengthened and repaired the wall, crenels and horse ramps of the fort, and rebuilt the Overhanging (*Xuanbi*) Great Wall.

From 2005 on, the State Council approved and implemented *Overall Work Plan for Great Wall Proctection Projects (2005-2014),* and the central government appropriated cultural heritage conservation related special funds totalling around RMB 1.9 million to implement 218 projects regarding the conservation and maintenance of the walls, watchtowers, beacon towers and other structures of the Great Wall (Fig. 3-2), achieving repair and strengthening of walls totalling a length of 410 km and 1,402 single structures. These projects were distributed in all the 15 provinces (and autonomous regions and municipalities directly under the Central Government City) that the Great Wall passes through, and were associated with the Spring and Autumn and Warring States periods and the Qin, Han, Tang, Liao, Jin and Ming dynasties. Of the total length of the walls repaired, the brick wall sections of the Ming Great Wall repaired accounted for more than 10%.

[27] Shen Zhaoyang et al.: *The Qinhuangdao Great Wall*. Local Chronicles Press, 2002

从1952年至1985年的35年间，嘉峪关市（原酒泉县辖地，1965年设市）利用国家经费和地方政府自筹资金先后对嘉峪关关城和周边长城进行了18次维修，修复了嘉峪关城楼、修缮了关城南北两翼长城、游击将军府、井亭、关帝庙等古建筑，重新油漆彩绘了关城古建筑，加固维修了关城城墙、垛口、马道，重修了悬壁长城。

2005年以来，国务院批准实施了《长城保护工程（2005—2014年）总体工作方案》，中央财政拨付文物保护专项资金约19亿元，组织开展了长城墙体、敌楼以及关堡、烽火台等本体保护维修项目218项（图3-2），维修、加固长城墙体410千米、单体建筑1402处，工程范围覆盖了长城资源分布的全部15个省（自治区、直辖市），涉及春秋战国、秦、汉、唐、辽、金、明等各个时代。其中，明长城砖城墙段落维修工程量超过墙体维修长度的10%。

2006年以来先后实施的山海关、嘉峪关长城保护工程，最大限度地保留了不同时期的重要历史遗存和信息，有效改善了遗产保护状况和环境景观。北京、河北等省市加大了对长城抗战遗址保护力度。此外各地还实施了一批环境整治、遗产监测、展示以及保护性设施建设等工程，消除了一大批突出的安全隐患，一批重要长城点段向社会开放，在推动地方经济社会发展中发挥了独特的作用。

与此同时，近10年来，长城保护工程措施和形式逐渐呈多样化、综合性的特点。除本体保护工程之外，各地还开展了一批载体保护、防洪工程、安防工程、消防工程、围栏工程、环境整治、遗产监测等项目，有效改善了遗产保护状况和环境景观。

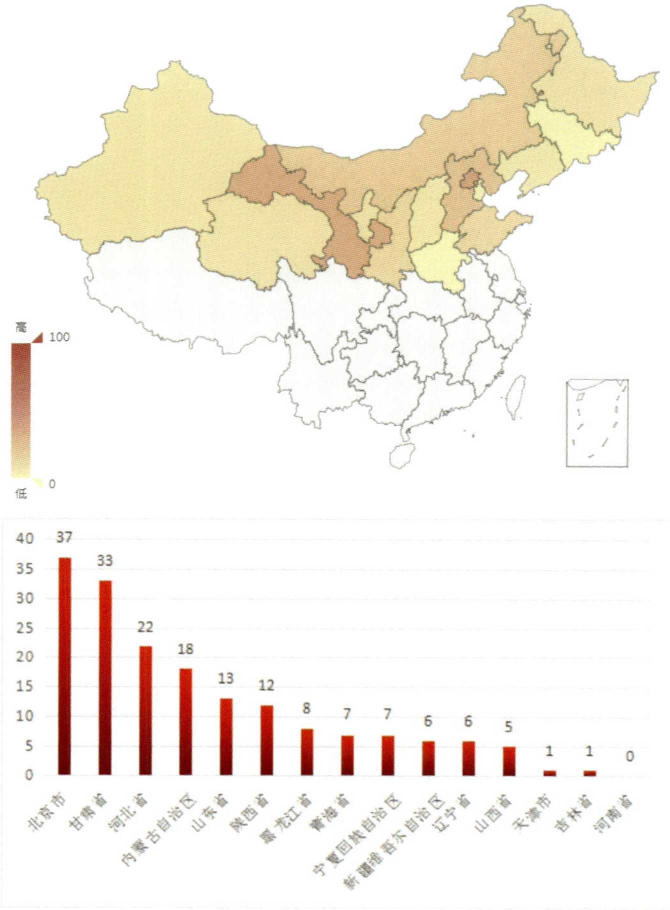


图 3-2
2006 年以来长城保护维修工程数量分省统计图

Fig. 3-2
Numbers of Great Wall Conservation and maintenance projects in each province since 2006

Shanhai Pass and Jiayu Pass Great Wall Conservation Projects implemented successively from 2006 on helped maximally conserve important historical heritage objects from different periods and their information, and helped effectively improve heritage conservation and environmental landscapes. Beijing, Hebei and other provinces and municipalities strengthened the conservation of Great Wall sites associated with the War of Resistance against Japan. In addition, a number of projects regarding environmental improvement, heritage monitoring and presentation, protective structure construction or other aspects were implemented across China, helping eliminate a large number of potential safety hazards; a number of important Great Wall sites and sections were opened to the public, helping promote local economic and social development.

Meanwhile, in the past nearly 10 years, measures used in and forms of Great Wall Conservation Projects gradually became diverse and comprehensive. Besides projects regarding the conservation of the Great Wall itself, a number of projects regarding the conservation of Great Wall supports, flood control, security, fire control, fencing, environmental improvement, heritage monitoring and other aspects were implemented across China, effectively improving heritage conservation and environmental landscapes.

## 第二节 长城保护维修组织管理

※ 实施程序——工程立项、勘察设计、技术审核、工程实施、竣工验收
根据长城文物保护单位的级别，依法履行相关审批手续

※ 过程监管——立项、勘察设计方案方面加强专业审核
保护工程实施过程中持续的巡视和检查
保护工程竣工后组织开展竣工验收

### 一、保护维修工作流程

我国已经建立起较为完善的文物保护工程管理相关制度和标准规范体系。尤其近几年，国家文物局出台了一系列文物保护工程实施的规范性文件。《文物保护工程勘察设计深度要求》（办保函〔2013〕375 号）《文物保护工程勘察设计资质管理办法（试行）》（文物保发〔2014〕13 号）《文物保护工程施工资质管理办法（试行）》（文物保发〔2014〕13 号）《文物保护工程监理资质管理办法（试行）》（文物保发〔2014〕13 号）《全国重点文物保护单位文物保护工程申报审批管理办法》（文物保函〔2014〕64 号）《全国重点文物保护单位文物保护工程检查管理办法（试行）》（文物保发〔2016〕26 号）《全国重点文物保护单位文

# Section 2 Organization and Management of Great Wall conservation and maintenance

- Implementation procedures—project initiation, survey and design, technical review, project implementation, and acceptance upon completion
  Legal examining and approving formalities based on the level of the Great Wall conservation entity
- Process supervision—strengthened professional review of project initiation and survey and design plans
  Continuous inspection and examination during conservation project implementation
  Acceptance upon completion after completion of a conservation project

## I. Conservation and maintenance workflow

China has established a rather complete cultural heritage conservation project management system and relevant standards. In particular, in recent years, the State Administration of Cultural Heritage has issued a series of cultural heritage conservation project implementation standards, such as *In-Depth Requirements for the Survey and Design of Cultural Heritage Conservation Projects* (B.B.H [2013] No. 375), *Measures for the Administration of Qualifications to Survey and Design Cultural Heritage Conservation Projects (Trial)* (W.W.B.F. [2014] No. 13), *Measures for the Administration of Qualifications to Construct Cultural Heritage Conservation Projects (Trial)* (W.W.B.F. [2014] No. 13), *Measures for the Administration of Qualifications to Supervise Cultural Heritage Conservation Projects (Trial)* (W.W.B.F. [2014] No. 13), *Measures for the Administration of Application and Approval of Cultural Heritage Conservation Projects Regarding Major Historical and Cultural Sites Protected at the National Level* (W.W.B.F. [2014] No. 64), *Measures for the Administration of Inspection of Cultural Heritage Conservation Projects Regarding Major Historical and Cultural Sites Protected at the National Level (Trial)* (W.W.B.F. [2016] No. 26), and *Interim Measures for the Management of Acceptance of Completed Cultural Heritage Conservation Projects Regarding Major Historical and Cultural Sites Protected at the National Level* (W.W.B.F. [2016] No. 343). These relevant systems and

物保护工程竣工验收管理暂行办法》（文物保函〔2016〕343 号）等。这些相关制度和标准规范对文物保护工程的各环节都做出了具体、有针对性的规定。近期，针对部分省（自治区、直辖市）的部分文物保护工程项目不同程度地存在国家重点文物保护专项补助资金结转结余的问题，国家文物局还印发了《关于进一步规范国家重点文物保护专项补助资金管理、提高使用绩效的通知》（文物办发〔2017〕5 号），提出了进一步规范文物保护项目资金管理，提高资金使用规范性、安全性、有效性的相关要求。

根据上述文件的规定，长城保护维修工程在实施过程中经过工程立项、勘察设计、工程实施和监理、竣工验收等环节。工程立项方案、勘查设计方案、工程实施方案等，根据文物保护单位级别和工程性质，依法履行审批手续。在勘察设计阶段，为保证工程能够客观反映长城的历史信息，需要专业机构进行必要的前期专项调查、考古勘探，明确相关点段的结构、形制、材料及病害情况。长城保护维修工程的具体实施由具体承担相关点段管理职责的地方文物行政部门负责组织实施和监督管理。根据《中华人民共和国招投标法》及各地相关规定，长城保护维修工程经费如达到一定的额度，需要经过公开招标的方式确定施工单位和监理单位。工程施工过程中，由具有相应资质的第三方专业机构进行监理，全程监督工程实施，确保施工单位严格按照批复同意的设计方案实施工程；工程完工 1 年以后、1 年 3 个月之内，由地方文物行政部门对工程的质量和效果进行初验并报原审批单位进行竣工验收。

长城是我国重要的跨区域、超大型线性文化遗产，我国已经组织实施了山海关、嘉峪关等一大批长城保护维修项目，取得了重要的阶段性成果。在此工作基础上，考虑到长城保护的重要性和特殊性，为进一步规范长城保护维修工程立项、勘察设计、施工及验收等相关工作，国家文物局制定了《长城保护维修工作指导意见》。针对长城保护维修过程中存在的问题，从保护维修的原则、工程立项、前期勘察与评估、设计方案编制、工程技术措施等方面做出了详细的规定。

standards provide specific, pertinent rules for every steps involved in cultural heritage conservation projects. Recently, to address carry-overs and balances of cultural heritage conservation subsidies for major historical and cultural sites protected at the national level incurred from some cultural heritage conservation projects in some provinces (and autonomous regions and municipalities directly under the Central Government), the State Administration of Cultural Heritage issued *Circular on Further Regulating Cultural Heritage Conservation Subsidies for Major Historical and Cultural Sites Protected at the National Level and Using Them More Efficiently* (W.W.B.F. [2017] No. 5), requiring that cultural heritage conservation project funds be further regulated and their use be safer and more effective.

As stipulated in the abovementioned documents, a Great Wall conservation and maintenance project is implemented following such steps as project initiation, survey and design, project implementation and supervision, and acceptance upon project completion. The project initiation plan, the survey and design plan, the project implementation plan and the like are examined and approved according to law based on the level of the cultural heritage conservation entity and the nature of the project. Upon survey and design, to ensure that the project retains the historic information of the Great Wall, a professional organ is needed to conduct necessary preliminary special investigation and archaeological exploration to identify the structure and materials of and damage to the site or section. A Great Wall conservation and maintenance project should be implemented and supervised by the local cultural heritage administration responsible for managing the corresponding site or section. In accordance with Law of the People's Republic of China on Tenders and Bids and relevant local regulations, when the funds for a Great Wall conservation and maintenance project reach a certain amount, an open tender is required to choose the construction unit and the supervision unit. A qualified third-party professional organ is needed to supervise the construction of the project to ensure that the construction unit implements the project in strict accordance with the approved design plan; within three months following one year after the completion of the project, the local cultural heritage administration should preliminarily inspect the quality and results of the project and report to the authority that approved the project for acceptance of the completed project.

The Great Wall is an important cross-regional, ultra-large linear cultural heritage object in China. China has implemented an array of Great Wall conservation and maintenance projects such as those regarding Shanhai Pass and Jiayu Pass, making important progress in the current stage of the campaign. Based on this, the State Administration of Cultural Heritage, in view of the

针对 2016 年出现的辽宁绥中明长城修缮不当等问题，国家文物局一方面严把长城保护维修工程审批关，对工程立项、方案设计等进行严格审核。对于存在暂不具备实施条件、不符合保护理念和长城保护特点或主要保护措施尚待商榷情况的，从严把关，慎重决策；另一方面，组织中国文化遗产研究院开展了《长城保护维修工程施工相关技术规范前期研究》，通过对我国部分长城维修工程现场进行深入调查与保护研究工作，梳理了近十年来的长城保护工作，分析了其中的经验与不足，为长城保护制定相关标准规范提供了充分的依据，并提出了前期、中期、远期工作计划。为国家文物局开展长城保护技术相关标准规范编制工作提供了重要基础支撑。

## 二、保护维修工程管理

近年来，国家文物局还加大了对长城保护工程的“事中、事后”管理力度。国家文物局委托中国文化遗产研究院，组织专家开展长城保护维修工程工地巡视、检查，近年来累计实施工地检查 15 次，检查长城保护维修工程 70 余项，对工程实施过程给予技术指导，及时发现并解决工程存在的各类问题，推动长城保护维修工程实施水平提升。同时，国家文物局还委托中国文物信息咨询中心，对部分省（自治区、直辖市）实施完成并提出验收申请的长城保护维修工程开展竣工验收工作。全过程监管力度的不断加强，确保了山海关、嘉峪关长城保护维修工程等一批长城重大文物保护工程的质量和实施效果。从实地检查情况来看，各地实施长城保护维修工程的工作程序、技术措施、实施管理等方面，总体上较好地遵循了相关规章制度的规定和标准规范的要求，长城保护维修各项工程的总体实施情况较好，消除了一大批长城重要点段的安全隐患。

importance and particularity of Great Wall conservation and in order to further regulate project initiation, survey and design, construction, acceptance and other work related to Great Wall conservation and maintenance projects, formulated *Guidance on Conservation and Maintenance Work of the Great WallConservation and maintenance,* which covers conservation and maintenance principles, project initiation, preliminary investigation and appraisal, design plan devising, technical methods and other aspects.

To address improper repair of the Ming Great Wall in Suizhong, Liaoning in 2016 and other problems, the State Administration of Cultural Heritage, on the one hand, was strict in approving Great Wall conservation and maintenance projects, approving project initiation, plans and others, and was cautious of approving those projects that were temporarily unfeasible, were against the conservation philosophy and the particularity of Great Wall conservation or involved disputable conservation measures; and, on the other hand, let the Chinese Academy of Cultural Heritage conduct *Preliminary Studies of Technical Specifications Regarding the Construction of Great Wall Conservation and maintenance Projects,* which review Great Wall conservation efforts in the past nearly 10 years through in-depth investigation of the sites of some Great Wall repair projects across China and conservation studies, analyze the experiences and deficiencies involved, providing sufficient basis for preparing Great Wall conservation related standards, and propose preliminary, medium-term and long-term working plans, thus effectively supporting the State Administration of Cultural Heritage to prepare Great Wall conservation technology related standards.

## II. Management of conservation and maintenance projects

In recent years, the State Administration of Cultural Heritage has also strengthened management during and after Great Wall Conservation Projects. Commissioned by the State Administration of Cultural Heritage, the Chinese Academy of Cultural Heritage organized experts to inspect the construction sites of Great Wall conservation and maintenance projects. In recent years, they have inspected construction sites 15 times, inspected 70 odd Great Wall conservation and maintenance projects, provided technical guidance and solved problems during the implementation of projects, helping improve the implementation of Great Wall conservation and maintenance projects. Meanwhile, the State Administration of Cultural Heritage commissioned China Cultural Heritage Information and Consulting Centre to accept completed Great Wall conservation and maintenance projects in some provinces (autonomous regions and municipalities directly under the Central Government). With increasingly strengthened whole-process

河北省秦皇岛市山海关区山海关长城保护维修工程实施过程中，河北省人民政府在工程立项之初，就成立了协调推进领导小组，负责专门协调处理维修方案审批、专项资金落实等具体工作。河北省文物局对设计、施工、监理的每个环节严格把关，督导检查；组织专家对山海关关城城墙施工图设计进行了评审，并严格按照相关法律法规的规定，委托招标代理单位，面向全国具有文物保护工程施工一级资质的施工单位开展公开招标，监理单位和大宗材料的采购也根据国家相关程序通过招标确定。河北省纪检监察部门则对工程全过程进行了跟踪监督。在工程建设过程中，现场项目部、监理单位和质量监督站多次组织对“隐蔽性工程”的内检，发现问题，并及时通知施工单位进行整改。河北省文物局还邀请北京市文物建筑质量监督站，对山海关古城墙保护工程进行质量监督，定期进行质量巡检，责成监理单位坚持现场旁站，全面巡视，确保工程质量和安全。随着工程进展，国家文物局有关领导多次视察工地，并组织国内文物建筑、考古、工程地质、长城研究等方面有关专家进行巡视检查和业务指导，并陆续对一些工程进行了阶段性检查和验收。

## 三、建设项目工程管理

近年来，涉及长城保护范围或建设控制地带范围的大型基础设施建设或其他建筑、设施建设工程项目（以下简称“长城涉建项目”）管理进一步规范。根据中国文化遗产研究院2012年开展的《长城保护管理专题调研报告》[28]的统计数据显示，2000-2011年间，国家文物局审批长城相关方案222项，其中长城涉建项目达到132项，占全部项目的近60%。值得注意的是，2006年之前，审批长城涉建项目仅21项，而2006年至2011年间，长城涉建项目项目数量激增109项。（表3-1）

---

[28] 李大伟：《长城保护管理专题调研报告》，内部资料。

supervision, the quality and implementation of a number of major Great Wall cultural heritage conservation projects, such as those regarding the Shanhai Pass and Jiayu Pass Great Walls, were secured. As seen from site inspections, Great Wall conservation and maintenance projects across China were largely properly implemented by properly following relevant rules, regulations and standards in terms of working procedures, technical methods and management, eliminating the potential safety hazards to a large number of major Great Wall sections.

During the implementation of the conservation and maintenance project regarding the Shanhai Pass Great Wall in Shanhaiguan District, Qinhuangdao City, Hebei Province, Hebei Provincial People's Government, as early as upon project initiation, established a leading group for coordination and acceleration to coordinate and handle repair plan approval, reception of special funds and other specific work. Hebei Provincial Administration of Cultural Heritage directed design, construction and supervision, organized experts to review the design of the construction drawing of the city wall of the Shanhai Pass fort, and commissioned a tendering agency to invite construction units across China having Class A qualifications for cultural heritage conservation project construction to bid in strict accordance with relevant laws and regulations; the choice of the supervision unit and the procurement of bulk materials were also done through public bidding. Hebei's provincial discipline supervision and inspection department tracked and supervised the project. During project construction, the on-site project department, the supervision unit and the quality supervision station frequently organized the internal inspection of "hidden subprojects" and promptly instructed the construction unit to solve the problems found. Hebei Provincial Administration of Cultural Heritage also invited Beijing Municipal Heritage Building Quality Supervision Station to supervise the quality of the Shanhai Pass city wall conservation project and inspect its quality regularly, and instructed the supervision unit to stand by on site, so as to ensure project quality and safety. With the progress of the project, leaders from the State Administration of Cultural Heritage inspected the construction site many times and organized Chinese experts in heritage buildings, archaeology, engineering geology, Great Wall studies and other aspects to inspect and direct the project and successively inspect and accept some subprojects.

## III. Management of construction projects

In recent years, the management of large infrastructure construction or other building or facility construction projects within Great Wall conservation boundaries or buffer zones (hereinafter referred to as "construction projects within Great Wall conservation boundaries or buffer zones") has been further regulated.

**表 3-1：2000—2011 年长城保护方案审批类型数量一览表**

Table 3-1: Types and numbers of Great Wall conservation schemes approved during 2000-2011

| 项目类型<br>Project type | 2000 | 2001 | 2003 | 2004 | 2005 | 2006 | 2007 | 2008 | 2009 | 2010 | 2011 | 合计<br>Total |
|---|---|---|---|---|---|---|---|---|---|---|---|---|
| 涉及长城本体的建设工程<br>Construction projects involving the Great Wall itself | 0 | 1 | 3 | 7 | 12 | 10 | 15 | 14 | 12 | 33 | 25 | 132 |
| 长城本体保护与环境整治工程<br>Projects regarding the conservation of the Great Wall itself and its environmental improvement | 4 | 1 | 0 | 7 | 4 | 3 | 12 | 9 | 8 | 11 | 31 | 90 |
| 合计<br>Total | 4 | 2 | 3 | 14 | 16 | 13 | 27 | 23 | 20 | 44 | 56 | 222 |

这一情况的出现，主要受到 2006 年颁布的《长城保护条例》的影响。《条例》第十二条明文规定：“任何单位或者个人不得在长城保护总体规划禁止工程建设的保护范围内进行工程建设……进行工程建设应当绕过长城。无法绕过的，应当采取挖掘地下通道的方式通过长城；无法挖掘地下通道的，应当采取架设桥梁的方式通过长城。任何单位或者个人进行工程建设，不得拆除、穿越、迁移长城。”

进入 90 年代之后，各类建设活动与长城保护的矛盾开始显现。特别是一些如公路、铁路和输油管道等大型基础设施建设项目频繁穿越长城。由于 2006 年之前没有相应的法律条款加以约束，这些工程出于节约成本的考虑，往往忽视长城保护的需要，采取直接在长城上开豁口的方式进行，对长城造成了直接破坏。2006 年《长城保护条例》颁布之后，通过不断加强宣传和管理力度，加大对违法案件的执法力度，使得长城涉建项目相关单位的长城保护意识显著提升，项目报审数量显著增长。与此同时，长城涉建项目均按照《条例》要选择挖掘地下通道或采取架设桥梁的方式通过长城，直接穿过、破坏长城的现象已经基本杜绝。

According to *Report of Investigation of the Great Wall Conservation Management* [28] developed by the Chinese Academy of Cultural Heritage in 2012, during 2000-2011, the State Administration of Cultural Heritage approved 222 Great Wall related schemes, including 132 construction projects within Great Wall conservation boundaries or buffer zones, accounting for nearly 60% of all the projects. It is worth noting that before 2006, only 21 construction projects within Great Wall conservation boundaries or buffer zones were approved, while during 2006-2011, 109 construction projects within Great Wall conservation boundaries or buffer zones were approved, marking a sharp increase. (Table 3-1)

This occurred primarily due to the promulgation of *Regulation on the Conservation of Great Wall* in 2006. Article 12 of the *Regulations* says: "No entity or individual is allowed to construct projects within the conservation boundaries defined in the Master plan of Great Wall conservation within which project construction is prohibited... Projects to be constructed should bypass the Great Wall; if impossible, a passage underneath the Great Wall should be dug to cross the Great Wall; if it is impossible to dig a passage underneath the Great Wall, a bridge should be built to cross the Great Wall. No entity or individual, upon project construction, should demolish, pass the project through or move the Great Wall."

From the 1990s on, the construction of projects began to conflict with Great Wall conservation. In particular, some highways, railways, oil pipelines and other large infrastructure construction projects frequently crossed the Great Wall. As no legal provisions were in place before 2006 to prohibit this, these projects, in view of cost effectiveness, were usually constructed by neglecting Great Wall conservation and digging holes in the Great Wall, causing direct damage to the Great Wall. After the promulgation of *Regulation on the Conservation of Great Wall* in 2006, by raising public awareness, strengthening management and further cracking down on illegal activities, the Great Wall conservation awareness of the entities associated with construction projects within Great Wall conservation boundaries or buffer zones was remarkably improved, and the number of projects reported for approval markedly increased. Meanwhile, all construction projects within Great Wall conservation boundaries or buffer zones cross the Great Wall by digging underground passages or building bridges in accordance with the Regulations, and largely there is no project directly crossing and causing damage to the Great Wall.

[28] Li Dawei: *Report of Investigation of Great Wall Conservation Management*, unpublished data.

# 第三节 长城保护维修理念共识

- 施工原则——不改变原状、最小干预、使用恰当的保护技术
- 技术需求——针对不同材质、保存状况和病害采取相应的措施
- 技术方法——现状保护、抢险加固为主；“局部加固”“重点修复”
  “古建修缮”和“遗址保护”的不同思路
  本体保护、环境整治、灾害预防的综合考虑
  针对土遗址、石砌、包砖建筑采用不同的技术手段

## 一、保护维修原则

长城是一个由多种设施共同构成的防御体系，这些遗存多位于山地、河谷、荒漠、草原等自然条件严酷之处，管理、维修的难度大、成本高。更为重要的是，长城是千百年来，自然侵蚀、人为因素共同作用形成的以遗址形态为主、文化景观特征突出的遗产。对这种类型遗产的保护，要尊重长城的保存现状，不可能进行全线修复或复原，也不宜全面开放进行参观游览，以避免对长城遗产的真实性和完整性造成破坏。

这就需要在实施长城保护工程的实施过程中做到因地制宜，坚持科学的原则和理念。通过多年的保护维修实践，长城保护维修理念的社会共识已经逐渐形成。长城保护要遵循文物保护原则和文物管理工

## Section 3 Great Wall Conservation and Maintenance Philosophy and Consensus

- Construction principles—retaining historic condition, minimal intervention, and use of appropriate conservation technology
- Technical needs—corresponding measures for different materials, states of preservation and damage
- Technical methods—primarily conservation on an as-is basis and emergency strengthening; "partial strengthening" and "major restoration"

  Different ideas for "traditional architecture repair" and "archaeological site conservation"

  Comprehensive consideration of the conservation of the Great Wall itself, environmental improvement and disaster prevention

  Different technical methods for earthen archaeological sites and stone and brick enclosed structures

### I. Conservation and maintenance principles

The Great Wall is a defence system consisting of various kinds of facilities. Most of these remains are located on mountains or grasslands, or in valleys, deserts or other natural harsh areas, making management and repair very difficult and costly. More importantly, the Great Wall is a cultural heritage object exposed to natural erosion and man-made damage in centuries and appearing primarily as archaeological sites and markedly as cultural landscapes. Therefore, the Great Wall should be conserved by respecting its current state of preservation, and should not be fully restored and opened to tourists, so as to avoid damage to the authenticity and integrity of the Great Wall.

This requires adjusting measures to local conditions and adhering to scientific principles and philosophies in implementing Great Wall Conservation Projects. Through many years of conservation and maintenance efforts, a social

作程序，应当始终坚持“不改变原状”“最小干预”和“使用恰当的保护技术”。[29] 2014年国家文物局下发的《长城保护维修工作指导意见》（以下简称《意见》），对这些保护原则、理念和做法在长城保护维修工程方面的具体要求进行了细化，提出了比较有针对性的明确要求。

《意见》指出，长城保护维修工程技术措施应以消除威胁长城结构安全隐患为主要目标，保证长城结构稳定，保护长城遗存的真实性、完整性和延续性，并应具备必要性、可行性和可操作性。

首先，对于地面仍存有建筑的长城段落，严格遵循不改变文物原状和最小干预的原则进行维修加固，严格保持其原形制、原结构，保证长城结构安全，最大限度保存历史信息，妥善保护长城沧桑古朴的历史环境风貌；

第二，对于历史上地面部分已坍塌或消失的长城遗址，实施遗址原状保护，通过局部整理归安和日常养护避免残损加剧，不在原址重建或进行大规模修复；

第三，对于面临自然灾害威胁的长城段落，加强预警监测，控制安全隐患，必要时可设置有针对性的保护性设施，缓解灾害风险压力，避免自然灾害的直接破坏；

第四，对于价值突出，或与重大历史事件有密切联系，具有展示潜力的长城点段，在严格保护其原形制、原结构的基础上，结合展示服务的需求，可适度进行局部修复展示。

第五，对于经过评估存在结构性病害、可能坍塌消失等重大问题的长城，首先采取物理支护措施进行临时性保护，并由具备资质专业机构制定抢险加固方案，按照“最小干预”的原则，对存在问题的部位进行维修加固，但不得进行形制的修复或复原。

最后，对于大量散布在人烟稀少地区、展示潜力不大的长城，工作重点是做好长城标识说明，加强日常巡查和养护。

---

[29] 国际古迹遗址理事会中国国家委员会：《2015中国文物古迹保护准则》，9-12页。

consensus on the philosophy of Great Wall conservation and maintenance has gradually been achieved. Great Wall conservation should follow cultural heritage conservation principles and cultural heritage management procedures, and should be subject to "retaining historic condition", "minimal intervention" and "use of appropriate conservation technology"[29]. *Guidance on Conservation and Maintenance Work of the Great WallConservation and maintenance* (hereinafter referred to as the *Guidance*) issued by the State Administration of Cultural Heritage in 2014 contain pertinent, specific requirements of these conservation principles, philosophies and measures in Great Wall conservation and maintenance projects.

The *Guidance* points out that Great Wall conservation and maintenance projects related technical methods should primarily be used to eliminate potential hazards threatening the safety of Great Wall structures, secure the stability of Great Wall structures, retain the authenticity, integrity and continuity of Great Wall remains, and should be necessary, feasible and operable.

First, Great Wall sections having structures above ground should be repaired and strengthened by strictly following the principle of retaining the historic condition of the cultural heritage object and minimal intervention, and strictly retaining their original structures, so as to secure the safety of Great Wall structures, maximally retain historic information, and properly preserve the historic and environmental features of the Great Wall;

Second, Great Wall sites with above-ground parts collapsed or disappeared should be conserved as is and further damage should be avoided through partial reinstallation and routine maintenance; there should be no reconstruction on original sites or massive restoration;

Third, for Great Wall sections threatened by natural disasters, prewarning and monitoring should be strengthened, potential safety hazards should be controlled, and pertinent protective structures can be provided when necessary, so as to alleviate risks from disasters and avoid direct damage caused by natural disasters;

Fourth, Great Wall sites and sections having outstanding value or being closely associated with significant historical events and having the potential for presentation can properly be partially restored for presentation on the basis of strict conservation of their original structures and taking into account presentation service needs.

---

[29] ICOMOS China: *Principles for the Conservation of Heritage Sites in China 2015*, pp. 9-12

## 专栏：文物保护维修工作原则阐释[30]

不改变原状：不改变文物原状的原则可以包括保存现状和恢复原状两方面内容。

必须保存现状的对象有：1. 古遗址，特别是尚留有较多人类活动遗迹的地面遗存；2. 文物古迹群体的布局；3. 文物古迹群中不同时期有价值的各个单体；4. 文物古迹中不同时期有价值的各种构件和工艺手法；5. 独立的和附属于建筑的艺术品的现存状态；6. 经过重大自然灾害后遗留下有研究价值的残损状态；7. 在重大历史事件中被损坏后有纪念价值的残损状态；8. 没有重大变化的历史环境。

可以恢复原状的对象有：1. 坍塌、掩埋、污损、荒芜以前的状态；2. 变形、错置、支撑以前的状态；3. 有实物遗存足以证明原状的少量的缺失部分；4. 虽无实物遗存，但经过科学考证和同期同类实物比较，可以确认原状的少量缺失的和改变过的构件；5. 经鉴别论证，去除后代修缮中无保留价值的部分，恢复到一定历史时期的状态；6. 能够体现文物古迹价值的历史环境。

最小干预：采用的保护措施，应以延续现状，缓解损伤为主要目标。

这种干预应当限制在保证文物古迹安全的限度上，必须避免过度干预造成对文物古迹价值和历史、文化信息的改变。作为历史、文化遗存，文物古迹需要不断的保养、保护。任何保护措施都应为以后的保养、保护留有余地。凡是近期没有重大危险的部分，除日常保养以外不应进行更多的干预。必须干预时，附加的手段应只用在最必要部分。

预防性保护是指通过防护和加固的技术措施和相应的管理措施减少灾害发生的可能、灾害对文物古迹造成损害、以及灾后需要采取的修复措施的强度。

使用恰当的保护技术：指对文物古迹无害，同时能有效解决文物古迹面临的问题，消除潜在威胁，改善文物古迹保存条件的技术。

应当使用经检验有利于文物古迹长期保存的成熟技术，文物古迹原有的技术和材料应当保护。对原有科学的、利于文物古迹长期保护的传统工艺应当传承。所有新材料和工艺都必须经过前期试验，证明切实有效，对文物古迹长期保存无害、无碍，方可使用。所有保护措施不得妨碍再次对文物古迹进行保护，在可能的情况下应当是可逆的。增补和加固的部分应当可以识别，并记入档案。

在具体组织实施长城保护维修工作的过程中，要始终坚持现状保护的总体思路。按照上述保护维修理念共识，在继续做好文物本体抢险加固、消除安全隐患的基础上，根据长城的结构特点、保存现状和结构稳定性情况，针对“古建筑”类长城和“遗址”类长城的不同特点，坚持“局部加固”与“重点修复”相结合的思路，因地制宜、适当地选取长城保护维修的策略和工程技术措施，使长城保护不利的情况尽快得到扭转。

[30] 国际古迹遗址理事会中国国家委员会：《2015中国文物古迹保护准则》，9-12页。

## Explanation of cultural heritage conservation and maintenance principles [30]:

Retaining historic condition: The principle of retaining historic condition involves either preserving existing condition or reinstating historic condition.

The existing condition of the following must be preserved: 1. Archaeological sites and ruins, particularly those with aboveground remnants; 2. the overall design and layout of architectural ensembles within a site; 3. individual components of significance from different periods within architectural ensembles; 4. components and artisan techniques from different periods that have significance for a site; 5. works of art, either independent or associated with a building; 6. damaged remnants of a site resulting from natural disasters, that retain research value; 7. damaged remnants resulting from important historical events, that have acquired commemorative significance; and 8. historic settings that have not undergone major change.

Reinstatement of a site to its historic condition is permitted in the following instances: 1. where collapse, burial, damage, or abandonment has occurred; 2. where deformation, incorrect placement, or bracing has occurred; 3. where there exist sufficient physical remains to reveal the historic condition of a small number of missing parts; 4. where there are no physical remains to reveal the original condition of a small number of missing or altered components, but where after scientific investigation and comparison with components of the same type and period, the original condition can be determined; 5. where, following appraisal, parts of a site that do not have historical value because of later interventions are removed so that the site can be returned to its historic condition at a specified period in the past; and 6. if reinstatement enables the historic setting to reveal the values of the site.

Minimal intervention: The main goals of conservation and management measures are to preserve a site's existing condition and to slow deterioration.

Intervention should be restricted to the minimum required to ensure conservation. Excessive interventions must be avoided as these may affect the values of a site as well as its historic and cultural information. A heritage site needs continuous maintenance and conservation. Conservation measures should not compromise future treatment. Apart from routine maintenance, there should be no intervention on parts of a building or site that are not at imminent risk of damage. When intervention is required it should be applied where it is most needed.

Preventive conservation is the use of technical measures such as physical conservation and strengthening, as well as management measures, to diminish the possibility of damage from disasters or reduce the amount of repair needed should a disaster occur.

Use of appropriate conservation technology: Appropriate conservation technology is one that will not damage or be detrimental to a site, while providing an effective solution to problems, preventing potential threats, and improving the state of preservation.

Technology that is tried and proven and is beneficial to the long-term preservation of a site should be used. Evidence of original technology and historic materials should be conserved. Traditional craftsmanship that contributes to the site's long-term preservation should be maintained. New materials and techniques may only be used after they have been tested and proven effective, and should not be detrimental or cause long-term damage. Conservation measures should not preclude future interventions and should be reversible when conditions permit. All added and strengthened components should be distinguishable and must be documented in the site's archives.

[30] ICOMOS China: *Principles for the Conservation of Heritage Sites in China 2015*, pp. 9-12

图 3-3
包砖长城病害举例——风化剥落、风蚀凹进、地基沉降（左：张依萌 拍摄；右：河北省文物局 提供）

Fig. 3-3
Instances of damage to brick enclosed Great Wall sections—weathering-caused peeling off, wind erosion-caused denting, and settlement of foundation (left: photo by Zhang Yimeng; right: provided by Hebei Provincial Administration of Cultural Heritage)

## 二、维修技术要求

### （一）破坏影响因素与病害

长城的破坏影响因素包括自然和人为两类。自然因素包括风、水、生物、地质环境等，具体表现在风沙侵蚀、降雨或洪水冲刷、冰雪冻融、动物筑巢或踩踏、植物根系生长或苔藓滋生、泥石流、地震等地质灾害；人为因素包括刻画、攀爬踩踏、耕种、取土、私拆长城砖石、在长城本体上掏窑洞或私搭乱建、开矿、基础设施建设破坏等等。（图 3-3、3-4、3-5）

受上述因素影响导致的长城病害包括：

1、结构稳定性病害。包括裂隙发育、坍塌、地基不均匀下沉、整体倾斜、滑坡等；

2、水病害。包括夯土软化、基础酥碱、本体水冲沟等；

3、风化病害。主要表现为墙体结构缺失、表面凹进、墙体外皮砖石酥碱剥落、夯土膨胀脱落等。

材质与病害的多样性，是长城保护工程技术需要重点解决的问题，对长城保护技术的使用也提出了更高的要求。这就要求在开展长城保护维修的时候，就必须根据实际情况，有针对性的采取科学合理的工程技术方法。

Fifth, for Great Wall sections which, after assessment, are found to have structural damage and may collapse and disappear or have other major problems, physical supporting measures should be taken first for temporary conservation, and qualified professional organs should develop emergency strengthening schemes to repair and strengthen the weak parts with "minimal intervention" and without structural restoration.

Finally, for those many Great Wall sections located in sparsely populated areas having little potential for presentation, the key work is to properly provide Great Wall signs and strengthen routine inspection and maintenance.

When organizing the implementation of Great Wall conservation and maintenance work, should adhered to the overall idea of conservation on an as-is basis, continued to properly conduct emergency strengthening of cultural heritage objects and eliminate potential safety hazards in accordance with the above-mentioned conservation and maintenance philosophy and consensus, adhered to the idea of "partial strengthening" and "major restoration" based on the structural characteristics, existing conditions of conservation and structural stability of the Great Wall and the different characteristics of Great Wall sections appearing as "ancient architectural structures" and those appearing as "archaeological sites", and adjusted Great Wall conservation and maintenance strategies and engineering and technical methods to local conditions, thus reversing the unfavourable situation of Great Wall conservation.

图 3-4
石砌长城病害举例——酥碱坍塌、植物侵害
（李大伟 拍摄）

Fig. 3-4
Instances of damage to stone Great Wall sections—efflorescence and collapse, damage caused by plants (photo by Li Dawei)

图 3-5
土筑长城病害举例——裂隙发育、风力掏蚀
（陕西省文物局 提供）

Fig. 3-5
Instances of damage to earthen Great Wall—fracture development, undercutting by wind (provided by Shaanxi Provincial Administration of Cultural Heritage)

考虑到自然环境与长城保护关系密切。国家文物局要求长城保护维修应与环境治理相结合。在开展本体保护维修工作中，应对影响将要实施保护维修的长城本体或载体安全的地质、水文等环境因素进行勘察、评估，并依据现状勘察评估结果，开展专项工程设计，优先解决直接影响长城安全的重大环境影响问题。

（二）保护维修技术方法

由于地域和功能限制，长城的建造采取因地制宜就地取材的做法，反映了各地不同时期的建造工艺和水平，就材料而言，有土（夯土、土坯、垡子等）、砖（青砖）、石（条石、片石、块石）、植物（红柳、胡杨、梭梭木、芦苇夹土、砂）等不同材质。就建筑工艺而言，有砌筑、夯筑、坯筑、堆筑、混筑、干垒、挖掘等方式。不同的破坏影响因素对不同材质长城造成的影响各异，导致的病害也不同。这就要求在开展长城保护维修的时候，就必须根据实际情况，有针对性的采取科学合理的工程技术方法。

我国强调长城保护维修必须保持长城的原形制、原结构，优先使用原材料、原工艺。只有传统工艺作法无法达到长城本体安全的技术要求时，才可考虑采用新技术和新材料，且必须在设计方案编制阶段完成室内实验和现场试验，实（试）验结论及评价报告应随保护维修工程设计方案上报并经审批后方能实施。

针对长城的不同影响因素和病害，要采用相应的技术手段进行保护。通过多年的实践，已经总结出了一些较常用的长城保护工程技术方法。如：针对动物和游人的踩踏，可以在长城本体外一定距离加装围栏进行隔离；针对植物侵害，可以进行植被修剪、清除或限制生长；针对裂隙发育，可以采取外部支护、内部灌浆或打锚杆的方式进行加固；针对坍塌、结构缺失的情况，土遗址可以用土坯或夯土补筑，砖石结构可以将散落的建筑材料按照原状进行归安和补砌；表面凹进，可以进行补砌或局部替换等等。

这些方法在具体工程实施过程中，需要具体分析，进行灵活运用。如陕西省的明长城建安堡保护加固工程，在对遗址顶部和四面生长根系发达的植被进行清理时，清除墙体上根系发达的灌

## II. Technical requirements for maintenance

### (I) Destructive impacts and damage

Destructive impacts on the Great Wall include natural and man-made ones. Natural destructive impacts include wind, water, organisms, geological environment and others, specifically such as wind and sand erosion, rainfall or flood erosion, ice and snow freezing and thawing, animal nesting or treading, plant root or moss growth, debris flow, earthquakes and other geological disasters; man-made destructive impacts include scrawling, climbing and treading, tilling, earth cutting, removing bricks or stones from the Great Wall without permission, digging cave dwellings into the Great Wall or constructing buildings on the Great Wall without permission, mining, damage caused by infrastructure construction and others. (Figs. 3-3, 3-4, 3-5)

Damage to the Great Wall caused by the above-mentioned impacts include:

1. Damage to structural stability, including fracture development, collapse, uneven settlement of foundation, overall leaning, landslides and others;

2. Damage by water, including rammed earth softening, foundation efflorescence, gullies in the Great Wall and others;

3. Damage by weathering, primarily appearing as absences of wall structures, surface denting, efflorescence and coming off of wall enclosing bricks or stones, swelling and coming off of rammed earth and others;

The diversity of materials and damage is a key technical issue to be addressed in Great Wall Conservation Projects, and poses higher requirements for the use of Great Wall conservation technology. This requires the use of pertinent scientific and reasonable engineering and technical methods upon Great Wall conservation and maintenance.

In view of the close relationship between the natural environment and Great Wall conservation, the State Administration of Cultural Heritage requires that Great Wall conservation and maintenance be integrated with environmental governance. Upon conservation and maintenance of the Great Wall itself, geological, hydrology and other environmental factors that affect the safety of the Great Wall section or its support to be conserved and repaired should be investigated and assessed, special engineering design should be conducted based on the results of the investigation and assessment of the existing condition to first address major environmental effects directly affecting the safety of the Great Wall.

### (II) Conservation and maintenance related technical methods

Due to regional and functional restrictions, the Great Wall was built using

图 3-6
建安堡墙体植被清理（陕西省文物局 提供）

Fig. 3-6
Removal of vegetation from the wall of Jian'anbao (photo by Shaanxi Provincial Administration of Cultural Heritage)

木及乔木，对于根系短小的植被则予以保留，一方面能防止雨蚀风蚀引起墙体顶面的水土流失，避免对墙体的二次破坏，起到一定的保护作用，另一方面又能保持建安堡沧桑古朴的风貌。

该工程还对夯土墙体进行了局部的原工艺补夯，对原先在夯土墙体上掏挖的窑洞进行了支护和土坯回填，对城门洞内缺失的表面砖进行补砌，对风蚀凹进严重的条石基础进行了替换。（图3-6、3-7、3-8）

又如宁夏回族自治区的三关口长城、甘肃省敦煌汉长城、新疆维吾尔自治区的吐鲁番、哈密等地烽燧在实施保护工程过程中，

图 3-7
建安堡墙体局部进行原工艺补夯（陕西省文物局 提供）

Fig. 3-7
Additional ramming of part of the wall of Jian'anbao using originally used workmanship (photo by: Shaanxi Provincial Administration of Cultural Heritage)

图 3-8
建安堡城门砖补砌与基础条石替换（陕西省文物局 提供）

Fig. 3-8
Addition of bricks to the city gate of and replacement of boulder strips of the foundation of Jian'anbao (photo by: Shaanxi Provincial Administration of Cultural Heritage)

locally available materials which reflect construction techniques and levels in different periods. The materials include earth (rammed earth, adobe, upturned soil and others), bricks (blue bricks), stones (boulder strips, flagstones and rubbles), plants (rose willows, diversiform-leaved poplars, sacsaoul, reeds clamping earth, and sand) and others. The construction techniques include laying bricks or stones, ramming, building by using adobe, piling, building by using different methods, building by using tamped clay, digging and others. Different destructive impacts differently affected Great Wall sections built of different materials and caused different damage. This requires the use of pertinent scientific and reasonable engineering and technical methods upon Great Wall conservation and maintenance.

China stresses that Great Wall conservation and maintenance must be conducted by retaining the original structure of the Great Wall and maximally using originally used materials and workmanship. Only when traditional workmanship cannot secure the safety of the Great Wall itself can new techniques and materials be considered, and indoor experiments and field tests must be completed during design plan development; experimental (test) conclusions and evaluation reports should be reported to the leadership together with conservation and maintenance project design plans and be implemented only after approval.

Different impacts on and damage to the Great Wall should be addressed using corresponding technical methods. Some commonly used Great Wall conservation related engineering and technical methods have been identified in many years of practice. Here are some examples: to address animal and tourist treading, fencing can be installed some distance from the Great Wall; to address damage by plants, plants can be trimmed or removed, or their growth can be

对夯土长城综合采用了裂隙灌浆、孔洞填补、土坯补砌、顶面防水和加装护栏等技术方法，最大限度排除了长城的安全隐患，并保持了长城的原始风貌。（图 3-9、3-10、3-11、3-12）

另外，北京市怀柔区的河防口长城保护工程等一批新近完成的长城保护工程均坚持了最小干预的原则，同时考虑了长城的可观赏性，修复效果良好。（图 3-13）

图 3-9
陕西明长城建安堡城墙裂隙灌浆

Fig. 3-9
Fracture grouting of the city wall of Jian'anbao of the Ming Great Wall in Shaanxi

图 3-10
宁夏回族自治区永宁县三关口长城墙体孔洞填补与加装围栏前后效果对比（左：宁夏回族自治区长城资源调查队 拍摄；右：张依萌 拍摄）

Fig. 3-10
The Sanguankou Great Wall in Yongning County, Ningxia Hui Autonomous Region: before and after filling of a hole in the wall and fencing (left: photo by the Team for Investigation of Great Wall Resources in Ningxia Hui Autonomous Region; right: photo by Zhang Yimeng)

restricted; to address fracture development, strengthening can be achieved by external supporting, grouting or anchoring; to address collapse and structural absences, an earthen site can be patched using adobe or rammed earth, and scattered building materials can be reinstalled and added as in their historic conditions in the case of a brick or stone structure; and a dented surface can be patched or partially replaced or otherwise.

These methods should be flexibly used through concrete analyses upon project implementation. For example, in the project regarding the conservation and strengthening of the Jian'anbao Ming Great Wall in Shaanxi Province, when removing the plants with developed root systems on the top and four sides of the site, shrubs and arbours with developed root systems on the wall were removed, while plants with short root systems were retained, so that on the one hand soil erosion on the top of the wall and secondary damage to the wall caused by rain and wind erosion can be avoided, and on the other hand, the historic features of Jian'anbao can be retained.

图 3-11
敦煌汉长城烽燧土坯补砌基础（敦煌研究院提供）

Fig. 3-11
Patched adobe built foundation of a beacon tower of the Han Great Wall in Dunhuang (provided by the Dunhuang Academy)

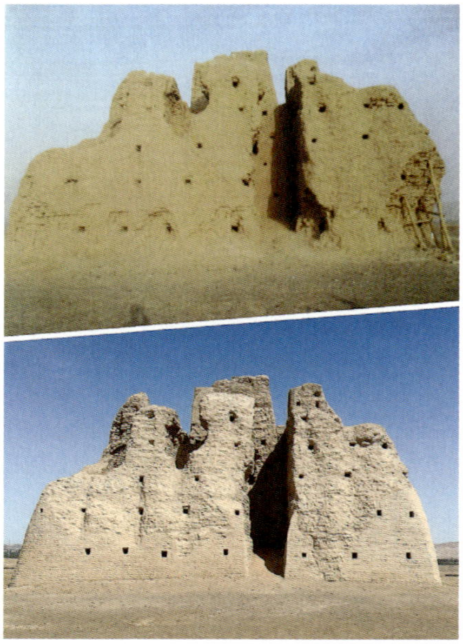

图 3-12
新疆维吾尔自治区吐鲁番烽火台 修缮前后对比（上：新疆维吾尔自治区长城资源调查队 拍摄；下：张依萌 拍摄）

Fig. 3-12
A beacon tower in Turpan, Xinjiang Uygur Autonomous Regions: before and after maintenance (upper: photo by the Team for Investigation of Great Wall Resources in Xinjiang Uygur Autonomous Region; lower: photo by Zhang Yimeng)

图 3-13
北京市怀柔区河防口村东 028 号敌台 修缮前后对比（上：北京市长城资源调查队 拍摄；下：张依萌 拍摄）

Fig. 3-13
Watchtower No. 028 east of Hefangkou Village, Huairou District, Beijing City: before and after maintenance (upper: photo by the Team for Investigation of Great Wall Resources in Beijing City; lower: photo by Zhang Yimeng)

## 专栏：文物保护工程的主要分类

《文物保护工程管理办法》（中华人民共和国文化部令第 26 号）规定：文物保护工程分为：保养维护工程、抢险加固工程、修缮工程、保护性设施建设工程、迁移工程等。

（一）保养维护工程，系指针对文物的轻微损害所做的日常性、季节性的养护。

（二）抢险加固工程，系指文物突发严重危险时，由于时间、技术、经费等条件的限制，不能进行彻底修缮而对文物采取具有可逆性的临时抢险加固措施的工程。

（三）修缮工程，系指为保护文物本体所必需的结构加固处理和维修，包括结合结构加固而进行的局部复原工程。

（四）保护性设施建设工程，系指为保护文物而附加安全防护设施的工程。

（五）迁移工程，系指因保护工作特别需要，并无其他更为有效的手段时所采取的将文物整体或局部搬迁、异地保护的工程。

The project also involved partial additional ramming of the rammed earth built wall using originally used workmanship, supporting and adobe backfilling of the cave dwellings dug into the rammed earth built wall, adding of missing surface bricks into the opening of the city gate, and replacing of weathered, severely dented boulder strips of the foundation. (Figs. 3-6, 3-7 and 3-8)

Also, when the projects regarding the conservation of the Sanguankou Great Wall in Ningxia Hui Autonomous Region, the Han Great Wall in Dunhuang, Gansu Province, and beacon towers in Turpan, Hami and other areas of Xinjiang Uygur Autonomous Region were implemented, fracture grouting, hole filling, adobe adding, roof waterproofing, fencing and other technical methods were comprehensively used on rammed earth built Great Wall sections, maximally eliminating potential safety hazards to the Great Wall and retaining the historic features of the Great Wall. (Figs. 3-9, 3-10, 3-11 and 3-12)

In addition, the project regarding the conservation of the Hefangkou Great Wall in Huairou District, Beijing City and other recently completed Great Wall Conservation Projects followed the principle of minimal intervention and took into account the beauty of the Great Wall, and achieved good restoration results. (Fig. 3-9)

## Main types of cultural heritage conservation projects:

*Measures for the Management of Cultural Heritage Conservation Projects* (Order No. 26 of the Ministry of Culture of the People's Republic of China) says that cultural heritage conservation projects can be classified into maintenance projects, emergency strengthening projects, repair projects, protective structure construction projects, relocation projects and others.

(i) Maintenance projects are projects involving routine and seasonable maintenance in the case of slight damage to cultural heritage.

(ii) Emergency strengthening projects are projects involving the use of reversible temporary emergency strengthening measures when cultural heritage objects are in severe emergences and cannot be completely repaired due to limited time, technology, funds or other restrictions.

(iii) Repair projects are projects involving structural strengthening and repair required for cultural heritage conservation, including partial restoration projects associated with structural strengthening.

(iv) Protective structure construction projects are projects involving the addition of safety conservation structures for cultural heritage conservation.

(v) Relocation projects are projects involving whole or partial relocation and nonlocal conservation of cultural heritage to meet special conservation needs when there are no other measures that are more effective.

【摘要】

成立于2006年的中国文化遗产研究院长城保护研究室是国家级长城专业研究机构；随着“长城保护工程”的开展，公立研究机构、高校长城研究逐渐繁荣，并逐步形成了专业研究团队；民间力量长期深度参与长城研究，也取得大量成果。

17世纪以来，海内外学者已经开始从研究的角度关注长城。300余年来，长城研究在历史、地理、民俗、建筑、考古、志书编纂等领域取得了大量成果。

“长城保护工程”实施以来，长城的历史理论、科技保护等研究工作也取得丰硕成果，长城保护技术、大型遗产管理策略、地理信息技术等研究日益受到重视。国家文物局组织实施长城资源调查相关资料和研究报告的编辑、出版，各省（自治区、直辖市）陆续编辑、出版省级调查报告12部。北京、天津、内蒙古、吉林、山东、河南、陕西、宁夏、新疆等地结合资源调查、规划编制、保护维修等进行长城考古勘探、发掘，并出版相关报告21部。2007年以来，长城建筑与军事聚落研究兴起。空间信息技术于20世纪80年代开始应用于长城保护管理，在“长城保护工程”实施过程中得到了推广，建立了全面、精确的长城资源数据库，并以此为基础开发了“长城资源保护管理信息系统”，为海量长城资源数据的科学、高效和信息化管理，公共信息发布，以及下一步长城世界遗产监测预警平台和预警体系建设奠定了基础。中国科学院利用遥感技术对消失于地表的明长城开展了无损探测研究，成功获取了试点区域明长城空间位置和沿线环境与景观格局的变化信息。以“长城文化创新”项目为代表，一些社会团体与科研机构也对长城保护工作应用数字技术进行了积极探索。

据不完全统计，1936年-2014年间发表的长城相关研究文章38858篇。其中哲学与人文社会科学研究文章8000余篇。绝大多数为基础研究成果，应用型研究成果在“长城保护工程”实施以来明显增加。

# 第四章
# 长城研究与成果展示

## Chapter 4
## The Great Wall Research and Achievements

[Abstract]

The Great Wall Conservation Research Office of Chinese Academy of Cultural Heritage founded in 2006 is a professional national research institution of the Great Wall; with the proceeding "Great Wall conservation Project", public research institutions and collage research on the Great Wall have gradually been flourishing, and professional research teams have been formed; Civil power has participated in the research on the Great Wall for a long time and made a lot of achievements.

Since the 17th century, Chinese and foreign scholars have paid attention to the Great Wall from the perspective of research. During more than 300 years, the research on the Great Wall has made a lot of achievements in the fields of history, geography, folklore, architecture, archeology and compilation of chronicles.

Since the implementation of the Great Wall conservation Project, the researches on the historical theory, science and technology Conservation of the Great Wall have also made fruitful achievements. The researches on the Conservation technology of the Great Wall, the management strategy of large-scale heritages, and geographic information technology have been paid increasing attention. The State Administration of Cultural Heritage organized the compilation and publication of relevant documents and study reports on the resources investigation of the Great Wall. All provinces, (autonomous regions and municipalities directly under the central government) compiled and published 12 provincial-level investigation reports in succession. Beijing, Tianjin, Inner Mongolia, Jilin, Shandong, Henan, Shaanxi, Ningxia, Xinjiang and other places made archaeological exploration and excavation of the Great Wall combined with resource investigation, planning compilation, Conservation and maintenance, and published 21 relevant reports. Since 2007, the study on the architecture and military settlement of the Great Wall got popular. Spatial information technologies began to be applied in the Conservation of the Great Wall since the 1980s', and promoted in the process of the "Great Wall conservation Project". It established a comprehensive and accurate resource database of the Great Wall, and developed the "Great Wall Resources Conservation and Management Information System" based on it, which laid the foundation for the scientific, efficient and information management of massive Great Wall resource data, the release of public information, and the construction the Great Wall world heritage monitoring and warning platform and warning system for the next step. Chinese Academy of Sciences made nondestructive exploration study on the Ming Great Wall which disappeared on the ground by remote sensing technology, and successfully obtained the spatial location of the Ming Great Wall in the pilot area and the information about the changes in the surrounding environment and landscape patterns. Represented by the project of "Great Wall Cultural Innovation", some social groups and scientific research institutions also made active exploration on the application of digital technology in the Conservation of the Great Wall.

According to incomplete statistics, 38,858 research articles related to the Great Wall were published during 1936 – 2014, including more than 8,000 research articles on philosophy and humanities and social science. The vast majority made basic research achievements, and application-based research achievements have been significantly increasing since the implementation of the "Great Wall conservation Project".

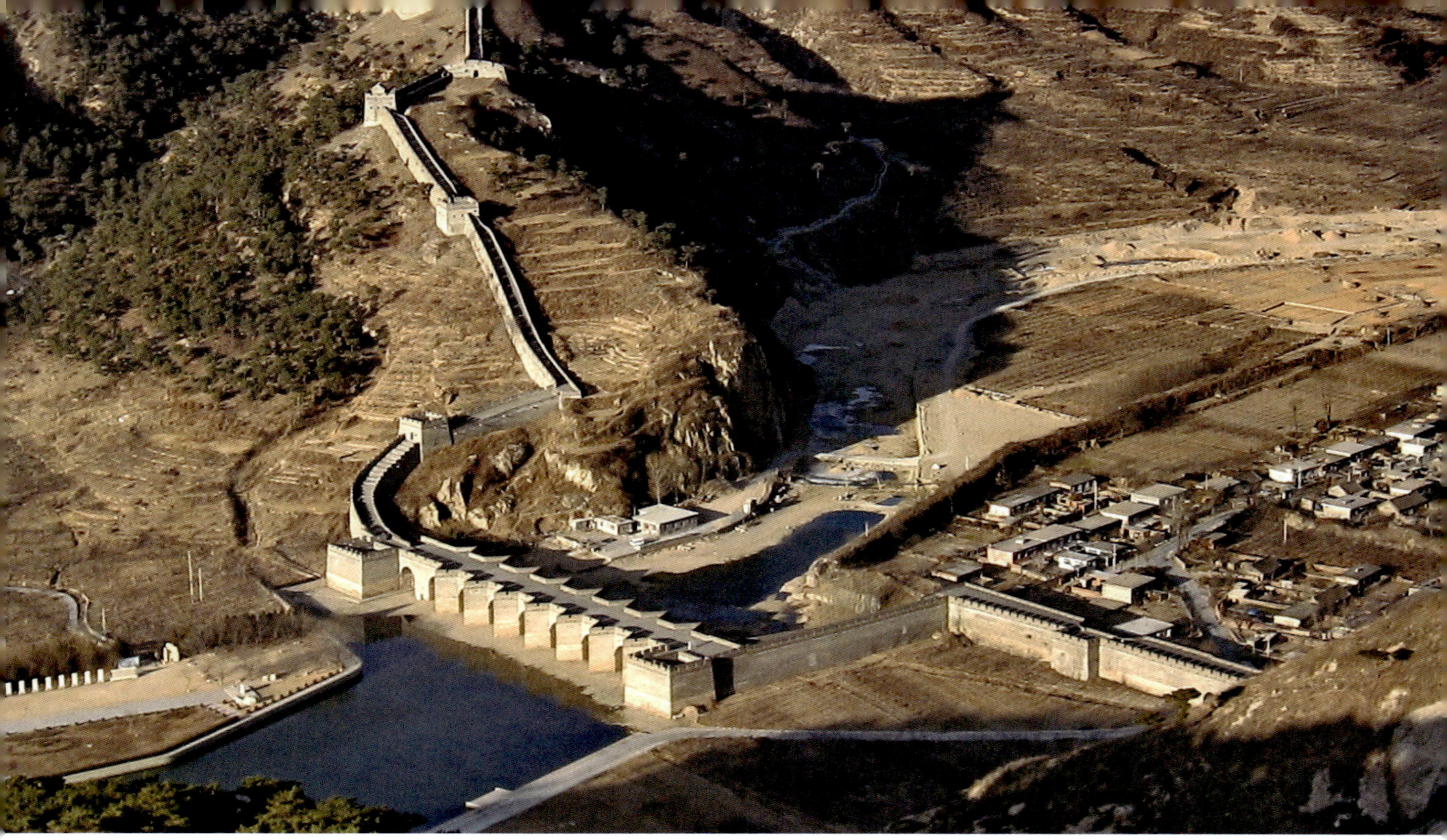

辽宁绥中九门口长城（严欣强 拍摄）

The Great Wall in Jiumenkou, Suizhong, Liaoning (Photo by Yan Xinqiang)

## 第一节 长城研究队伍

※ 专业长城研究机构——“长城保护工程”实施平台、以应用研究为特色

※ 国家级长城数据中心、管理中心、咨询中心

※ 公立科研机构、高校研究团队——发挥专业特长，研究“专”、“精”

※ 社会研究力量——热情高，影响大，参与深，理论指导和专业方法欠缺

### 一、专业长城保护管理研究机构

#### （一）机构设置与职能

中国文化遗产研究院长城保护研究室，原为成立于 2006 年的中国文化遗产研究院“长城保护工程”项目管理小组，2017 年改为现名。（本报告中的所介绍的工作和引用的数据截止 2016 年，根据实际情况，仍称“长城项目组”），是国家级长城保护研究专业机构，负责具体实施长城保护工程相关工作，是长城保护工程实施的国家级平台。

## Section 1 The Great Wall Research Team

- Professional Great Wall research institutions - implementation platform of the "Great Wall Conservation Project" characterized by application-based researches
- National Great Wall data center, management center and consultation center
- Public research institutions and college research teams – take advantage of professional expertise and make "specialized" and "intensive" researches
- Social research force -- high enthusiasm, great influence, deep involvement, in lack of theoretical guidance and professional methods

### I. Professional research institutions on the Great Wall conservation and management

#### (I) Institutional settings and functions

The Great Wall Conservation Research Office of Chinese Academy of Cultural Heritage was the former "Great Wall Conservation Project" project management team of Chinese Academy of Cultural Heritage was established in 2006 and renamed in 2017. (The work and data introduced in this report are all before 2016, so it's still called the "Great Wall Project Team" according to the actual situation) hereafter referred to as the "Great Wall Project Team"). It is a national professional research agency on the Great Wall conservation, responsible for the specific implementation of the Great Wall Conservation Project; moreover, it's a national platform for the implementation of the Great Wall Conservation Project.

In 2006, the State Administration of Cultural Heritage founded the leadership team of the "Great Wall Conservation Project", "responsible to solve the major problems in the process of the Great Wall conservation, decide the

2006年，国家文物局成立了“长城保护工程”领导小组，“负责研究解决长城保护中的重大问题，确定长城保护的指导原则和工作方针，决策有关重大事项”；[31]领导小组下设办公室，“负责组织各有关部门实施长城保护工程，部署各项具体工作，指导和督促落实《总体工作方案》”；[32]办公室在中国文化遗产研究院[33]下设“长城保护工程”项目管理小组，“负责具体实施领导小组办公室部署的‘长城保护工程’的有关工作”。[34]

从那时起，长城项目组即配备具有博士、硕士学历的考古、历史、管理、工程技术等各方面人员。2014年之后，虽然“长城保护工程”已经结束，但国家文物局长城保护管理工作更为繁重，长城项目组开始承担越来越多的长城保护研究工作，目前编制内业务人员4名、长期聘用专业人员1名，共5人组成。

长城项目组依托于院综合科研与技术平台，在国家文物局指导下，先后承担了长城保护工程管理、长城资源调查与认定、长城资源保护管理信息系统建设与平台维护、长城历史文献综合整理、长城保护法律法规与政策研究、长城保护条例专项执法督察、长城世界遗产监测方法研究、长城综合保护与利用研究、长城保护管理专业培训、长城保护管理公众宣传教育、长城研究的国际学术交流等工作，协助国家文物局在全国长城保护管理工作中发挥业务统筹、指导与协调的核心作用，在长城保护研究中取得突出成果，为促进长城保护工作的不断提升发挥了重要作用。

---

[31] 国家文物局：《关于成立“长城保护工程”领导小组和项目管理小组的通知》，文物保函[2006]601号。

[32] 国家文物局：《关于成立“长城保护工程”领导小组和项目管理小组的通知》，文物保函[2006]601号。

[33] 时称中国文物研究所。

[34] 国家文物局：《关于成立“长城保护工程”领导小组和项目管理小组的通知》，文物保函[2006]601号。

guiding principles and work guidelines of the Great Wall conservation, and make decision about major issues" [31]; an office was established under the leadership team, "responsible to organize the relevant departments to implement the Great Wall Conservation Project, deployment specific work, guide and supervise the implement of the *Overall Work Program*" [32]; the office established the project management team of the "Great Wall Conservation Project" under Chinese Academy of Cultural Heritage [33], responsible for the implementation of the specific work related to the 'Great Wall Conservation Project' deployed by the leadership team office" [34].

Since then, the Great Wall project team employed personnel with doctor or master's degree on archeology, history, management, engineering and other specialties. After 2014, although the "Great Wall Conservation Project" was finished, the State Administration of Cultural Heritage faced even heavier tasks of the Great Wall conservation and management, and the Great Wall project team began to assume increasing tasks of the Great Wall conservation research. Currently it consists of 5 members including 4 formal business personnel and 1 long-term employed professional.

Depending on the comprehensive scientific research and technology platform of the institute, under the guidance of the State Administration of Cultural Heritage, the Great Wall project team undertook the Great Wall Conservation Project management, the Great Wall resources investigation and identification, the construction and platform maintenance of the Great Wall resources conservation and management information system, the comprehensive sorting of the Great Wall historical documents, researches on the Great Wall conservation laws, regulations and policies, special law enforcement supervision of the Great Wall conservation ordinance, researches on the Great Wall World Heritage monitoring methods, researches on the Great Wall comprehensive conservation and utilization, the professional training on the Great Wall conservation and management, public education on the Great Wall conservation and management, international academic exchanges on the Great Wall researches and other work. It assisted the State

[31] State Administration of Cultural Heritage: *the Notice on Founding the Great Wall Conservation Project" Leading Team and Project Management Team*, Cultural Heritage Bao Han No. [2016] 601

[32] State Administration of Cultural Heritage: *the Notice on Founding the Great Wall Conservation Project" Leading Team and Project Management Team*, Cultural Heritage Bao Han No. [2016] 601

[33] The former Chinese Academy of Cultural Relics.

[34] State Administration of Cultural Heritage: *the Notice on Founding the Great Wall Conservation Project" Leading Team and Project Management Team*, Cultural Heritage Bao Han No. [2016] 601

### （二）研究特色

除了进行传统文史研究之外，长城保护管理研究是长城项目组的特色工作。长城项目组结合国家文物局委托的大量长城日常业务管理工作，重视开展长城基础研究、应用研究和标准规范研究，培育以长城保护管理研究为核心的科研方向和研究团队，在提高长城管理业务水平的同时，成为国内长城保护管理应用研究的骨干队伍。

中国文化遗产研究院承担的社科基金重大项目《大遗址保护行动跟踪研究》中，长城项目组承担了长城案例研究工作。以长城价值研究为基础，对“十一五”以来期间长城保护规划实施、管理体制机制、文化建设等各项工作进行综合跟踪研究和评估。认为“十一五”以来的长城保护管理工作取得了巨大的成绩，同时也存在一些问题，主要表现在观念和体制机制两方面。长城自身的特点决定了对长城保护需要在国家层面进行统筹协调，优化配置有限资源，加强理论建设，进一步完善管理制度。同时应充分利用社会资源，充分调动公众参与长城保护的积极性。

通过多年的努力和积累，以长城项目组为核心的文研院科研队伍，也成长为全国长城保护研究工作的中坚力量。

一是初步成为长城综合数据中心。长城项目组积累了较为全面、系统、综合的长城数据，包括全国长城历史文献、资源调查数据，长城资源认定数据，长城保护管理业务数据，包括长城保护管理机构、负责人、长城保护员、长城保护规划与保护工程实施状况、四有工作情况、长城专项法规、违法破坏事件、旅游景区情况、经费投入情况等各方面的数据，而且这些数据全部与认定编码和地理数据挂接，具备查询、检索、统计、辅助决策功能，并初步实现动态更新机制，为国家长城保护管理决策、各级长城保护管理和科学研究提供了重要基础，全国长城综合数据中心的框架初步形成。

Administration of Cultural Heritage to play a core role of business overall planning, guidance and coordination in the national Great Wall conservation and management, made outstanding achievements in the researches on the Great Wall conservation, and played an important role in the improvement of Great Wall conservation.

### (II) Characteristics of the Study

In addition to the traditional literature and history studies, the study on the Great Wall conservation and management is a special task of the Great Wall project team. Combining with a lot of daily management of the Great Wall commissioned by the State Administration of Cultural Heritage, Great Wall project team pays attention to basic study, application-based study and standard specification study of the Great Wall, develops the study orientation and team around the study of the Great Wall conservation and management. In the improvement of the Great Wall business management, it becomes the backbone team in the application-based study of China's Great Wall conservation and management.

In the *Tracking Study of Da Yi Zhi*, a major project on social science fund undertaken by Chinese Academy of Cultural Heritage, the Great Wall project team undertook the case study task of the Great Wall. Based on the value study of the Great Wall, it made comprehensive tracking study and evaluation on the Great Wall conservation planning implementation, management system and mechanism, cultural construction and other work during the period of "the Eleventh Five-year Plan". It believes that the Great Wall conservation and management during the period of "the Eleventh Five-year Plan" made great achievements, but there are still some problems, mainly in two aspects, conception and mechanism.

The characteristics of the Great Wall itself determines that the conservation the Great Wall need coordination and planning at the national level to optimize the allocation of limited resources, strengthen the theoretical construction, and further improve the management system. At the same time, we should make full use of social resources, and mobilize the enthusiasm of the public to participate in the conservation of the Great Wall.

Over years of efforts and accumulation, the scientific research team of Chinese Academy of Cultural Heritage around the core of the Great Wall project team also has developed into the backbone strength of the study on the Great Wall conservation.

Firstly, it became a preliminary comprehensive data center of the Great Wall. The Great Wall project team accumulated a comparatively complete, systematic and comprehensive data of the Great Wall, including the historical documents

二是逐步成为长城保护专业管理中心。长城是我国体量最大的文化遗产，横跨我国整个北部疆域 15 个省市区，社会经济自然条件复杂，国际国内影响巨大，其保护管理是国家文物行政主管部门历来的工作重点。长城项目组在长城的整体保护、分级管理体制中发挥了关键的承上启下专业作用。通过长城保护规划编制和协调、长城保护维修技术方案审核组织、工程现场检查指导组织、专项调研咨询与评估、长城信息系统建设运行、宣传教育、人员管理与培训等工作的开展，一方面为国家长城保护管理提供了有力的专业支持，另一方面同长城沿线各地建立起了顺畅的工作机制和合作关系。目前长城项目组已经越来越多地起到了长城保管理工作行业引领和组织协调的重要作用，全国长城保护专业管理中心的地位初步形成。

图 4-1
中国文化遗产研究院长城保护研究室全体成员合影（周魁英 拍摄）

Fig. 4-1
The staff of Great Wall Concervation Research Office of Chinese Academy of Cultural Heritage (by Zhou Kuiying) of Cultural Heritage (by Zhou Kuiying)

of the Great Wall in whole China, resource investigation data, the Great Wall resource identification data, the Great Wall conservation management data, including various data such as the Great Wall conservation management agencies, responsible persons, the Great Wall protectors, the Great Wall conservation planning and the implementation conservation projects, "Four basic works", special laws and regulations on the Great Wall, violation events, tourist attractions and funding investment. Moreover, all the data are linked with the identified codes and geographical data, with searching, retrieval, statistics and auxiliary decision-making function, and the preliminary dynamic update mechanism was realized to provide an important foundation for the national decision-making of the Great Wall conservation management, the Great Wall conservation management and scientific study at all levels. The preliminary framework of the national Great Wall comprehensive data center was completed.

Secondly, it gradually became a professional management center of the Great Wall conservation. The Great Wall is China's largest-sized cultural heritage, across 15 provinces, cities and regions among the whole northern China, with complicated social and economic conditions, making great influences in China and overseas. The conservation and management have been the main focus of national administrative departments of cultural heritage. The Great Wall project team has played a key role as a professional connection link in the overall conservation of the Great Wall and the hierarchical management system. Through the compilation and coordination of the Great Wall conservation planning, audit organization of the Great Wall conservation and maintenance technical program, organization of project on-site supervision and guidance, consultation and evaluation of special studies, construction and operation, publicity and education, personnel management and training of the Great Wall information system; on the one hand, it provided strong professional supports for China's Great Wall conservation and management, and on the other hand, it established smooth working mechanism and cooperation with various places along the Great Wall. At present, the Great Wall project team is playing an increasingly important role of guidance and coordination in the conservation and management of the Great Wall. It has become a preliminary professional management center of the Great Wall conservation.

Thirdly, it is a research and consulting center of the Great Wall conservation. Depending on the comprehensive research advantage of the Chinese Academy of Cultural Heritage, the Great Wall project team combined the professional management work of the Great Wall conservation with studies, and through special, sustained and multi-disciplinary management investigation of the Great Wall conservation, consultation and study, it got to know the

三是作为长城保护研究咨询中心。长城项目组依托于中国文化遗产研究院的综合科研优势，将长城保护专业管理工作与研究相结合，通过开展专项、持续、多学科交叉的长城保护管理调研、咨询和研究，比较全面和深入地了解我国长城历史分布、保存现状、保护管理、工程技术特点，形成了不同于传统长城历史研究和专题研究的独特研究方向，重点开展以长城保护管理需求为中心的相关基础研究、应用研究和标准规范研究，取得了一系列长城保护管理研究成果，培养了一支热爱长城、了解长城的综合科研队伍，长城保护研究咨询中心的团队初步形成。

## 二、公立科研机构、高校的专业团队

2005 年以来，长城研究呈现较为显著的变化是长城研究专业团队纷纷形成。天津大学建筑学院张玉坤教授的团队从建筑学的角度对军事聚落体系进行多年的专项研究；敦煌研究院发挥土遗址研究的优势，对敦煌地区汉长城的监测、保护工程技术进行了系统研究和实验，并将研究成果实际应用到敦煌地区的长城保护工作中。

西北大学段清波、徐卫民、王建新等教授的研究团队，对中国长城历史发展的研究，尤其是秦汉长城、丝绸之路与长城的关系研究方面成果突出，完成了教育部哲学社会科学重大课题攻关项目《中国历代长城研究》。

## 三、社会长城研究力量

长期以来，以中国长城学会、长城小站等为代表的很多民间团体、组织和学者积极参与长城研究，持续开展了大量专题研究工作，形成了一批研究成果。其中也涌现出成大林、董耀会、威廉·林赛等一批民间长城研究者；此外，长城沿线各地还有一大批民间学者、爱好者也对长城进行了大量的研究工作。但这些研究力量较为分散，较之专业学术机构的研究而言，其研究在专业理论指导和专业方法方面有所欠缺。

historical distribution, current situation, conservation and management, engineering technical characteristics of the Great Wall in China, and formed a special study orientation different from the traditional Great Wall historical study. It put the emphasis on the relevant basic study, application-based study and standard and specification study around the management demands of the Great Wall conservation, made a series of achievements in the study of the Great Wall conservation management, and cultivated an integrated research team loving and understanding the Great Wall. A preliminary team of the Great Wall conservation, study and advisory center was formed.

## II. Public scientific research institutions and professional teams in colleges

Since 2005, a significant change in the Great Wall study is the formation of professional teams of the Great Wall study. Professor Zhang Yukun's team from the School of Architecture of Tianjin University has made special study on military settlement system for many years in the architectural view; Dunhuang Academy took the advantages in the study of earthen sites to make systematical studies and experiments on monitoring and conservation engineering technology of the Han Great Wall in Dunhuang area, and actually applied the study achievements in the Great Wall conservation in Dunhuang area.

Professor Duan Qingbo, Xu Weimin and Wang Jianxin's study teams from Northwest University made outstanding achievements in the study on the development history of China's Great Wall, especially the Great Wall of the Qin and Han Dynasties, and the relationship between the Silk Road and the Great Wall. They completed a key project of philosophy and social science research of the Ministry of Education, *Study on Great Wall of Successive Chinese dynasties.*

## III. Social organizations of the Great Wall study

For a long time, many civil societies, organizations and scholars represented by the Great Wall Society of China and the Great Wall Station participated in the Great Wall study, carried out a large number of special studies, and made some achievements. A group of Great Wall scholars in folk emerged such as Cheng Dalin, William Lindesay; In addition, a large number of folk scholars and enthusiasts along the Great Wall also made a lot of studies on the Great Wall. However, these study forces are separated and in lack of professional theoretical guidance and professional method compared with the studies of professional academic institutions.

## 第二节 “长城保护工程”实施以前的长城研究概述

※ 研究领域广泛——历史、地理、民俗、建筑、考古、志书编纂等

※ 以基础研究为主要方向，多学科背景的专题研究、应用性研究起步

### 一、国内研究

#### （一）早期历史考据研究

17 世纪—18 世纪。这一阶段的长城研究，以历史考据为主。明清时期，关于长城的文献大量出现，除官修的《明史》《大清一统志》等，以及各地编纂的方志之外，一些记载长城的专门志书、文集、笔记，对长城的沿革、布局、走向进行了详尽的描述。

明末清初，部分学者开始关注旧朝边疆史，其中就包括了对长城进行文献考证。顾炎武的《日知录》、顾祖禹的《读史方舆纪要》分别对长城的起源、沿革进行了讨论。乾隆时期，乾嘉学派开始抛开政治，对长城进行更加细致和严谨的史地考证。杨守敬等人在《历代舆地沿革险要图》上以乾嘉学派的考据为基础，首次对历代长城进行了全面绘制，可视为这一阶段长城研究的总结。国学大师王国维对金界壕的建筑、布局和性质也进行了探讨。

# Section 2 Overview of previous Great Wall study before the implementation of "Great Wall Conservation Project"

- Extensive study fields covering history, geography, folklore, architecture, archaeology, and chorography compilation, etc.
- Take basic study as the main orientation, and start from multi-disciplinary thematic study and application-based studies

## I. Domestic studies

### (I) History study in early period

The 17th --18th century. The Great Wall studies during this stage are mainly based on historical studies. A lot of literature about the Great Wall was made during the Ming and Qing Dynasties. In addition to the official *History of the Ming Dynasty, the Chronicle of the Qing Dynasty* and the local chronicles of various areas, some special chronicles, essays and records of the Great Wall also made detailed description about the evolution, layout and direction of the Great Wall.

In the late Ming and early Qing dynasties, some scholars began to pay attention to the history of the frontier in previous dynasties due to political consideration, which included the literature investigation on the Great Wall. Gu Yanwu's *Daily Understanding* and Gu Zuyu's *Essentials of Historical Geography* respectively discussed the Great Wall's origin and evolution. In the period of Qianlong Emperor, Qianjia School began to make more detailed and rigorous historical and geographical investigation regardless the political elements. In the *Maps of Major Ancient Geography Evolutions*, Yang Shoujing and others

## （二）历史地理学研究

19 世纪末以来，受到边疆危机的加剧和西方探险家来华考察的刺激，中国学者掀起了一阵边疆考察的热潮。屠寄于 1897 年起受清政府命令，主持黑龙江舆图测绘，其间详细考察了东北部地区的金界壕，是较早关注金界壕的学者之一。1914 年，张相文考察西北，作《长城考》，及《中国地理沿革史》，通过实地考察与文献相结合的方式甄别了战国、秦、明三代长城，为长城历史地理学研究之始。20 世纪上半叶，一批学者运用中国传统历史研究方法分别对长城建制沿革进行了系统的文献考证。王国良的《中国长城沿革考》、[35] 寿彭飞的《历代长城考》、[36] 张维华的《中国古代长城建置考》、[37] 顾颉刚、史念海的《中国疆域沿革史》[38] 等历史地理学著作陆续面世，标志着长城历史地理学的成熟。

[35] 王国良、寿鹏飞：长城研究资料两种（中国长城沿革考 历代长城考），（台北）明文书局，1982 年。
[36] 王国良、寿鹏飞：长城研究资料两种（中国长城沿革考 历代长城考），（台北）明文书局，1982 年。
[37] 张维华：《中国长城建置考》，中华书局，1979 年。
[38] 顾颉刚、史念海：《中国疆域沿革史》，商务印书馆，1938 年。

drew comprehensive maps of the Great Wall in various dynasties for the first time based on the investigation of Qianjia School, which could be regarded as a summary of the Great Wall study in this stage. Wang Guowei, a master of Chinese culture, also discussed the construction, layout and nature of the Jin Jiehao (the great wall built in Jin dynasty).

**(II) Historical and geographical studies**

Since the end of the 19th century, stimulated by the intensification of the border crisis and Western explorers' investigation in China, Chinese scholars set off an upsurge of border investigation. Appointed by the Qing government in 1897, Tu Ji presided over the mapping of Heilongjiang. During this period, as one of the scholars concerned about the Jin Jiehao in earlier period, he made detailed investigations on the Jin Jiehao in northeastern China. In 1914, Zhang Xiangwen visited northwest China, and wrote *the Investigation on the Great Wall* and *the History of Chinese Geography Evolution*, which distinguished the Great Wall in three dynasties, the Warring States period, Qin and Ming dynasties, by the combination of field investigation and literature, as a start of historical geography study of the Great Wall. In the first half of the twentieth century, a group of scholars respectively made systematic literature investigations on the system evolution of the Great Wall by means of traditional Chinese historical *study methods. Wang Guoliang's Study on the Evolution of the Great Wall* [35] , Peng Shoufei's *Investigation on Great Wall in Various Dynasties* [36], Zhang Weihua's *Investigation on the Establishment of Ancient Chinese Great Wall* [37], Gu Jiegang and Shi Nianhai's *History of Chinese Territorial Evolution* [38] and other historical geography books were published in succession, symbolizing the maturity of the Great Wall historical geography study.

---

[35] Wang Guoliang, Shoupeng Fei: Two kinds of Great Wall research data (Investigation on the evolution of China Great Wall; Investigation on the Great Wall of Various Dynasties), Taipei: Mingwen Book Store, in 1982.

[36] Wang Guoliang, Shoupeng Fei: Two kinds of Great Wall research data (Investigation on the evolution of China Great Wall; Investigation on the Great Wall of Various Dynasties), Taipei: Mingwen Book Store, in 1982.

[37] Zhang Weihua: *Investigation on the Establishment of Ancient Chinese Great Wall*, Beijing: Zhonghua Book Company, in 1979.

[38] Gu Jiegang & Shi Nianhai: *History of Chinese Territorial Evolution*, Commercial Press, in 1938.

### （三）民俗学、建筑学研究

这一时期，以吴立模、[39]顾颉刚[40]为代表的学者对各地孟姜女故事进行搜集、整理、对比，研究其演变，认为孟姜女的故事源于《左传》杞梁妻故事，开创了长城的民俗学研究。至20世纪50-60年代，孟姜女研究进一步发展，路工从阶级斗争的观点出发，否定了顾颉刚的观点；钟敬文、[41]魏建功、[42]刘半农、[43]日本学者饭仓照平、[44]苏联汉学家李福清[45]等人就孟姜女故事的形成时代展开了探讨。

建筑学家梁思成、[46]刘敦桢[47]等人则开始梳理和研究历代长城建筑材料与结构。罗哲文首先从建筑学的角度对长城进行了比较系统的考察和研究，[48]并在此基础上提出浙江台州府城是明长城的“师范和蓝本”的观点。[49]

### （四）简牍学与考古学研究

“简牍学”的开创，与长城研究密不可分。1914年，王国维、罗振玉等国学大师用新出简牍材料研究西北地区的汉代长城，著成《流沙坠简》，考释了斯坦因挖掘获取的588枚（件）记录西北长城军事档案的汉晋简牍，成为中国近代最早研究简牍的著作。

---

[39] 吴立模：《孟姜女故事的转变》，《星海》，1923年12月1日。

[40] 顾颉刚：《孟姜女故事研究集》，上海古籍出版社，1984年。

[41]《为孟姜女冤案平反——批驳“四人帮”追随者的谬论》，《人民文学》1979年7月号。

[42] 魏建功：《杞梁妻姓名的递变与哭崩之城的递变》，收录于顾颉刚、钟敬文：《孟姜女故事论文集》，中国民间文学出版社，1983年，p44。

[43] 刘半农：《敦煌写本中之孟姜女小唱》，《歌谣》周刊第83号，1925年。

[44] a《关于孟姜女》，《文学》，1958年8月号。b《孟姜女故事的原型》，东京都立大学《人文学报》第25号。

[45] 李福清：《万里长城的传说与中国民间文学的体裁问题》，（莫斯科）东方文学出版社，1961年。

[46] 梁思成：《中国建筑史》，285页，百花文艺出版社，1998年。

[47] 刘敦桢：《中国古代建筑史》，62页，中国建筑工业出版社，2003年。

[48] a 文物编辑委员会：《中国长城遗迹调查报告集》，文物出版社，1981年。b 罗哲文：《长城》，北京出版社，1982年。

[49] 罗哲文：《江南八达岭，巍巍临海城》，《风景名胜》2009年第11期。

### (III) Folklore and architecture studies

During this period, the scholars represented by Wu Limo [39] and Gu Jiegang [40] collected, collated and contrasted the story of Widow Meng Jiang from various places and studied the evolution. They believed that the story originated from the story of Qi Liang's wife in *Zuo Zhuan*, and initiated the folklore study of the Great Wall. In the 1950s and 1960s, the study on Widow Meng Jiang was further developed. Lu Gong denied the opinion of Gu Jiegang from the view of class struggle; Zhong Jingwen [41], Wei Jiangong [42], Liu Bannong [43], and Japanese scholar Iigura [44], Russian Sinologist Boris Lyvovich Riftin [45] and some others discussed about the formation era of Widow Meng Jiang's story.

Architects Liang Sicheng [46], Liu Dunzhen [47] and some others began to sort out and study the building materials and structures of the ancient Great Wall. Luo Zhewen for the first time made systematic investigation and study on the Great Wall from the perspective of architecture [48], and proposed that Taizhou City in Zhejiang is the "model and blueprint" of the Ming Great Wall [49] on this basis.

### (IV) Bamboo Slip and Archeology Studies

The initiation of "study of bamboo slips" is inseparable with the Great Wall study. In 1914, Wang Guowei, Luo Zhenyu and some other Chinese culture masters studied the Han Great Wall in northwest China by newly unearthed bamboo slips, and wrote *Bamboo Slips in Sand*, which studied the 588 pieces of bamboo slips on the northwest Great Wall military archives from the Han and Jin dynasties unearthed by Marc Aurel Stein, as the earliest book on the study of bamboo slips in modern China.

[39] Wu Limo: *Changes of Widow Meng Jiang's Story and Xinghai*, on December 1, 1923.

[40] Gu Jiegang: *Collection of Studies on Widow Meng Jiang's Story*, Shanghai: Shanghai Ancient Books Publishing House, in 1984.

[41] *Redress for Widow Meng Jiang's Grievances; Criticism on the fallacies of the "Gang of Four"'s Followers*, *People 's Literature* issue of July 1979.

[42] Wei Jiangong: Gradual Change of Qi Liang's Wife'S Name and the City Wall Collapsed by Weeping, included in Gu Jiegang & Zhong Jingwen's *Essays of Widow Meng Jiang's Stories*, Beijing: China Folk Literature Publishing House, in 1983, p44.

[43] Liu Bannong: *Widow Meng Jiang's Song in Dunhuang Written Books*, *Ballad* weekly issue No. 83, in 1925.

[44] A. *About Widow Meng Jiang*, *Literature*, issue of August, 1958. B. *Prototype of Widow Meng Jiang's Story*, Tokyo Metropolitan University *Journal of Humanities* No. 25.

[45] Li Fuqing: *The Legend of The Great Wall and the Genre of Chinese Folk Literature*, Moscow: Oriental Literature Publishing House, in 1961.

[46] Liang Sicheng: *History of Chinese Architecture*, Baihua Literature and Art Publishing House, in 1998, p285.

[47] Liu Dunzhen: *History of Ancient Chinese Architecture*, Beijing: China Architecture and Industry Press, in 2003, p62.

[48] A. Cultural Relics Editor Committee: *Investigation Reports on China Great Wall Sites*, Cultural Relics Press, in 1981. B. Luo Zhewen: *the Great Wall*, Beijing: Beijing Publishing House, in 1982.

[49] Luo Zhewen: *Badaling in Jiangnan; Towering Linhai City*, *Scenery* issue 11 in 2009.

20世纪20年代，考古学引入中国，并迅速生根。作为中瑞西北考察团成员的黄文弼，利用现代考古学方法对内蒙古地区长城进行了测量、发掘和时代判断，指出了长城建筑“就地取材”的特点。1930-1934年，黄文弼在新疆罗布泊北岸的汉塞遗址进行发掘，获取汉代木简71枚。[50] 1944-1945年，中央研究院历史语言研究所、中央博物院筹备处、中国地理研究所、北京大学文科研究所四单位也曾合组西北科学考察团，在甘肃、新疆两地进行考察，调查发掘了汉代的玉门关和长城遗址。40年代，李文信、佟柱臣等人对燕秦长城、金界壕进行考察和发掘，首次运用考古学的方法对长城进行断代和确定走向。

1956-1959、1981-1985、2007-2008年开展的三次全国文物普查中，各地陆续发现了一批长城遗迹。其中，1956年起实施的首次全国文物普查中，北京、河北、甘肃等地即将明长城作为调查重点。1979年，国家文物事业管理局在内蒙古自治区呼和浩特市召开了“全国长城保护研究工作座谈会”。此次会议提出了三项任务：第一，对长城进行全面普查；第二，对长城历史文献加以系统的整理、汇集；第三，开展对长城的政治、经济、中西交通、文化、民族关系等研究。会后，各省（自治区、直辖市）积极响应，陆续开展了一系列长城普查和保护工作。1979-1984年，结合第二次全国文物普查，各地对重要区域的春秋战国长城、秦汉长城、明长城和金界壕等遗址进行调查，出版了《中国长城遗迹调查报告集》，对我国长城资源有了进一步认识。

---

[50] 黄文弼：《罗布淖尔考古记》（北平）国立北京大学出版部，1948年。

In the 1920s, archeology was introduced into China and quickly took root.

As a member of the Scientific Mission to North-western China, Huang Wenbi made measure, excavation and dating judgment on the Great Wall in Inner Mongolia by means of modern archeological methods, and pointed out the characteristics of "taking local materials" of the Great Wall. During 1930-1934, Huang Wenbi excavated the Hansei site on the north bank of Lop Nur in Xinjiang and obtained 71 pieces of Ham bamboo slips[50]. During 1944-1945, the Institute of History and Philology of the Academia Sinica, the Preparatory Office of the Central Museum, the Institute of Geography of the Chinese Academy of Sciences, and the Institute of Liberal Arts, Peking University also jointly organized the Scientific Mission to North-western China to investigate in Gansu and Xinjiang. They investigated and excavated the sites of Yumen Pass and the Great Wall from the Han Dynasty. In the 1940s, Li Wenxin, Tong Zhuchen and some others made investigation and excavation on the Yan Qin Great Wall and the Jin Jiehao, when they made dating and determined the direction of the Great Wall by means of archaeological methods for the first time.

In the three national cultural heritage investigations during 1956-1959, 1981–1985 and 2007-2008, a number of Great Wall remains were discovered in various places. Among them, in the first national cultural heritage investigation since 1956, the Ming Great Wall was regarded as the focus investigation site in Beijing, Hebei and Gansu. In 1979, the State Administration of Cultural Heritage held a "Symposium on the National Great Wall Conservation Study" in Hohhot, Inner Mongolia Autonomous Region. The symposium put forward three tasks: firstly, a comprehensive census of the Great Wall; secondly, systematic collation and collection of the Great Wall historical documents; thirdly, the studies on the politics, economy, Chinese-Western transportation, culture, and ethnic group relationship of the Great Wall. After that, all the provinces (autonomous regions and municipalities) made positive responses and carried out a series of Great Wall census and conservation in succession.

During 1979-1984, combining with the second national cultural heritage investigation, all the regions made investigations on the Great Wall sites from the Spring and Autumn and Warring States, the Qin and Han dynasties, and the Ming dynasty and the Jin Jiehao in important areas, and published the Investigation Reports Collection of the Great Wall Sites, which deepened the understanding of China's Great Wall resources.

---

[50] Huang Wenbi: Archeology in Lop Nor (M), Peking, National Peking University Publishing Department, in 1948.

比较系统的区域考古调查工作，直至20世纪70年代末才逐渐展开。1973年，甘肃省革委会组织甘肃省博物馆及酒泉地区各地县文物部门联合对汉长城肩水金关遗址进行了发掘。20世纪70-90年代，甘肃省文物考古研究所对河西走廊地区的汉代长城遗迹进行了系统考古调查；[51] 20世纪80-90年代，甘肃省、内蒙古自治区陆续发掘了肩水金关、甲渠候官、[52] 悬泉置[53] 等汉长城遗址，再次获取大批汉简；陈梦家、陈直等古文字学家通过对汉简的考释，进一步搞清了居延遗址的长城布局，并加深了对汉代西北地区长城沿线军事与社会生活的认识。河北省在1981年组织了专门的长城考察队，用七年时间，对明蓟镇长城进行了详细的调查与测绘。[54]（表4-1）

（五）多学科背景的专题研究

1949年之后，长城研究领域不断拓宽。长城开始摆脱了就事论事的研究模式，被纳入社会学、经济学、军事学、农学、甚至政治学框架下进行讨论，空间上，研究对象从长城扩展到“长城地带”。受科学研究服务建设的思潮影响，侯仁之、史念海、景爱等历史地理学家开始关注西北地区长城沿线的生态环境与气候变迁。20世纪80年代，长城被联合国教科文组织列入《世界遗产名录》以后，长城研究日渐兴起，中国学者对长城进行概念和价值研究。尽管目前工作不多，但此项研究的不断深入，必将对长城概念与价值的进一步探讨，将对于长城保护管理工作的范围和定位产生影响。此外，长城沿线各地还涌现出一批长城研究学者并成为长城研究领域不可忽视的力量。

（六）保护理论与技术研究

20世纪80年代甘肃、内蒙古、河北等地的长城调查在“全国长城保护研究工作座谈会”召开的背景下展开。

[51] 吴礽骧：《河西汉塞调查与研究》，文物出版社，2005年。
[52] 中国社会科学院考古研究所：《居延汉简甲乙编》，中华书局，1980年。
[53] 何双全：《甘肃敦煌汉代悬泉置遗址发掘简报》，《文物》2000年第5期。
[54] 河北省文物研究所：《明蓟镇长城1981—1987年考古报告》，文物出版社，2012年。

Relatively systematic regional archaeological investigation gradually started in the late 1970s. In 1973, the Gansu Provincial Revolutionary Committee organized the Gansu Provincial Museum and county cultural heritage administrations in Jiuquan area jointly excavated the site of Jianshui Jinguan of the Han Great Wall. During the 1970s-1990s, Gansu Provincial Institute of Cultural Relics and Archeology made a systematic archaeological investigation on the Han Great Wall sites in the Hexi Corridor area[51]; During the 1980s-1990s, Gansu Province and Inner Mongolia Autonomous Region excavated Jianshui Jinguan, Jiaqu Houguan [52], Xuanquanzhi [53] and other Han Great Wall sites and obtained a lot of bamboo slips from the Han dynasty again; Chen Mengjia, Chen Zhi and some other experts on ancient characters further understood the Great Wall layout of Juyan site and deepened the knowledge of military and social life along the Great Wall in northwest China in the Han dynasty by means of the interpretation of the bamboo slips the Han dynasty. Hebei Province organized a special Great Wall expedition team in 1981, and made detailed investigation and mapping on the Great Wall in Mingji County in seven years [54]. (Table 4-1).

### (V) Thematic studies on multidisciplinary background

After 1949, the field of the Great Wall study was continuously widened. The study of the Great Wall began to get rid of single model and be discussed in the framework covering sociology, economics, military science, agriculture, and even political science. In the term of space, the study object was extended from the Great Wall to the "Great Wall zone". Influenced by the thought of scientific study serving construction, historical geographers such as Hou Renzhi, Shi Nianhai and Jing Ai began to pay attention to the ecological environment and climate changes along the Great Wall in northwest China. In the 1980s, after the Great Wall was included in the World Heritage List by the UNESCO, the Great Wall study gradually got prosperous. Chinese scholars made concept and value study on the Great Wall. Although the current workload was not so much, the increasingly deepening study and further discussion on the concept and value of the Great Wall would definitely influence the scope and positioning of the Great Wall conservation management. In addition, a group of scholars on Great Wall study also emerged in various places along the Great Wall and they became indispensible power in the field of the Great Wall study.

[51] Wu Rengxiang: *Investigation and Research on Hexi Han Passes*, Cultural Relics Publishing House, in 2005.

[52] Institute of Archeology of Chinese Academy of Social Sciences: *Juyan Han Bamboo Slips Volume A & B*, Zhonghua Book Company, in 1980.

[53] He Shuangquan: *Briefing on the Excavation of Dunhuang Han Dynasty Xuanquanzhi Site in Gansu*, *Cultural Relics* issue 5 in 2000.

[54] Hebei Institute of Cultural Relics: *Archaeological Report on Mingji Town Great Wall 1981-1987*, Cultural Relics Press, in 2012.

## 表 4-1："十一五"之前部分重要长城考察活动与研究成果一览表

| 重要考察活动 | 时间（年度） | 成果 | 出版时间 |
| --- | --- | --- | --- |
| 斯坦因第二次中亚考察 | 1906 ~ 1908 | 《西域考古记》 | 1921 |
| 盖洛长城考察 | 1908 | 《中国长城》 | 1909 |
| 斯坦因第三次中亚考察 | 1913 ~ 1916 | 《亚洲腹地考古图记》 | 1924 |
| 中瑞西北考察团贝格曼额济纳河流域调查 | 1928 ~ 1933 | 索马斯特罗姆《内蒙古额济纳河流域考古报告》；《居延汉简甲乙编》 | 1956 ~ 1958 |
| 中研院等四单位西北考察团向达、夏鼐、阎文儒甘肃烽燧调查 | 1944 ~ 1945 | 夏鼐《新获之敦煌汉简》；阎文儒《河西考古杂记（上、下）》 | 1961/ 1986 ~ 1987 |
| 汉长城肩水金关遗址发掘 | 1973 | 《肩水金关汉简（壹－伍）》 | 2011-2016 |
| 甘肃省文物考古研究所河西走廊汉代长城调查 | 1979 | 吴礽骧《河西汉塞调查与研究》 | 2005 |
| 河北省文物研究所明蓟镇长城调查 | 1981-1987 | 《明蓟镇长城 1981-1987 年考古报告》 | 2012 |
| 董耀会、吴德玉、张元华等明长城考察 | 1984 ~ 1987 | 《明长城考实》 | 1988 |
| 地质矿产部地质遥感中心北京地区长城遥感调查 | 1984 | 《北京地区长城航空遥感调查》 | 1987 |
| 李文龙战国中山长城考察 | 1988 | 《保定境内战国中山长城调查记》 | 2001 |
| 地质矿产部地质遥感中心宁夏地区长城遥感调查 | 1990 ~ 1992 | 《宁夏长城航空遥感调查研究》 | 1994 |
| 李逸友等对内蒙古地区长城的考察 | 1996-1997 | 《中国北方长城考述》 | 2001 |
| 成大林等长城资源调查前期调研 | 2003 | 《长城保护、管理和研究现状调查及对策研究》 | 内部参考资料 |
| 唐晓峰、陈品祥等北京地区北齐长城调查 | 2004 | 《北京北部山区古长城遗址地理踏查报告》 | 2009 |

Table 4-1: List of some important investigations on the Great Wall and the achievements before the "Eleventh Five-Year Plan"

| Important investigations | Time (Year) | Achievement | Publication Time |
|---|---|---|---|
| Stein's second investigation on Central Asia | 1906 ~ 1908 | *Archaeological Records of the Western Regions* | 1921 |
| Gairo's investigation on the Great Wall | 1908 | *The Great Wall of China* | 1909 |
| Stein's third investigation on Central Asia | 1913 ~ 1916 | *Archaeological Pictorial of Inner Asia* | 1924 |
| *The Scientific Mission to North-Western China's investigation on Bergman Ejina River Basin* | 1928 ~ 1933 | Sommar Strom's *Archaeological Report on Ejina River Basin, Inner Mongolia; Chapter 1 &2 of Juyan Han Bamboo Slips* | 1956 ~ 1958 |
| Xiang Da, Xia Nai and Yan Wenru of Chinese Academy of Sciences and other three units northwest delegation's investigation on Fengsui, Gansu | 1944 ~ 1945 | Xia Nai's *Newly Obtained Dunhuang Han Bamboo Slips; Yan Wenru's Hexi Archaeological Records (Chapter 1 & 2)* | 1961/ 1986 ~ 1987 |
| Site excavation of Jianshui Jinguan of the Han Great Wall | 1973 | *Han Bamboo Slips from Jianshui Jinguan (Chapter 1-5)* | 2011-2016 |
| Gansu Provincial Institute of Cultural Relics and Archeology's investigation on the Han Great Wall in Hexi Corridor | 1979 | Wu Rengxiang's *Investigation and Study on Hexi Han Passes* | 2005 |
| Hebei Provincial Institute of Cultural Relics's investigation on the Great Wall in Mingji Town | 1981-1987 | *Archaeological Report of 1981-1987 on the Ming Ji zhen Great Wall in Mingji Town* | 2012 |
| Dong Yaohui, Wu Deyu and Zhang Yuanhua's investigation on the Ming Great Wall | 1984 ~ 1987 | *Study on the Ming Great Wall* | 1988 |
| Geological Remote Sensing Center of the Ministry of Geology and Mineral Resource's remote sensing investigation on the Great Wall in Beijing area | 1984 | *Aviation Remote Sensing Investigation Report on the Great Wall in Beijing Area* | 1987 |
| Li Wenlong's investigation on Zhongshan Great Wall from the Warring States Period | 1988 | *Investigation Report on Zhongshan Great Wall from the Warring States Period in Baoding* | 2001 |
| Geological Remote Sensing Center of the Ministry of Geology and Mineral Resource's remote sensing investigation on the Great Wall in Ningxia area | 1990 ~ 1992 | *Aviation Remote Sensing Investigation and Studies on the Great Wall in Ningxia Area* | 1994 |
| Li Yiyou's investigation on the Great Wall in Inner Mongolia | 1996-1997 | *Investigation on the Great Wall in Northern China* | 2001 |
| Cheng Dalin's preliminary investigation on the Great Wall resources | 2003 | *Investigation 2003 On the Current Situation Investigation and Solution on the Great Wall Conservation, Management and Study* | internal reference |
| Tang Xiaofeng and Chen Pinxiang's investigation on the North Qi Great Wall in Beijing area | 2004 | *Investigation 2004 " Geographical Investigation Report on the Ancient Great Wall Sites in the Northern Mountain area of Beijing* | 2009 |

这一时期，长城保护研究发展起来，具体内容包括：

（1）长城保护理论、政策研究。主要就当前长城保护管理中的热点、难点问题进行研究，通过对长城保护、管理和研究现状的调查研究，分析问题产生原因，提出解决问题的对策建议。

（2）长城保护与利用模式研究。对长城保护与利用的现有模式进行调研分析，做出综合性评估，探索符合国情的可持续发展的长城保护与合理利用模式。

（3）长城保护技术研究。现存长城建造于不同时代，分布于不同地域，所处的自然环境各不相同，其建筑形式、所用材料、技术多种多样。因此，需要进行有针对性的保护技术研究。

**（七）志书编纂**

自明代以来，长城志书成为中国方志系统的重要组成部分。如明代的《宣府镇志》《两镇三关通志》《四镇三关志》《延绥镇志》；清代的《山海关志》等均对明长城的修建过程、建置沿革、关隘布局等进行了详细的描述，留下了丰富的史料。在当代，尤其是 20 世纪 80 年代以来，各地也积极编纂长城志书。

1984、1988 年，《山海关长城志》[55]《天津黄崖关长城志》[56]分别出版；2008 年北京市地方志编纂委员会编纂出版了《北京志·长城志》；2015 年，河北省地方志编纂委员会编纂出版了《河北省志·长城志》。两部志书分别收录了北京市、河北省长城资源调查的最新数据，成为区域长城研究史料的重要集成。

1994 年，由中国长城学会组织罗哲文、董耀会等编纂出版了《长城百科全书》。较为全面汇总、整理了当时人们对长城的认识。全书分为总论、长城区域历史、长城区域地理、长城区域军事、长城

[55] 郭述祖：《山海关长城志》，河北省地名志办公室，1984 年。
[56] 天津市“爱我中华，修我长城”活动指导委员会办公室：《天津黄崖关长城志》，天津古籍出版社，1988 年。

## (VI) Studies on the conservation theory and technology

In the 1980s, the Great Wall investigations of Gansu, Inner Mongolia, Hebei and other places were launched under the background of the "National Symposium on the Great Wall Conservation Study".

During this period, the Great Wall conservation study was developed, with the specific contents including:

(1) Studies on the Great Wall conservation theories and policies. It's mainly to study the hot issues and difficulties in current Great Wall conservation management, to analyze the causes of the problems and put forward suggestions to solve them through the investigation on the current Great Wall conservation, management and studies.

(2) Studies on the Great Wall conservation and utilization model. It's to investigate and analyze the existing model of the Great Wall conservation and utilization and make comprehensive assessments. It's to explore the sustainable models of the Great Wall conservation and utilization in line with China's national conditions.

(3) Studies on the Great Wall conservation technology. The existing Great Walls were built in various times and distributed in various regions, where the natural environment is different, and architectural forms, materials and technologies varied. Therefore, it's necessary to make targeted studies on conservation technology.

## (VII) Chronicle compilation

Since the Ming dynasty, the Great Wall chronicle has become an important part of Chinese local chronicle system, such as the Chronicle of Xuanfu Town, the Chronicles of Two Towns and Three Passes, the Chronicles of Four Towns and Three Passes and the Chronicle of Yansui Town in the Ming dynasty, and the Chronicle of Shanghaiguan in the Qing dynasty all made detailed description on the construction process, system evolution and pass layout of the Ming Great Wall, and left a wealth of historical data. In the contemporary times, and especially since the 1980s', the compilation of the Great Wall chronicle has got active in various places.

*The Chronicle of Shanhai Pass Great Wall* [55] and *the Chronicle of Huangyaguan Great Wall in Tianjin* [56] were published in 1984 and 1988 respectively; Beijing Local Chronicles Compilation Committee compiled and published the *Chronicle of Beijing; the Great Wall* in 2008; Hebei Local Chronicle Compilation Committee compiled and published the *Chronicle of Hebei Province; the Great Wall* in 2015. These two books included the latest data of the investigation on Beijing and Hebei Great Wall resources, as an important integration of historical data on the regional Great Wall studies.

[55] Guo Shuzu: *Chronicle of Shanhaiguan Great Wall*, Hebei Local Chronicle Office, in 1984.

[56] Tianjin "Love Our China; Repair Our Great Wall" Leading Committee Office: *the Chronicle of Huangyaguan Great Wall in Tianjin*, Tianjin Ancient Books Publishing House, in 1988.

区域民族、长城区域人物、长城建筑、长城关隘、长城区域经济、长城文学艺术、长城旅游等部分，从宏观到微观，系统介绍了长城的有关知识，成为20世纪90年代至2006年之前，长城研究的重要参考文献。

## 二、海外研究

国外学者开展的长城研究起源于17世纪。主要有以下两方面内容：

### （一）长城的实地考察、测绘与考古

1687年，法国人张诚（Jean-Francois · Gerbillon）在实地考察基础上写成《对大鞑靼的历史考察概述》，对长城的材质进行了相对客观、全面的描述，成为第一份比较专业的长城学术研究成果。

两年后，康熙帝命在华西方传教士绘制《皇舆全览图》。该图以三角测量的方法标绘了长城沿线300余处关堡，成为长城精确测绘之始。

18世纪以降，长城考察在来华西方人士中开始流行。来自英国、法国、俄国、芬兰、瑞典、匈牙利、德国、美国及日本等国家的探险家和学者纷纷踏足长城，并开展相关研究。美国人威廉埃德加盖洛（William · Edgar · Geil）[57]是首位走完长城全程的西方学者，在行程中，他还发现了青海长城。他在实地考察的基础上，于1909年出版《中国长城》一书，对长城的起源、历史文化和军事体系进行了全面的讨论，可视为西方第一部长城专著。

英国探险家马尔克·奥莱尔·斯坦因（Marc · Aurel · Stein）[58]和瑞典考古学家沃尔克·贝格曼（Warlock · Bergman）等人较早关注长城考古。在20世纪的前30年间，他们先后对甘肃、内蒙古地区的居延汉代长城遗址进行了考古发掘和测绘，对居延遗址汉代

[57]〔美〕盖洛：《中国长城》，山东画报出版社，2006年。

[58]〔英〕斯坦因著、向达译：《西域考古记》，商务印书馆，2013年；〔英〕奥雷尔·斯坦因著、艾力江译《亚洲腹地考古图记》，广西师范大学出版社，2004年。

In 1994, Great Wall Society of China organized Luo Zhewen, Dong Yaohui and some others to compile and publish *the Great Wall Encyclopedia*. It could be regarded as the first comprehensive summary and sorting of people's understanding of the Great Wall at that time. The book included preface, the Great Wall regional history, the Great Wall regional geography, the Great Wall regional military, the Great Wall regional ethnic group, the Great Wall regional characters, the Great Wall buildings, the Great Wall passes, the Great Wall regional economy, the Great Wall literature and art, and the Great Wall tourism, with systematic introduction of the relevant knowledge about the Great Wall from macro to micro perspectives. It was an important reference literature on the Great Wall study during the 1990s'-2006.

## II. Overseas studies

The Great Wall studies by foreign scholars originated in the 17th century, mainly including the following two aspects:

### (I) Field investigation, mapping and archaeology on the Great Wall

In 1687, the French Jean-Francois Gerbillon wrote *Overview of the History Investigation on the Great Tartar* on the basis of field investigation, making relatively objective and comprehensive description of the material of the Great Wall, as the first professional academic study achievement on the Great Wall.

Two years later, Emperor Kangxi ordered the Western missionaries to draw the Overall Map. This map includes more than 300 passes and for tresses along the Great Wall by triangulation mapping, as a start of accurate mapping of the Great Wall.

Since the 18th century, the Great Wall investigation began to get popular in Westerners in China. Adventurers and scholars from Britain, France, Russia, Finland, Sweden, Hungary, Germany, the United States, Japan and other countries set foot at the Great Wall for study. William Edgar Geil [57] from the USA was the first Western scholar who traveled the whole length of the Great Wall. He discovered the Qinghai Great Wall in his travel. On the basis of field investigation, he published the book *The Great Wall of China* in 1909, providing a comprehensive discussion on the origins, history, culture and military system of the Great Wall, as the first Western monograph on the Great Wall.

British explorer Marc Aurel Stein [58] and the Swedish archaeologist Warlock Bergman and some others were concerned about the Great Wall Archeology in early time. In the first 30 years of the 20th century, they made archaeological excavation and mapping on Juyan sites of the Han

[57] [US]Geil: *The Great Wall of China*, Shandong Pictorial Publishing House, in 2006.

[58] [UK] Written by Stein, and translated by Xiang Da: *Archaeology in the Western Regions*, the Commercial Press, in 2013; [UK] Written by Aurel Stein, and translated by Ai Lijiang *Archaeological Map of Asian Inland*, Guangxi Normal University Press, in 2004.

长城的布局有了比较清楚的认识，并且采集到 1 万余枚记录汉代长城军事档案的简牍，即后世所说的“居延汉简”，成为重要的考古研究材料。法国汉学家埃玛纽埃尔-爱德华·沙畹（Emmanuel-èdouard·Chavannes）[59]和他的学生马伯乐（Henri· Maspero）[60]对斯坦因所获的汉简进行了最早的释读。

（二）长城理论研究

20 世纪以前的西方世界，主要将长城视为边界，认为起到隔绝文明，孤立主义的作用。

20 世纪初以来，海外的长城研究方兴未艾。其中以美国学者成就最为突出。1934 年，美国学者欧文·拉铁摩尔在其著作《中国的亚洲内陆边疆》一书中提出了“长城边疆”理论，从地缘政治角度出发，认为长城的核心不是“隔绝”，而是“过渡”与“互动”。他对东北、内蒙古、新疆、西藏等地的生态环境、民族、生产方式、社会形态、历史演进等方面进行了深入考察，揭示了上述四个边疆地区与内地的互动关系，讨论了中国内陆边疆历史的丰富多样性，《中国的亚洲内陆边疆》成为长城研究的必读书目。他所提出的“中国边疆理论”，[61]也一度成为海外长城研究的标准范式。

20 世纪 80 年代以来，受西方后现代主义思潮影响，林蔚（Arthur Waldron）提出了从政治史的角度研究长城的新思路。[62]以他的《长城：从历史到神话》为代表，一批学者开始批判拉铁摩尔的学说，甚至对“长城”这一概念进行质疑和解构。

然而林蔚等人的观点并未根本动摇“中国边疆”理论的基础。该理论强调历史的动态变化和政治因素，体现了长城的复杂性，仍是当代西方长城研究的主流理论。但他对于长城概念的质疑，确实为长城的研究带来了新的启发。

[59]〔法〕沙畹：《奥莱尔·斯坦因在东土耳其斯坦沙漠中所获汉文文书考释》，牛津大学出版社，1913 年。

[60]〔法〕马伯乐：《斯坦因第三次中亚考察所获汉文文书》，伦敦，1953 年。

[61]〔美〕拉铁摩尔著，唐晓峰译：《中国的亚洲内陆边疆》，江苏人民出版社，2005 年。

[62]〔美〕林蔚著，石云龙、金鑫荣译：《中国长城：从历史到神话》，江苏教育出版社，2008 年。

Great Wall in Gansu and Inner Mongolia in succession, and got a clear understanding of the layout of the Han Great Wall in Juyan sites. They collected more than 10,000 pieces of bamboo slips recording the military archives of the Han Great Wall, namely the later well-known "Juyan Han Bamboo Slips", as important archaeological study materials. French sinologist Emmanuel-èdouard Chavannes [59] and his student Henri Maspero [60] made the earliest interpretation of Stein's Han bamboo slips.

### (II) Theory study on the Great Wall

The Western world before the 20th century mainly regarded the Great Wall as a border, believing that it plays the role of civilization separation and isolationism.

Since the early 20th century, overseas study on the Great Wall was still in prosperity. Among them the achievements of US scholars were most outstanding. In 1934, US scholar Owen Rattimore put forward the theory of "Great Wall Frontier" in his book *Inner Asion Frontier of China,* believing that the core of the Great Wall is not "isolation" but "transition" and "interaction" from the geopolitical point of view. He made in-depth investigations on the ecological environment, ethic group, mode of production, social form and historical evolution in northeast China, Inner Mongolia, Xinjiang and Tibet, and revealed the interaction between the four frontier regions and the inland, and discussed the diversity of China's inland frontier history. *Inner Asion Frontier of China* became a must-read book for the Great Wall study. His "Theory of China's Frontier" [61] also became a standard model of overseas study on the Great Wall.

Since the 1980s, influenced by the Western postmodernism, Arthur Waldron proposed a new idea of the Great Wall study from the perspective of political history [62]. Represented by his *the Great Wall: From History to Myth*, some scholars began to criticize the theory of Lattimore, and even questioned and deconstructed the concept of "the Great Wall".

However, Arthur Waldron's point of view did not fundamentally shake the theory of "Great Wall Frontier". This theory emphasizes the dynamic changes and political factors of history, and embodies the complexity of the Great Wall. It's still the mainstream theory of contemporary Western study on the Great Wall. But his questioning against the concept of the Great Wall indeed brought new inspiration for the Great Wall study.

[59] [France] Chavannes: *Investigation and Interpretation of Han Books Obtained in the East Turkestan Desert by Aurel Stein*, Oxford University Press, in 1913.

[60] [France] Maspero: *Han Books Obtained in Stein's Third Central Asian Investigation*, London, in 1953.

[61] [US] Written by Lattimore and translated by Tang Xiaofeng: *China's Asian Inland Frontier*, Jiangsu People's Publishing House, in 2005.

[62] [US] Written by Arthur Waldron, and translated by Shi Yunlong and Jin Xinrong: *China Great Wall: from History to Mythology*, Jiangsu Education Press, in 2008.

# 第三节 “长城保护工程”实施以来的长城研究进展

※ 研究领域——史学理论研究进一步发展
※ 保护理论政策和应用技术研究兴起
※ 学科导向的专题研究繁荣
※ 研究手段——多学科参与、新方法应用

## 一、长城历史理论研究

“长城保护工程”实施以来，史学理论研究进一步发展。中国学者赵现海撰写的《明代九边长城军镇史》批判继承了国外的“高边疆”理论“中国边疆理论”“区域社会史”观念等边疆研究理论，并进行改良，提出“长城制度史”研究模式。首次从整体上对明长城军事制度进行了系统考察；讨论了处于核心边疆的明代九边军镇建立、发展过程，长城建筑与防御模式的兴起与变化，及其与明朝政权兴亡、东北亚地缘格局变化的关系；从地理的角度，对中国古代历史变迁给出了整体性的诠释；从世界史的视野出发，检讨了明代九边长城军镇防御模式对于近世中国疆域界定与近代化进程的整体影响。他的新作《明长城时代的开启》则从微观的角度，以河套地区明长城防线的演变为线索，提出“外边疆”“内边疆”等概念，探讨长城的社会史问题，可以说是长城历史研究理论方法的重要新成果。

# Section 3: The progress of the Great Wall study since the implementation of the "Great Wall Conservation Project"

- Study field -- further development of historical theory study
- Rise of conservation theory policies and application-based technology study
- Prosperity of subject-oriented special study
- Study methods -- participation of various disciplines and application of new methods

## I. Historical Theory Study on the Great Wall

Historical theory study was further developed since the implementation of "Great Wall Conservation Project". Chinese scholar Zhao Xianhai wrote *the History of Nine Frontier Fortifications in the Great Wall Region of Ming Dynasty,* which critically inherited the foreign theories of "high frontier", "China's frontier", the concept of "regional social history" and other frontier study theories, improved them and proposed the study model of the "Great Wall system History". It made systematic study on the military system of the Great Wall on the whole for the first time; it discussed the establishment and development process of the nine frontier fortification of the Ming dynasty in the core frontier, the rise and change of the architecture and defense mode of the Great Wall, and its relationship with the rise and fall of the Ming Dynasty regime and the change of the geographical pattern in Northeast Asia; it made holistic interpretation of the historical changes in ancient China from the perspective of geography; it discussed the overall influence of the defense model of the nine frontier fortification in the great wall region of Ming dynasty on the definition of modern China's territory and modernization process from the perspective of world history. His new book the Begin of the Ming Great Wall Era put forward the concepts of "outside frontier" and "inner frontier" based on the evolution of the Ming Great Wall defense line in Hetao Region from micro perspective, and discussed the social history of the Great Wall. it's regarded as an important new achievement of the theoretical methodology of the Great Wall historical study.

美国学者狄宇宙（Nicola Di Cosmo）则对长城起源及其背后的社会动因开展研究，提出“汉族扩张论”。他对汉代与匈奴的关系，及长城在其中所扮演的角色的解读，十分具有冲击力和颠覆性。[63]

## 二、长城考古研究

“长城保护工程”实施以来，长城考古在规模、目标和领域方面都有明显的变化。在“长城保护工程”框架下开展的长城资源调查工作，其主要目的是服务于长城的保护管理。

2007 年至 2010 年，经国务院同意，国家文物局统一组织开展了长城资源调查。这是首次由中国政府统一组织在长城沿线各省（自治区、直辖市）全面开展的一次长城资源调查，此次调查获得了大量的长城资源一手资料。为加强长城科学研究，丰富社会各界对长城的认识，2011 年国家文物局发布《长城资源调查报告编写体例（试行）》。对长城资源调查报告的体例、主要内容等进行规范，积极推动、指导各地开展各个时代长城资源调查报告的编写。目前，各省已经编写出版长城资源调查报告 12 部，各省调查报告仍在陆续出版之中。（表 4-2）

由中国文化遗产研究院负责编写的《明长城资源调查报告（暂定名）》也已经完成了初稿。该报告首次将明长城作为一个整体，系统梳理明长城资源调查数据，并按照长城资源认定分类标准，对明长城涉及的 20000 余处墙体、壕堑、单体建筑、关堡和相关遗存进行了考古类型学分析，是迄今为止明长城考古研究最完整的材料，以下会有专门介绍，此不赘述。

[63]〔美〕宇宙著，贺严、高书文译：《古代中国与其强邻》，中国社会科学出版社，2010 年。

US scholar Nicola Di Cosmo studied the origin of the Great Wall and its social motivation, and put forward the theory of "the Han nationality expansion". His interpretation of the relationship between the Han dynasty and the Huns, and the role of the Great Wall in this relationship is very shocking and subversive [63].

## II. Archaeological study on the Great Wall

Since the implementation of the "Great Wall Conservation Project", the Great Wall archeology obviously changed in size, goal and field. The resource investigation on the Great Wall in the framework of "Great Wall Conservation Project" is mainly for the purpose of serving the conservation management of the Great Wall.

During 2007-2010, with the consent of the State Council, the State Administration of Cultural Heritage organized the resource investigation on the Great Wall. This is the first all-round resource investigation on the Great Wall organized by the Chinese government in all the provinces (autonomous regions and municipalities) along the Great Wall. A lot of first-hand information about the resources of the Great Wall was obtained in this investigation. In order to strengthen scientific study on the Great Wall and enrich the community's understanding of the Great Wall, the State Administration of Cultural Heritage released the Preparation System of the Resource Investigation Report on the Great Wall (Trial Edition) in 2011. It regulated the form and main content of the resource investigation report on the Great Wall, and actively promoted and guided various places to compile the resource investigation reports on the Great Wall in each dynasty. Until now, various provinces have compiled and published 12 resource investigation reports on the Great Wall, and more provincial investigation reports are still in publication. (Table 4-2)

[63] [US] Written by Cosmo, and translated by He Yan and Gao Shuwen: *Ancient China and Its Strong Neighbors*, China Social Science Press, in 2010.

## 表 4-2：长城资源调查报告出版情况统计简表

| 省份 | 报告名称 | 编著单位 | 出版社 | 出版年度 |
|---|---|---|---|---|
| 天津市 | 《天津市明长城资源调查报告》 | 天津市文物局、天津市文化遗产保护中心、天津市明长城资源调查队 | 文物出版社 | 2012 |
| 河北省 | 《河北省明长城资源调查报告—来源县卷》 | 河北省文物局 、河北省古代建筑保护研究所、河北省明长城资源调查队 | 文物出版社 | 2010 |
| 内蒙古自治区 | 《内蒙古自治区长城资源调查报告—明长城卷》 | 内蒙古自治区文化厅（文物局）、内蒙古自治区文物考古研究所 | 文物出版社 | 2013 |
| | 《内蒙古自治区长城资源调查报告—东南部战国秦汉长城卷》 | 内蒙古自治区文化厅（文物局）、内蒙古自治区文物考古研究所 | 文物出版社 | 2014 |
| | 《内蒙古自治区长城资源调查报告—北魏长城卷》 | 内蒙古自治区文化厅（文物局）、内蒙古自治区文物考古研究所 | 文物出版社 | 2014 |
| 辽宁省 | 《辽宁省长城资源调查报告》 | 辽宁省文物局 | 文物出版社 | 2011 |
| 吉林省 | 《吉林省长城资源调查报告》 | 吉林省文物局 | 文物出版社 | 2015 |
| 陕西省 | 《陕西省明长城资源调查报告．营堡卷》 | 陕西省考古研究院 | 文物出版社 | 2011 |
| | 《陕西省明长城资源调查报告》 | 陕西省考古研究院 | 文物出版社 | 2015 |
| | 《陕西省早期长城资源调查报告》 | 陕西省考古研究院、西北大学文化遗产学院 | 文物出版社 | 2015 |
| 青海省 | 《青海省明长城资源调查报告》 | 青海省文物管理局、青海省文物考古研究所 | 文物出版社 | 2012 |
| 新疆维尔自治区 | 《新疆维吾尔自治区长城资源调查报告》 | 新疆维吾尔自治区文物局 | 文物出版社 | 2014 |

Table 4-2: Summary of the publication of resource investigation reports on the Great Wall

| Province | Report title | Compiler | Publishing house | publishing year |
|---|---|---|---|---|
| Tianjin City | *Resource Investigation Reports on the Ming Great Wall in Tianjin City* | Tianjin Bureau of Cultural Relics, Tianjin Cultural Heritage Conservation Center, and Tianjin Resource Investigation Team on the Ming Great Wall | Cultural Relics Press | 2012 |
| Hebei Province | *Resource Investigation Reports on the Ming Great Wall in Hebei Province – Volume of Laiyuan County* | Hebei Bureau of Cultural Relics, Hebei Ancient Building Conservation and Research Institute, and Hebei Resource Investigation Team on the Ming Great Wall | Cultural Relics Press | 2010 |
| Inner Mongolia Autonomous Region | *Resource Investigation Reports on the Ming Great Wall in Inner Mongolia Autonomous Region -- Volume of the Ming Great Wall* | Inner Mongolia Autonomous Region Department of Culture (Bureau of Cultural Relics), and Inner Mongolia Autonomous Region Institute of Cultural Relics and Archeology | Cultural Relics Press | 2013 |
| | *Resource Investigation Reports on the Ming Great Wall in Inner Mongolia Autonomous Region -- Volume of the Warring States, Qin and Han Great Wall in Southeast China* | Inner Mongolia Autonomous Region Department of Culture (Bureau of Cultural Relics), and Inner Mongolia Autonomous Region Institute of Cultural Relics and Archeology | Cultural Relics Press | 2014 |
| | *Resource Investigation Reports on the Ming Great Wall in Inner Mongolia Autonomous Region -- Volume of the Northern Wei Great Wall* | Inner Mongolia Autonomous Region Department of Culture (Bureau of Cultural Relics), and Inner Mongolia Autonomous Region Institute of Cultural Relics and Archeology | Cultural Relics Press | 2014 |
| Liaoning Province | *Resource Investigation Reports on the Great Wall in Liaoning Province* | Resource Investigation Reports on the Great Wall in Liaoning Province | Cultural Relics Press | 2011 |
| Jilin Province | *Resource Investigation Reports on the Great Wall in Jilin Province* | Jilin Bureau of Cultural Relics | Cultural Relics Press | 2015 |
| Shaanxi Province | *Resource Investigation Reports on the Ming Great Wall in Shaanxi Province -- Volume of Yingbao* | Shaanxi Provincial Research Institute of Archaeology | Cultural Relics Press | 2011 |
| | *Resource Investigation Reports on the Ming Great Wall in Shaanxi Province* | Shaanxi Provincial Institute of Archeology | Cultural Relics Press | 2015 |
| | *Resource Investigation Reports on the Great Wall of Early Period in Shaanxi Province* | Shaanxi Provincial Institute of Archeology, and Cultural Heritage Institute of Northwest University | Cultural Relics Press | 2015 |
| Qinghai Province | *Resource Investigation Reports on the Ming Great Wall in Qinghai Province* | Qinghai Provincial Administration Bureau of Cultural Relics, and Qinghai Provincial Institute of Cultural Relics and Archeology | Cultural Relics Press | 2012 |
| Xinjiang Uygur Autonomous Region | *Resource Investigation Reports on the Great Wall in Xinjiang Uygur Autonomous Region* | Xinjiang Uygur Autonomous Region Bureau of Cultural Relics | Cultural Relics Press | 2014 |

西北大学段清波、徐为民主编的《中国历代长城发现与研究》以长城资源调查材料为基础，结合长城文献的梳理工作，把历代长城分为战国长城、秦长城、汉长城、魏晋南北朝长城、隋长城、唐长城、辽长城、金长城、明长城、清柳条边等10个时期的长城进行分时段研究，全面总结过去的长城研究成果，提出长城研究的不足和发展方向，为今后的研究提供了全面、可靠、学术价值高的资料。

此外，近年来还出现了配合长城风景区规划、保护规划和保护工程前期勘探开展的一些考古研究。

如北京市配合慕田峪长城风景名胜区总体规划开展了地下文物勘探与试掘；[64] 山东省，配合齐长城保护规划编制，于2014、2015年度对黄岛区多段齐长城遗址开展了发掘勘探工作，并形成了年度报告[65]等；除辽宁省、天津市、河北省、内蒙古自治区、陕西省、青海省、新疆维吾尔自治区等省出版了长城资源调查报告外，20世纪80年代河北省文物考古研究所对蓟镇长城的调查报告，也于2012年出版。此外，北京市、[66]河南省、[67]宁夏回族自治区、[68]新疆维吾尔自治区[69]等发表有专题性的调查与发掘简报，辽宁、吉林、黑龙江等省发表有多篇总结性研究成果，另外，山东、陕西省等省配合保护规划编制工作进行了前期勘察，并编写了勘察报。研究成果共计21部、篇。

[64] 北京市文物研究所：《关于慕田峪长城风景名胜区总体规划地下文物调查的报告》，2013年，内部资料。

[65] a 青岛市文物保护考古研究所：《2014年齐长城——黄岛段考古调查勘探工作报告》，2014年1月20日。内部资料。b 青岛市文物保护考古研究所：《2015年齐长城考古调查勘探工作报告》，2015年5月11日。内部资料。

[66] 北京市文物研究所，延庆县文物管理所：《北京市延庆县四海镇火焰山营盘遗址发掘简报》，《北京文博》2007年3期。

[67] a 赵杰：《明代河南省长城考察简报》，《华夏考古》2012年第4期。b 李一丕等：《豫南地区楚长城资源调查与发掘取得突破》，《中国文物报》2011年9月30日，005版。

[68] 宁夏回族自治区文物考古研究所、内蒙古鄂托克前旗文化局、灵武市文物管理所：《宁夏回族自治区灵武市古长城调查与试掘》，《考古与文物》2006年2期。

[69] 邢春林，程建军：《新疆渭干河西岸唐代烽燧遗址的调查与研究》，《"丝绸之路与龟兹中外文化交流"学术研讨会论文集》，2010年8月19日。

The first draft of *Resource Investigation Reports on the Ming Great Wall (Tentative Name)* compiled by Chinese Academy of Cultural Heritage was also completed. The report regards the Great Wall as a whole for the first time. It made systematic sorting on the resource investigation data of the Ming Great Wall, and made archaeological typology analysis on more than 20,000 walls, trenches, monolithic buildings, forts and relevant remains related to the Great Wall in accordance with the resources identification and classification standards of the Great Wall. It is the most complete material of the archaeological study on the Ming Great Wall so far. There is special introduction in the following chapter.

*Discovery and Study on China's Ancient Great Wall* compiled by Duan Qingbo and Xu Weimin from Northwest University classified the ancient Great Wall into the Warring States Great Wall, the Qin Great Wall, the Han Great Wall, Wei, Jin and the Northern and Southern Dynasties Great Wall, the Sui Great Wall, the Tang Great Wall, the Liao Great Wall, the Jin Great Wall, the Ming Great Wall and the Qing Wicker based on the resource investigation materials on the Great Wall combing with the sorting of the Great Wall literature and made sectional study on these ten periods. It summarizes the achievements of the Great Wall studies in the past and puts forward the shortcomings and development orientations of the Great Wall study, to provide all-round and reliable data with high academic value for the future studies.

In addition, in recent years there are some archaeological studies coordinating with the Great Wall scenic area planning, conservation planning and pre-exploration for conservation projects.

For example, to coordinate with the overall planning of Mutianyu Great Wall Scenic Area, Beijing City made underground cultural relics exploration and trail excavation[64]; to coordinate with the compilation of the Qi Great Wall conservation planning, Shandong Province made exploration and excavation on many sections of Qi Great Wall sites in Huangdao District in 2014 and 2015, and completed annual reports[65]; Liaoning Province, Tianjin, Hebei Province, Inner

[64] Beijing Institute of Cultural Relics: *Report on the Underground Cultural Relics Investigation of the Master Planning of Mutianyu Great Wall Scenic Area*, in 2013, internal information.

[65] A. Qingdao Institute of Cultural Relics Conservation and Archeology: *2014 Report on the Archaeological Investigation and Exploration in Qi Great Wall – Huangdao Section*, on January 20, 2014. Internal Information. B. Qingdao Institute of Cultural Relics Conservation and Archeology: *2014 Report on the Archaeological Investigation and Exploration in Qi Great Wall*, on May 11, 2015. Internal Information.

吉林省为配合保护规划编制工作，经国家文物局批准，2011年、2013年和2014年，分别对唐代老边岗土墙和延边长城进行了局部考古发掘，确认了唐代老边岗土墙内侧挖壕、外侧筑墙的构筑方式、老边岗土墙为文献记载的高句丽千里长城以及延边长城的始建年代等问题，为长城资源调查报告的编写和保护规划编制提供了资料。[70]

内蒙古自治区乌拉特中旗乌不浪口东段秦汉长城修缮工程中，考古清理了乌不浪口段西侧71米长城的基础遗址，发现了营盘（暂定）毛石基础，并针对考古发现调整补充了设计方案，对遗址基础进行加固，内侧做防水隔离层，保护清理后的遗址原地表。[71]

陕西省为配合款贡城保护修缮工程中，先后两次对款贡城进行考古调查勘探，完整揭露了墙体，并详细勘察了整个城址现存状况。

新疆维吾尔自治区吐鲁番市境内烽燧保护修缮工程对部分烽燧和戍堡也开展了前期考古清理工作，明确了布局，为科学修缮奠定了基础。（图4-2）

图4-2
新疆维吾尔自治区七泉湖烽燧保护工程前期考古清理现场俯瞰（新疆维吾尔自治区文物局 提供）

Fig. 4-2
Overlook of the pre-archaeological clean-up site of the beacon tower conservation project of Qiquan Lake, Xinjiang Uygur Autonomous Region (provided by Xinjiang Uygur Autonomous Region Bureau of Cultural Relics)

## 三、长城保护技术研究

现存长城建造于不同时代，分布于不同地域，所处的自然环境各不相同，其建筑形式、所用材料、技术多种多样。长城保护技术研究多结合长城修缮工程进行，目的在于有针对性研究和提升长城保护技术。

[70]《吉林省长城保护工程（2010–2014年）总结报告及“十三五”工作计划》。
[71]《乌拉特中期长城保护情况汇报》。

Mongolia Autonomous Region, Shaanxi Province, Qinghai and Xinjiang Uygur Autonomous Region published resource investigation reports on the Great Wall. In addition to these, the investigation report on the Jizhen Great Wall by Hebei Province Institute of Archaeology in the 1980s' was also published in 2012. Besides, Beijing City[66], Henan Province[67], Ningxia Hui Autonomous Region[68] and Xinjiang Uygur Autonomous Region[69] published thematic investigation and excavation briefings, Liaoning, Jilin and Heilongjiang published a number of summary study achievements. In addition, Shandong and Shaanxi Province carried out preliminary surveys to coordinate with the compilation of conservation planning, and compiled survey report. Study achievements totally include 21 chapters and articles.

To coordinate with the compilation of conservation planning, approved by the State Administration of Cultural Heritage, Jilin Province made partial archaeological excavations of the Tang Laobiangang Wall and Yanbian Great Wall respectively in 2011, 2013 and 2014, confirmed the building method of the Tang Laobiangang Wall by inside trench and outside wall, the fact that Laobiangang Wall is the Goguryeo Great Wall recorded in the literature, and the building date of Yanbian Great Wall, which provided data for the compilation of the resource investigation reports on the Great Wall and the conservation planning.[70]

In the renovation project of the east part of the Qin and Han Great Wall at Wubu Langkou, Urad Zhongqi, Inner Mongolia Autonomous Region, the archaeological team cleaned up the base site of 71-meter Great Wall at the west side of Wubu Langkou, and discovered base of Yingpan (tentative) Stone, and adjusted additional the design program according to the archaeological discoveries to reinforce the foundation of the site and add waterproof isolation layer inside to protect the original site ground after the clean-up.

To coordinate with Kuangong City conservation and renovation project, Shaanxi Province made archaeological investigations and explorations twice, completely exposed the wall, and made a detailed investigation on the existing situation of the whole city.[71]

The beacon tower conservation and renovation project in Turpan City, Xinjiang Uygur Autonomous Region also made pre-archaeological and clean-up work on some beacon towers and castles, and made clear the layout, which laid the foundation for scientific renovation (Fig 4-2).

[66] Beijing Institute of Cultural Relics, Yanqing County Institute of Cultural Relics Management: *Briefing on the Excavation of Yingpan Site in Huoyan Mountain, Sihai Town, Yanqing County, Beijing City, Beijing Cultural Heritage* issue 3 in 2007.

[67] A. Zhao Jie: *Briefing on the Investigation of Henan Great Wall in the Ming Dynasty, Chinese Archeology* issue 4 in 2012. B. Li Yipi and others: *Breakthroughs in the Resource Investigation and Excavation of Chu Great Wall in South Henan, Chinese Cultural Relics News*, edition 005on September 30, 2011.

[68] Ningxia Hui Autonomous Region Institute of Cultural Relics and Archeology, Inner Mongolia Etuokeqianqi Bureau of Culture, Lingwu Institue of Cultural Relics Management: Investigation and Trail Excavation on the Ancient Great Wall in Lingwu City, Ningxia Hui Autonomous Region, Archeology and Cultural Relics, issue 2 in 2006.

[69] Xing Chunlin & Cheng Jianjun: *Investigation and Study on the Tang Beacon Site in the West Bank of Weigan River in Xinjiang, Academic Seminar Symposium on the "Cultural Exchanges betwen Silk Road and Kucha*, on August 19, 2010.

[70] *Summary Report and the "Thirteen Five" Work Plan of the Great Wall Conservation Project in Jilin Province (2010-2014)*

[71] *Report on the Mid-term Great Wall conservation of Ulat*

## （一）空间信息技术应用

### 1、以遥感为基础的长城空间考古

早在20世纪80年代末90年代初，地质矿产部就相继对北京市、[72]宁夏回族自治区[73]的明长城进行过区域性的航空遥感调查，用以掌握长城长度、分布与保存状况。在对北京长城的遥感调查过程中，成功发现了“北京节”敌台，确定了明代“内长城”与“外长城”的分界点。这些工作为长城资源调查工作积累了经验。

2000年以来，以遥感为基础、融合了考古、GPS和地理信息技术的空间考古技术发展起来。对长城这样环境复杂多样的遗产进行大尺度研究方面，空间考古具有很大优势。

2012年，中国科学院遥感与数字地球研究所（简称中科院遥感所）开始利用空间考古技术参与丝绸之路沿线的遥感考古。2013年，中科院遥感所研究员、联合国教科文组织国际自然与文化遗产空间技术中心副主任王心源主持的丝绸之路瓜州－敦煌（沙洲）空间遥感考古项目取得重大进展。王心源的团队通过遥感技术与传统考古手段和野外调查相结合，在丝绸之路瓜州至敦煌（沙洲）段一处消失古绿洲新发现多处与长城相关的古遗址。而此前考古工作者用了近十年时间才在戈壁滩找到巴州古城。

---

[72] 曾朝铭，顾巍：《北京地区长城航空遥感调查》，《文物》1987年7期。

[73] 黎风、顾巍、曹灿霞：《宁夏长城航空遥感调查研究》，《国土资源遥感》，1994年3期。

## III. Studies on the Great Wall conservation technology

Existing Great Walls were built in different times and distributed in different regions, with various natural environment and diverse architectural forms, materials and technologies. The studies on the Great Wall conservation technology were mostly made combining with the Great Wall renovation project, in order for targeted studies and improvement of the Great Wall conservation technology.

### (I) Application of space information technology

1. Space archaeology on the Great Wall based on remote sensing

As early as the late 1980s and early 1990s, the Ministry of Geology and Mineral Resources made a regional aerial remote sensing survey on the Ming Great Walls in Beijing[72] and Ningxia Hui Autonomous Region[73], to know the length, distribution and preservation of the Great Wall. In the process of remote sensing investigation on Beijing Great Wall, the "Beijing Jie" enemy station was successfully discovered, and the demarcation point between the "inner Great Wall" and "outer Great Wall" in the Ming dynasty was distinguished. These work accumulated experience for the resource investigation on the Great Wall.

Since 2000, spatial archaeological technologies based on remote sensing, integrating archaeological, GPS and geographic information technology was developed. Spatial archeology enjoys a great advantage in large-scale study on complex and diverse heritage sites such as the Great Wall.

In 2012, the Institute of Remote Sensing and Digital Earth of the Chinese Academy of Sciences (hereinafter referred to as RADI) began to apply space archaeological technology in the remote sensing archeology along the Silk Road. In 2013, the Silk Road Guazhou-Dunhuang (Shazhou) remote sensing archeology project hosted by Wang Xinyuan, a researcher at the RADI and the deputy director of the International Center on Spatial Technologies for Natural and Cultural Heritage under the Auspices of UNESCO, made significant progress. Wang Xinyuan's team discovered many ancient sites related ancient the Great Wall at a disappeared ancient oasis in Guazhou-Dunhuang (Shazhou) section of the Silk Road through the combination of the remote sensing

[72] Zeng Zhaoming & Gu Wei: *Aviation Remote Sensing Investigation on the Great Wall in Beijing Area*, *Cultural Relics*, issue 7 in 1987.

[73] Li Feng, Gu Wei & Cao Canxia: *Aviation Remote Sensing Investigation and Study on the Great Wall in Ningxia*, *Remote Sensing of Land Resources*, issue 3 in 1994.

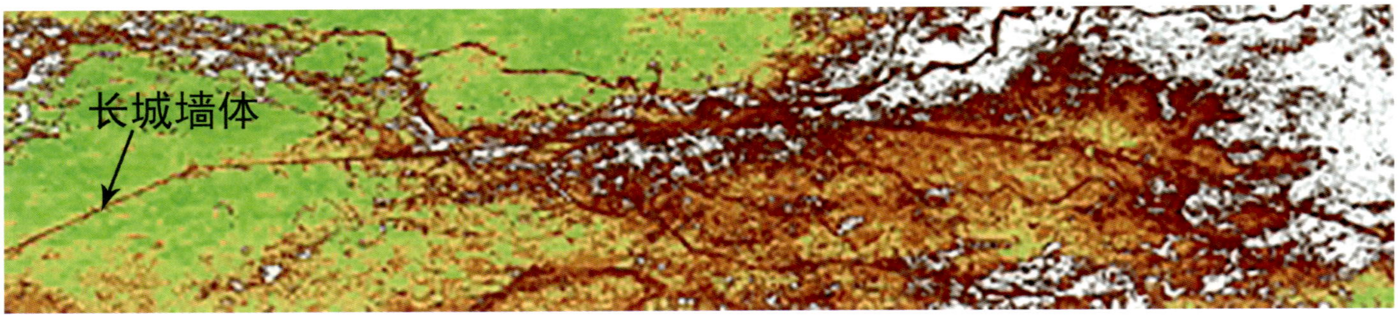


图 4-3
资源三号卫星 2m 分辨率图像遥感解译获得的汉长城遗址及其特征（图片来源：光明网 http://epaper.gmw.cn/gmrb/html/2013-11/02/nw.D110000gmrb_20131102_1-12.htm?div=-1）

Fig. 4-3
Site of the Han Great Wall and its characteristics obtained through the remote sensing interpretation of Resource 3# satellite's 2m resolution image (Source: Gmw.cn http://epaper.gmw.cn/gmrb/html/2013-11/02/nw.D110000gmrb_20131102_1-12.htm?div=-1)

瓜州—至敦煌（沙洲）是丝绸之路的一段重要干道，对于研究我国古代丝绸之路交通史、研究生态环境变化具有重要的价值。2013 年 10 月 13-14 日，中科院遥感所、兰州大学、甘肃省文物考古研究所、瓜州县文物局（博物馆）、联合国教科文组织国际自然与文化遗产空间技术中心联合组成的科学考察队，在通过遥感技术对瓜—沙段影像分析的基础上，对疑似考古点进行了实地考察和验证。此次考察确认新发现了 5 处古城遗址，2 处民居村落中的 13 处房址遗迹，1 段古渠道遗迹、1 条古道遗迹和 1 处陶窑遗址。2015 年 4 月，该团队基于高分辨率卫星图像，通过人机交互解译，从全局尺度揭示了位于新疆塔里木盆地南缘的丝绸之路重镇——米兰遗址灌溉系统的详细结构。研究人员在东西长约 6 公里，南北宽约 5 公里范围内发现了由 1 条干渠、7 条支渠和大量斗渠、毛渠组成的灌溉系统。据遥感影像估算，当时可供利用的绿洲资源达 8000 至 10000 公顷。

据考证，米兰遗址为《汉书 · 西域传 · 鄯善国》记载的楼兰古国的伊循城。元凤四年（前 77 年），汉朝应楼兰的请求派军队到此屯田戍守。米兰遗址附近的汉代长城烽燧很可能就是这一时期在此修筑的。米兰灌溉系统的发现，对于研究丝绸之路瓜沙段线路走向、长城军事与后勤系统、沿线古环境演变具有重要意义。（图 4-3、4-4）

图 4-4
丝绸之路空间遥感考古发现的古城（图片来源：甘肃省文物局官网 http://www.gsww.gov.cn/Web_DetailPic.aspx?id=11713）

Fig. 4-4
Ancient city discovered through the Silk Road space remote sensing archaeology (Source: official website of Gansu Provincial Bureau of Cultural Relics Http://www.gsww.gov.cn/Web_DetailPic.aspx?id=11713)

technology and traditional archaeological methods and field investigation. Prior to this, archaeologists spent nearly a decade to find the ancient city of Bavaria in the Gobi Desert.

Guazhou-Dunhuang (Shazhou) is an important section of the Silk Road, with high value for the study the transportation history of ancient Silk Road and the changes of ecological environment. In October 13-14, 2013, a scientific research team jointly organized by the RADI, Lanzhou University, Gansu Provincial Institute of Cultural Relics and Archeology, Guazhou County Bureau of Cultural Relics (Museum) and the International Center on Space Technologies for Natural and Cultural Heritage under the Auspices of UNESCO made field investigation and verification on suspected archaeological sites based on the movie analysis of Guazhou-Dunhuang (Shazhou) section through remote sensing technology. The investigation confirmed the five newly-discovered sites of ancient cities, 13 sites of residential houses in 2 villages, 1 site of ancient channel, 1 site of ancient road and 1 site of pottery kiln. In April 2015, based on high-resolution satellite images, through the human-computer interaction interpretation, the team revealed the detailed structure of the irrigation system of Milan site – an important town on the Silk Road in the south of Tarim Basin, Xinjiang from in global scale. Researchers discovered the irrigation system consisting of 1 main canal, 7 branch canals and a large number of lateral canals and sublateral canals in a scope 6 km long from the east to the west and 5 km wide from the north to the south. According to estimation of remote sensing images, the available oasis resources reached 8,000 to 10,000 hectares at the time.

According to the study, the site of Milan was Yixun City of ancient Loulan recorded in *the Book of Former Han; the Western Regions; Shanshan State.* In the fourth year of Yuan Feng period (77 BC), the Han dynasty sent troops to garrison this region in response to Loulan's request. The beacon tower of the Han Great Wall near by the site of Milan was probably built in this period. The discovery of the Milan irrigation system is of great significance to the study on the direction of the Silk Road at Guazhou- Shazhou section, military and logistics system of the Great Wall, and ancient environmental evolution along this line. (Fig 4-3, 4-4)

2、长城资源测绘

长城资源调查范围覆盖东经 130.5° -75.2°，北纬 32.5° - 50.3°，高程海拔 0-3400 米，地域面积超过 4 万平方公里。调查范围之广、难度之高，调查数据量之大，前所未有。对长城这样超大型的文化遗产，传统的文物调查手段难以支撑，需要探索更加高效和精确的新调查方法。空间信息技术的发展，使这一目标的实现成为可能。

### 专栏：空间信息技术

空间信息技术（Spatial Information Technology）自 20 世纪 60 年代兴起后，得到迅速发展和应用。通过全球卫星定位系统（Global Positioning Systems，GPS）、地理信息系统（Geographic Information System，GIS）和遥感技术（Remote Sensing，RS）等空间信息技术，结合计算机技术和通讯技术，将人类活动及其自然环境的各类信息进行数字化采集、量测、分析、存储、管理、展示和应用，极大提升了人类认识世界的能力，拓展了研究领域。

2006 年，国家文物局和国家测绘地理信息局签署协议，开展了首次战略合作，采取“文物定性，测绘定量”的方式共同开展长城资源调查。测绘人员在野外调查现场，使用全球卫星定位系统（GPS）手持终端、红外测距仪等设备采集坐标，确定长城遗存与调查者所选择的参照物（村庄、公路铁路、河流、附近其他长城遗存等）之间的距离，对长城遗存进行精确定位，并现场填写电子调查日志与调查登记表。专业测绘人员还使用 AutoCAD 软件对保存较好或有突出特点的单体建筑、关堡、有特点的城墙、马面、相关遗存等进行测绘制图，用激光雷达对重要遗存进行三维扫描和建模。

### 2. The Great Wall resource mapping

The resource investigation on the Great Wall covers a scope from 130.5 °-75.2 ° east longitude to 32.5 ° -50.3 ° north latitude, and the elevation of 0-3,400 meters, a geographical area of more than 40,000 square kilometers. The wide investigation scope, degree of difficulty and the amount of data are unprecedented. It's difficult to support the extraordinary large-scale cultural heritage such as the Great Wall by traditional cultural relics investigation means. It's necessary to explore more efficient and accurate new investigation methods. The development of spatial information technology makes this goal possible.

### Special column: Spatial information technology

After spatial information technology got prosperous in the 1960s', it has been rapidly developed and applied. Through spatial information technologies such as Global Positioning Systems (GPS), Geographic Information System (GIS) and Remote Sensing (RS), combining with computer technology and communication technology, digital collection, measurement, analysis, storage, management, display and application of all kinds of information about human activities and the natural environment greatly enhanced human's ability to understand the world and expanded the field of study.

In 2006, the State Administration of Cultural Heritage and National Administration of Surveying, Mapping and Geoinformation signed an agreement to carry out the first strategic cooperation and make resource investigation on the Great Wall by means of "cultural relics qualitative analysis and mapping quantitative analysis". Mapping personnel collects coordinate information by GPS, handheld terminal, infrared range finder and other devices in field investigation site to determine the distance between the site of Great Wall and the selected references (such as village, highway and railway, river, and other sites of Great Wall nearby), find exact location of the Great Wall sites and fill out the electronic investigation log and investigation registration form on the site. Professional surveying and mapping personnel even measures and draws maps for monolithic buildings, forts, special city walls, bastions and related remains well preserved or with prominent features with AutoCAD, and makes three-dimensional scanning and modeling for important remains with laser radar.

## 专栏：长城资源调查编码规则说明

像长城这样大规模的文物调查，又有很多单位和人员参加，必须有统一的标准要求。

国家文物局在测绘部门的协助下，制定了一套长城调查编码，用 18 位数字来对应每一段长城的所在行政区、类别、时代、材质和编号等信息，这样一来，所有调查过的长城点段就能进行统一编目，并且基本信息也可以通过编码一目了然。

2007 年，国家文物局与国家测绘局联合编制并印发了《长城资源调查文物编码规则》，并收录在《长城资源调查工作手册》中。根据规则要求，编码由地域区划代码 6 位＋类别代码 6 位＋时代码 2 位＋顺序码 4 位组成。若长城从 A（省县）进入 B（省县）又折返至 A（省县）的情况，由调查单位对所辖段长城编码。调查单位双方必须共同认定该段长城唯一的起点、终点。

测绘人员采用遥感影像解译、数字摄影测量等技术方法分别对墙体、界壕壕堑、单体建筑、关堡、相关遗存等五类长城遗存的专题数据，以及明长城沿线两侧各 1 千米、早期时代长城沿线两侧各 5 千米范围内的居民点（城市、乡镇、行政村、自然村）、道路（各级公路、铁路、乡间小路）、桥梁等基础设施，主要的河流、山脉以及地形地貌、自然景观等基础地理数据进行采集、识别和测量，并用 arcGIS 等软件对其进行加工处理，制作了包括明长城 1 米分辨率数字正射影像（DOM）、1:10000 数字高程模型（DEM）和 1:10000 数字线划图（DLG）数据，以及秦汉及其他时代长城 2.5 米分辨率 DOM、1:50000 DEM、1:50000 DLG，最终绘制完成了精确的长城资源分布图，全面展现了历代长城的分布、构成和走向，获取了误差不超过 4‰的全国、分省、分时代、材质等的长城精确长度，以及各类遗存数量、保存状况等丰富信息。（图 4-5、4-6、4-7）

基于空间信息技术制作的历代长城分布电子地图可在计算机上按照任意比例缩放，相较于传统绘图，打破了绘图单位面积表现内容的限制，大大增加了图像的信息量，精度亦为人工测量所无法企及，使图像在长城研究中能够发挥更大作用。

图 4-5
慕田峪长城数字正射影像（DOM）、数字高程模型（DEM）和数字线划图（DLG）

Fig. 4-5
DOM, DEM and DLG of Mutianyu Great Wall

## Special column: Rules on the code of the Great Wall resource investigation

There must be a unified standard for such large-scale cultural relics investigation as the Great Wall with the participation of many units and people.

With the assistance of the surveying and mapping department, The State Administration of Cultural Heritage formulated the investigation code of the Great Wall, by using 18 digits to represent the information including the administrative district, category, time, material and serial number of each section of the Great Wall. As a result, all the investigated sections of the Great Wall can collected into unified catalogs, and the basic information can also be known at a glance of the code.

In 2007, the State Administration of Cultural Heritage and National Administration of Surveying, Mapping and Geoinformation jointly compiled and published *the Rules on the Cultural Heritage Code of the Great Wall Resource Investigation included in the Work Note of the Great Wall Resource Investigation*. According to the rules, the code consists of 6 digits representing the geographical area, 6 digits representing the category, 2 digits representing the time and 4 digits representing the sequence. If a section of Great Wall extends from A (province/ county) into B (province/ county) and turns back to A (province/ county) situation, the investigation unit determine the code of the part under the jurisdiction. The two sides of the investigation units must jointly determine the only starting point and end of this section of Great Wall.

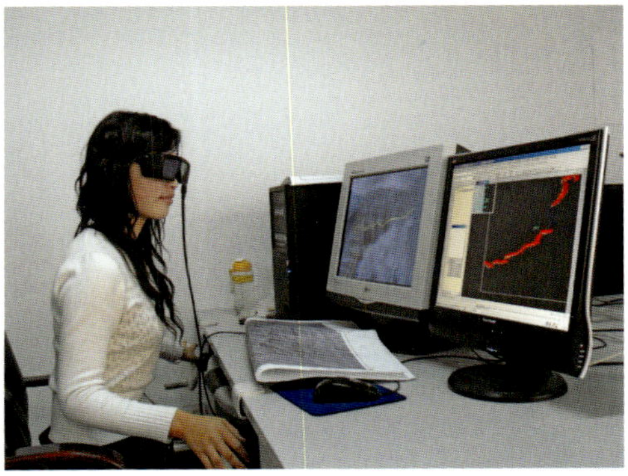

图 4-6
宁夏长城资源测绘内业作业

Fig. 4-6
Operation in Ningxia Great Wall Resources Surveying and Mapping Institute

The surveying and mapping personnel applies remote sensing image interpretation, digital photogrammetry and other technical methods to respectively collect, identify and measure the thematic data of five categories of the Great Wall remains, namely the walls, trenches, monolithic buildings, forts and related remains, and the residential sites (including cities, towns, administrative villages and natural villages), ways (including highways, railways, country roads at all levels), bridges and other infrastructure in the scope of 1 km from both sides of the Ming Great Wall and 5 km from both sides of earlier Great Walls, main rivers, mountains, topography and landform, natural landscape and other basic geographical data, and applies arcGIS and other software for processing to make 1 meter resolution digital orthoimage (DOM), 1: 10000 digital elevation model (DEM) and 1: 10000 digital line graphic (DLG) date of the Ming Great Wall, as well as 2.5 m resolution DOM, 1: 50000 DEM and 1: 50000 DLG of the Great Wall from the Qin and Han and other dynasties. Finally, they completed a precise Great Wall resources distribution map, showing the distribution, composition and direction of the ancient Great Walls from various dynasties, and obtained the precise length data of the Great Wall of the whole country, each province, each dynasty, and various materials with the error rate lower than 4 % and other information such as the quantity and preservation of all kinds of remains. (Figs 4-5, 4-6, and 4-7)

Digital maps of the ancient Great Wall distribution based on spatial information technology can be freely zoomed in and out by any proportion on the computer. Compared with traditional drawings, it broke through the restriction of contents in unit area and greatly increased the information inn the image. Its accuracy is also much higher than artificial measurement, so that the image can play a greater role in the Great Wall study.

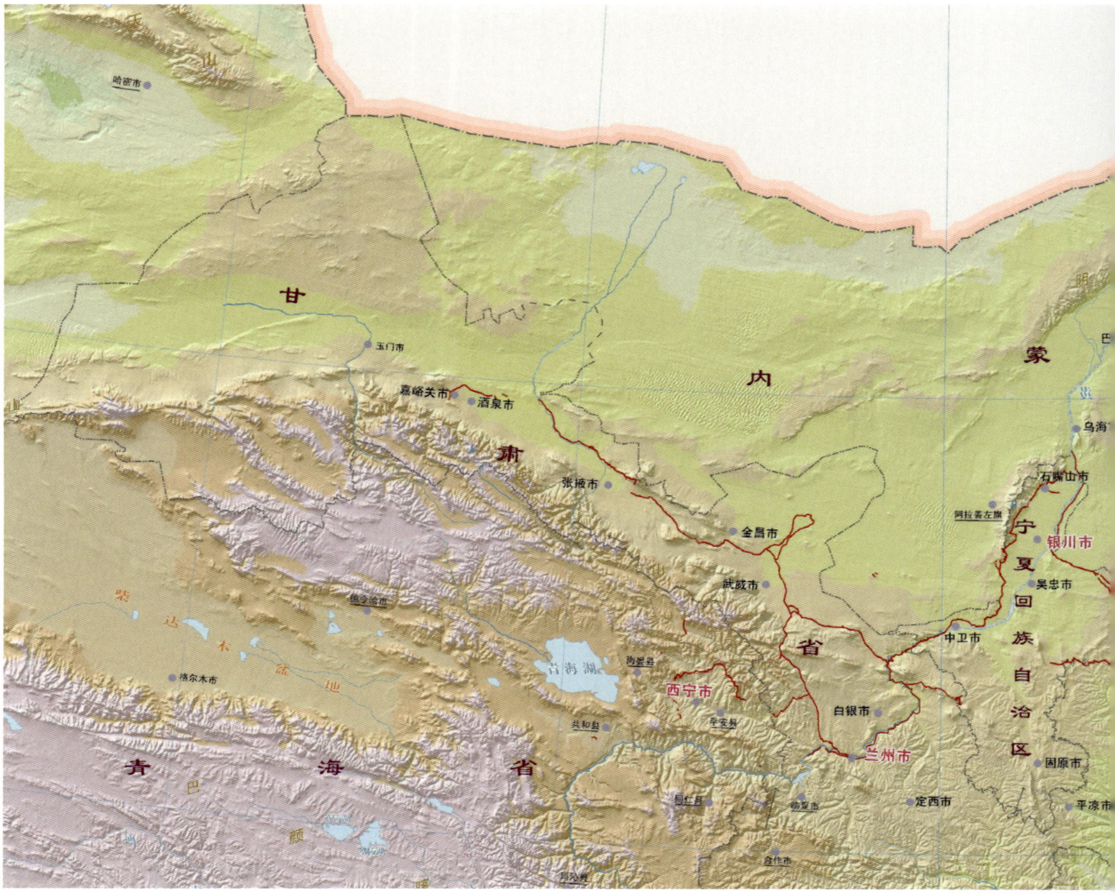


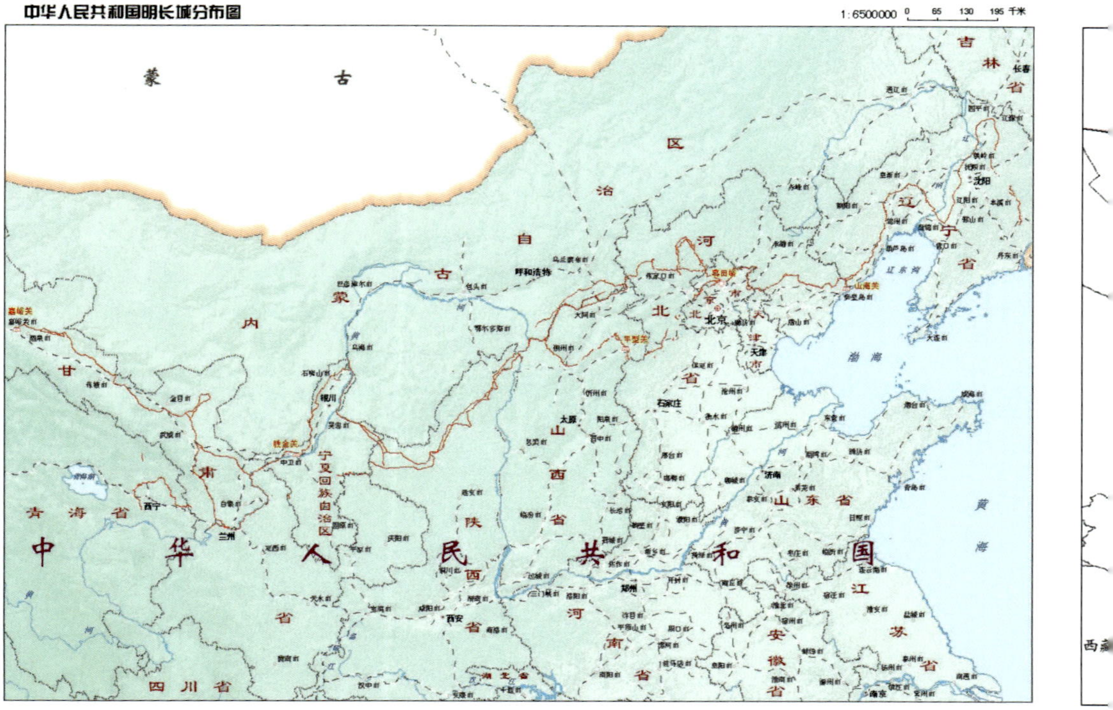


图 4-7.2
使用 arcGIS 软件绘制的长城资源分布图（政区图）

Fig. 4-7.2
Great Wall resource map (administrative map) drawn with arcGIS

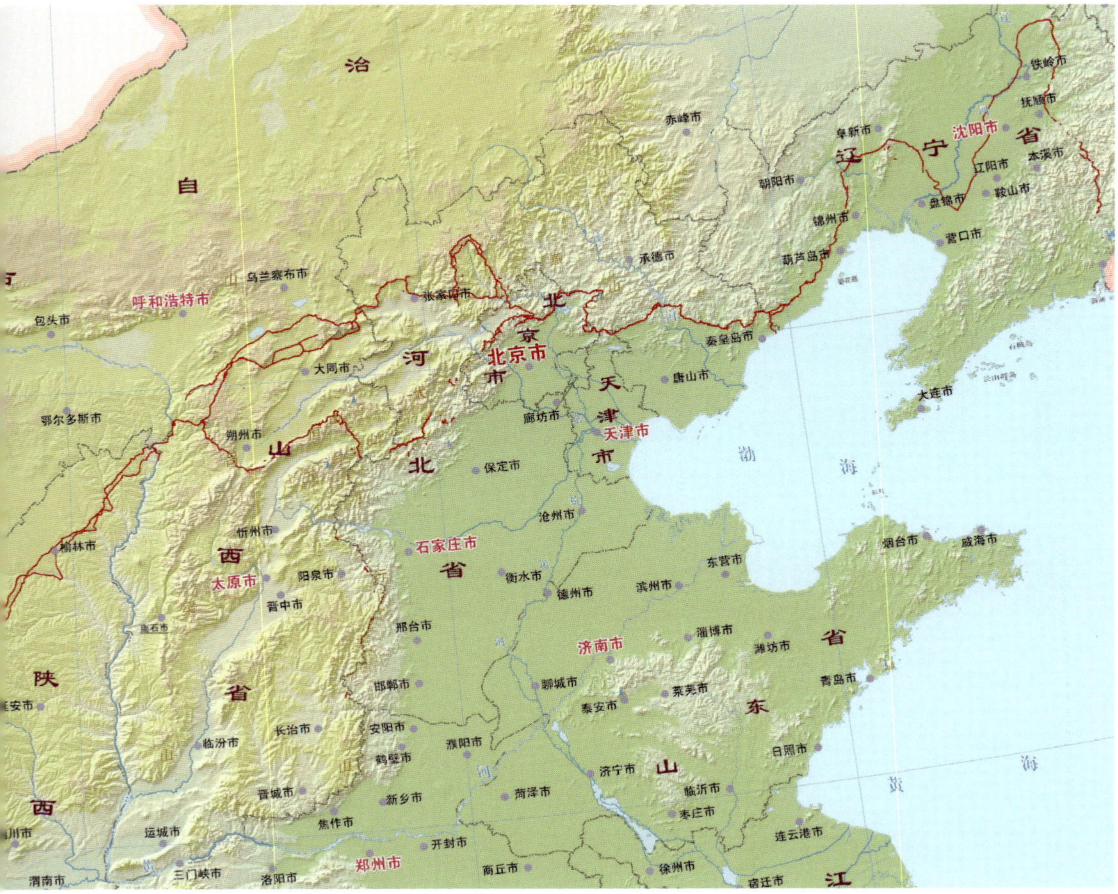


图 4-7.1
使用 arcGIS 软件绘制的长城资源分布图（地形图）

Fig. 4-7.1
Great Wall resource map (topographic map) drawn with arcGIS

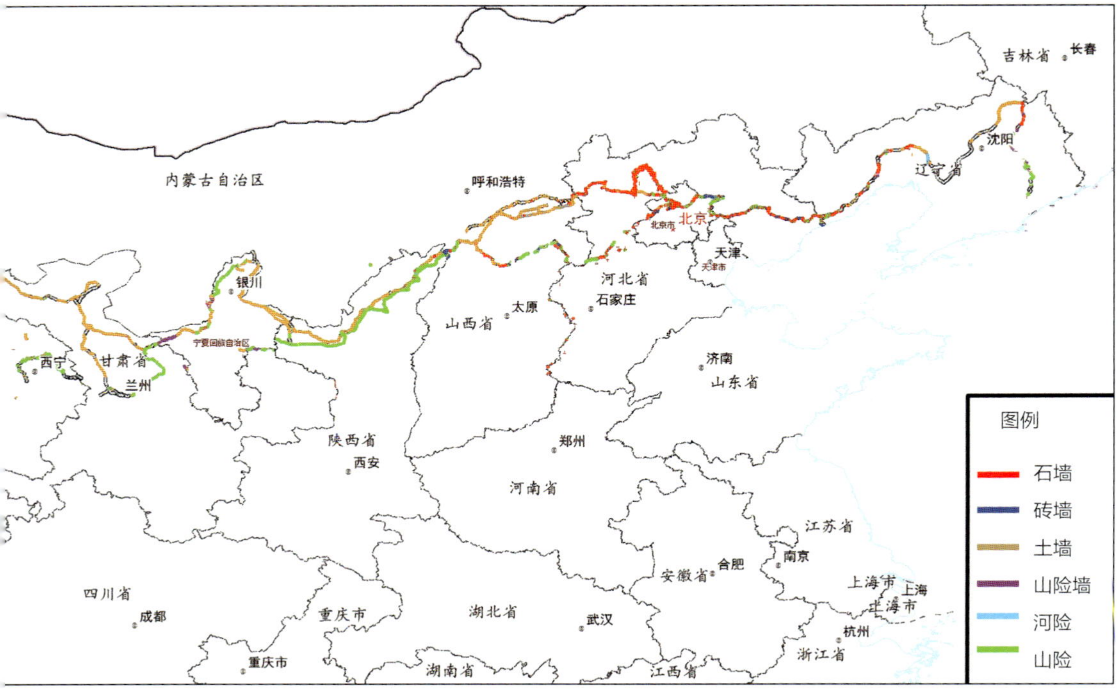


图 4-7.3
使用 arcGIS 软件绘制的长城资源分布图（材质分布图）

Fig. 4-7.3
Great Wall resource map (material distribution map) drawn with arcGIS

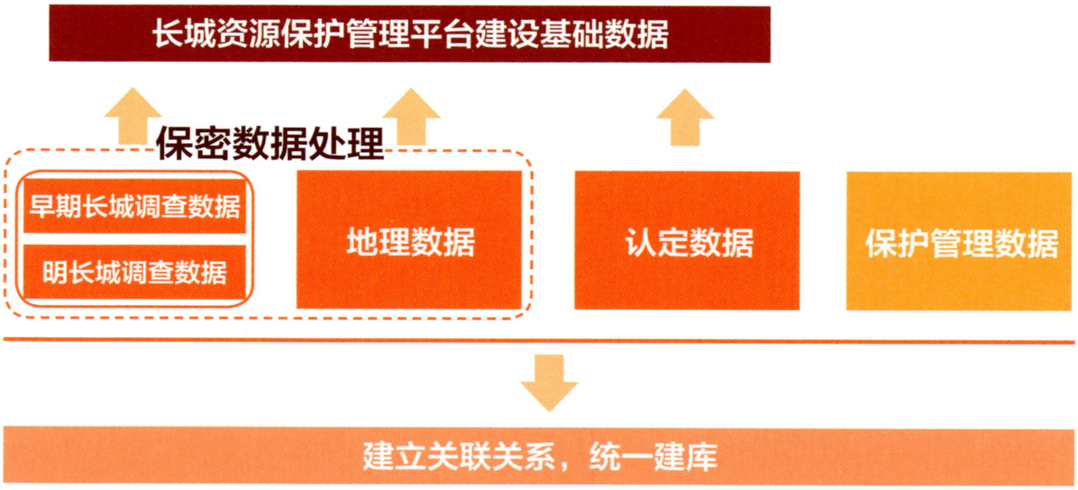


3、长城数据库与信息系统建设

受国家文物局委托，中国文化遗产研究院与国家基础地理信息中心开展合作，基于长城资源调查成果建立了长城资源信息数据库，并采用 GIS、数据库、多媒体和互联网等方面的先进技术，设计与构建了可实现多条件查询、实时更新、实时监测的长城资源保护管理信息系统。

该信息系统包括各时期长城资源调查数据，长城认定数据和长城保护管理业务数据，包括长城保护规划、长城保护工程、涉及长城保护范围的建设工程等项目数据，以及长城日常养护、“四有”档案、执法巡查、案件督查及相关法律文件、长城资源利用（旅游、宣传教育等）等，实现了各类数据之间的交互查询和检索。

信息系统建立了数据管理、数据应用和公众服务三个子系统。数据管理系统主要对长城资源数据进行存储、更新；数据应用系统用于长城保护管理业务，包括的填报、审核、查询、复杂统计、地图定位、地图制作与浏览等；公众服务子系统即面向社会开放的“中国长城遗产”网站（http://www.greatwallheritage.cn），已于 2016 年 12 月 1 日正式上线。（图 4-8、4-9、4-10）

图 4-8
长城资源保护管理信息系统数据结构

Fig. 4-8
Data structure of the Great Wall resource conservation management information system

### 3. Construction of the Great Wall database and information system

Under the commission of the State Administration of Cultural Heritage, the Chinese Academy of Cultural Heritage has cooperated with the National Geomatics Center of China to establish the Great Wall Resource Information Database based on the achievements of the Great Wall resource investigation. They designed and built the Great Wall resource conservation management information system available to multi-condition search, real-time update and real-time monitoring by applying GIS, database, multimedia and Internet and other advanced technologies.

The information system includes the Great Wall resource investigation data in various periods, the Great Wall identification data and the Great Wall conservation management business data, including the Great Wall conservation planning, the Great Wall Conservation Project, construction related to the Great Wall conservation zone and other project data, and the Great Wall daily maintenance, "four basic works"" archives, law enforcement inspection, case supervision and related legal documents, the Great Wall resources utilization (in tourism, publicity and education, etc.), and it achieved interactive search and retrieval among different kinds of data.

The information system establishes three subsystems namely data management, data application and public service. Data management system is mainly to store and update the Great Wall resource data; data application system is for the Great Wall conservation management business, including application, audit, searching, complex statistics, map positioning, map drawing and browsing; public service subsystem is "the Great Wall Heritage of China" website (http://www.greatwallheritage.cn) open to the public was officially launched on December 1, 2016. (Figs 4-8, 4-9, 4-10)

In addition, based on many years of studies on the Ming Great Wall, the School of Architecture of Tianjin University established the Great Wall Geographic Information Database, and collected, stored, managed, calculated, analyzed, displayed and described the geographical distribution data, element mapping information and historical information of the Ming Great Wall and its military defense settlement.

The civil Great Wall enthusiasts from an NGO called "the Great Wall Station" collect and organize the Great Wall resource data through a variety of channels in spare time. They established the Great Wall historical literature database, the Great Wall architecture and geographic information database, the Great Wall inscriptions database, the Great Wall expert database, and the Great Wall video database, etc. They are all open to the public and on real-time updates;

此外，天津大学建筑学院基于多年的明长城研究，建立了明长城地理信息数据库，对明长城及其军事防御聚落的地理分布数据、要素测绘信息和历史信息进行采集、储存、管理、运算、分析、显示和描述；

长城小站的民间长城爱好者利用业余时间通过各种渠道收集整理长城资源数据，建立了长城历史文献数据库、长城建筑与地理信息数据库、长城碑刻铭刻数据库、长城专家数据库、长城视频数据库等等，并向社会开放实时更新。

图 4-9
升级后的长城资源保护管理信息系统主页面

Fig. 4-9
Upgraded main page of the Great Wall resource conservation management information system

图 4-10
“中国长城遗产”网主页面

Fig. 4-10
Web page of "the Great Wall Heritage of China"

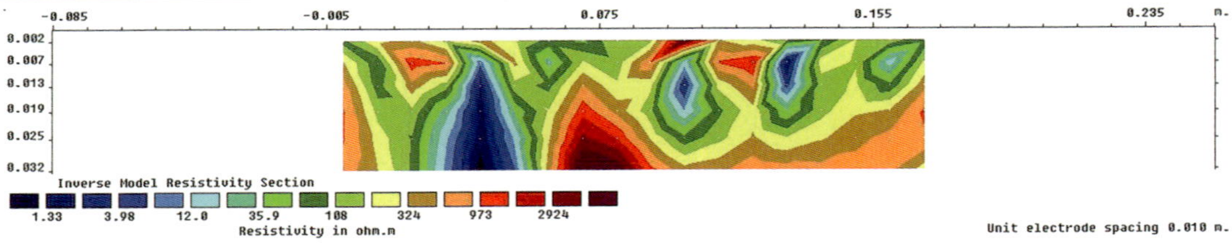


4、长城数字化展示

中国科学院等科研机构也在空间信息技术应用于长城保护方面进行了有益尝试。2016年10月18日，中国科学院等科研单位与中国长城学会合作，启动了“长城文化创新”项目，拟结合航拍、激光扫描、空地遥感、3D、多媒体、虚拟现实等现代技术把长城及周围设施进行数字化，并建立相关数据库，形成数字化虚拟的网上长城博物馆。该项目把长城文化研究学术领域的丰厚成果通过新媒体、新手段让更多的青年人了解和认识长城，激发大众热爱祖国和长城文化，参与到保护长城的行动中来。

## （二）长城保护维修技术研究

“长城保护工程”实施以来，长城保护维修技术研究蓬勃发展。尤其是西北地区土遗址保护技术研究，取得了较大进展。西北大学、敦煌研究院等科研机构纷纷开展了长城土遗址保护技术的专项研究工作。如：敦煌地区汉长城保护工程采用现代科技手段进行了充分的前期研究和试验。敦煌研究院的科研人员采用高密度电法、面波仪、探地雷达、热红外仪、微波仪、声波仪、全站仪、电导率仪和便携式显微镜等相关设备，探测城墙及烽燧土体存在的变形、空鼓、裂隙发育程度及具体位置，为后期病害成因分析和保护维修方案的制订提供技术参数。

在此基础上，通过室内、室外试验和数值分析对遗址本体夯砌补支顶加固、灌浆、锚固、表面防风化等修复技术及工艺进行研发和完善，并在长城本体上进行小面积试点观测，确定修复效果良好后，推广应用到长城土体保护修复实际工作中。（图 4-11）

图 4-11
敦煌汉长城利用高密度电法进行无损墙体检测（敦煌研究院 提供）

Fig. 4-11
Non-destructive wall testing on the Dunhuang Han Great Wall with high-density electricity method (provided by Dunhuang Academy China)

4. Digital display of the Great Wall

Chinese Academy of Sciences and other scientific research institutions also made useful attempts for the application of space information technology in the Great Wall conservation. On October 18, 2016, Chinese Academy of Sciences and some other scientific research units cooperated with the Great Wall Society of China to launch the "Great Wall Cultural Innovation" project. It's to digitize the Great Wall and the surrounding facilities combining with modern technologies such as aerial photography, laser scanning, open space remote sensing, 3D, multi-media and virtual reality, and establish relevant database, to form a digital virtual online Great Wall museum. The project spreads the great achievements in the academic field of Great Wall cultural study, and helps more young people to know the Great Wall through new media and new methods, stimulates the public to love the motherland and the Great Wall culture, and participate in the actions of the Great Wall conservation.

**(II) Study on the Great Wall conservation and maintenance technologies**

Since the implementation of the "Great Wall Conservation Project", the study on the Great Wall conservation and maintenance technologies has been flourishing. Especially the study on the northwest China earthen site conservation technologies has made great progress. Northwest University, Dunhuang Academy China and other scientific research institutions all made special studies on the Great Wall earthen site conservation technology. For example, modern scientific and technological methods were applied in the Han Great Wall Conservation Project in Dunhuang area to make a completed pre-research and testing. Scientific personnel of Dunhuang Academy China applied high-density electricity, surface wave instrument, ground penetrating radar, thermal infrared instrument, microwave instrument, acoustic instrument, total station instrument, conductivity meter and portable microscope and other related instruments to detect deformation, hollowing, crack development degree and specific location of the Great Wall and beacon towers. It provides technical parameters for the late analysis on the cause of damages and the formulation of the conservation and maintenance programs.

On the basis of this, through the indoor and outdoor experiment and numerical analysis, the repair technologies and techniques such as the roof reinforcement, grouting, anchoring and surface anti-weathering of the main body of the site were developed and improved, and small-area pilot observation was carried out on the Great Wall, to determine the positive effect of remediation to promote the application of the Great Wall to protect the actual work. (Fig 4-11)

## 四、长城保护工程技术标准规范研究

长城建造历史悠久，不同时代长城的建造材料、工艺、形制差异很大，现状保存程度和病害成因各异，这给长城保护工程施工及其管理带来很大困难。

长城保护维修工程从 1952 开始，已开展 60 多年，尤其近 10 多年来，长城保护维修力度加大，每年都有大量保护维修项目。多年来从勘察、设计、施工、监理等工作流程一直在使用文物行业或者建设、水利、地震等部门制定的技术标准和规范，而这些技术标准和规范都有其不同的适用范围，对长城而言，并非完全适用。

随着国家对长城保护工作的重视，长城保护工程数量呈逐年激增趋势，为了弥补长城保护工程技术标准规范缺失的问题，有针对性地对长城保护工程实施过程中各项技术措施制定相应的标准，规范和指导工程实施，有必要制定专门的长城施工技术标准，这对指导长城保护维修工程各项技术实施的科学化、规范化，保障长城保护工程科学健康发展，提高长城保护工程施工水平具有重要意义。

### 1、研究背景与过程

2016 年，国家文物局下发了《关于开展 2016 年度行业标准制修订计划项目申报工作的通知》（办博函〔2016〕796），以此为契机，在国家文物局的支持下，由全国文物保护标准化技术委员会秘书处组织，中国文化遗产研究院联合河北古代建筑保护研究所、兰州大学联合承担了《长城维修工程施工技术规程》编制工作。结合项目，中国文化遗产研究院进行了“长城保护工程技术标准规范研究”。

### 2、研究进展与阶段性成果

2016 年 9 月 1 日，“长城保护工程技术标准规范研究”项目正式启动，并召开第一次专家研讨会，讨论了项目的定位、分类、深度等问题。编写组根据专家意见形成了《长城维修工程施工技术规程》编制大纲，并于 2016 年 10 月 14 日召开了第二次专家讨论会，邀请国家文物局、故宫博物院、中国文化遗产研究院、河北省古建所、辽宁有色勘察院等单位的 10 多位专家参加会议，对《长城保护工程施工技术规程》编制大纲的定位、结构、内容、深度等方面进行讨论。专家一致认为，项目应首先编制具有指导意见性质的长城维修施工技术操作指南，以满足目前长城保护施工过程中亟需的管理和技术要求。根据专家意见，编写组对大纲进行修改完善后，着手开展编制工作，至 2016 年 12 月 1 日，《长城维修工程施工技术操作指南》（以下简称《操作指南》）初稿完成。（表 4-3）

## IV. Study on the standards and norms of the Great Wall conservation engineering technology

The construction of the Great Wall enjoys a long history. The building materials, technologies and shapes of the Great Walls in different times are greatly different, and the current status of preservation and causes of damages widely vary, which make great difficulties to the construction and management of the Great Wall Conservation Project.

Great Wall conservation and maintenance project started from 1952 and has been carried out for more than 60 years. Especially in the recent 10 years, increasing efforts were made on the Great Wall conservation and maintenance, and a large number of conservation and maintenance projects every year. Over the years, the survey, design, construction, supervision and other work processes have been following the technical standards and norms formulated by the departments of cultural relics or construction, water conservancy and earthquake. These technical standards and norms are for different scopes of application and not entirely applicable for the Great Wall.

With China's attention to the conservation of the Great Wall, the number of the Great Wall Conservation Projects has been increasing year by year. In order to make up for the problem of missing standards and norms of the Great Wall conservation engineering technology, and formulate corresponding standards aiming at various technical measures in the process of the Great Wall Conservation Projects to standardize and guide the implementation of the projects, it is necessary to formulate a special standard for Great Wall technology construction. It is significant for the scientific and standardized implementation of various technologies in the Great Wall conservation and maintenance projects, ensuring the scientific and healthy development of the Great Wall Conservation Projects, and improving the construction level of the Great Wall Conservation Projects.

### 1. Background and process of study

In 2016, the State Administration of Cultural Heritage issued *the Notice on Carrying out the Application for the 2016 Professional Standard Revision and Formulation Program* (No. B.B.H. [2016] 216). Taking this opportunity, with the support of the State Administration of Cultural Heritage, organized by the secretary department of the National Heritage Conservation Standardization Technical Committee, Chinese Academy of Cultural Heritage jointly with Hebei Ancient Building Conservation Research Institute and Lanzhou University undertook the formulation of *the Construction Technical Regulations on the Great Wall Maintenance Projects*. Combining with the projects, the Chinese Academy of Cultural Heritage carried out the "study on the technical standards and norms of the Great Wall Conservation Project".

### 2. Progress and stage achievements of study

On September 1, 2016, the project of "study on the technical standards and norms of the Great Wall Conservation Projects" officially started, and held the first expert seminar, to discuss the positioning, classification and depth of the projects. The formulation team wrote the compilation outline of *the Construction Technical Regulations on the Great Wall Maintenance Projects* according to the expert comments. On October 14, 2016, they held the second expert seminar, and invited more than 10 experts from the State Administration of Cultural Heritage, the National Palace Museum, Chinese Academy of Cultural Heritage, Hebei Academy of Ancient Building, Liaoning Institute of Nonferrous Survey and other units attending it, discussed the

首先，《操作指南》确定了适用范围、对象和基本原则；

第二，《操作指南》将长城保护维修工程划分为准备、施工、验收等三个阶段，并对每个阶段的工作提出了具体的管理和技术要求；

第三，《操作指南》按照石结构、土结构、砖结构混筑结构等类别，对长城的本体与附属设施结构进行了分类；

第四，《操作指南》根据不同的长城类型，对维修施工用料、工程用水、各项工艺进行了细致规定。

**表 4-3：《长城维修工程施工技术操作指南》目录**

Table 4-3: Content of *the Operation Guideline on the Construction Technology of the Great Wall Maintenance Projects*

| | |
|---|---|
| 第一章　总则<br>Chapter 1 General | 1.1 范围<br>1.1 Scope |
| | 1.2 对象<br>1.2 Objects |
| | 1.3 基本原则<br>1.3 Basic principles |
| 第二章<br>施工阶段划分及各阶段管理工作要求<br>Chapter 2<br>Division of Construction Stages and Requirements on the Management in Each Stage | 2.1 施工准备阶段<br>2.1 Construction preparation stage |
| | 2.2 施工阶段管理要求<br>2.2 Management requirements for construction stage |
| | 2.3 验收阶段管理要求<br>2.3 Management requirements for inspection and acceptance stage |
| 第三章<br>长城本体及附属设施结构分类<br>Chapter 3<br>Structural classification of the Great Wall itself and ancillary facilities | （件附录 A）<br>(See Appendix A) |

第四章
工程材料技术要求
Chapter 4 Technical requirements for engineering materials

- 4.1 总体要求
  4.1 General requirements
- 4.2 石材
  4.2 Stone
- 4.3 砖
  4.3 Brick
- 4.4 土料
  4.4 Earth
- 4.5 石灰
  4.5 Lime
- 4.6 土坯
  4.6 Adobe
- 4.7 其他材料
  4.7 Other materials

第五章
施工工艺技术要求
Chapter 5 Technical requirements for construction technology

- 5.1 总体要求
  5.1 General requirements
- 5.2 清理
  5.2 Cleaning
- 5.3 归安
  5.3 Recovery
- 5.4 砌筑
  5.4 Masonry
- 5.5 夯筑
  5.5 Ramming
- 5.6 裂隙灌浆
  5.6 Fissure grouting
- 5.7 墙面剔补
  5.7 Wall repair
- 5.8 锚固
  5.8 Anchoring

第六章 附则
Chapter 6 Supplementary Provisions

第七章 附录
Chapter 7 Appendix

- A 术语
  A Terminology
- B 长城结构分类
  B Structure Classification of the Great Wall

positioning, structure, content and depth of the compilation outline of *the Construction Technical Regulations on the Great Wall Maintenance Projects*. All experts agreed that the project needs an operation guide for the Great Wall maintenance construction technology with the nature of guidance comments first to meet the urgent need of management and technical requirements in the process of current Great Wall conservation construction. According to the expert comments, the compilation team began to proceed with the compilation after the revision of the outline. On December 1, 2016, the first draft of *the Operation Guideline on the Construction Technology of the Great Wall Maintenance Projects* (hereinafter referred to as *Operation Guideline*) was completed.

Firstly, the *Operation Guideline* determined the application scope, object and basic principles;

Secondly, the *Operation Guideline* divided the Great Wall conservation and maintenance projects into three stages, namely preparation, construction and warranty period, and proposed specific management and technical requirements for each stage;

Thirdly, the *Operation Guideline* classified the structures of the Great Wall itself and the ancillary facilities in accordance with the structural categories of the stones, earth, bricks, masonry with stones and bricks;

Fourthly, the *Operation Guideline* made meticulous regulations for the materials of maintenance construction, water use of project and various processes based on different types of the Great Walls.

在此基础上，课题组将编制完成《长城维修工程施工操作规程》，成为长城保护维修领域的行业标准。

### 专栏：长城保护维修施工工艺介绍

（1）归安：指将可明确原位置的塌落构件归位至原位置，或将不稳定状态的结构归位至稳定状态以防塌落的维修措施。

（2）砌筑：指用砖或石材按照一定的规则进行垒砌的工艺；

（3）夯筑：指用土料进行分段、分层夯打的建筑工艺；

（4）裂隙灌浆：特指将浆液注入结构裂隙中，以阻塞降水沿裂隙入渗通道和改善结构力学性能的维修措施；

（5）墙面剔补：特指对城墙墙体面层结构实施局部修缮的维修措施。仅适用于砖结构长城墙体；

（6）锚固：指在长城结构不稳定、整体变形严重的土结构或混筑结构长城墙体上插入锚杆具进行牵拉固定的隐蔽工程．

## 五、文化遗产监测管理与研究

### （一）世界遗产定期报告

长城作为世界遗产，其保护管理工作也要按照世界遗产的标准开展。

1994 年起，世界遗产委员会确立了每 6 年提交遗产地定期报告的制度。定期报告的内容包括了遗产地基本信息，组织管理机构情况、影响因素的变化（包括自然与人为因素）、保护管理和监测情况（保护措施、保护计划、财政与人力资源、科研、教育、旅游等），并要求遗产地根据这些数据进行遗产地的总体评估，提出工作优化需求。2011 年，国家文物局组织完成了长城世界文化遗产第二轮定期报告及回顾性突出普遍价值申明、地图绘制工作。

On this basis, the project team will finally complete the compilation of the *Construction Operation Regulations on the Great Wall Maintenance Projects*, as the industry standard in the field of the Great Wall conservation and maintenance.

### Special column: Introduction to the construction process of the Great Wall conservation and maintenance

(1) Recovery: It refers to the maintenance measure of recovering the collapsed component whose original position can be found to its original position, or recovering the structure in unstable state to a stable state to prevent from collapse.

(2) Masonry: It refers to the process of masonry with brick or stone in accordance with certain rules;

(3) Ramming: It refers to the ramming process with earth materials in several sections and layers;

(4) Fissure grouting: It specially refers to the maintenance measure of infusing the grout into the structural fissures in order to block the precipitation from infiltrating into the channel from the fissure and improve the mechanical properties;

(5) Wall repair: It specifically refers to the maintenance measure of partial repair on the surface structure of the wall. It's only applicable for the Great Wall in brick structure;

(6) Anchoring: It refers to the hidden engineering of inserting anchoring rods on the unstable or severely deformed Great Wall structure in earth structure or mixed structure for traction fixation.

## V. Monitoring management and study on the cultural heritage

### (I) World Heritage Periodic Report

As a world heritage site, the conservation and management of the Great Wall should be carried out in accordance with the standard of world heritage.

Since 1994, the World Heritage Committee has established a system for submitting a periodic report on the world heritage site every six years. The content of the report includes the basic information of the heritage site, the situation of the organization and management organizations, the change of the influencing factors (including natural and human factors), conservation management and monitoring (including conservation measures, conservation plans, finance and human resources, scientific research, education and tourism, etc.). It's required that the heritage sites should make overall assessment based on these data and propose optimization requirements. In 2011, the State Administration of Cultural Heritage organized and completed the second round of periodic report, retrospective OUV statement and mapping of the Great Wall world cultural heritage.

## 专栏：世界遗产监测与定期报告制度

根据英汉词典的解释，“监测”（monitor）有“监听、监视、监控、追踪、检查”等含义。

文化遗产监测，就是对文化遗产破坏风险进行管控。其基本内涵，是“利用多种科技手段对文化遗产的价值载体及其风险因素进行周期性、系统性和科学性的观测、记录和分析”。[74]

1994 年，经世界遗产委员会主席团大会讨论，世界遗产监测工作被正式列为世界遗产委员会职责，成为世界遗产保护工作的一项制度。《保护世界自然与文化遗产公约》要求缔约国各世界遗产地以 6 年为周期向世界遗产委员会提供本遗产地的评估报告。报告内容包括《公约》实施情况及遗产地的保护管理和监测工作具体情况，并对结果进行总结并提出相应的对策。

世界遗产监测属于一种管理手段，可以说是对遗产管理的管理。其目的在于根据周期性获取的世界遗产本体及遗产地环境的相关信息，开展预防性保护。

21 世纪初，我国正式引入了文化遗产监测的概念，并将其作为一项独立的工作。

2006 年 11 月 4 日和 12 月 8 日，国家文物局先后颁布了《中国世界文化遗产保护管理办法》和《中国世界遗产监测巡视管理办法》；次年 11 月出台《世界文化遗产监测规程（征求意见稿）》，成为中国世界遗产监测工作的指导文件。

根据《国家文物博物馆事业发展“十二五”规划》要求，“十二五”期间中国的世界遗产监测工作有四大任务：一是构建法规体系；二是完善工作机制；三是加强能力建设；四是建立信息系统。

各遗产地在“十一五”期间国家制定的世界遗产监测各项法律规范的基础之上，陆续出台遗产地的监测管理办法，世界遗产监测的国家——遗产地两级法规体系逐步形成。

### （二）长城监测预警系统与监测预警体系建设

为配合开展长城监测预警体系预研究工作，长城项目组在中国文化遗产院科研经费支持下，先后开展了多项研究课题。

《长城监测预警体系建设预研究》在长城遗产地调研的基础上，结合其他世界遗产地遗产监测情况调研，了解目前世界遗产监测的基本方法、经验等，搜集、整理国际、国内世界遗产保护领域关于预防性保护、风险管理、防灾减灾的研究资料。一方面，对文化遗产监测现状进行研究、评估。总结世界文化遗产监测的经验做法，评估其监测工作中所采用的技术手段；另一方面，理清长城遗产特性和管理特点，分析长城监测体系建设的实际需求。

[74] 朱水涌：《武夷山世界文化遗产的监测与研究》，厦门大学出版社，2008 年。

## Special column: World Heritage Monitoring and Periodic Report System

According to the explanation in English-Chinese dictionary, "monitor" means "audio monitoring, video monitoring, supervising, tracking and inspection".

Cultural heritage monitoring is the management and control on the risks of damages to the cultural heritage sites. Its basic connotation is "periodic, systematic and scientific observation, recording and analysis on the value carrier and its risk factors of cultural heritage sites by means of a variety of scientific methods".[74]

In 1994, after the discussion of presidium meeting of the World Heritage Committee, cultural heritage monitoring was officially included in the responsibilities of the World Heritage Committee and became a system of world heritage conservation. *Convention Concerning the Conservation of the World Natural and Cultural Heritage* required all the world heritage sites of the member states to submit an assessment report of the site to the World Heritage Committee every six years. The report should cover the implementation of the convention and the specific situation of the conservation management and monitoring on the heritage site, summarize the results and puts forward corresponding solutions.

World heritage monitoring is a kind of management tool which can be regarded as the management of heritage management. The aim is to carry out preventive conservation on the basis of periodically obtained relevant information on the world heritage and the environment of the heritage site.

In the early 21st century, China formally introduced the concept of cultural heritage monitoring and regarded it as an independent work.

On November 4 and December 8, 2006, the State Administration of Cultural Heritage promulgated the Measures on the Administration of China World Cultural Heritage Conservation and the *Measures on the Administration of China's World Heritage Monitoring and Inspection. In November the following year, Monitoring Procedures of World Cultural Heritage (Exposure Draft)* was issued and became the guidance of China's world heritage monitoring.

According to the requirements of the "Twelfth Five-Year Plan" of National Cultural Relics Museum Development, China's world heritage monitoring in the period of the "Twelfth Five-Year Plan" includes four major tasks. The first is to establish a regulatory system; the second is to improve the working mechanism; the third is to strengthen capacity construction; and the fourth is to establish an information system.

On the basis of the state-formulated legal norms on the world heritage monitoring in the period of the "Eleventh Five-Year Plan", the heritage sites issued the monitoring and management methods on the heritage sites in succession, and the regulatory system of world heritage monitoring on the two levels state-heritage site was gradually established.

### (II) The Great Wall monitoring and early warning system and its construction

To cooperate with the pre-study on the Great Wall monitoring and early warning system, the Great Wall project team has carried out a number of study subjects with the research funding support of Chinese Academy of Cultural Heritage.

On the basis of the investigation of the Great Wall heritage sites, combining with the investigations on the monitoring of other world heritage sites, *the Pre-study on the Great Wall Monitoring and Early Warning*

[74] Zhu Shuiyong: *Monitoring and Study on Wuyi Mountain World Cultural Heritage*, Xiamen University Press, in 2008.

《线性文化遗产破坏风险评估与监测方法研究——以居延长城甘肃金塔段为例》课题，针对长城遗产监测进行了深入调查和研究，从不同的专业角度对长城的价值与构成、威胁长城遗产的各因素进行评估，并对其存状进行实时监控，规避破坏风险，为合理的保护管理和利用长城资源提供科学、有效、符合国情及长城保护管理实际的理论技术指导。以甘肃省金塔县为试点，长城项目组进行了长城破坏风险因素识别与风险评估。通过大范围、长时段的长城保存状态变化情况分析，可以评估不同地区的长城破坏风险，确定下一步工作中的长城保护重点。（图 4-12）

《重大文化遗产地综合保护与利用研究——长城重要点段保护监测与利用试点》课题，主要针对长城文化遗产的特点，研发基于长城信息系统 GIS 平台的便携式终端技术，并根据长城沿线社会经发展水平、长城分布地理环境等因素，选取部分长城重点地区进行试点部署，为长城保护和利用管理工作探索信息效率更高、运行成本更低、适用范围更宽、服务群体更广的信息管理技术，全面提升我国长城文化遗产保护、研究、管理水平。2016 年已经开展大量实地调研，并确定张家口市崇礼区为试点地，签订合作协议，与国信司南公司签订协议共同开发监测移动终端，积极推动长城监测试点工作的逐步开展。

长城项目组还与长城小站等组织、张保田等民间爱好者合作，长期致力于长城老照片考证、长城资源调查影像复拍对比等工作，为下一步长城监测工作的开展积累了大量宝贵的基础数据。

目前，在长城保护管理信息系统的基础上，国家文物局也已启动了包括长城在内的世界文化遗产监测平台和监测体系建设工作。2012 年，中国世界文化遗产监测预警总平台和通用平台正式上线，开始对全国 40 余处世界遗产地进行监测数据的采集工作，迄今为止，数据总量已经累计超过 20Tb。（图 4-13）在国家文物局的指导下，2016 年，长城项目组在充分调研的基础上，与国信司南（北京）地理信息技术有限公司开发了配合长城执法巡查与长城保护员巡查工作使用，并与长城资源保护管理信息系统相关联的长城监测巡检系统 APP。（图 4-14）

图 4-12
金塔县长城哨马营城堡券门变化情况（上图：斯坦因 拍摄，1906 年；下图：张依萌 拍摄，2013 年）

Fig. 4-12
Changes in the arch gate of Shaomaying Fort of Jinta County Great Wall (The figure above: Stein, in 1906; the figure below: Zhang Yimeng, in 2013)

*System* got to know the basic methods and experience of current world heritage monitoring, collect and sorted out the study data related to preventive conservation, risk management, disaster prevention and mitigation in the field of China and foreign world heritage conservation. On one hand, research and evaluation are made for the cultural heritage monitoring. We'll summarize the experience and practices of the monitoring to world cultural heritages to evaluate the technical means applied in the evaluation and monitoring. On the other hand, we'll clarify the properties and management characteristics of the Great Wall and analyze the actual demands of the construction of the Great Wall monitoring system.

The subject of *On the Risk Assessment and Monitoring Methods of Linear Cultural Heritage Destruction - Taking Jinta Section of Juyan Great Wall* in Gansu as an Example made in-depth investigation and research on the Great Wall heritage monitoring, and assessed the Great Wall's value and the constitution and all the factors threatening the Great Wall heritage from various professional perspectives. It makes real-time monitoring on it to avoid the risk of damage, and provides scientific and effective theoretical technological guidance in line with the national conditions and the reality of the Great Wall conservation management for reasonable conservation management and utilization of the Great Wall resources. Based on the Jinta County in Gansu Province as a pilot, the Great Wall Project Team carried out the Great Wall damage risk factor identification and risk assessment. Through the analysis on the changes of the Great Wall preservation status in a large scope over a long period of time, it is possible to assess the damage risk of the Great Wall in different regions and determine the focus of the Great Wall conservation in the next step (Fig 4-12).

The subject of *On the Comprehensive Conservation and Utilization of Major Cultural Heritage Sties -- Conservation Monitoring and Utilization Pilot of Important Great Wall Sites and Sections* mainly researches and develops portable terminal technology based on the Great Wall information system GIS platform aiming at the characteristics of the Great Wall cultural heritage, and selects some key areas of the Great Wall for pilot deployment according to the social economic development level along the Great Wall and geographical environment of the Great Wall distribution to explore information management technologies with higher information efficiency, lower operating costs, wider application scope and larger service groups for the Great Wall conservation and utilization management, and to enhance the conservation, research and management level of China's Great Wall cultural heritage.

In 2016, a large number of field investigations were carried out, and Chongli District, Zhangjiakou City was nominated as a pilot site. The cooperation agreement was signed with Geo-compass to jointly develop mobile monitoring terminals, and actively promote the Great Wall monitoring pilot to gradually proceed.

Great Wall project team also cooperates with organizations such as the Great Wall Station and private enthusiasts such as Zhang Baotian for long-term commitment to the survey of old photos, the Great Wall, the Great Wall resource investigation and image shooting comparison, which accumulated a lot of valuable basic data for the next step of the Great Wall monitoring work.

At present, on the basis of the Great Wall conservation and management information system, the State Administration of Cultural Heritage has also started the construction of the monitoring platforms and systems for world cultural heritage sites including the Great Wall. In 2012, China's world cultural heritage monitoring

图 4-13
中国世界遗产监测预警总平台遗产信息地图界面

Fig. 4-13
The interface of heritage information map on China world heritage monitoring and warning general platform

2016 年，结合“长城执法专项督察”工作，国家文物局牵头，长城项目组参与了陕西省府谷县“明长城无人机 + 卫星遥感监测试点”工作，对全县明长城 140 千米墙体、169 座烽火台，84 处敌台马面，16 座关堡及 12 处相关遗存进行了无人机和卫星影像综合监测，涉及范围约 1200 平方公里。

通过将无人机获取的高分辨率正射影像与 2008-2008、2015-2016 年两期卫星影像匹配、叠加、对比，提取两个时间段长城遗存本体及环境变化信息。

其中，北侧长城遗址采用“刀锋”固定翼无人机系统在约 65 千米长城、69 平方千米范围内进行作业，获取空间分辨率 0.159 米、像素为 7360*4912

图 4-14
长城监测巡检系统 app 界面

Fig. 4-14
The interface of Great Wall monitoring patrol system app

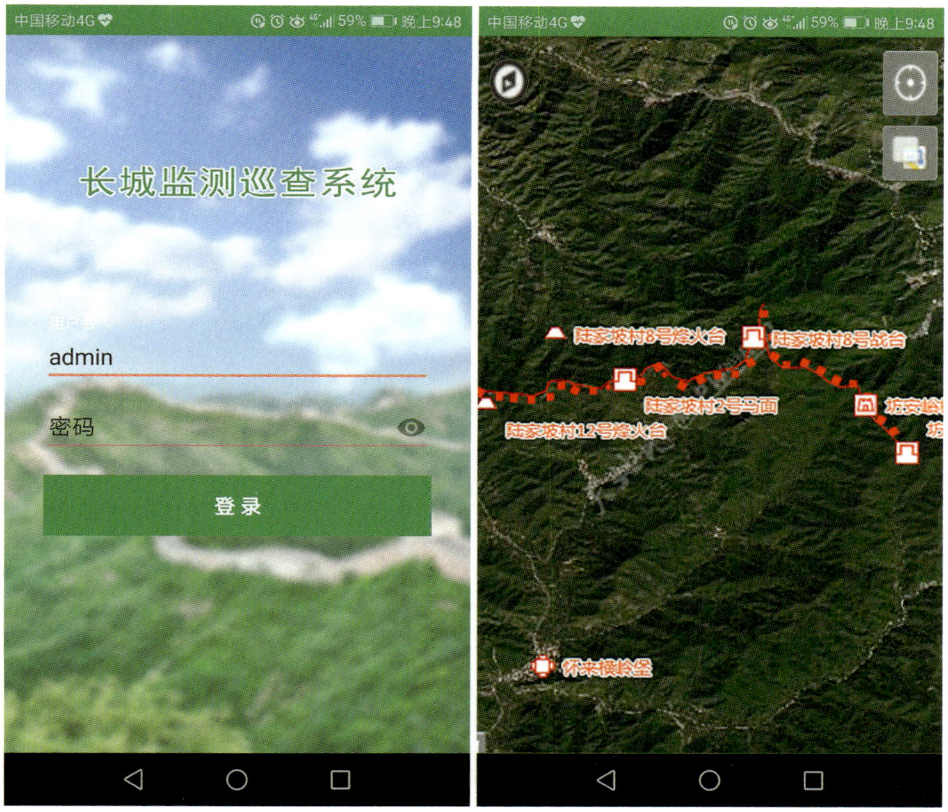


and warning general platform and universal platform were officially launched, and began the collection of monitoring data for more than 40 world heritage sites throughout China. So far, the total amount of data has been accumulated to be more than 20Tb. (Fig 4-13). Under the guidance of the State Administration of Cultural Heritage, the Great Wall project team, on the basis of sufficient investigation, developed the Great Wall monitoring and inspection system app coordinating with the Great Wall law enforcement inspection and the Great Wall conservation inspector work, associated with the Great Wall resource conservation management information system jointly with Geo-compass (Beijing) Geographic Information Technology Co. in 2016. (Fig 4-14)

的影像；南侧长城遗址采用“大疆精灵 3”四旋翼无人机系统进行散点作业，获取空间分辨率 0.10 米、像素 4000*3000 的影像。

卫星影像采用 CGC2000 坐标系和 1985 国家高程基准，主要通过公司存档数据、市场采购等方式获得。（表 4-4）

**表 4-4：卫星影像数据指标统计表**

Table 4-4: Satellite Image Data Indicators

| 卫星数据 Satellite data | 数据指标 Data indicators | |
|---|---|---|
| | 空间分辨率 Space resolution | 幅宽（千米 * 千米） Width (km * km) |
| QuickBird | 全色 0.61 米多光谱 2.44 米 Panchromatic 0.61 meters Multi-spectral 2.44 m | 16.5*16.5 |
| WorldView01/02 | 全色 0.46 米多光谱 1.8 米 Panchromatic 0.46 meters Multi-spectral 1.8 m | 16.5*16.5 |
| GF2 | 全色 0.8 米都光谱 4 米 Panchromatic 0.8 meters Multi-spectral 4 m | 45*45 |

此外，还从国家测绘地理信息局和各省测绘主管部门申请了府谷县长城沿线两侧 1 公里范围内的数字正射影像（DOM）、数字线划图（DLG）和数字高程模型（DEM）作为正射纠正基准控制资料。

通过对获取的府谷县无人机影像和卫星数据进行标准化处理和内业解译，获取了如下监测数据：

In 2016, combining with the "Great Wall Law Enforcement Special Inspection", the State Administration of Cultural Heritage led the Great Wall project team to participate in "the Great Wall UAV + satellite remote sensing monitoring pilot" in Fugu County, Shaanxi Province. It made comprehensive monitoring by UAV and satellite image for 140 km walls, 169 beacon towers, 84 enemy platform bastions, 16 forts and 12 related remains covering a range of about 1,200 square kilometers.

By matching, overlapping and comparing the high-resolution orthophotic images obtained by UAVs with the satellite images of two periods 2008-2008 and 2015-2016, it took the information of the Great Wall remains and environmental changes in these two periods.

Among them, for the Great Wall site in the north side, "blade" fixed-wing UAV system was in the operation covering the scope of about 65 km Great Wall and 69 square kilometers area to obtain images at spatial resolution of 0.159 meters and the pixel of 7360 * 4912; for the Great Wall in the south site, "DJ PHANTOM3" four-rotor UAV system was in scatter operations to obtain images at spatial resolution of 0.10 m and the pixel of 4000 * 3000.

The satellite images are based on the CGC2000 Coordinate System and the 1985 National Elevation Benchmark, mainly obtained through company archival data and market purchases, etc. (Table 4-4).

In addition, they also applied DOM (digital ortho image), DLG (digital line graphic) and DEM (digital elevation model) within 1 km from both sides of the Fugu County Great Wall to the National Administration of Surveying, Mapping and Geoinformation and the provincial authorities of surveying and mapping as the control data for orthorectification correction reference.

Through the standardized process and professional interpretation of the UAV images and satellite data obtained in Fugu County, they obtained the following monitoring data:

During 2008-2016, totally 7 sites in the Ming Great Wall in Fugu County disappeared, including 1 wall and 1 beacon tower naturally collapsed, 2 beacon towers and 3 enemy platforms destroyed by urban and rural construction; other 10 sites were changed; and the remaining 327 sites remain unchanged. It's verified by field procedure (Table 4-5, 4-15).

## 表 4-5：府谷长城 2008-2016 年变化情况统计表
Table 4-5: Change Statistics of Fugu Great Wall during 2008 - 2016

| 类型 Type | 总数 Total quantity | 未变化 Unchanged | 变化 Changed | 消失 Disappeared | 变化率 Change rate | 消失率 Disappearance rate |
|---|---|---|---|---|---|---|
| 烽火台 Beacon tower | 169 | 166 | 0 | 3 | 0.00% | 1.78% |
| 敌台马面 Enemy platform bastion | 84 | 77 | 4 | 3 | 4.76% | 3.57% |
| 关堡 Fort | 16 | 15 | 1 | 0 | 6.25% | 0.00% |
| 墙体 Wall | 63 | 59 | 3 | 1 | 4.76% | 1.59% |
| 其他遗存 Wall | 12 | 10 | 2 | 0 | 16.67% | 0.00% |
| 合计 Total | 344 | 327 | 10 | 7 | 2.91% | 2.03% |

2008 年 -2016 年间，府谷县境内明长城共消失遗迹 7 处，包括自然坍塌的墙体、烽火台各 1 处，因城乡建设而破坏的烽火台 2 处，敌台 3 处；另有 10 处发生了变化；其余 327 处未变化。经外业核查无误（表 4-5、图 4-15）。

以上数据是通过一次工作来检验两个时期的长城变化情况，识别了部分破坏风险，但要对长城破坏进行有效进行预警，还需要通过长期、多次的监测工作积累数据，总结规律[75]。

与此同时，国家文物局也鼓励各地开展监测工作试点。目前，嘉峪关、玉门关已经初步建成世界遗产监测中心，前者已于 2012 年率先建成了“嘉峪关世界文化遗产监测预警平台”，对嘉峪关关城进行结构稳定性和环境监测，并以嘉峪关关城木结构建筑和夯土墙体的结构稳定性监测为主。（图 4-16）此外，北京八达岭长城、河北山海关长城、金山岭长城、新疆维吾尔自治区的克孜尔尕哈烽火台等段点也不同程度地开展了监测工作。

[75] 国家文物局：陕西省府谷县用长城无人机+卫星遥感监测试点项目总结报告。

The above data is to verify the changes of the Great Wall between two periods through one-time work. It identified some risks of damage, but for effective early warning on the damage of the Great Wall, it needs to accumulate data and summarize the regularity through many times of monitoring work for a long term[75].

At the same time, the State Administration of Cultural Heritage also encourages local areas to carry out monitoring pilots. At present, world heritage monitoring centers were preliminarily built in Jiayu Pass and Yumen'guan. The former built the "Jiayu Pass World Cultural Heritage Monitoring and Early Warning Platform" in 2012 for the structural stability and environmental monitoring on Jiayu Pass City Wall, mainly focusing on the structural stability monitoring on the wooden structure buildings and rammed earth walls of Jiayu Pass City Wall. (Fig 4-16) In addition, monitoring work was also carried out with varying degrees on the Badaling Great Wall in Beijing, Shanhai Pass Great Wall in Hebei, Jinshanling Great Wall, Kizil Ga Kazakh Beacon Tower in Xinjiang Uygur Autonomous Region and other sits and sections.

图 4-15
府谷县境内明长城烽火台2016年无人机影像与2008年卫片对比

Fig. 4-15
Comparison between the UAV image in 2016 and satellite photo in 2008 of the beacon tower of the Ming Great Wall in Fugu County

[75] State Administration of Cultural Heritage: unmanned aerial vehicles for the Great Wall of Fugu County, Shaanxi + conclusive report of the satellite remote sensing monitoring pilot project

上述工作为长城监测体系的建立积累了丰富的技术经验。长城资源保护管理信息系统的建立，是实现长城信息管理的第一步。目前，国家文物局正在组织中国文化遗产研究院等专业机构在长城资源保护管理信息系统基础上，研究、建立长城监测预警平台，协助开展长城的世界遗产监测工作。通过长期采集长城本体与环境数据，并进行数据分析评估，提前发现长城破坏风险，并结合长城执法巡查督察、长城保护员制度和各种技术手段，对长城进行综合预防性保护，变被动保护为主动保护。

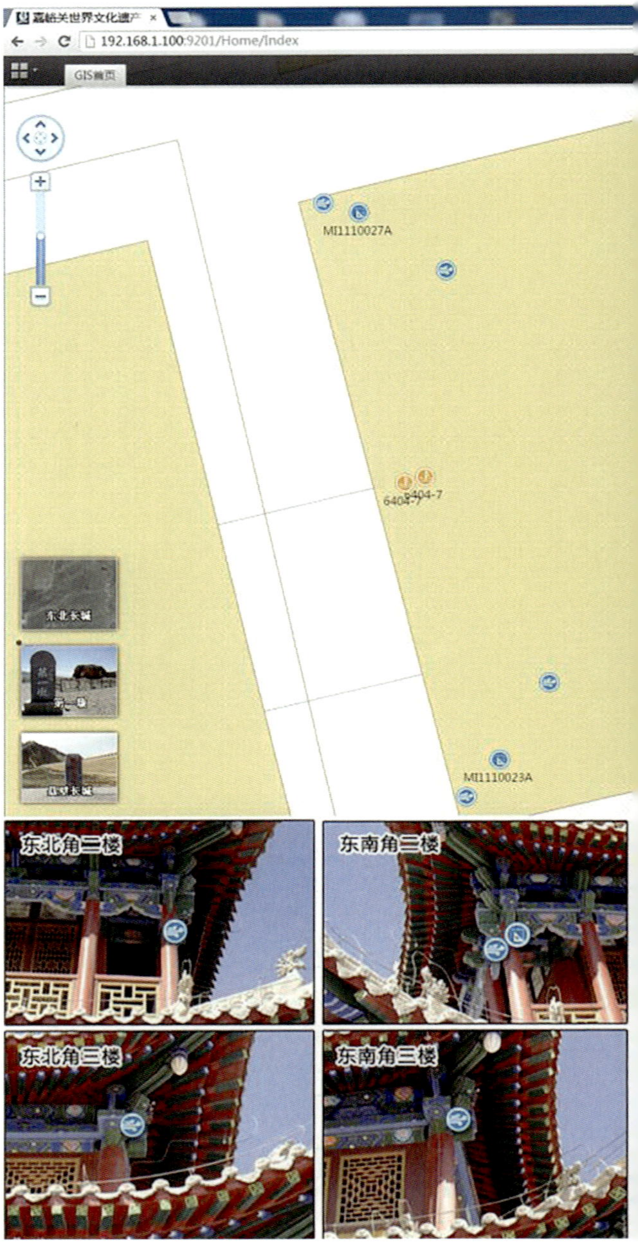


图 4-16
嘉峪关世界文化遗产监测系统传感器分布页面
（嘉峪关世界文化遗产监测中心 提供）

Fig. 4-16
Sensor distribution of Jiayu Pass World Cultural Heritage Monitoring System (provided by Jiayu Pass World Cultural Heritage Monitoring Center)

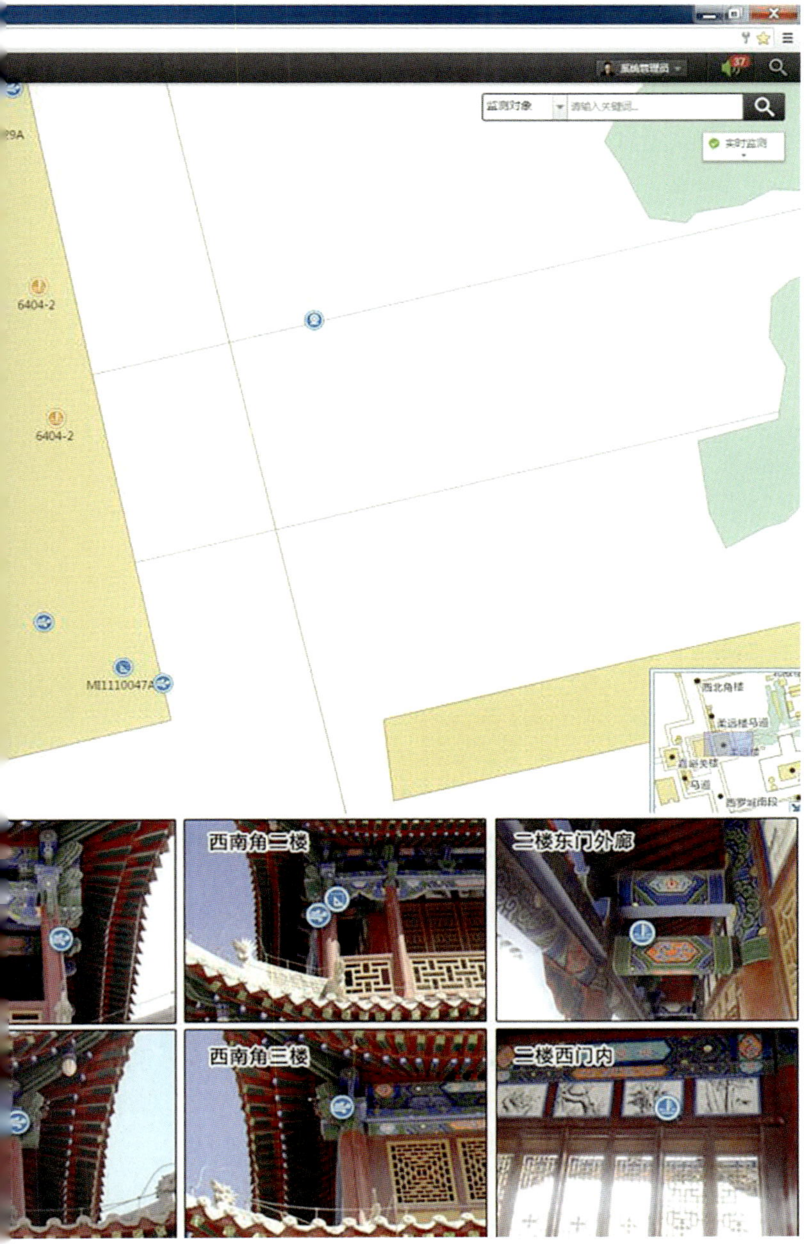


The above work has accumulated rich technical experience for the establishment of the Great Wall monitoring system. The establishment of the management of the Great Wall resource conservation information system is the first step to realize the information management of the Great Wall. At present, the State Administration of Cultural Heritage is organizing the Chinese Academy of Cultural Heritage and other professional institutions to study and establish the Great Wall monitoring and early warning platform based on the management of the Great Wall resource conservation information system, and give assistance in the world heritage monitoring work of the Great Wall.

Through the long-term collection of the Great Wall and its environmental data, data analysis and evaluation, they can detect damage risks on the Great Wall in early time, and make comprehensive preventive conservation of the Great Wall combining with the Great Wall law enforcement inspectors, the Great Wall guard system and a variety of technical means to convert passive conservation into initiative conservation.

## 六、长城军事聚落与防御体系研究

2007 年开始，天津大学建筑学院的张玉坤教授及其团队开始从建筑的角度对明长城关堡的军事防御体系进行研究，取得了一系列的成果，完成学位论文、专著等 20 余部，发表学术论文 40 余篇。

### （一）明长城防御体系研究

对长城及其军事聚落的空间分布规律、层次与系统进行分析，并绘制完成明长城军事防御聚落分布图。提出了“长城秩序带”的概念。（图 4-17、4-18）

图 4-17
明长城军事防御聚落分布图
（北京建筑大学 提供）

Fig. 4-17
Map of the Ming Great Wall military defense settlement distribution (provided by Beijing University of Architecture)

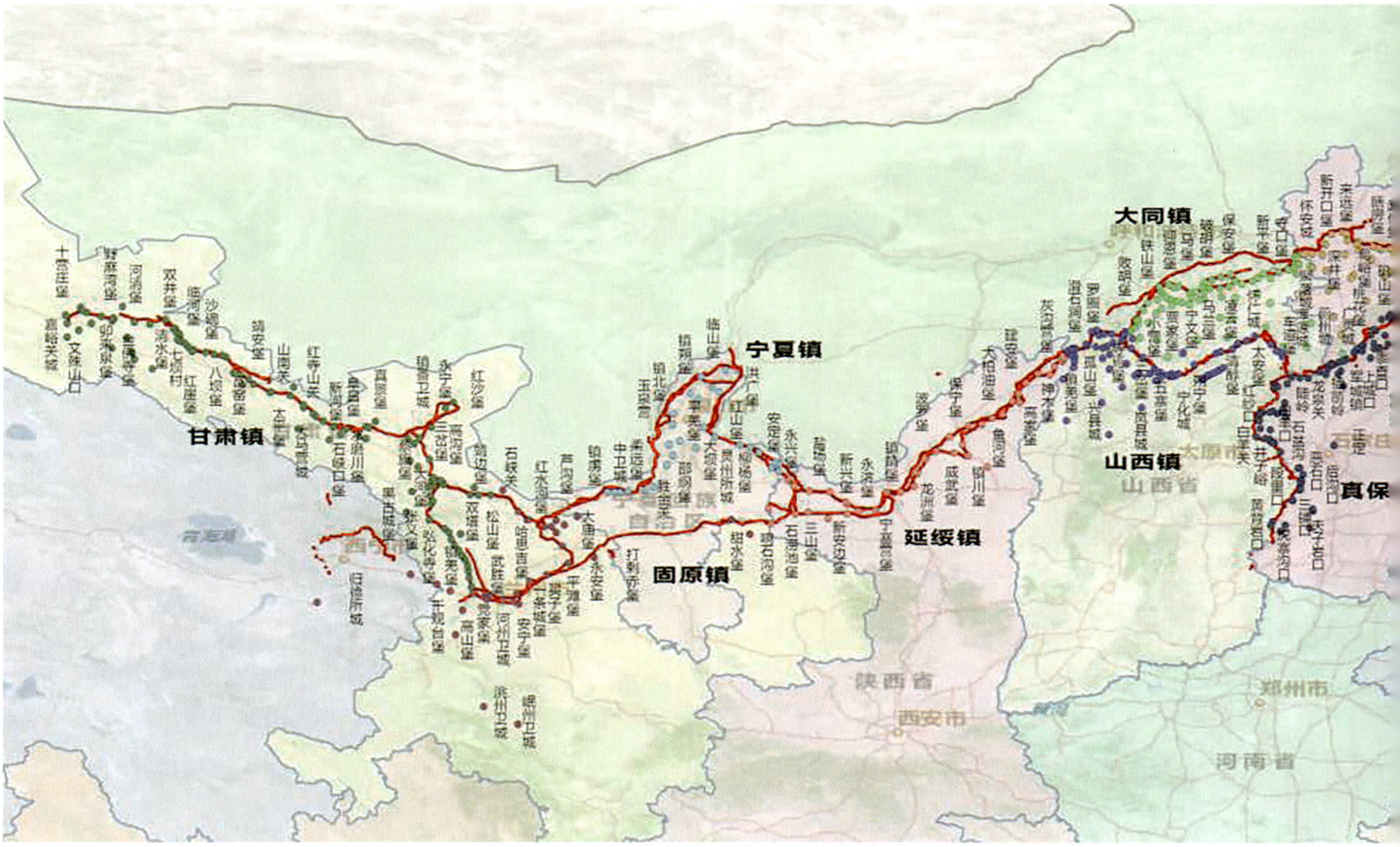

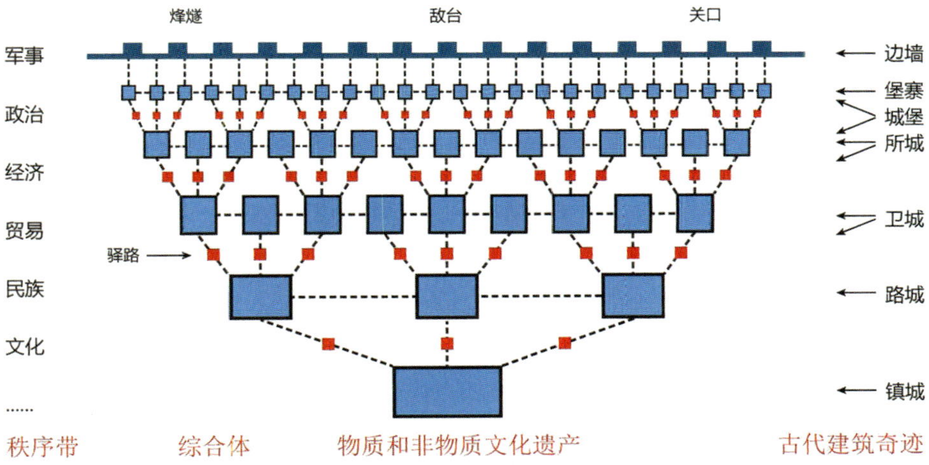


图 4-18
秩序带——明长城防御体系概念图
（北京建筑大学 提供）

Fig. 4-18
Order zone-- concept map of the Ming Great Wall defense system (provided by Beijing University of Architecture)

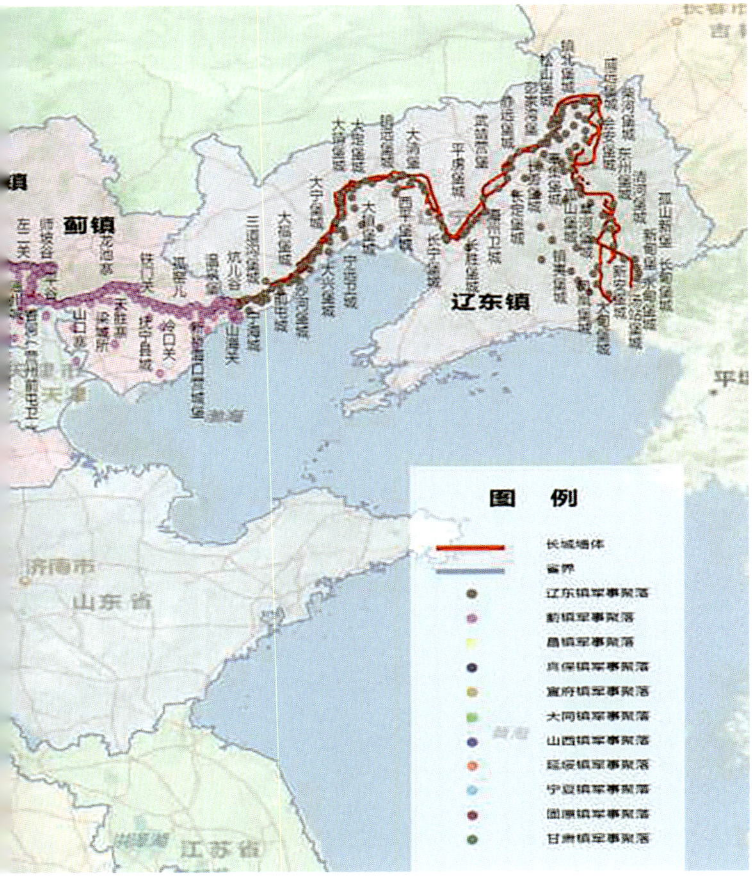


## VI. Study on the Great Wall Military Settlement and Defense System

Since 2007, Professor Zhang Yukun of the School of Architecture of Tianjin University and his team began to study the military defense system of the Ming Great Wall forts from the perspective of architecture, and got a series of achievements. They completed more than 20 theses and monographs, and published more than 40 academic papers.

### (I) Study on the Ming Great Wall defense system

It analyzed the spatial distribution regularity, levels and system of the Great Wall and its military settlement, and completed the map of the Great Wall military defense settlement distribution. It put forward the concept of "Great Wall Order Zone". (Figs 4-17, 4-18)

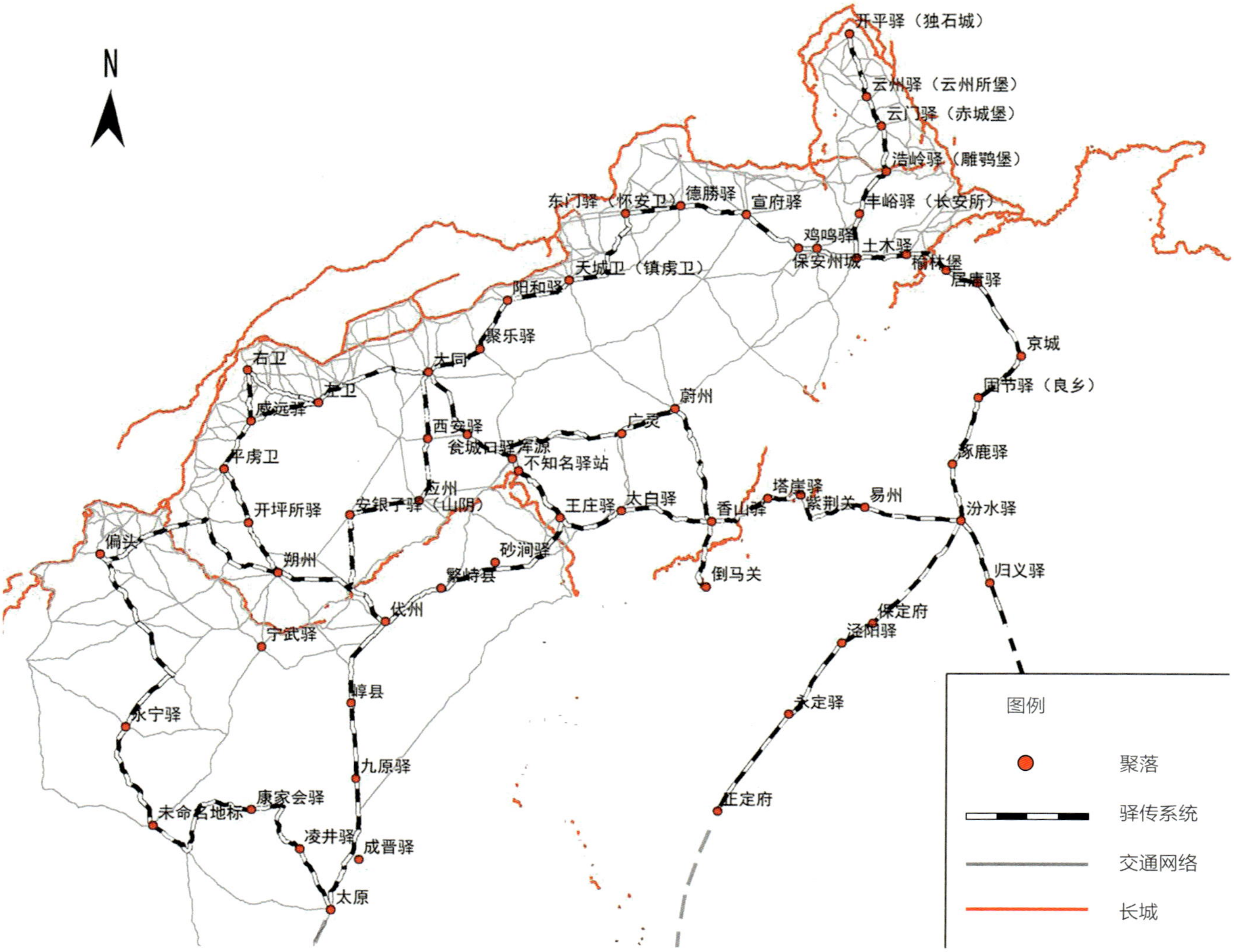


## （二）明长城九边军事聚落的专题研究

图 4-19
宣大山西三镇驿传系统整体布局
（北京建筑大学 提供）

Fig. 4-19
Overall layout of the postal delivery system of Xuanda Shanxi three towns (provided by Beijing University of Architecture)

天津大学建筑学院对明长城九边各镇防御体系和军事聚落都进行了专题研究。如曹迎春以宣府、大同、山西三镇为研究对象，基于长城历史资料、现代研究成果、实地调研及试验数据，综合运用 GIS 空间分析技术、数学以及统计学方法，定量化揭示了三镇防御体系的宏观系统关系，包括布局时空演化、烽传线路与道路分布关系等等。（图 4-19）

### (II) Special study on the nine frontier military settlement in the Ming Great Wall region

The School of Architecture of Tianjin University made special studies on the defense systems and military settlements of all the nine frontier towns in the Ming Great Wall region. For example, Cao Yingchun selected three towns, Xuanfu, Datong and Shanxi as the study objects. Based on the historical data, modern research results, field investigation and experimental data of the Great Wall, he quantitatively revealed the macro-system relationship of the defense systems of the three towns including space-time evolution of the layout, beacon pass route and the relationship of road distribution, etc. by applying GIS spatial analysis technology, mathematics and statistical methods. (Fig 4-19)

## VII. The compilation of the Ming Great Wall Resources Investigation Report

The Great Wall resource investigations obtained the most comprehensive and complete data of the Great Wall resources so far, among which the Ming Great Wall is well preserved and the investigation data is also more systematic. Therefore, the State Administration of Cultural Heritage commissioned Chinese Academy of Cultural Heritage to carry out the compilation of *the Ming Great Wall Resources Investigation Report (tentative name)* throughout China, to sort out and grasp the first hand investigation data on the Ming Great Wall.

The compilation of *the Ming Great Wall Resources Investigation Report (tentative name)* started in 2011. Chai Xiaoming, the associate director of Chinese Academy of Cultural Heritage at that time (now the director of Chinese Academy of Cultural Heritage) was the editor, and all members of the Great Wall project team participated in the compilation.

First of all, the compilation team determined the report compilation outline, compilation system and division of tasks after several meetings. *The Ming Great Wall Resources Investigation Report (tentative name)* was divided into six parts and fifteen chapters according to the basic system of archaeological excavation report.

Part 1 Introduce the general situation of the Great Wall investigation, including the origin of the investigation, the investigation process and methods;

Part 2 Review the investigation and research history the Ming Great Wall, including a brief research history and literature in summary;

Part 3 Introduce the historical evolution of the Great Wall and the characteristics of the geographical environment;

Part 4 The most important content of the report. It introduces the achievements of the Great Wall resource investigation, including the general situation of the Great Wall resources, the constitution of the Great Wall (including the wall, trench, enemy platform, bastion, water sluice, trail and other wall facilities), the beacon tower, fort and the related remains, relics and inscription descriptions of the Ming Great Wall;

Part 5 Introduce the current preservation and management of Ming Great Wall. The report is for the Great Wall researchers and also for the professional Great Wall cultural relics management personnel throughout China. Therefore, the end of the report introduces the current preservation and problems of the Ming Great Wall, including the current situation, cause of the damages and current management of the Great Wall. This is a characteristic of this report.

Part 6 Summary of the whole report.(Table 4-6)

## 七、《明长城资源调查报告》编写

长城资源调查工作获取了迄今最全面、最完整的长城资源数据，其中明长城整体保存程度较好，调查数据也比较系统。因此，国家文物局委托中国文化遗产研究院进行全国《明长城资源调查报告（暂定名）》的编写，从整体上梳理和把握明长城的第一手调查材料。

《明长城资源调查报告（暂定名）》的编写工作始于2011年，时任中国文化遗产研究院副院长柴晓明（现为中国文化遗产研究院院长）担任主编，长城项目组全体人员参与编写。

首先，编写组经过多次会议研究确定了报告编写提纲、编写体例和任务分工。《明长城资源调查报告（暂定名）》按照考古发掘报告的基本体例，分为六篇十五章。

第一篇，介绍明长城调查工作概况，包括调查工作的缘起、调查过程及方法等；

第二篇，回顾明长城调查与研究史，包括研究简史和文献综述；

第三篇，介绍明长城历史沿革与地理环境特点；

第四篇是报告最重要的内容，即明长城资源调查成果介绍。包括明长城资源概况、明长城本体（墙体、壕堑，敌台、马面、水关、步道等墙体设施）构成、明长城烽火台、关堡及相关遗存、遗物和题记描述；

第五篇，介绍明长城保护管理现状。报告除了面向长城研究人员，也面向全国长城专业文物管理人员。因此报告的末尾，分专章介绍了明长城保存现状及问题，包括长城本体现状、损毁原因和管理现状等内容，这是本报告的特色；

第六篇为全报告的总结。（表4-6）

表 4-6：《明长城资源调查报告（暂定名）》目录及负责人

Table 4-6: Content and person in charge of *the Ming Great Wall Resources Investigation Report (tentative name)*

| 篇目<br>Part | 章节<br>Chapter | 负责人<br>Person in charge |
|---|---|---|
| 第一篇 明长城调查工作概况<br>Part 1 General situation of the Great Wall investigation | 第一章 明长城调查缘起<br>Chapter 1 Origin of the Ming Great Wall investigation<br>第二章 明长城调查及其方法<br>Chapter 2 Investigation of the Great Wall and the methods | 柴晓明<br>Chai Xiaoming |
| 第二篇 明长城调查与研究回顾<br>Part 2 Reviews of the Ming Great Wall investigation and research | 第一章 调查研究简史<br>Chapter 1 Brief history of investigation and research | 李文龙<br>Li Wenlong |
| | 第二章明长城文献综述<br>Chapter 2 Overview of the Ming Great Wall literature | 刘文艳<br>Li Wenlong |
| 第三篇 明长城历史沿革及地理环境<br>Part 3 Historical evolution and geographical environment of the Ming Great Wall | 第一章 历史沿革<br>Chapter 1 Historical evolution<br>第二章 地理环境及特点<br>Chapter 2 Geographical environment and characteristics | 李大伟<br>Li Dawei |
| 第四篇 明长城调查成果<br>Part 4 Achievements of the Ming Great Wall investigation | 第一章 明长城概况<br>Chapter 1 Overview of the Ming Great Wall | 李文龙<br>Li Wenlong |
| | 第二章 明长城本体的构成<br>Chapter 2 Composition of the Great Wall main body | 张依萌<br>Zhang Yimeng |
| | 第四节 明代长城烽火台<br>Section 4 Beacon tower of the Ming Great Wall | 刘文艳<br>Liu Wenyan |
| | 第三章 明长城关堡<br>Chapter 3 Forts of the Ming Great Wall | 许慧君<br>Xu Huijun |
| | 第四章 明长城防御体系的相关遗存<br>Chapter 4 Defense system and related remains of the Ming Great Wall<br>第五章 遗物与题记<br>Chapter 5 Relics and Inscription | 王继红<br>Wang Jihong |
| 第五篇 明长城保存现状及其问题<br>Part 5 Current preservation and problems of the Ming Great Wall | 第一章 长城本体现状<br>Chapter 1 Current situation of the Great Wall main body<br>第二章 损毁原因<br>Chapter 2 Causes of damages<br>第三章 管理现状<br>Chapter 3 Current management | 李大伟<br>Li Dawei |
| 第六篇 结论<br>Part 6 Conclusion | | 柴晓明<br>Chai Xiaoming |

图 4-20
《明长城资源调查报告（暂定名）》编写组讨论长城分布图绘制工作（张依萌 拍摄）

Fig. 4-20
The compilation team of *the Ming Great Wall Resources Investigation Report (tentative name)* is discussing the drawing work of the Great Wall distribution map (photo by Zhang Yimeng)

在此基础上，编写组花费近四年时间对全国十个省（自治区、直辖市）202 个县提交的详略不一，内容庞杂的近 30000 份长城资源调查登记表，按照统一标准规范进行系统整理，通过人工核对、电话询问、实地调研相结合的方式进行查缺补漏和数据核实，对个别重复调查或存在矛盾的材料一一进行甄别。在整理材料的同时，即着手按照考古报告的要求进行标本卡片制作、标本分型分式、文本写作和绘图、排图工作，并以每周例会的形式管理编写进度。

目前，报告已经完成了包括近 40 万字、200 余幅图片，50 余张表格，千余张照片的初稿，预计 2018 年之前正式出版。（图 4-20 、4-21）

需要指出的是，《明长城资源调查报告（暂定名）》是一份学术研究性质的著作，以长城资源调查而非认定数据为基础进行编写，以客观介绍材料为目的，同时也融合了长城项目组的一些基本观点，因此在明长城的长度、遗存数量等数据和标本描述与长城资源认定数据存在一定的差异。

图 4-21
《明长城资源调查报告（暂定名）》分型定式举例——砖砌空心敌台内部结构平面型式

Fig. 4-21
Example of form classification in the Ming Great Wall Resources Investigation Report (tentative name) -- the plane type of internal structure of brick-built hollow enemy platform

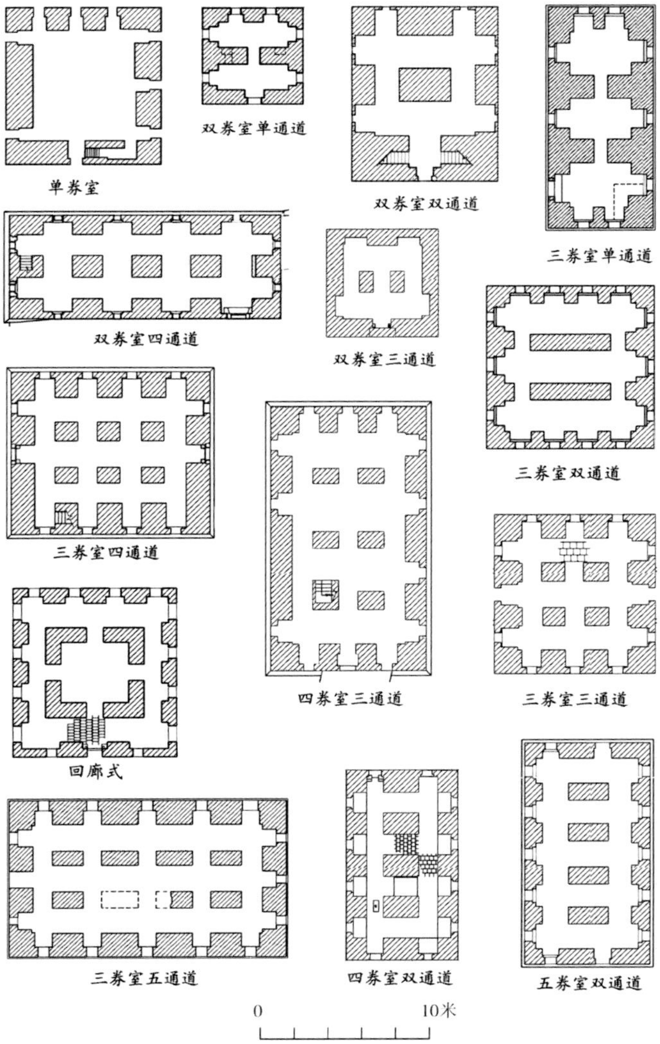


On this basis, the compilation team spent nearly four years on nearly 30,000 Great Wall resource investigation forms for 10 provinces (autonomous regions and municipalities) and 202 counties in different lengths with multifarious contents. They made systematic processing in accordance with uniform standards, made up the deficiencies and verified the data through the combination of manual check, telephone inquiries, field investigation and research, and reexamined a few repeatedly investigated or contradictory data one by one. In the process of sorting out the data, they started to make the specimen cards, specimen classification, text writing and drawing and drawing layout in accordance with the requirements of the archaeological report, and managed the compilation progress in the form of weekly regular meetings.

Until now, the first draft of the report has been completed, including nearly 400 thousand words, more than 200 pictures, more than 50 sheets, more than a thousand photos. It is expected to be formally published before 2018. (Figs. 4-20, 4-21)

It should be pointed out that *the Ming Great Wall Resources Investigation Report (tentative name)* is a book on academic research, written on the basis of the Great Wall resource investigation rather than the identified data, for the purpose of objective introduction materials. At the same time, it also integrates some basic view points of the Great Wall project team, so on the data such as the length of the Great Wall and the quantity of remains and specimen description, there are some differences with the identified Great Wall resource data.

## 八、《中国长城志》编纂

“长城保护工程”的开展，带动了民间长城研究的热情。2007 年，中国长城学会开始了《中国长城志》的编纂工作，成立了编辑部，同时聘请北京师范大学历史学院、中央民族大学历史学院、人民教育出版社历史编辑室、中国人民大学国学院、北京大学、中国文物学会等专业机构的长城研究专家，以及中国地方志指导小组办公室方志学专家共同组成了专家组，对志书的编写工作提供专业建议和业务指导。

《中国长城志》是第一部以民间力量为主导编纂的大型文物类志书。全书分为十卷，成书约 2300 万字。《中国长城志》采用述、记、志、传、图、表、录七种体编撰，分为《图志》《总述—大事记》《环境—经济—民族》《建筑》《边镇—关隘—堡寨》、《考古—保护—研究》《军事》《人物》《文献》《文学艺术》和《附录》等十一卷，每卷分别聘请各领域的专家作为主编，分别组织编写工作。

其中：《图志》卷，包括按时代和行政区收集和制作的长城舆图、历史地图、长城现状测绘图；

《总述—大事记》卷，概括全志各卷内容，介绍长城的基本概念、价值、历史地位与作用、长城保护概况，梳理长城建筑发展脉络和长城大事记等；

《环境—经济—民族》卷，记载长城沿线环境、经济、民族情况；

《建筑》卷，介绍长城的选址、布局、结构、材质和建造工艺方法等内容；

《边镇—关隘—堡寨》卷，对长城沿线的关隘、城堡及军事聚落、军事建制进行梳理；

《考古—保护—研究》卷，介绍长城考古发现、遗迹的走向、分布及现代科技手段应用于长城考古研究和保护管理的情况；

《人物》卷，整理和介绍长城相关的将领、官吏、工匠等人物；

《军事》卷，介绍长城军事史、防御体系、历代战争和国家

## VIII. Compilation of the *Chronicles of China Great Wall*

The Great Wall Conservation Project inspired the enthusiasm of the civil study on the Great Wall. In 2007, the Great Wall Society of China started the compilation of *the Chronicles of China Great Wall*. They established the editorial department, and invited the experts on the study of the Great Wall from professional institutions such as the History College of Beijing Normal University, the History College of the Central University for Nationalities, the Historical Editing Office of the People's Education Publishing House, the National College of Renmin University of China, Peking University, and Cultural Relics Society of China, as well as the expert Fang Zhixue from Chinese Local Chronicles Leader Team Office to form an expert team to provide professional advice and business guidance for the compilation of the book.

*The Chronicles of China Great Wall* is the first large-scale chronicles on cultural relics compiled mainly by civil power. The book includes ten volumes, with about 23 million words. *The Chronicles of China Great Wall* is compiled in the forms of narration, records, chronicles, biography, drawing, table and analects. It includes eleven volumes namely *Drawing Chronicle, Summary - Memorabilia, Environment - Economy - Ethnic Groups, Buildings, Frontier Towns – Passes – Forts, Archaeology - Preservation - Research, Military, Characters, Documentation, Literature and Art* and *Appendix*. Experts in various fields were invited as the editor respectively for each volume to organize the compilation separately.

Among them, the volume *Drawing Chronicle* includes the Great Wall maps, historical map and mapping graphs of current situation of the Great Wall collected and made by dynasty and administrative area;

The volume *Summary – Memorabilia* sums up the contents of all the volumes, and introduces the basic concepts, values, historical status and roles, preservation overview, building development and major historical events of the Great Wall;

The volume *Environment - Economy – Ethnic Groups* records the environment, economy and ethnic groups along the Great Wall;

The volume of *Buildings* introduces the location, layout, structure, material and building techniques and methods of the Great Wall;

The volume of *Frontier Towns – Passes – Forts* sorts out the passes, forts, military settlements and military systems along the Great Wall;

The volume of *Archaeology - Preservation – Research* introduces the archaeological discoveries of the Great Wall, the direction and distribution of remains, and application of modern technology in archaeological research and conservation and management of the Great Wall;

The volume *Characters* sorts out and introduces generals, officials, craftsmen and other characters related to the Great Wall;

The volume *Military* introduces the military history, defense system, wars and

战略等；

《文献》卷，收录史书、方志、笔记中历代长城相关记载、长城志书等文献并进行校注；

《文学艺术》卷，收录长城诗词歌赋、神话传说、摄影绘画作品等内容；（表 4-7）

## 表 4-7：长城志各卷主编情况一览表

| 卷名 | 主编 | 职称 / 职务 |
|---|---|---|
| 《图志》 | 陈军 | 国家基础地理信息中心 总工程师 |
| 《总述 - 大事记》 | 董耀会 | 中国长城学会 常务副会长 |
| 《环境 - 经济 - 民族》 | 李宏滨 | 中央民族大学 教授 |
| | 唐晓峰 | 北京大学 教授 |
| 《建筑》 | 汤羽扬 | 北京建筑大学 教授 |
| 《边镇 - 关隘 - 堡寨》 | 张玉坤 | 天津大学建筑学院 教授 |
| 《考古 - 保护 - 研究》 | 朱筱新 | 北京教育学院 教授 |
| 《人物》 | 毛佩琦 | 中国人民大学 教授 |
| 《军事》 | 刘庆 | 解放军军事科学院 研究员 |
| 《文献》 | 向燕南 | 北京师范大学 教授 |
| 《文学艺术》 | 孙志升 | 秦皇岛日报社 高级记者 |
| | 苏君里 | 河北科技师范学院 教授 |

national strategies in various dynasties of the Great Wall;

The volume *Documentation,* includes the relevant records of the ancient Great Wall in historical books, local chronicles and notes, chronicles of the Great Wall and some other documents with annotation;

The volume *Literature and Art* includes poetry and songs, myths and legends, photographic and paintings works of the Great Wall;

Table 4-7: List of editors of the *Chronicles of China Great Wall*

| Volume | Editors | Title/Position |
|---|---|---|
| *Drawing Chronicle* | Chen Jun | Chief Engineer of National Basic Geographic Information Center |
| *Summary – Memorabilia* | Dong Yaohui | Executive vice president of Great Wall Society of China |
| *Environment - Economy – Ethic Groups* | Li Hongbin | Professor of Central University for Nationalities |
| | Tang Xiaofeng | Professor of Peking University |
| *Buildings* | Tang Yuyang | Professor of Beijing University of Architecture |
| *Frontier Towns – Passes – Forts* | Zhang Yukun | Professor of School of Architecture, Tianjin University |
| *Archaeology - Preservation - Research* | Zhu Xiaoxin | Professor of Beijing Institute of Education |
| *Characters* | Mao Peiqi | Professor of Renmin University of China |
| *Military* | Liu Qing | Researcher of People 's Liberation Army Academy of Military Sciences |
| *Documentation* | Xiang Yannan | Professor of Beijing Normal University |
| *Literature and Art* | Sun Zhisheng | Senior reporter of Qinhuangdao Daily News |
| | Su Junli | Professor of Hebei Normal University of Science and Technology |

## 第四节 长城研究成果分析

※ 在“中国知网”上以“长城”为关键词搜索，可得 1915-2016 年间发表的文章 84729 篇

※ 长城相关哲学与人文社会科学研究论文占全部文章数的不到 10%，其中超过 60% 发表于 2006 年 -2016 年间

※ 2006 年以来，受“长城保护工程”实施影响，成果猛增，但仍以文史研究为主

“长城保护工程”总体工作方案提出“加强长城保护科学研究，完成长城及其保护管理研究课题”的任务。从近十年来的长城保护科学研究课题情况来看，当前长城研究以基础研究为主，应用研究相对较少。其中，长城应用研究应主要就当前长城保护管理中的热点、难点问题进行研究，以优化长城保护管理工作为目的，为政府决策及相关工作提供科学依据和理论支持，科研成果也将实际应用于长城保护管理工作中，主要研究方向包括：长城保护、管理、监测现状、问题及对策研究，即通过对长城保护、管理和研究现状的调查研究，全面、深入了解其中存在的主要问题，分析问题产生原因，提出解决问题的对策建议，为制定长城保护管理各环节的工作标准与技术规范奠定基础；长城利用模式研究，即对长城开发利用的现有模式进行调研分析，做出综合性评估，探索符合国情的可持续发展的长城保护与合理利用模式。此外，“长城保护工程”总体工作方案还提出设立国家级的“长城及其保护管理研究”综合研究课题，具体内容包括中国历代长城研究、长城保护理论政策研究、长城保护技术研究三大部分内容，由国家牵头开展长城相关研究。

根据不完全统计，在长城沿线各省（自治区、直辖市）政府和有关部门主导开展的长城研究方面，2005-2014 年间，各地共出版长城调查报告、研究专著和完成课题研究报告 72 部（篇），其中专著有 24 部，长城调查报告（含简报）有 25 部（篇），共开展了长城研究课题 23 项。其中甘肃省最多，有 7 项，山西省有 6 项。国家级科研项目有 5 项；省部级科研项目有 10 项；其他各级科研项目有 6 项；其他项目有 3 项。（表 4-8）

# Section 4 Analysis on the Study Achievements of the Great Wall

- Search the keyword "Great Wall" on "CNKI.NET", and 84,729 articles published during 1915-2016 are available
- Papers on the philosophy and humanities and social science related to the Great Wall accounted for less than 10% of all the articles, among which more than 60% were published during 2006 - 2016
- Since 2006, influenced the by implementation of the "Great Wall Conservation Project", the achievements increased rapidly but still mainly on the study of literature and history

The overall work program of the "Great Wall Conservation Project" proposed the task "to strengthen the Great Wall conservation and scientific research and to complete the research projects on the Great Wall and its conservation management". The situation of research projects on the Great Wall and its conservation management in the past decade indicates that the current Great Wall researches are mainly around basic researches and relatively less about application-based researches. Among them, the application-based researches on the Great Wall are mainly on currently hot and difficult issues in the Great Wall conservation and management for the purpose of optimizing the Great Wall conservation and management to provide scientific basis and theoretical support for government decision-making and related work. The achievements of scientific research will also be applied in actual work of the Great Wall conservation and management. The main research directions include the current situation, problems and solutions of the Great Wall conservation, management and monitoring, namely, to get all-round and in-depth understanding of the main problems through investigation and study on the current Great Wall conservation, management and researches, analyze the causes and put forward suggestions to solve the problem, to lay the foundation for the formulation of the work standards and technical specifications in each process of the Great Wall conservation and management; utilization model study on the Great Wall, namely, research and analysis and comprehensive assessment on the current models of the Great Wall development and utilization. Explore a model of conservation and reasonable utilization of the Great Wall in line with the national conditions and sustainable development. In addition, the overall work program of "Great Wall Conservation Project" proposed to establish national comprehensive research subject on "the Great Wall and study on the conservation and management", including three parts of study Great Wall of successive Chinese dynasties in various dynasties, on the Great Wall conservation theories and policies, and on the Great Wall conservation technologies. The country leads the subject to carry out the studies related to the Great Wall.

## 表 4-8：长城保护科研成果统计表
Table 4-8: Scientific research achievements on the Great Wall conservation

| 行政区划 Administrative division | 专著 Monograph | 调查报告[76] Investigation report[76] | 研究课题报告 Research subject report | 总计 Total |
|---|---|---|---|---|
| 北京市 Beijing | 2 | 1 | 0 | 3 |
| 天津市 Tianjin | 4 | 1 | 0 | 5 |
| 河北省 Hebei Province | 3 | 1 | 4 | 8 |
| 山西省 Shanxi Province | 1 | 0 | 6 | 7 |
| 内蒙古自治区 Inner Mongolia Autonomous Region | 4 | 7 | 1 | 12 |
| 辽宁省 Liaoning Province | 1 | 2 | 1 | 4 |
| 吉林省 Jilin Province | 0 | 1 | 0 | 1 |
| 黑龙江省 Heilongjiang Province | 0 | 0 | 0 | 0 |
| 山东省 Shandong Province | 0 | 0 | 0 | 0 |
| 河南省 Henan Province | 1 | 2 | 2 | 5 |
| 陕西省 Shaanxi Province | 2 | 4 | 2 | 8 |
| 甘肃省 Gansu Province | 4 | 1 | 7 | 12 |
| 青海省 Qinghai Province | 0 | 2 | 0 | 2 |
| 宁夏回族自治区 Ningxia Hui Autonomous Region | 2 | 1 | 0 | 3 |
| 新疆维吾尔自治区 Xinjiang Uygur Autonomous Region | 0 | 2 | 0 | 2 |
| 合计 Total | 24 | 25 | 23 | 72 |

[76] 调查报告的统计截止 2016 年，其他项截止 2014 年。

According to incomplete statistics, on the Great Wall studies carried out by the governments and relevant departments of the provinces (autonomous regions and municipalities directly under the central government) along the Great Wall, totally72 investigation reports and research monographs of the Great Wall have been published and research reports were completed during the period of 2005-2014, including 24 monographs, 25 the Great Wall investigation reports (including briefings), and 23 research projects on the Great Wall. Among them, 7 are from Gansu Province, which is the most, and 6 are from Shanxi Province. There are 5 national scientific research projects; 10 provincial and ministerial scientific research projects; 6 other scientific research projects at lower levels; and 3 other projects. ( Table 4-8).

With respect to the papers on the Great Wall researches, we take the data published by CNKI.NET as an example. Search the keyword "Great Wall" on CNKI.NET, and 84,729 articles published during 1915-2016 are available (Fig 4-2). If search the keyword "Great Wall research", we can get 38,858 results. In particular, if search a series of keywords related to the "Great Wall" in the catalogs of "philosophy and humanities" and "social sciences", carefully compare and discriminate all the results are exclude the data unrelated to the Great Wall research and repeated data, we can see that there are 8,359 articles related to the Great Wall research were published during 1936-2014, accounting for less than 10% of all the articles, among which articles published in the period during 2006-2016 account for 63.6% of all the articles. According to the papers searched on CNKI.NET, the contents include the researches on both traditional history and culture and on the conservation management and development and utilization of the Great Wall. Most of them are basic researches on the history and culture of the Great Wall. If limit the keywords to the "Great Wall Management" and "Great Wall Conservation", there are only 2599 and 1869 relevant articles. The articles on the theme of the Great Wall are far more than the professional research achievements of the Great Wall, which reflects the wide social influence of the Great Wall from one perspective; On the other hand, the relevant documents of the Great Wall conservation is far less than the total research achievements on the Great Wall, which indicates that the relevant research on the Great Wall conservation and management still has great potential for further development. (Fig 4-2, Table 4-9).

---

[76] The statistics of the investigation report are until 2014 and the other items are until 2014.

就长城研究论文而言，以中国知网公开发布数据为例。在中国知网中以“长城”为关键词进行搜索，1915-2016 年间发表的文章 84729 篇（图 4-22）。如果以“长城研究”为关键词进行搜索，则能得到 38858 条结果。具体到以“长城”相关的一系列关键词在“哲学与人文科学”、“社会科学”文献分类目录下进行搜索，再对全部结果进行仔细的比对、甄别，并排除了与长城研究无关，以及重复数据之后，可知 1936 年 -2014 年间发表的长城相关研究文章 8359 篇，占全部文章数的不到 10%，其中发表于 2006 年 -2016 年间的文章占全部研究文章总数的 63.6%。根据中国知网检索的论文内容来看，研究内容上既有传统的历史文化研究，也有长城保护管理和开发利用方面的研究，其中绝大部分属于长城历史文化方面的基础研究。若将关键词限定在“长城管理”和“长城保护”，则仅有相关文献 2599 篇和 1869 篇。以“长城”为主题的文章数量远远超过长城专业研究成果的数量，这从一个侧面反映了长城的社会影响之广泛；另一方面，长城保护相关文献数量远远少于长城研究成果总数，则说明了长城保护管理的相关研究仍然具有较大的发展潜力。（图 4-22，表 4-9）

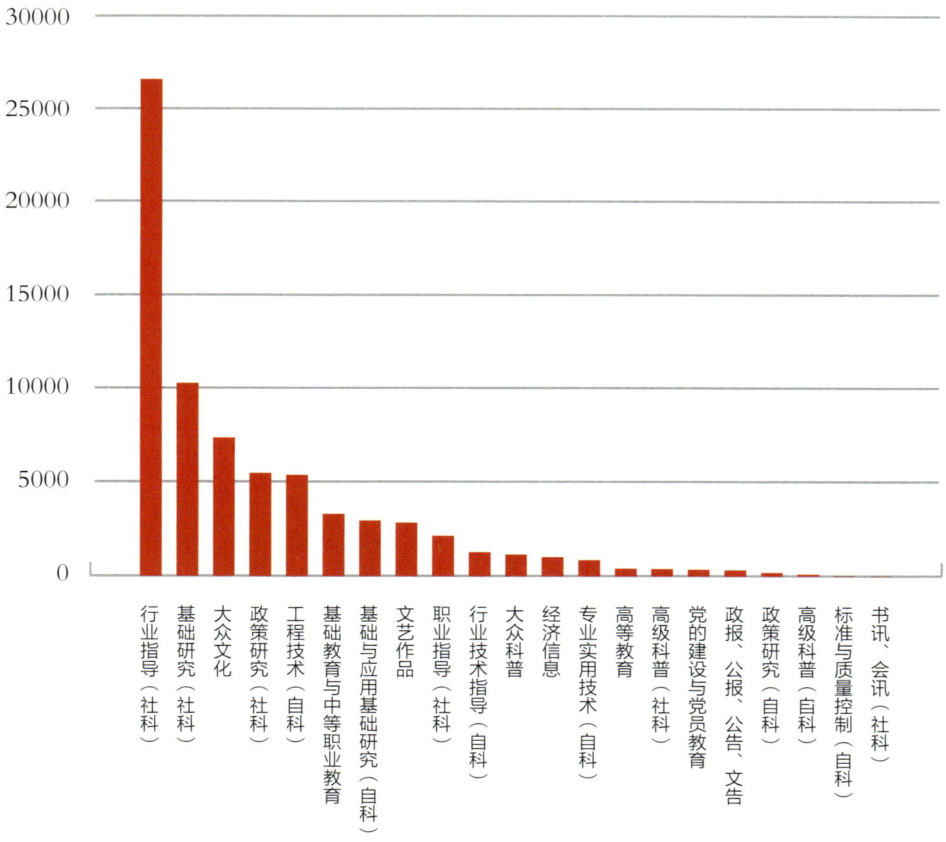


图 4-22
中国知网“长城”相关文献数量分类统计图表（1915-2016 年）

Fig. 4-2
Classification statistics chart of the documentation related to "the Great Wall" on CNKI.NET (1915 - 2016)

## 表 4-9：中国知网长城研究相关文献分类统计表（1936 ~ 2016 年）

Table 4-9: Classification statistics table of the documentation related to the Great Wall research on CNKI.NET (1936 ~ 2016)

| 年份<br>Year | 开发利用类<br>Development and utilization | 保护管理类<br>Conservation and management | 历史文化类<br>History and culture | 合计<br>Total |
|---|---|---|---|---|
| 1936-1949 | 0 | 0 | 1 | 1 |
| 1950-1978 | 0 | 2 | 56 | 58 |
| 1979 | 3 | 3 | 11 | 17 |
| 1980 | 2 | 1 | 10 | 13 |
| 1981 | 4 | 0 | 18 | 22 |
| 1982 | 4 | 2 | 29 | 35 |
| 1983 | 1 | 5 | 29 | 35 |
| 1984 | 1 | 3 | 35 | 39 |
| 1985 | 6 | 6 | 47 | 59 |
| 1986 | 3 | 2 | 35 | 40 |
| 1987 | 4 | 4 | 44 | 52 |
| 1988 | 9 | 4 | 34 | 47 |
| 1989 | 6 | 3 | 58 | 67 |
| 1990 | 1 | 9 | 67 | 77 |
| 1991 | 5 | 4 | 44 | 53 |
| 1992 | 5 | 6 | 59 | 70 |
| 1993 | 10 | 8 | 49 | 67 |
| 1994 | 16 | 17 | 130 | 163 |
| 1995 | 9 | 22 | 134 | 165 |
| 1996 | 5 | 4 | 110 | 119 |
| 1997 | 7 | 12 | 135 | 154 |
| 1998 | 12 | 11 | 144 | 167 |
| 1999 | 8 | 13 | 86 | 107 |
| 2000 | 14 | 14 | 129 | 157 |
| 2001 | 16 | 18 | 118 | 152 |
| 2002 | 15 | 21 | 176 | 212 |

| | | | | |
|---|---|---|---|---|
| 2003 | 21 | 36 | 179 | 236 |
| 2004 | 32 | 42 | 171 | 245 |
| 2005 | 36 | 84 | 296 | 416 |
| 2006 | 44 | 162 | 363 | 569 |
| 2007 | 45 | 139 | 433 | 617 |
| 2008 | 22 | 88 | 330 | 440 |
| 2009 | 51 | 78 | 344 | 473 |
| 2010 | 37 | 81 | 288 | 406 |
| 2011 | 48 | 82 | 276 | 406 |
| 2012 | 57 | 137 | 291 | 485 |
| 2013 | 44 | 109 | 272 | 425 |
| 2014 | 53 | 75 | 281 | 409 |
| 2015 | 89 | 157 | 356 | 602 |
| 2016 | 39 | 156 | 287 | 482 |
| 合计 | 784 | 1620 | 5955 | 8359 |

注：数据根据中国知网统计结果整理。其中，开发利用类检索关键词：长城＋旅游、长城＋开发、长城＋利用；保护管理类检索关键词：长城＋保护、长城＋管理、长城＋政策、长城＋法规、长城＋法律、长城＋应用、长城＋监测；历史文化类检索关键词：长城＋关、长城＋堡、烽火台、烽燧、长城＋遗址、长城＋考古、长城＋文化、长城＋历史、长城＋调查、长城＋地理

Remark: The data are sorted out according to the statistics of CNKI.NET. The keywords for development and utilization include the Great Wall + tourism, the Great Wall + development, the Great Wall + utilization; the keywords for conservation and management include the Great Wall + conservation, the Great Wall + management, the Great Wall + policy, the Great Wall + law and regulation, the Great Wall + law, the Great Wall + application, the Great Wall + monitoring; the keywords for history and culture include the Great Wall + pass, The Great Wall + fort, beacon tower and beacon fire, the Great Wall + site, the Great Wall + archaeology, the Great Wall + culture, the Great Wall + history, the Great Wall + investigation, and the Great Wall + geography

总体来讲，长城保护管理理论政策研究仍然薄弱。数量上，在8359篇各类长城研究文章中，涉及长城保护管理方面的应用性研究文章在1994年开始显著增长，至2006年达到峰值，这应当与“长城保护工程”的实施有关。但这类文章总数仅1600余篇，占全部论文的不到五分之一；开发利用类文章数量更少，仅784篇，占全部论文数量的不到十分之一。这可以表现出研究者的一种倾向，即仍然以传统的长城历史文化考证为侧重点，对保护管理理论政策和开发利用研究的重视程度尚待进一步提升。（图4-23）

conservation and management increased significantly since 1994 and reached the peak value in 2006, which should be influenced by the implementation of "the Great Wall Conservation Project". However, the total quantity of such articles is only 1,600, accounting for less than one-fifth of all papers; the articles on development and utilization are even less, and the quantity is only 784, accounting for less than one-tenth of all papers. It indicates a tendency of the researcher, namely, they still focus on the investigations on the traditional history and culture of the Great Wall, and more emphasis needs to be further put on the studies on the conservation and management theories and policies and development and utilization (Fig 4-3).

图 4-23
中国知网长城研究相关文献分类折线统计图（1979 ~ 2016 年）

Fig. 4-23
Classification statistics broken line graph of the documentation related to the Great Wall research on CNKI.NET (1979 ~ 2016)

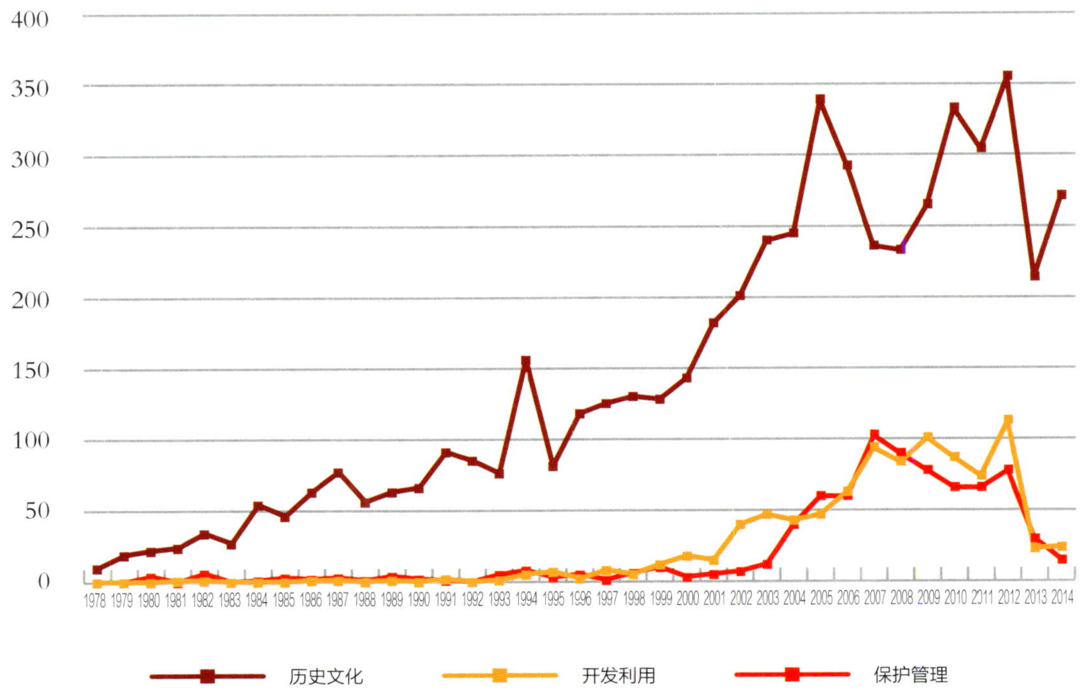

【摘要】

从1952年北京修复居庸关、八达岭等长城点段并对公众开放起，长城沿线各省（自治区、直辖市）陆续开始了对长城的保护维修和旅游开放。截至目前，全国以长城为核心展示或依托长城兴建的参观游览区92处，其中以长城展示为核心的专门景区45处，长城专题博物馆、陈列馆8家。八达岭、慕田峪、金山岭、九门口、镇北台、嘉峪关等长城重要点段已成为长城旅游代表性景区，“不到长城非好汉”为国内外游客所传诵。2005～2015年，据不完全统计，八达岭长城接待游客7650多万人次，年接待游客近800万人次，门票收入超过24亿元；甘肃嘉峪关长城景区共接待游客550多万人次，门票收入将近4.5亿元，成为当地经济社会发展的支柱产业。长城旅游与丝路旅游、沙漠旅游、草原旅游有机结合，带动了红色旅游、研学旅游、乡村旅游等蓬勃发展，有力扩大了公共文化供给，改善了长城沿线生态环境，推动了区域经济增长及国家扶贫攻坚战略的实施。与此同时，长城成为世界了解古代中国与现代中国的金色名片。仅八达岭自开放以来已接待各国元首、政府首脑500多位，成为中国政府与世界各国友好交往的重要场所。

# 第五章
# 长城旅游与宣传教育

# Chapter 5
# Great Wall Tourism and the Promotion of and Education in Great Wall Conservation Awareness

[Abstract]

Since 1952, when Beijing restored Juyong Pass, Badaling and other Great Wall sites and sections and opened them to the public, the provinces (autonomous regions and municipalities directly under the Central Government) that the Great Wall passes through have successively conserved and repaired many Great Wall sections and opened them to tourists. So far, there are 92 sightseeing areas across China primarily presenting the Great Wall or making use of it, including 45 scenic areas primarily presenting the Great Wall, and 8 Great Wall themed museums and exhibition halls. According to incomplete staticstics, Badaling, Mutianyu, Jinshanling, Jiumenkou, Zhenbeitai, Jiayu Pass and other major Great Wall sites and sections have become representative scenic areas featuring Great Wall tourism, and the saying "he who does not reach the Great Wall is not a true man" has become popular among global tourists. During 2005-2015, the Badaling Great Wall received more than 76.5 million person-times of tourists, representing annual reception of nearly 8 million person-times of tourists, and achieved income from tickets of more than RMB 2.4 billion; the Jiayu Pass Great Wall scenic area in Gansu received more than 5.5 million person-times of tourists, and achieved income from tickets of nearly RMB 450 million, significantly supporting local economic and social development. The integration of Great Wall tourism, Silk Road tourism, desert tourism and grassland tourism helped drive the development of red tourism, study tours, rural tourism and the like, enrich public culture, improve the ecological environments of the areas along the Great Wall, and promote regional economic growth and the implementation of China's poverty relief strategy. Meanwhile, the Great Wall has become a major attraction through which the rest of the world gets to know ancient and modern China. Since being opened to tourists, Badaling alone has received 500 odd heads of state and government, becoming an important place where the Chinese government meets with guests from abroad.

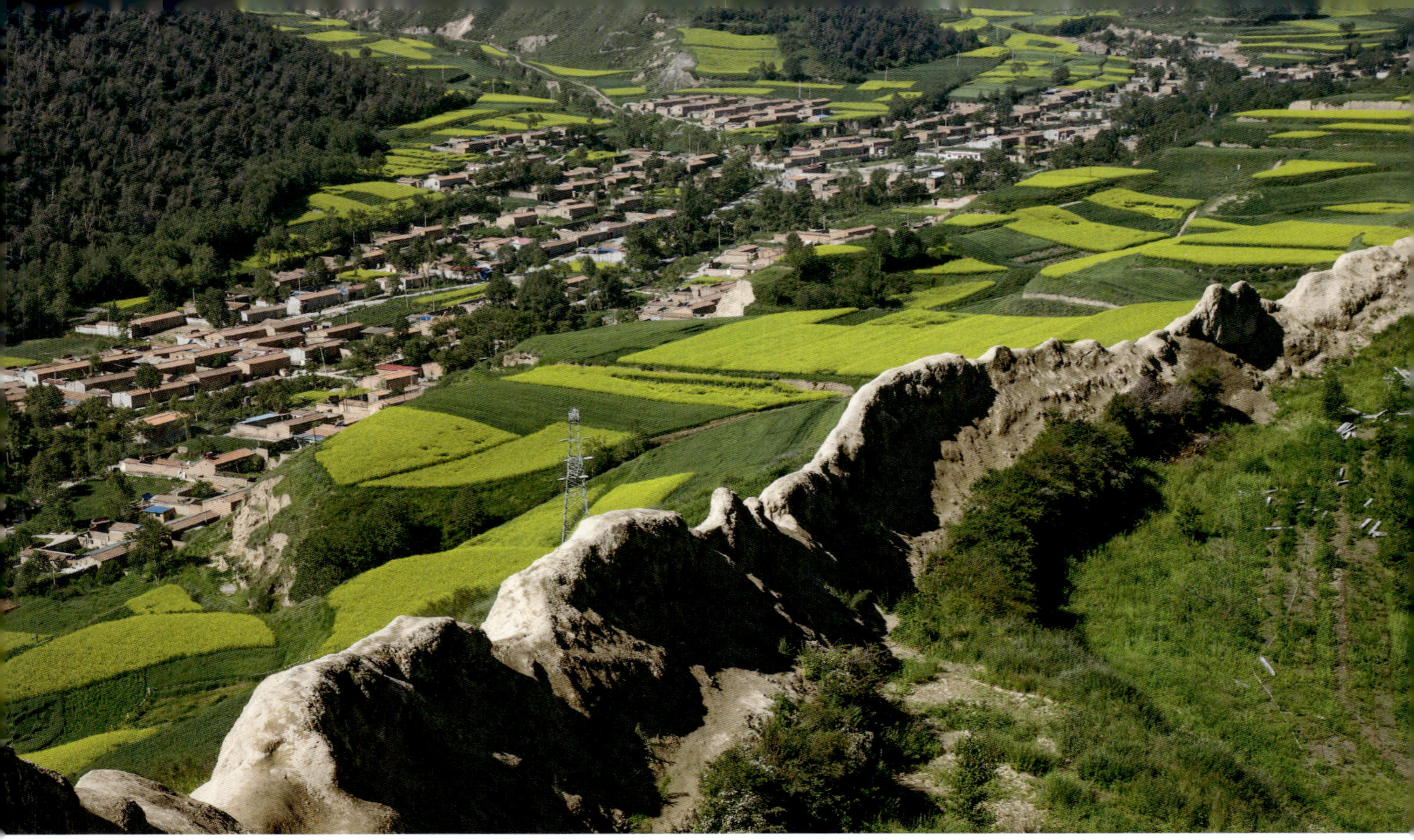

青海大通明长城（杨越峦 拍摄）

The section of the Great Wall of the Ming Dynasty in Datong, Qinghai (Photo by Yang Yueluan)

## 第一节 长城旅游基本情况

※ 相关规定——开辟长城旅游景区须在文物部门备案

※ 景区数量——92 处长城景区，包括专门景区 45 处，综合景区 47 处

※ 十年数据——1,073,541 人次游览，354,660 万元收入

长城凝结着中国古代劳动人民的心血和智慧，积淀着中华文明博大精深、灿烂辉煌的文化内涵，已经成为中华民族的象征。与此同时，经历 2400 余年人类、自然因素的共同作用和岁月洗礼，造就了具有独特审美价值的长城文化景观，使得长城成为海内外游客向往的旅游目的地。发展长城旅游，对于向全世界人民展示中华民族的精神品质和价值追求，具有独特的作用。

1952 年，时任政务院副总理的郭沫若先生对八达岭长城提出了“修复长城，向游人开放”的建议，1953 年修复后，对游客开放，1958 年，首次接待国内外游人参观游览。今天，长城旅游已成为发展中国与世界旅游产业的重要资源之一，为长城沿线居民带来了切实利益，社会经济效益显著。2005-2012 年间，除 2007 年和 2009 年外（2007 年参观人次排名第 7、2009 年门票收入排名第 6），其参观人次与门票收入都位列全国文物保护单位前三甲。

## Section 1 Overview of Great Wall Tourism

* Relevant regulations—the establishment of a Great Wall scenic area should be filed with the corresponding cultural heritage authority
* Number of scenic areas—92 Great Wall scenic areas, including 45 themed scenic areas and 47 comprehensive scenic areas
* From 2005 to 2015—1,073,541 person-times of visitors, and income of RMB 3,546.6 million

The Great Wall is a product of the painstaking efforts and wisdom of ancient Chinese labourers, and represents part of the brilliant Chinese culture. It has become a symbol of China. Meanwhile, more than 2,400 odd years of man-made and natural impacts made the Great Wall a unique, aesthetic historic and cultural landscape and a world-famous tourist destination. Developing Great Wall tourism can help communicate the spirit and values of the Chinese nation to the rest of the world.

In 1952, Mr. Guo Moruo, then vice premier, proposed the suggestion "conserving cultural heritage, restoring the Great Wall and opening it to tourists" to Badaling Great Wall. The Badaling Great Wall was opened to tourists after restoration in 1952 and received global tourists in 1958. Today, Great Wall tourism has become an important source of Chinese and global tourism, benefiting inhabitants along the Great Wall and bringing remarkable social and economic benefits. During 2005-2012 (excluding 2007, when the Great Wall ranked $7^{th}$ in terms of person-times of tourists, and 2009, when it ranked $6^{th}$ in terms of income from tickets), the Great Wall ranked among the top three Historical and Cultural Sites Protected at the National Level in terms of person-times of tourists and income from tickets.

Besides the Badaling Scenic Area, a number of other scenic areas featuring Great Wall related historic and cultural presentation and tourism were designated in areas along the Great Wall. It was found through field investigation, Web searches and identification with the cultural heritage administrations of the 15 provinces (autonomous regions and municipalities directly under the Central Government) that the Great Wall passes through that by 2014, a total of 92 Great Wall scenic areas along the Great Wall were designated across China (Fig. 5-1).

除八达岭景区外，长城沿线各地还开辟了一批以长城历史文化展示和游览为主要内容的景区。通过实地调研和网络信息检索，并与长城沿线 15 省（自治区、直辖市）文物行政部门核实，截止 2014 年，长城沿线各地共设立长城景区 92 处。（图 5-1）

依据长城在景区中的角色，可将长城景区分为两类：长城专题景区和综合性景区。长城专题景区有 45 处，主要指长城作为展示主题的景区，如八达岭、山海关、北京云蒙山长城遗址公园、黑龙江齐齐哈尔金长城遗址公园等；长城综合性景区有 47 处，主要指景区范围内有长城、但不以长城作为唯一展示对象的综合性景区，如闾山森林公园景区、镇北堡西部影视城等。（表 5-1）

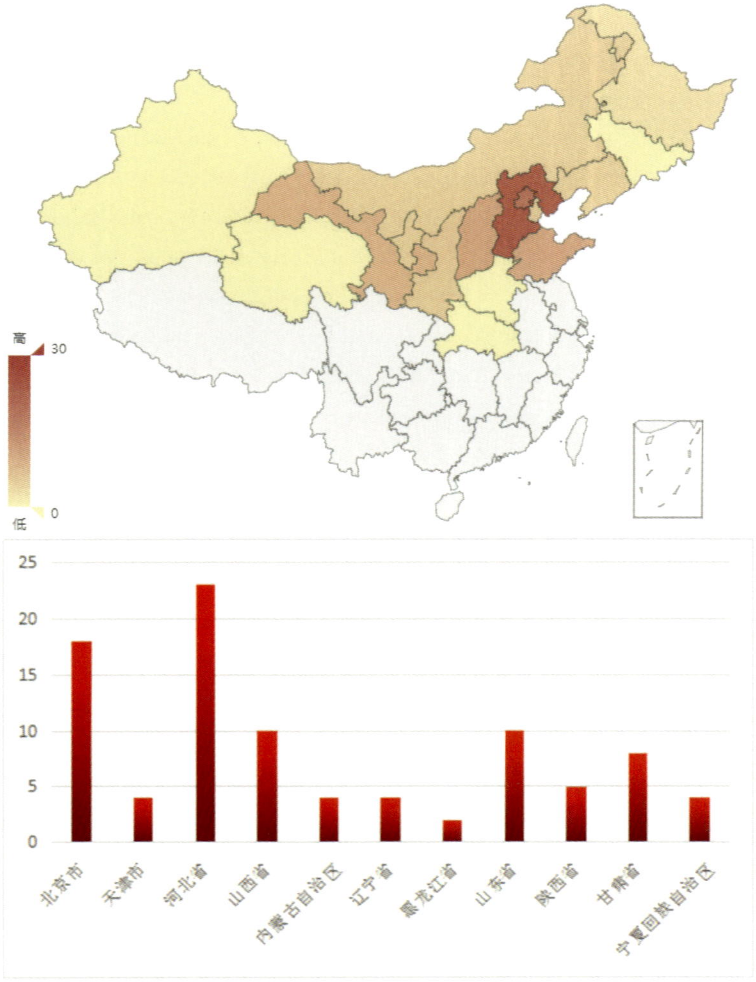


图 5-1
全国长城参观游览区数量统计图

Fig. 5-1
Number of Great Wall sightseeing areas across China

Based on the role that the Great Wall plays in a scenic area, Great Wall scenic areas can be classified into two types: Great Wall themed scenic areas and comprehensive Great Wall scenic areas. There are 45 Great Wall themed scenic areas, which primarily refer to scenic areas in which the Great Wall is presented as the theme, such as the Badaling, Shanhai Pass and Yunmengshan Great Wall Archaeological Parks in Beijing, and the Jin Great Wall Archaeological Park in Qiqihar, Heilongjiang; and 47 comprehensive Great Wall scenic areas, which primarily refer to comprehensive scenic areas in which the Great Wall is not the only attraction presented, such as Lüshan Forest Park Scenic Area and Zhenbeipu West Studio (Table 5-1).

## 表 5-1：长城景区分类统计表
Table 5-1: Great Wall scenic areas: classified

| 地区 Region | 长城专题景区 Great Wall themed scenic areas | 长城综合性景区 Comprehensive Great Wall scenic areas | 合计 Total |
|---|---|---|---|
| 北京市 / Beijing City | 11 | 7 | 18 |
| 天津市 / Tianjin City | 1 | 3 | 4 |
| 河北省 / Hebei Province | 12 | 11 | 23 |
| 山西省 / Shanxi Province | 5 | 5 | 10 |
| 内蒙古自治区 / Inner Mongolia Autonomous Region | 1 | 3 | 4 |
| 辽宁省 / Liaoning Province | 2 | 2 | 4 |
| 黑龙江省 / Heilongjiang Province | 1 | 1 | 2 |
| 山东省 / Shandong Province | 2 | 8 | 10 |
| 陕西省 / Shaanxi Province | 4 | 1 | 5 |
| 甘肃省 / Gansu Province | 6 | 2 | 8 |
| 宁夏回族自治区 / Ningxia Hui Autonomous Region | 0 | 4 | 4 |
| 合计 / Total | 45 | 47 | 92 |

根据功能和管理部门的不同，在 92 处长城景区中，有国家级风景名胜区 8 处，省级风景名胜区 8 处；国家森林公园 8 处；国家级自然保护区 5 处；国家级水利风景区 2 处；国家地质公园 8 处。[77] 经过旅游质量评定的 A 级以上景区 46 处。其中有 16 处景区具有身份分类重叠的特点。（表 5-2）

## 表 5-2：长城景区身份 / 级别重叠情况统计简表

Table 5-2: Great Wall scenic areas having multiple identities/levels

| 地区 Region | 景区名称 Scenic area name | AAAAA 级 AAAAA level | AAAA 级 AAAA level | AAA 级 AAA level |
|---|---|---|---|---|
| 北京市 Beijing City | 云蒙山长城遗址公园 Yunmengshan Great Wall Archaeological Park | | | ☆ |
| | 八达岭——十三陵风景名胜区 Badaling-Ming Tombs Scenic Area | ☆ | | |
| | 八达岭国家森林公园 Badaling National Forest Park | | | ☆ |
| 河北省 Hebei Province | 苍岩山风景名胜区 Cangyanshan Scenic Area | | ☆ | |
| | 青山关风景名胜区 Qingshanguan Scenic Area | | ☆ | |
| | 阜平天生桥风景区 Tianshengqiao Scenic Area, Fuping County | ☆ | | |
| | 野山坡风景名胜区 Yeshanpo Scenic Area | ☆ | | |
| 山西省 Shanxi Province | 恒山风景名胜区 Mount Heng Scenic Area | | ☆ | |
| | 杀虎口风景名胜区 Shahukou Scenic Area | | ☆ | |
| | 山西芦芽山国家级自然保护区 Luya Mountain National Natural Reserve, Shanxi | | ☆ | |
| 内蒙古自治区 Inner Mongolia Autonomous Region | 内蒙古克什克腾国家地质公园 Keshiketeng National Geological Park, Inner Mongolia | | ☆ | |
| | 呼和浩特市乌素图国家森林公园 Wusutu National Forest Park, Hohhot City | | | ☆ |
| 辽宁省 Liaoning Province | 医巫闾山风景名胜区 Yiwulü Mountain Scenic Area | | ☆ | |
| 黑龙江省 Heilongjiang Province | 镜泊湖风景名胜区 Jingbo Lake Scenic Area | ☆ | | |
| 宁夏回族自治区 Ningxia Hui Autonomous Region | 宁夏沙坡头国家级自然保护区 Shapotou National Natural Reserve, Ningxia | ☆ | | |
| | 水洞沟 Shuidonggou | ☆ | | |

[77] 根据郭凡礼、黎雪荣、周思然、马荣主编《2016–2020 年中国旅游景区深度分析及发展规划咨询建议报告》，2013 年 4 月电子版，中国投资咨询网，景区分为五类：其中风景名胜区（住房和城乡建设部管理和公布）；森林公园（国家林业部管理和公布）；自然保护区（国家环保总局管理和公布）；水利风景区（国家水利部管理和公布）；地质公园（国土资源部管理和公布）。

Having different functions and managed by different authorities, the 92 Great Wall scenic areas include 8 national scenic areas and 8 provincial scenic areas; 8 national forest parks; 5 national natural reserves; 2 national water conservancy scenic areas; and 8 national geological parks [77] . Among them, there are 46 scenic areas above the Class A level in terms of quality in tourism, including 16 scenic areas having multiple identities (Table 5-2).

| 国家级风景名胜区 National Scenic Area | 省级风景名胜区 Provincial scenic area | 国家森林公园 National forests park | 国家级自然保护区 National natural reserve | 国家级水利风景区 National water conservancy scenic area | 国家地质公园 National geological park |
|---|---|---|---|---|---|
| ☆ | | ☆ | | | ☆ |
| ☆ | | | | | |
| | | ☆ | | | |
| ☆ | | | | | |
| | ☆ | | | | |
| | | ☆ | | | ☆ |
| ☆ | | | | | ☆ |
| ☆ | | | | | |
| | ☆ | | | | |
| ☆ | | | ☆ | | |
| | | | | | ☆ |
| | | ☆ | | | |
| ☆ | | | ☆ | | |
| ☆ | | | | | ☆ |
| | | | ☆ | ☆ | |
| | | | | | ☆ |

[77] According to *Report of an In-Depth Analysis of and Suggestions for Development Planning of Chinese Tourist Scenic Areas during 2016-2020* chiefly compiled by Guo Fanli, Li Xuerong, Zhou Siran and Ma Rong, April 2013, electronic version, www.ocn.com.cn, scenic areas can be classified into five types: scenic areas (administered and designated by the Ministry of Housing and Urban-Rural Development); forest parks (administered and designated by the Ministry of Forestry); national reserves (administered and designated by the Ministry of Environmental Conservation); water conservancy scenic areas (administered and designated by the Ministry of Water Resources); and geological parks (administered and designated by the Ministry of Land and Resources).

表 5-3：2005-2015 年八达岭、嘉峪关、山海关长城景区参观游览人数统计表（单位：人次）

Table 5-3: Numbers of tourists received by Badaling, Jiayu Pass and Shanhai Pass Great Wall scenic areas during 2005-2015 (unit: person-times)

| 年份 Year | 八达岭 Badaling | 嘉峪关 Jiayu Pass | 山海关 Shanhai Pass | | | 合计 Total |
|---|---|---|---|---|---|---|
| | | | 老龙头 Laolongtou | 关城 the fort | 角山长城 the Jiaoshan Great Wall | |
| 2005 | 5191690 | 307227 | 616900 | 672300 | 不详 | 6788117 |
| 2006 | 5930888 | 388900 | 757500 | 635000 | 147400 | 7859688 |
| 2007 | 6234724 | 403600 | 807100 | 805900 | 不详 | 8251324 |
| 2008 | 5554499 | 301068 | 594400 | 541700 | 不详 | 6991667 |
| 2009 | 6898854 | 346362 | 890000 | 979300 | 167200 | 9281716 |
| 2010 | 6965452 | 406000 | 947900 | 991300 | 184600 | 9495252 |
| 2011 | 8033518 | 510000 | 1050000 | 1108800 | 180500 | 10882818 |
| 2012 | 7986443 | 657000 | 993900 | 1054000 | 143600 | 10834943 |
| 2013 | 7375168 | 570000 | 930000 | 1048900 | 121600 | 10045668 |
| 2014 | 8058397 | 610000 | 1107600 | 1183700 | 128200 | 11087897 |
| 2015 | 8324985 | 1016000 | 1279800 | 1256300 | 121200 | 11998285 |
| 合计 | 76554618 | 5516157 | 9975100 | 10277200 | 1194300 | 103517375 |

据不完全统计，2005 年到 2015 年间，八达岭、嘉峪关、山海关三地长城景区的游人人数就达到了 1,035,17375 人次。十年间长城旅游收入总额达到 357813.16 万元。通过对数据的年度分析可以看出，长城景区游客数量和收入基本呈逐年上升趋势。（表 5-3、5-4）

表 5-4：2005-2015 年八达岭、嘉峪关、山海关长城景区收入统计表（单位：万元）
Table 5-4: Income of Badaling, Jiayu Pass and Shanhai Pass Great Wall scenic areas during 2005-2015 (unit: RMB 10,000)

| 年份 Year | 八达岭 Badaling | 嘉峪关 Jiayu Pass | 山海关 Shanhai Pass | | | 合计 Total |
|---|---|---|---|---|---|---|
| | | | 老龙头 Laolongtou | 关城 fort | 角山长城 Jiaoshan Great Wall | |
| 2005 | 15167.33 | 1530.27 | 2469.22 | 2176.55 | 不详 | 21343.37 |
| 2006 | 17228.29 | 1986.72 | 2441.82 | 2093.06 | 257.24 | 24007.13 |
| 2007 | 20385.54 | 2886.26 | 2869.01 | 2296.55 | 不详 | 28437.36 |
| 2008 | 17922.74 | 2113.59 | 2043.69 | 1623.25 | 不详 | 23703.27 |
| 2009 | 21945.95 | 2109 | 3001.16 | 2959.18 | 618.78 | 30634.07 |
| 2010 | 22213.07 | 3199.37 | 3180.04 | 3361.29 | 407.72 | 32361.49 |
| 2011 | 25853.79 | 4256.05 | 3309.35 | 3651.22 | 407.94 | 37478.35 |
| 2012 | 25610.52 | 4840.92 | 3400.93 | 3778.15 | 290.85 | 37921.37 |
| 2013 | 23934.23 | 4847.67 | 3269.91 | 3780.78 | 283.74 | 36116.33 |
| 2014 | 25430.83 | 6047 | 4002.31 | 4198.27 | 455.64 | 40134.05 |
| 2015 | 26007.03 | 9791.8 | 4833.92 | 4653.94 | 389.68 | 45676.37 |
| 合计 | 241699.32 | 43608.65 | 34821.36 | 34572.24 | 3111.59 | 357813.16 |

According to incomplete statistics, during 2005-2015, Badaling, Jiayu Pass and Shanhai Pass Great Wall scenic areas totally received 103,517,375 person-times of tourists. In the decade, their income from Great Wall tourism totalled RMB 3,578,131,600. It can be seen from the data that the number of tourists received by Great Wall scenic areas and the income achieved largely increased year by year. (Tables 5-3 and 5-4).

# 第二节 长城宣传教育活动

※ 活动统计——387 次活动，309 家机构、1906522 人次参加
※ 官方活动——2009、2012 年长城长度新闻发布会
文化遗产日主题活动，颁发“长城保护员证”
文化遗产公开课——“长城脚下的课堂”活动

长城与中华民族的命运紧密联结在一起。长城蕴含着团结统一、众志成城的爱国主义精神，坚韧不屈、自强不息的民族精神，守望和平、开放包容的时代精神，历经岁月锤炼，已深深融入中华民族的血脉之中，成为实现中华民族伟大复兴的强大精神力量。大力开展宣传教育，传承与弘扬长城精神，始终是长城保护的首要之义。

2009 年和 2012 年，国家文物局分别组织两次长城资源调查成果新闻发布会，被人民日报、光明日报、中国文物报、中国文明网、新华网等国内多家报纸、网站转载，并在中央电视台新闻联播节目中播出，产生了较大的社会反响。其中，2009 年 4 月 18 日在北京八达岭长城，国家文物局和国家测绘局共同发布明长城长度数据调查成果——明长城总长 8851.8 千米，时任全国政协副主席王志珍、文化部部长蔡武、国家文物局局长单霁翔、国家测绘局局长徐德明、国家文物局副局长童明康、国家测绘局副局长李维森、北京市人民政府副秘书长侯玉兰及文物界专家代表、部分国家驻华使节、联合国教科文组织官员等出席仪式。2012 年 6 月 5 日，国家

## Section 2 Activities to Promote and Educate in Great Wall Conservation Awareness

- Statistics on activities—387 activities, 309 organs, and 1,906,522 person-times of participants
- Official activities—press conferences in 2009 and 2012 announcing the length of the Great Wall
  Themed activities on the Cultural Heritage Day; issuance of "Great Wall Conservator's Certificates"
  Open Courses on Cultural Heritage—"Classrooms at the Foot of the Great Wall"

The Great Wall is closely associated with the destiny of the Chinese nation. It symbolises unity and patriotism, the persistence and dauntlessness of the Chinese, peace, openness and inclusiveness. Promotion of and education in the spirit associated with the Great Wall is also an important part of Great Wall conservation.

In each of 2009 and 2012, the State Administration of Cultural Heritage (SACH) held a press conference to announce Great Wall resource survey results. This was reported by People's Daily, Guangming Daily, China Cultural Heritage Weekly, wenming.cn, xinhuanet.com and other newspapers and websites, and by CCTV, generating a great social influence. Specifically, on April 18, 2009, at the Badaling Great Wall in Beijing, the SACH and the National Administration of Surveying, Mapping and Geoinformation (NASMG) jointly announced that the total length of the Ming Great Wall, as surveyed, is 8,851.8 km. Wang Zhizhen, then vice chairman of the CPPCC, Cai Wu, then Minister of Culture, Shan Jixiang, then director of the SACH, Xu Deming, then director of the NASMG, Tong Mingkang, then deputy director of the SACH, Li Weisen, then deputy director of the NASMG, Hou Yulan, then deputy secretary general of the Beijing Municipal People's Government, experts and representatives from the cultural heritage community, some ambassadors to China, officials from UNESCO and others attended the ceremony. On June 5, 2012, at the Juyong Pass Great Wall in Beijing, the SACH held an event titled "'the Great Wall and the Soul of China'—Promotion of Great Wall Conservation Awareness and Announcement of Great Wall Resource Survey and Identification Results", to mark China's 7th "Cultural Heritage Day". Tong Mingkang, then deputy director

文物局在北京居庸关长城隆重举办“长城长 中华魂”——长城保护宣传暨长城资源调查和认定成果发布活动，拉开了庆祝我国第七个“文化遗产日”系列活动的序幕。时任国家文物局副局长童明康在活动中致辞，并公布了我国调查、认定的历代长城总长度——21196.18 千米。有关部委、北京市、各相关省级文物部门、专家学者和长城调查队员、长城保护员、志愿者的代表出席了活动。

2015 年 11 月、2016 年 9 月，国家文物局分别在北京八达岭森林公园、北京慕田峪长城和甘肃嘉峪关关城举办了“文化遗产公开课——长城脚下的课堂”公开课活动，由国家文物局领导、中国文化遗产研究院专业研究人员带领北京小学的学生爬上长城，讲授长城知识，宣传长城保护。其中，2016 年 9 月 20 日，正值《长城保护条例》经国务院常务会议审议通过 10 周年之际，国家文物局启动了长城文化遗产公开课系列活动，陆续在长城沿线 15 个省（自治区、直辖市）分会场举办了公开课。9 月 20 日、23 日，国家文物局顾玉才副局长、宋新潮副局长分别在慕田峪长城和嘉峪关长城向小学生讲授长城知识，宣传长城保护。国家文物局文化遗产公开课活动“从娃娃抓起”，为下一代宣传普及

图 5-2
国家文物局顾玉才副局长为同学们讲授长城知识（图片来源：央视网 http://news.cctv.com/2016/09/21/ARTIigSnGQTvsRctP2gyCZ1w160921.shtml）

Fig. 5-2
Deputy director of the SACH Gu Yucai was lecturing students on knowledge about the Great Wall (photo by: CCTV's website http: //news.cctv.com/2016/09/21/ARTIigSnGQTvsRctP2gyCZ1w160921.shtml)

图 5-3
国家文物局宋新潮副局长为北京小学的同学们授课（图片来源：国家文物局官网 http://www.sach.gov.cn/art/2015/11/30/art_723_126415.html）

Fig. 5-3
Deputy director of the SACH Song Xinchao was lecturing students from Beijing Elementary School (photo by: the SACH's website http: //www.sach.gov.cn/art/2015/11/30/art_723_126415.html)

of the SACH, made a speech and announced that the total length of the Great Wall, as surveyed, is 21,196.18 km. Representatives of ministries and commissions concerned, Beijing municipal and relevant provincial cultural heritage administrations, experts and scholars, Great Wall survey team members and Great Wall conservators and volunteers attended the event.

In each of November 2015 and September 2016, at the Badaling Forest Park in Beijing, the Mutianyu Great Wall in Beijing and the fort of Jiayu Pass in Gansu, respectively, the SACH provided “Open Courses on Cultural Heritage—Classrooms at the Foot of the Great Wall”, in which leaders from the SACH and researchers from the Chinese Academy of Cultural Heritage led students from Beijing Elementary School onto the Great Wall, lectured them on knowledge about the Great Wall and promoted Great Wall conservation awareness. Specifically, on September 20, 2016, which marked the 10$^{th}$ anniversary of the adoption of *Regulation on the Conservation of Great Wall* by the State Council, the SACH launched open courses on the Great Wall; later, the SACH successively provided these courses in the 15 provinces (autonomous regions and municipalities directly under the Central Government) that the Great Wall passes through. On September 20 and 23, at the Mutianyu Great Wall and the Jiayu Pass Great Wall, respectively, deputy directors of the SACH Gu Yucai and Song Xinchao lectured elementary school students on knowledge about the Great Wall, and promoted Great Wall conservation awareness. The SACH's open courses on cultural heritage were attempts to promote knowledge about the Great Wall and cultural heritage conservation awareness among children. (Figs. 5-2 and 5-3)

长城知识，培养文化遗产保护意识进行了有益尝试。（图5-2、5-3）

2016年11月30日-12月1日，国家文物局在河北金山岭长城举行纪念《长城保护条例》实施十周年系列活动，来自10余家中央部委、长城沿线15个省（自治区、直辖市）文物行政部门负责同志、专家，民间组织、志愿者和媒体记者200余人参加活动。此次活动上，国家文物局正式向社会发布了《中国长城保护报告》和改版后的中国长城遗产网（www.greatwallheritage.cn）。《中国长城保护报告》第一次以国务院文物行政部门的名义发布专项文物资源的保护管理状况，是国家文物局引导社会力量参与长城保护的一次积极行动，取得了良好的社会反响。

此次活动期间，国家文物局还组织长城沿线15个省（自治区、直辖市）文物行政部门负责同志和专家召开了长城保护维修研讨会，对当前长城保护维修项目中存在的问题进行了深入交流，对今后开展长城保护维修提出了意见建议。国家文物局还与华晨汽车集团签署了合作协议，支持该公司在2017年组织员工与车友开展长城保护志愿巡查活动，并建立长效合作机制。八达岭、慕田峪、居庸关、黄崖关、山海关、金山岭等京津冀长城保护管理机构发起成立了京津冀长城保护联盟，推动长城保护展示、宣传教育与研究工作协同发展，并发出了共同抵制长城旅游不文明行为的倡议。

2016年12月15日上午，国家文物局支持，中国文化遗产研究院、中国文物学会传统建筑园林委员会、北京建筑大学未来城市设计高精尖创新中心以及该校建筑遗产研究院联合主办，国内10余家参与长城保护规划与设计的单位共同协办的“万里长城，薪火相传——《长城保护条例》颁布10周年纪念展暨学术研讨会”在北京建筑大学举行。展览系统地回顾了《长城保护条例》颁布10年来，全国长城保护工作取得的成绩。学术研讨会上，国家文物局有关领导与各界专家学者就长城保护工作中的挑战与下一步工作的开展进行交流，探讨长城综合保护与利用方法等。（图5-4）

From November 30 through December 1, 2016, the SACH held events to mark the 10th anniversary of the implementation of *Regulation on the Conservation of Great Wall* at the Jinshanling Great Wall in Hebei. More than 200 people, including heads of 10 odd central ministries and commissions and of the cultural heritage administrations of the 15 provinces (autonomous regions and municipalities directly under the Central Government) that the Great Wall passes through, experts, those coming from non-governmental organisations, volunteers and journalists, participated in the events, during which the SACH officially issued *Report of the Conservation of the Great Wall* and the revised website www.greatwallheritage.cn. The *Report* was the first report of the conservation and management of a specific cultural heritage object issued in the name of the cultural heritage administration under the State Council, and was a proactive move by the SACH to encourage social involvement in Great Wall conservation, receiving a favourable social response.

During the events, the SACH also convened a symposium of the heads of and experts from the cultural heritage administrations of the 15 provinces (autonomous regions and municipalities directly under the Central Government) that the Great Wall passes through on Great Wall conservation and maintenance. They discussed outstanding problems in Great Wall conservation and maintenance projects and proposed suggestions for Great Wall conservation and maintenance in the future. The SACH also signed a cooperation agreement with Brilliance Auto Group to support Brilliance to organize its employees and Brilliance car owners to voluntarily inspect the Great Wall in 2017, and established a long-term cooperation mechanism with Brilliance. Great Wall conservation and management organs associated with Badaling, Mutianyu, Juyong Pass, Huangyaguan, Shanhai Pass, Jinshanling and other Great Wall sections in Beijing, Tianjin and Hebei established the Beijing-Tianjin-Hebei Great Wall Conservation Alliance to promote Great Wall presentation, promotion of and education in Great Wall conservation awareness and Great Wall studies, and to say no to uncivilized behaviour by Great Wall tourists.

On the morning of December 15, 2016, supported by the SACH and cosponsored by the Chinese Academy of Cultural Heritage, the Traditional Building and Garden Committee of China Cultural Heritage Society, Beijing Advance Innovation Centre for Future Urban Design at Beijing University of City Engineering and Architecture (BUCEA) and the Academy of Architectural Heritage at BUCEA, with the assistance of 10 odd entities involved in Great Wall conservation planning and design, an exhibition and symposium titled “the Great Wall, a Cultural Heritage Object” to mark the 10th anniversary of the *promulgation of Regulation on the Conservation of Great Wall* was held at BUCEA. The exhibition systematically reviewed achievements in Great Wall conservation in the decade after the promulgation of the *Regulations*. At the symposium, leaders from the SACH, experts and scholars discussed challenges to and future work to be done in Great Wall conservation, as well as measures to comprehensively conserve and use the Great Wall and other things. (Fig. 5-4)

图 5-4
“万里长城，薪火相传”——《长城保护条例颁布十周年》纪念展开幕式现场（图片来源：北京建筑大学新闻网 http://xww.bucea.edu.cn/tgx/91726.htm）

Fig. 5-4
Opening ceremony of the exhibition titled “the Great Wall, a Cultural Heritage Object” to mark the 10th anniversary of the promulgation of *Regulation on the Conservation of Great Wall* (Photo by: BUCEA's website http: //xww.bucea.edu.cn/tgx/91726.htm)

除国家文物局以外，长城沿线各地和各种社会团体、组织开展的长城宣传教育活动也日益增多。据各地文物部门上报“长城资源保护管理信息系统”的数据统计，2005-2015 年，长城沿线各地政府和有关部门组织开展的各类保护、宣传、教育等活动 387 次，309 家机构参与其中，参与总人数达到 1,906,522 人次。在 387 次活动中，有 317 次为以长城保护为主题的宣传教育活动，主要包括长城保护知识宣传、文物保护普法教育、长城历史文化艺术的宣传展示等。活动参与者既包括各级政府、文物行政部门、企事业单位、民间团体、新闻媒体，也包括来自社会各界的长城爱好者和志愿者。其中，具有官方性质的长城保护管理宣传活动在“长城保护工程”实施期间得到大力的推动和发展。活动组织者的主要力量是各级文物局、文物保护管理所、博物馆以及科研机构，总计达到 176 个，占全部活动组织机构的近六成。其次是 41 个各级党委、人民政府、各部委和职能部门等占有相当大的比例，达到 13.3%。长城保护工作得到中国政府的大力支持。（图 5-5）长城保护宣传教育和利用活动次数在“长城保护工程”实施期间都有逐年增长的趋势。（图 5-6）

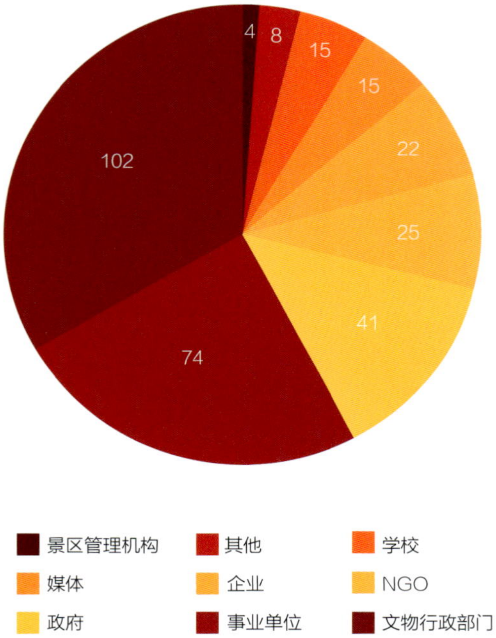


图 5-5
长城保护宣传教育活动参与机构类别数量统计饼状图

Fig. 5-5
Pie chart showing the types and numbers of organs participating in activities to promote and educate in Great Wall conservation awareness

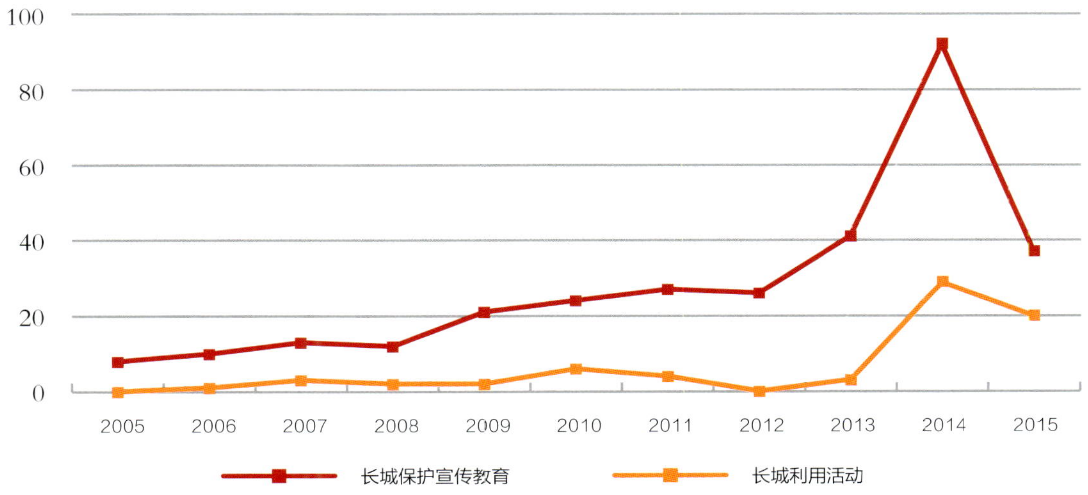


图 5-6
长城保护宣传教育活动年度次数统计折线图

Fig. 5-6
Line chart showing the times of activities to promote and educate in Great Wall conservation awareness each year

Besides those carried out by the SACH, activities to promote and educate in Great Wall conservation carried out in the areas along the Great Wall and by mass organizations across China have also increased. According to statistics reported into the "the Great Wall Conservation and Management Information System" by cultural heritage administrations across China, during 2005-2015, governments and departments concerned in the areas along the Great Wall organized a total of 387 activities regarding conservation, promotion of and education in conservation awareness and other aspects, involving 309 organs and 1,906,522 person-times of participants. Of the 387 activities, 317 were activities to promote and educate in Great Wall conservation, primarily involving promotion of knowledge about Great Wall conservation, popularization of cultural heritage conservation related laws, and promotion and presentation of Great Wall related history, culture and art. Participants in the activities included governments and cultural heritage administrations at all levels, enterprises and institutions, nongovernmental organisations, and news media organizations as well as Great Wall enthusiasts and volunteers from all walks of life. Among them, official activities to promote Great Wall conservation and management were promoted during the implementation of the "Great Wall Conservation Project". The activities were organized primarily by cultural heritage administrations at all levels, museums and research institutions, which totalled 176 and accounting for nearly 60% of all organizers, and then by Party committees and people's governments at all levels, ministries, commissions and functional departments, which accounted for 13.3% of all organizers. Great Wall conservation was greatly supported by the Chinese government (Fig. 5-5). During the implementation of the "Great Wall Conservation Project", the frequency of activities to promote and educate in Great Wall conservation awareness and to use the Great Wall largely increased year by year (Fig. 5-6).

2016 年，中国文物保护基金会发起“保护长城 加我一个”活动，积极探索社会力量参与长城保护的新模式。这是公众参与长城保护的第一次公募活动，也是文物保护领域第一次采用“互联网 + 公益”方式进行公募。截至 2017 年 3 月，该公募活动已经吸引超过 17 万余人参与，已募集善款 200 余万元。本次长城公募所募得的资金，用于河北省宽城县和迁西县喜峰口长城段落修缮，计划修缮长城墙体 1050 米。此外，中国文物保护基金会还采取了腾讯公益慈善基金会为主，联合其他互联网企业共同捐资的方式，对北京市怀柔区箭扣长城段落进行修缮。两段长城公募资金募集使用情况将及时在中国文物保护基金会微信公众号和腾讯公益平台上公示，接受社会监督。本次公募活动设计了一系列让捐赠者参与的活动，如邀请部分捐赠者烧制长城砖、攀登长城等，为捐赠者提供更多亲近长城、了解长城的渠道，让大家能够更近距离、更深层次地了解长城。

中国文化遗产研究院与中国教育学会培训中心合作，从 2013 年起，连续两年在长城脚下开展了世界文化遗产长城志愿者活动，来自 14 个国家的青年参与其中。2013 年 8 月，中国文化遗产研究院成员张依萌应邀赴马来西亚世界遗产地马六甲市参加了中国教育学会培训中心与马来西亚、印度尼西亚文化遗产管理机构联合举办的第一届“Ma-Chn-Do”（马来 - 中国 - 印尼）世界遗产志愿者活动，期间对志愿者做了长城历史文化和长城资源调查方面的科普讲座，加深了志愿者对长城的了解，获得了良好的宣传效果，同时也扩大了长城的影响；2014 年夏，时任中国文化遗产研究院院长刘曙光（现任国家文物局副局长）代表中国的文化遗产研究机构参加了在中国金山岭长城举办的第二届“Ma-Chn-Do”志愿者活动开幕式，与各国青年志愿者进行交流，并邀请参加该活动的联合国教科文组织世界遗产中心项目负责人 Camela Quin 女士参观了中国文化遗产研究院，介绍了中国的长城保护管理工作情况。（图 5-7）

图 5-7
第二届“Ma-Chn-Do”志愿者活动开幕式

Fig. 5-7
Opening ceremony of the Second “Ma-Chn-Do” World Heritage Volunteers Program

In 2016, China Foundation for Cultural Heritage Conservation launched the campaign titled "Let Me Participate in Great Wall Conservation", proactively exploring a new mode of social involvement in Great Wall conservation. This was the first fund-raising campaign regarding Great Wall conservation and the first fund-raising campaign regarding cultural heritage conservation based on "Internet + public good". By March 2017, more than 170,000 people participated in the campaign, and RMB 2 million odd yuan were raised. The funds raised this time were used to repair the Xifengkou Great Wall in Kuancheng County and Qianxi County, Hebei Province, with walls totalling a length of 1,050 m planned to be repaired. In addition, China Foundation for Cultural Heritage Conservation repaired the Jiankou Great Wall in Huairou District, Beijing City using donations primarily from Tencent Charity Foundation and also from other Internet companies. The use of the funds raised for the two Great Wall sections will be announced on the public WeChat account of China Foundation for Cultural Heritage Conservation and the Tencent Charity Platform for social supervision. This fund-raising campaign provided activities involving donators, such as firing Great Wall bricks and climbing the Great Wall, allowing donators to get closer to and know more about the Great Wall.

From 2013 on, Chinese Academy of Cultural Heritage and the Training Centre of the Chinese Society of Education carried out activities involving Great Wall volunteers for two consecutive years at the foot of the Great Wall. The volunteers included young people from 14 countries. In August 2013, Zhang Yimeng, a member of Chinese Academy of Cultural Heritage, was invited to participate in the First "Ma-Chn-Do" (Malaysia-China-Indonesia) World Heritage Volunteers Program cosponsored by the Training Centre of the Chinese Society of Education and Malaysian and Indonesian cultural heritage administrations in Malacca, Malaysia. During the program, project team members lectured volunteers on the history and culture of the Great Wall and Great Wall resource surveys, allowing volunteers to know more about the Great Wall. In summer 2014, Liu Shuguang, then president of the Chinese Academy of Cultural Heritage (now deputy head of the SACH), on behalf of Chinese cultural heritage research institutes, attended the opening ceremony of the Second "Ma-Chn-Do" (Malaysia-China-Indonesia) World Heritage Volunteers Program provided at the Jinshanling Great Wall in China to communicate with young volunteers from different countries, and invited Ms. Camela Quin, a participant from UNESCO World Heritage Centre, to visit the Chinese Academy of Cultural Heritage, and briefed her on China's Great Wall conservation and management efforts. (Fig. 5-7)

图 5-8
长城小站结合“家住长城边”助学活动向小学生宣讲长城知识（张俊 提供）

Fig. 5-8
The Great Wall Station was lecturing elementary school students on knowledge about the Great Wall in the campaign titled “Living by the Great Wall” to assist impoverished students (Photo by Zhang Jun)

自 20 世纪 80 年代以来，民间长城研究与保护力量迅速发展，越来越多的民间组织和个人积极开展长城保护宣传教育活动。如 1984 年出现的“爱我中华，修我长城”社会赞助活动引发了改革开放以来一次全社会保护长城的热潮；成大林、董耀会、威廉·林赛等人徒步行走长城，并随之投身于长城研究与保护工作之中，成为民间长城研究的著名学者；由北京地区长城爱好者成立于 1999 年的“长城小站”公益组织，长期致力于长城宣传教育、长城抗战研究、长城老照片复拍、长城沿线助学活动，是社会力量参与长城保护的代表。（图 5-8）

“国际长城之友协会”于 2004 年启动“万里长城百年回望”项目，对长城老照片进行复拍工作。2005 年 -2016 年间，协会在全国各地举办多次展览，展示长城文化，提高人们保护长城的意识；该协会还定期组织志愿者清理长城垃圾，普及保护长城与爱护环境的理念。（图 5-9、5-10）

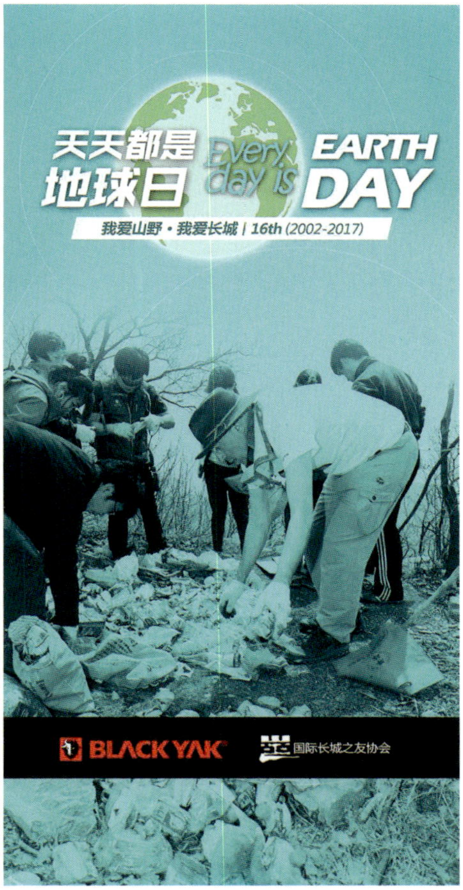


图 5-9
“我爱山野、我爱长城”长城捡拾垃圾主题活动海报（吴琪 提供）

Fig. 5-9
Poster of a campaign titled “I Love the Wilderness, I Love the Great Wall” to pick rubbish on the Great Wall (provided by Wu Qi)

图 5-10
国际长城之友协会创始人威廉・林赛在长城上捡拾垃圾

Fig. 5-10
William Lindesay, founder of the International Friends of the Great Wall, was picking rubbish on the Great Wall

From the 1980s on, nongovernmental forces engaged in Great Wall studies and conservation developed rapidly. More and more nongovernmental organisations and individuals proactively carried out activities to promote and educate in Great Wall conservation awareness. Examples include the donation campaign titled “Love China and Repair the Great Wall” initiated in 1984, which triggered an upsurge in Great Wall conservation after the inception of the reform and opening-up policy; Cheng Dalin, Dong Yaohui, Cheng Dalin, William Lindesay and others travelled along the Great Wall on foot and were engaged in Great Wall studies and conservation efforts, becoming famous scholars in unofficial Great Wall studies; “the Great Wall Station”, a public good organization established by Great Wall enthusiasts in Beijing in 1999, which is the representative of social forces participating in the Great Wall Conservation, has long been engaged in promotion of and education in the Great Wall, studies of War of Resistance against Japanese related history associated with the Great Wall, rephotographing of scenes depicted in old photos of the Great Wall, and efforts to assist impoverished students in the areas along the Great Wall. (Fig. 5-8)

In 2004, the International Friends of the Great Wall (IFGW) launched a project named “A 100-Year Retrospect on the Great Wall” to rephotograph scenes depicted in old photos of the Great Wall. During 2005-2016, the IFGW held exhibitions across China to present Great Wall culture and improve Great Wall conservation awareness. The IFGW also regularly organized volunteers to pick rubbish on the Great Wall and promote Great Wall conservation and environmental conservation awareness. (Figs. 5-9 and 5-10)

河北省金山岭马拉松已经连续开展 5 届；秦皇岛市坚持每年在各长城景区、博物馆等地举办 6 场以上内容丰富、形式多样的临时展览，如《20 世纪文化名人中国梦图片展》《喜迎十八大、庆祝建国六十三周年精品珍邮展》《廉政文化警示案例漫画展》《“爱我中华、修我长城”三十年记忆长城修复回顾展》等。赤城县博物馆举办“保护长城，爱我家园”长城保护宣传活动。青龙满族自治县文保所通过举办《长城万里行 圆我中国梦》活动进行长城保护宣传；迁安市文保所与长城保护基金会、东方青年未来发展中心一起，举办了千名学子长城保护宣传大型徒步活动，进行长城徒步考察、长城保护宣传，通过图片展览、保护签名、讲解采访等形式，介绍长城资源情况，宣传长城是历史文化遗产，号召全民自觉保护。

山西省文物局积极支持成立了由山西省人大原副主任任会长、省文物局和各有关市政府、人大领导任副会长的山西省长城保护研究会。大同市、朔州市、忻州市等设区市分别成立了大同长城学会、大同长城保护与发展研究中心、朔州市长城保护研究会、忻州市长城学会等组织。他们通过办刊物、定期举办研讨会、组织长城考察、图片展览等活动，积极开展长城保护宣传与研究。如 2008 年，省文物局与山西省长城保护研究会和中国长城协会于 2008 年联合举办了《长城万里行——山西省书画采风》活动。国家文物局原局长张文彬和国内不少著名的书画家参加了这次活动。省电视台和各有关市的电视台、报纸等新闻媒体对这次活动进行了跟踪报道。2016 年 11 月 26 日，大同市人民政府、市委宣传部、市发改委、市文化局、市旅游局、市文物局、市体育总会共同支持下，中国长城学会、山西省长城保护研究会和大同长城学会在大同市共同举办了“2016 中国·大同首届长城文化节”启动仪式，来自大同市各相关部门和多家户外群体、公益组织等社会和界人士、千余人参加启动仪式。活动于 12 月 1 日持续至 18 日，内容包括长城徒步环保行、长城古堡文化讲座、长城研究论坛、“长城谣、大同颂”诗歌文艺晚会、长城摄影展和长城书画展等，取得了良好的社会反响。

山东沂水县文物管理所与捷安特活动俱乐部联合举办了齐长城“骑行”活动：相约齐长城，共护文化遗产。莒县文物局在莒县段齐长城修缮工程启动前，采取集中培训的方式对齐长城两侧违章建筑所有人宣传国家政策，进行齐长城违章建筑拆除宣传。岱岳区文物行政部门指导有关乡镇在坚持保护为主的前提下，充分利用齐长城资源优势，进行科学地开发利用。注重将文物保护与经济社会发展相结合，改善生态人文环境，加快文化、旅游等相关产业发展。

甘肃省发挥长城资源在传承历史文化、涵养民族精神等方面的独特作用，一是建成嘉峪关长城博物馆、玉门关陈列中心、阳关博物馆、山丹明长城陈列馆等长城展示设施，改善重点长城段落的基础设施，实施原状展示并对公众开放；二是以甘肃省简牍博物馆、嘉峪关长城研究所等为主要基地，并不断深化与国内外相关高校、科研院所的合作，大力推动长城学研究，出版了一批长城研究专著；三是通过举办展览、组织专题活动、制作发行影视传媒作品等途径，

Five Jinshanling Great Wall Marathon events have been held in Hebei Province; Qinhuangdao City held more than 6 diverse temporary exhibitions, such as *Chinese Dream Themed Picture Exhibition Involving Chinese Cultural Notables in the 20th Century, Exhibition of Rare Stamps to Mark the Upcoming 18th Party Congress and the 63rd Anniversary of the Founding of the PRC, Exhibition of Cartoons Depicting Cautionary Cases to Promote Honest and Clean Government, and Retrospective Show of Great Wall Restoration in the Past Three Decades in the "Love China and Repair the Great Wall" Campaign*, in Great Wall scenic areas, museums and other places, each year. Chicheng County Museum held an event titled "Conserve the Great Wall, Cherish My Homestead" to promote Great Wall conservation awareness. Qinglong Man Autonomous County Cultural Heritage Administration held an event titled "Travel along the Great Wall, My Chinese Dream Comes True" to promote Great Wall conservation awareness; Qian'an City Cultural Heritage Administration, working with Great Wall Conservation Foundation and Oriental Youth Future Development Centre, launched a hiking journey involving 1,000 students to visit the Great Wall and promote Great Wall conservation awareness, and presented Great Wall resources, promoted the Great Wall as a historical and cultural heritage object and promoted Great Wall conservation awareness through picture exhibitions, endorsing Great Wall conservation, explanations, interviews and other ways.

Shaanxi Culture Relics Bureau actively supported the establishment of Great Wall Conservation Research in Shanxi Province with the former vice chairperson of Shanxi Provincial People's Congress as the society's chairperson and leaders of the provincial cultural heritage bureau, relevant municipal governments and people's congress as the society's vice chairpersons. Datong, Shuozhou, Xinzhou and other cities with districts established Datong Great Wall Society, Datong Great Wall Conservation and Development Research Center, Great Wall Conservation Research in Shuozhou City, Xinzhou Great Wall Society and other organizations. By means of publications, seminars, field investigations and exhibitions, these organizations have actively carried out Great Wall conservation publicity and research. For example, in 2008, Shaanxi Culture Relics Bureau teamed up with Great Wall Conservation Research in Shanxi Province and Great Wall Society of China to hold the Travelling along the Great Wall: Shanxi Provincial Calligraphy and Painting Collection and Creation activity. Zhang Wenbin, former director-general of State Administration of Cultural Heritage, and quite a few famous calligrapher and artists attended the activity. Provincial TV stations, relevant cities' TV stations, newspaper and other news media made follow-up reports on the activity. On November 26, with the joint support of Datong People's Government, the Publicity Department of CPC Datong Committee, the Development and Reform Commission, the Cultural Bureau, the Tourism Bureau, the Cultural Heritage Bureau and the Sports Federation of Datong, Great Wall Society of China, Great Wall Conservation Research in Shanxi Province and Datong Great Wall Society jointly held the inauguration for the 2016 Datong(China) First Great Wall Cultural Festival with more than 1,000 participants from relevant departments, outdoor sports communities, welfare organizations and other walks of life of Datong. The activity, from December 1 to 18, consisted of Great Wall Hike for Environmental Conservation, Great Wall Castle Cultural Seminar, Great Wall Research Forum, Datong Odes to Great Wall Evening, Great Wall Photo Exhibition and Great Wall Calligraphy and Painting Exhibition etc. and received good social responses.

Shandong Yishui County Cultural Heritage Administration, working with Giant Club, launched a cycling tour along the Qi Great Wall titled "Meet at the Qi Great Wall, Jointly Conserve Cultural Heritage". Juxian County Administration of Cultural Heritage, before the project to repair the Juxian County section of the Qi Great Wall was initiated, communicated state policies to the owners of buildings constructed on both sides of the Qi Great Wall without licences before demolishing these buildings. Daiyue District Cultural Heritage Administration directed townships

图 5-11
宁夏回族自治区青铜峡市文物管理所倡导开展“三关口——北岔口明长城徒步穿越活动”（青铜峡市文物管理所 提供）

Fig. 5-11
The event named "Travelling across the Sanguankou-Beichakou Section of the Ming Great Wall on Foot" organized by Qingtongxia Municipal Cultural Heritage Administration of Ningxia Hui Autonomous Region (provided by Qingtongxia Municipal Cultural Heritage Administration)

开展多平台、多维度的宣传推介，扩大长城文化的影响力，特别是 2015 年大型纪录片《河西走廊》的播出，对长城文化起到了极大的宣传；四是积极挖掘长城的文化和旅游价值，推动长城资源与旅游的深度融合，嘉峪关关城、玉门关遗址等长城段落已经成为旅游热点和精品景区，有力地带动了地方社会经济发展。

宁夏回族自治区文物局积极组织各市县文物行政部门在每年的“文化遗产日”、“5.18 宁夏回族自治区长城保护宣传日”开展专题宣传。2014 年配合中国文物保护基金会完成 2014 千名学子徒步长城银川站宣传活动。采取制作宣传展板、印发宣传资料、利用微信、微博开展宣传教育活动。（图 5-11）

## 专栏：“文化遗产日”

2005 年底，国务院确定每年 6 月的第二个星期六是中国的文化遗产日。文化遗产日的设立，旨在营造保护文化遗产的良好氛围，提高公众对文化遗产保护重要性的认识，动员全社会共同参与、关注和保护文化遗产。

2006 年 6 月 10 日，我国迎来第一个文化遗产日。当年的主题是“保护文化遗产，守护精神家园”。此后每年的文化遗产日都会确定一个相应的主题，文物部门和社会各界都会在遗产日当天开展相应的主题活动。

2016 年 6 月 11 日，是第 10 个文化遗产日，主题确定为“让文化遗产融入现代生活”。国家文物局在主场城市承德举办了宣传活动。宣传口号包括：“保护文化遗产 创造美好生活”“为文保员点赞 向守护者致敬”“文化遗产无价宝 需要你我呵护好”“保护传统村落 留住最美乡愁”“避暑山庄：和合承德”等。

在河北承德市普宁寺广场举行的主场活动开幕式上，12 位长城保护员代表全国 15 个省（自治区、直辖市）的长城保护员获得国家文物局颁发的“长城保护员证”。同时，还领到了统一定制的服装。长城保护员从此有了正式的身份。

and towns concerned to make scientific use of Qi Great Wall resources when giving priority to their conservation; this integrates cultural heritage conservation with economic and social development in order to improve ecological and cultural environments and accelerate the development of culture, tourism and other relevant industries.

Gansu Province allowed Great Wall resources to play a unique role in inheritance of history and culture, cultivation of the national spirit and other aspects: 1) Jiayuguan Great Wall Museum, Yumenguan Exhibition Centre, Yangguan Museum, Shandan Ming Great Wall Exhibition Hall and other Great Wall presentation facilities were built, the infrastructure of key Great Wall sections was improved, and the sections are preserved in their original condition and are opened to the public; 2) Gansu Provincial Museum of Bamboo and Wooden Slips, Jiayuguan Great Wall Research Institute and other major bases were used and cooperation with global universities and research institutes was deepened to promote Great Wall studies, and a great number of books on Great Wall studies were published; 3) exhibitions and themed events were held, TV plays and films, especially *Hexi Corridor*, a full length documentary produced in 2015, were produced, and other means were used to promote Great Wall culture; and 4) the cultural and tourist value of the Great Wall was proactively explored, the in-depth integration of Great Wall resources and tourism was promoted, and the Jiayuguan fort, the Yumenguan site and other Great Wall sections have become popular tourist destinations and select scenic areas, helping promote local social economic development.

Ningxia Hui Autonomous Region Cultural Heritage Administration proactively organized its municipal and county cultural heritage administrations to promote Great Wall conservation awareness on each "Cultural Heritage Day" and "May 18, the Great Wall Conservation Awareness Promotion Day of Ningxia Hui Autonomous Region". In 2014, working with China Foundation for Cultural Heritage Conservation, the Administration organized the promotion event involving 2014 students who travelled through the Yinchuan station of the Great Wall. Display boards, printed materials, WeChat and Weibo were used to promote and educate in Great Wall conservation awareness. (Fig. 5-11)

### "Cultural Heritage Day":

At the end of 2005, the State Council decided that the second Saturday of each June would be China's Cultural Heritage Day, which was established to promote cultural heritage conservation awareness and encourage social involvement in cultural heritage conservation.

June 10, 2006 marked China's first Cultural Heritage Day, whose theme was "Conserve Cultural Heritage, Protect Our Spiritual Home". From then on, each Cultural Heritage Day was given a theme, and cultural heritage administrations and all walks of life would organize corresponding activities on the day.

June 11, 2016 marked China's 10th Cultural Heritage Day, whose theme was "Let Cultural Heritage Be Part of Modern Life". The State Administration of Cultural Heritage held a promotion event in Chengde, using such promotion slogans as "Conserve Cultural Heritage , Create a Good Life", "Applaud the Conservators, Salute the Guardians", "Cherish Our Invaluable Cultural Heritage", "Conserve Traditional Villages to Preserve Our Memories", and "the Mountain Resort: a Harmonious Chengde".

At the opening ceremony of the event held in the square of the Puning Temple in Chengde City, Hebei, 12 Great Wall conservators, on behalf of Great Wall conservators in 15 provinces (autonomous regions and municipalities directly under the Central Government), received "Great Wall Conservator's Certificates" and Great Wall inspector's uniforms from the State Administration of Cultural Heritage. From then on, Great Wall conservators were officially recognized.

【摘要】

过去十年，在党中央、国务院领导同志的亲自关心和国务院的统一部署下，国家文物局和长城沿线各地在长城保护管理方面开展了大量工作。经过不懈努力，长城保护工作取得了较大成绩，但与长城本身的特殊地位相比，长城保护管理工作仍有很大进步的空间。在新形势下，长城保护管理工作面临着一系列的挑战。

长城具有身份多重、本体与环境多样、保存状况和保护理念复杂的特点。保存至今的长城大多已坍塌或损毁，甚至地面建筑已经消失。因此长城保护常常被一些地政府忽视，对长城保护的重要性认识不足，责任落实、工作措施不到位，许多长城点段缺少必要的人员管理。同时，长城保护尚未成为民众的自觉行为，个别地方保护修复缺少有针对性的科学方案，施工管理过于粗放，质量不高，对长城本体和风貌造成影响。现代人为或自然破坏加剧，“野长城”游览需要加强服务引导。制约长城保护的诸多困难与问题尚未得到有效解决，保护形势依然不尽如人意。如何秉持科学的文物保护理念，采取有效措施，保护长城的历史、科学艺术价值的延续，妥善处理长城保护管理与沿线区域经济社会发展的矛盾，缓解和预防自然灾害威胁，遏制人为破坏，打击涉及长城的违法犯罪行为，是一项需要各级政府和全社会关注并付诸努力的艰巨任务。保护长城任重道远。

加强长城保护必须本着对历史负责，对人民负责的态度，进一步完善政策措施，加强科学统筹，加大保护力度，落实政府责任，依法严格保护，促进社会参与，弘扬长城精神，充分发挥长城在传承和弘扬中华优秀传统文化中的独特作用。

# 第六章
# 长城保护挑战与展望

## Chapter 6
## Great Wall Conservation: Challenges and Prospects

[Abstract]

In the last decade, supported by the Party Central Committee and leaders of the State Council and directed by the State Council, the State Administration of Cultural Heritage and the areas along the Great Wall made great efforts in Great Wall conservation and management, making remarkable achievements. However, compared with the special position of the Great Wall, Great Wall conservation and management still have great room for improvement. In face of the new situation, Great Wall conservation and management are facing a series of challenges.

The Great Wall has multiple identities; Great Wall sections and their environments are diverse, and their states of preservation and conservation philosophies are complex. Most surviving Great Wall sections have collapsed or been damaged and some of their aboveground structures even disappeared. Therefore, Great Wall conservation was often neglected by some local governments, which were not very aware of the importance of Great Wall conservation, did not fully fulfil their responsibilities for and take sufficient measures for Great Wall conservation, resulting in many Great Wall sites and sections not being managed by people. Meanwhile, the public's awareness of Great Wall conservation needs to be raised, and in few cases, local conservation and restoration were not provided with pertinent scientific schemes, and construction management was rough and not of high quality, affecting the Great Wall itself and its features. Modern man-made or natural damage to the Great Wall has become more serious; in "wild Great Wall" tourism, services and guidance should be strengthened. Many difficulties and problems in Great Wall conservation have not been effectively solved, and conservation is not satisfactory. Governments at all levels and the whole society need to strive to adhere to scientific cultural heritage conservation philosophies and take effective measures to preserve the historical, scientific and artistic values of the Great Wall, properly resolve the contradiction between Great Wall conservation and management and regional economic and social development of the areas along the Great Wall, alleviate and prevent damage caused by natural disasters, minimize man-made damage, and crack down on criminal acts associated with the Great Wall. Great Wall conservation is a long-term, arduous task.

To strengthen Great Wall conservation, we must be responsible for history and the people, further improve policies and measures, strengthen scientific planning and conservation efforts, allow governments to fulfil their responsibilities, conserve the Great Wall in strict accordance with law, promote social involvement, promote the spirit associated with the Great Wall, and let the Great Wall fully play its unique role in the inheritance and promotion of outstanding traditional Chinese culture.

山西偏关老牛湾明长城烽火台（杜震欣 拍摄）

The beach tower of the Great Wall of the Ming Dynasty in Laoniuwan, Pianguan Pass, Shanxi (Photo by Du Zhenxin)

## 第一节 保护管理视野下的长城特点

- 两种文物属性——“古建筑”还是“古遗址”？
- 两个遗产身份——文物保护单位 + 世界文化遗产
- 众多管理对象——四万余点段，数百个文物保护单位
- 多重管理系统——文物保护单位、旅游景区、自然保护区
- 自然环境多样——草原、森林、戈壁、沙漠，山地、丘陵、平原
- 社会环境复杂——人口分布不均，经济发展不平衡
- 保护管理需求——科学统筹，因地制宜

### 一、身份多重性

长城具有多重保护身份。1987 年，“中国长城”作为文化遗产类型列入《世界遗产名录》，其保护和管理受到国际社会的监督。1987 年纳入世界文化遗产范围的长城著名点段包括山海关、八达岭、嘉峪关，以及位于北京市、天津市、河北省、山西省、内蒙古自治区、辽宁省、吉林省、山东省、河南省、湖北省、湖南省、四川省、陕西省、甘肃省、青海省、宁夏回族自治区境内的部分长城遗存[78]。此外，

[78] 联合国教科文组织世界遗产委员会官网 http://whc.unesco.org/en/list/438.

# Section 1 The Characteristics of the Great Wall in Conservation and Management

- Two types of cultural heritage—a "traditional architectural structure" or an "archaeological site"?
- Two identities as a heritage site—a protected historical and cultural site + a World Heritage site
- Numerous objects of management—40,000 odd sites and sections, hundreds of protected historical and cultural sites
- Multiple management systems—protected historical and cultural sites, tourist scenic areas and nature reserves
- Diverse natural environments—grasslands, forests, deserts, mountainous regions, hills, and plains
- Complex social environments—uneven population distribution, imbalance in economic development
- Requirements for conservation and management—scientific overall planning, adjusting measures to local conditions

## I. Multiple identities

The Great Wall has multiple identities in terms of conservation. In 1987, "the Great Wall of China" was inscribed onto UNESCO's World Heritage List as a cultural heritage site, and its conservation and management began to be supervised by the international community. Famous Great Wall sites and sections inscribed onto UNESCO's World Heritage List in 1987 include Shanhai Pass, Badaling, Jiayu Pass and some other Great Wall remains located in Beijing City, Tianjin City, Hebei Province, Shanxi Province, Inner Mongolia Autonomous Region, Liaoning Province, Jilin Province, Shandong Province, Henan Province, Hubei Province, Hunan Province, Sichuan Province, Shaanxi Province, Gansu Province, Qinghai Province and Ningxia Hui Autonomous Region [78]. In addition, the components of the Silk Roads: The Routes Network of Chang'an-Tianshan Corridor, inscribed onto UNESCO's World Heritage List in 2014, also includes Great Wall remains such as the Yumen Pass and the Kizilgaha Beacon Tower. (Fig. 6-1)

In China's cultural heritage conservation system consisting of the *Law of the People's Republic of China on the Conservation of Cultural Relics* and other relevant laws and regulations, the identity of the Great Wall is a protected historical and cultural site and an immovable cultural heritage object. So far, among the Great Wall sections (including various Great Wall resources) identified by the State Administration of Cultural Heritage (SACH), 29 important Great Wall sites and sections with outstanding historical values and associated with major historical events and figures have been successively identified as major historical and cultural sites protected at the national level by the State Council. In addition, except for the few Great Wall sites and sections newly found in resource surveys, most Great Wall sections have successively been announced as sites protected at the

[78] The website of the UNESCO World Heritage Committee: http://whc.unesco.org/en/list/438.

2014 年，列入《世界遗产名录》的“丝绸之路：长安－天山廊道的路网 ”的遗产构成要素中，也包含玉门关、克孜尔尕哈烽燧等长城遗迹。（图 6-1）

图 6-1
克孜尔尕哈烽燧（张依萌 拍摄）

Fig. 6-1
The Kizilgaha Beacon Tower (photo by Zhang Yimeng)

在我国《中华人民共和国文物保护法》等相关法律法规所共同构成的中国文物保护体系中，长城的身份是文物保护单位和不可移动文物。至目前为止，经过国家文物局认定的长城（含各类长城资源）中，已有 29 处历史价值特别突出、与重大历史事件、人物相关联的长城重要点段被国务院陆续公布为全国重点文物保护单位；此外，除极少数经过资源调查新发现的点段以外，绝大多数的长城已按照“属地管理”原则，由各省（自治区、直辖市）陆续公布为省级文物保护单位。

关于长城的文物类型。《文物保护法》第三条将不可移动文物分为“古文化遗址、古墓葬、古建筑、石窟寺、石刻、壁画、近代现代重要史迹和代表性建筑”等类别。在国务院公布的 29 处长城全国重点文物保护单位中，有古建筑类 14 处，古遗址类 15 处。在第五批、第六批、第七批全国重点文物保护单位中，部分省（自治区、直辖市）长城作为古建筑被整体公布，但现存大部分长城遗存实际上已经成为遗址，地面建筑已是自然残损状态。（图 6-2）

此外，长城还列入多项保护计划。其中，“十一五”期间，国家文物局、财政部共同编制了《“十一五”期间大遗址保护总体规划》，长城被纳入第一批 100 处“大遗址”名单。另一方面，在我国众多的风景名胜区、自然保护区、森林公园、地质公园和旅游风景区，以及一部分农牧区域、工矿企业范围内，也分布着大量长城遗存，形成交叉管理、利用和开发局面。在长城保护管理方面，涉及多个利益相关者群体，管理主体多、管理理念、手段、方法、利益诉求各不相同，管辖权也存在一定程度的交叉，为进一步提高长城的保护管理整体水平带来挑战。

图 6-2
长城，古建筑还是古遗址？（左：张保田 拍摄，2007 年；右：张依萌 拍摄，2010 年）

Fig. 6-2
Is the Great Wall a traditional architectural structure or an archaeological site? (left: Zhang Baotian, 2007; right: Zhang Yimeng, 2010)

provincial level by corresponding provinces (autonomous regions and municipalities directly under the Central Government) in accordance with the principle of "localized management".

Concerning the type of cultural heritage site that the Great Wall belongs to, Article 3 of the *Law of the People's Republic of China on the Conservation of Cultural Relics* defines immovable cultural heritage as "sites of ancient culture, ancient tombs, traditional architecture, cave temples, stone carvings, mural paintings, and important historical sites and typical buildings of modern and contemporary times, etc." Of the 29 major historical and cultural sites of the Great Wall protected at the national level announced by the State Council, 14 are traditional architectural structures, and 15 are archaeological sites. Among the fifth, sixth and seventh batches of major historical and cultural sites protected at the national level, Great Wall sections in some provinces (autonomous regions and municipalities directly under the Central Government) were announced as traditional architectural structures. However, most surviving Great Wall remains have actually become archaeological sites, with their aboveground structures being naturally damaged. (Fig. 6-2)

In addition, the Great Wall has been included in many conservation plans. One is *Master Plan for the Conservation of Da Yi Zhi during the 11th Five-Year Plan Period* jointly developed by the SACH and the Ministry of Finance during the 11th Five-Year Plan period, in which the Great Wall is included in the first batch of 100 "Da Yi Zhi". On the other hand, many Great Wall remains are distributed in scenic areas, natural reserves, forest parks and geological parks, and in some agricultural and pastoral areas, as well as industrial and mining enterprises across China, resulting in overlapping management, use and development. Great Wall conservation and management involve multiple stakeholders and management entities who have different management philosophies, measures, methods and interests, and somewhat overlapping jurisdiction, posing challenges to further improving Great Wall conservation and management.

## 二、自然与人文环境多样性

长城自东部沿海延伸至西北内陆，其分布范围几乎覆盖了整个中国北方地区，经过的地区有草原、森林、戈壁、沙漠、山地、丘陵、平原等不同地质类型，主要受温带季风气候和温带大陆性气候影响。各地气候、水文条件各不相同。所处自然环境的复杂决定了不同地区的长城建筑材质和形制特色，并对长城的保护技术和理念提出了不同的要求。（图 6-3）

长城分布于中国北方 15 个省（自治区、直辖市）的 404 个县域，大型基础设施建设，如公路、铁路、油气管道布设等，在如此广阔的范围内，难免与长城发生交叉；其沿线所经过的各省（自治区、直辖市）的城乡人口密度、资源环境、产业结构、经济与社会发展水平差距很大。截止长城资源调查工作结束之时，长城沿线 404 个县域中，属于国家级贫困县的有 112 个，占长城分布县域数量的 27.5%。从整体上看，往往是人烟稀少地区或贫困地区长城资源反而更加丰富。人口和经济的不平衡性，导致长城的保护管理资源也不平衡。

## II. Diversity of Natural and Cultural Environments

The Great Wall extends from the east coast to the northwest hinterland, nearly passing through the whole northern China and through grasslands, forests, deserts, mountainous regions, hills, plains and other landforms, primarily in temperate monsoon climates and temperate continental climates. These areas have different climatic and hydrological conditions. Due to the complexity of their natural environments, Great Wall sections were built of different materials and have different structures, resulting in different requirements for Great Wall conservation technology and philosophies. (Fig. 6-3)

The Great Wall passes through 404 counties in 15 provinces (autonomous regions and municipalities directly under the Central Government) in northern China, where large-scale infrastructure projects, such as highways, railways and oil pipelines, may cross the Great Wall; and the provinces (autonomous regions and municipalities directly under the Central Government) that the Great Wall passes through differ greatly in population density, resources and environment, industrial structure, and the level of economic and social development. Upon completion of the Great Wall resource survey, of the 404 counties that the Great Wall passes through, 112 are national poor counties, accounting for 27.5% of all the counties that the Great Wall passes through. In general, sparsely populated areas or poor areas have richer Great Wall resources. Population and economic imbalances result in an imbalance in Great Wall conservation and management resources.

图 6-3
长城沿线自然景观

Fig. 6-3
Natural landscapes along the Great Wall

a 滨海（河北省长城资源调查队 提供，2007 年）
b 山地（辽宁省长城资源调查队 提供，2007 年）
c 草原（张依萌 拍摄，2012 年）
d 荒漠（张依萌 拍摄，2012 年）

| a | b |
|---|---|
| c | d |

## 三、保护管理理念复杂性

文物，是长城的基本身份。长城保护管理应当遵循文物保护的基本原则和方法。由于长城在公众的印象中一定程度上被过度概念化、符号化，导致人们忽略了长城作为文物的基本属性，而是将它作为一种工具或形象，由此对长城保护管理工作的方向和质量存在一些不理解或认识不到位的情况。

一方面，由于长城作为“古建筑”的形象深入人心，使得各地存在“八达岭化”的认识误区，导致一部分地方存在长城保护工作中“重建筑保护，轻遗址保护”的错误倾向。建筑保护与遗址保护在理念和方法上不同，以保护古建筑的方式保护古遗址，势必对文物本体的真实性和完整性造成负面影响。

另一方面，由于长城的规模极其庞大，沿线自然与人文环境十分复杂，完全依靠文物部门的现有力量对其进行全线的实时监控和管理是不可能的。同时，由于长城自身特征、保护状况等多样性，也决定了不可能采取不计成本的方式对长城进行全面修复，或采取“一刀切”的方式将类型丰富、保存状况各异、环境地域特色显著的长城遗存按照一个标准、要求进行一劳永逸的保护。

此外，长城不仅是一座建筑，更与其所在环境共同构成一个独特的文化景观。保护长城的环境与长城本体应当放在同等重要的位置，贯彻整体保护的理念。然而各地并没有充分认识到这一点，在开展城乡建设、长城保护的过程中，只关注长城建筑，而忽视了周边环境的协调与控制，割裂了长城墙体与构成长城防御体系的关堡、烽火台及其自然地理环境之间的有机联系，使长城的价值受到损害。

## III. Complexity of Conservation and Management Philosophies

The basic identity of the Great Wall is a cultural heritage site. Great Wall conservation and management should follow the basic principles and methods of cultural heritage conservation. As the Great Wall is somewhat excessively conceptualized and symbolized in public minds, people often neglect the basic identity of the Great Wall as a cultural heritage site and instead, deem it an instrument or image, and therefore may somewhat not understand or not fully understand the orientation and quality of Great Wall conservation and management efforts.

On the one hand, as the Great Wall is widely conceived as a "traditional architectural structure", it is misconceived as an extended Badaling section, and therefore some regions mistakenly tend to attach importance to the conservation of architectural structures and neglect the conservation of archaeological sites in Great Wall conservation. The conservation of architectural structures and that of archaeological sites are subject to totally different philosophies and methods. Conserving an archaeological site using measures that apply to a traditional architectural structure will certainly undermine the authenticity and integrity of the site.

On the other hand, as the Great Wall is enormous, and the natural and cultural environments it passes through are very complex, it is impossible to monitor and manage all Great Wall sections by totally relying on governments and cultural heritage administrations. Meanwhile, due to the diversity of the characteristics, states of conservation and other aspects of Great Wall sections, it is impossible to fully Repair the Great Wall without taking costs into account, or to conserve diverse types of Great Wall remains in different states of conservation and local environments by following the same standard and requirements.

In addition, the Great Wall is not only an architectural structure, but also a unique cultural landscape integrated with its environment. Equal importance should be attached to the conservation of the Great Wall's environment and that of the Great Wall itself, so that they are conserved as a whole. However, the regions that the Great Wall passes through did not fully realize this, and only paid attention to the architectural structures of the Great Wall and neglected the control of the surrounding environments, which should be in harmony with the Great Wall, during urban-rural development and Great Wall conservation, and disintegrated the relationship between the walls of the Great Wall, the forts and beacon towers, which are part of the defense system of the Great Wall, and their natural and geographical environments, thereby impairing the value of the Great Wall.

## 第二节 长城保护管理工作挑战

### 一、长城基础研究依然薄弱

一是关于长城概念和构成有待明确。对概念和构成的认识，也就是对保护对象的认识，是长城保护管理的基础。长期以来，“长城”并无公认的定义，其内涵和外延并不明晰。《长城保护条例》《长城资源调查工作手册》《长城资源认定资料手册》等文件均采用列举法来表述长城的构成，缺乏相应的概括和提炼；长城资源调查与认定工作基本摸清了长城的“家底”，搞清了长城资源的分布范围，但对长城资源的分类仍然是建立在调查所见遗迹的基础之上。今日的长城已是遗址状态，通过考古调查，我们无法完全了解长城的原貌。但鉴于其巨大的规模，随着研究的不断开展，我们很可能会不断发现新的长城资源类型，而长城的相关法律法规和管理制度需要保持一定的稳定性，不能经常变更，这就造成了长城管理制度滞后于管理需求的可能。

二是长城的价值有待进一步挖掘。长城列入世界遗产名录已经 30 年，世界遗产委员会当时对于长城的“突出普遍价值”的描述已经相对陈旧，并且在今天看来存在一定的错误。比如世界遗产委员会的评语中有“从月球上能看到的唯一人工建造物”语，即属于讹传。

随着我们对长城认识的拓展，其原有“突出普遍价值”描述已不适应其世界遗产身份，需要修订；作为长城保护管理理论基础的长城价值研究，也亟待深入。

## Section 2 Challenges Facing Great Wall Conservation and Management

### I. Basic studies of the Great Wall are still insufficient

First, the concept of the Great Wall needs to be clarified, and its components need to be identified. Knowledge about the concept and components of the Great Wall, or the objects of Great Wall conservation, is the basis of Great Wall conservation and management. For a long time, there has not been an established definition of the "Great Wall", whose connotation and denotation are not clarified. *Regulation on the Conservation of Great Wall, A Handbook of the Great Wall Resource Survey, A Handbook of the Data Used to Identify Great Wall Resources* and other documents equally list, rather than define Great Wall components; the survey and identification of Great Wall resources largely helped ascertain Great Wall resources and their distribution; however, the classification of Great Wall resources are still based on the remains found. As today's Great Wall is an archaeological site, we cannot fully ascertain what the Great Wall was like through archaeological investigations. However, as the Great Wall is enormous, with the furthering of studies, we may continually find new types of Great Wall resources, while Great Wall related laws and regulations and management systems need to remain somewhat steady and cannot be changed very often, resulting in Great Wall management systems possibly falling behind management needs.

Second, the value of the Great Wall needs to be further identified. As the Great Wall has been inscribed onto UNESCO's World Heritage List for 30 years, the World Heritage Committee's description of the "outstanding universal value" of the Great Wall is comparatively outdated, and has some errors as seen today. For example, the Committee said that the Great Wall is "the only work built by human hands on this planet that can be seen from the moon". This is not true.

As our knowledge has increased about the Great Wall, the original description of its "outstanding universal value" no longer suites the Great Wall as a World Heritage site, and needs to be revised; furthering of studies of the value of the Great Wall, as the theoretical basis of Great Wall conservation and management, is also urgently needed.

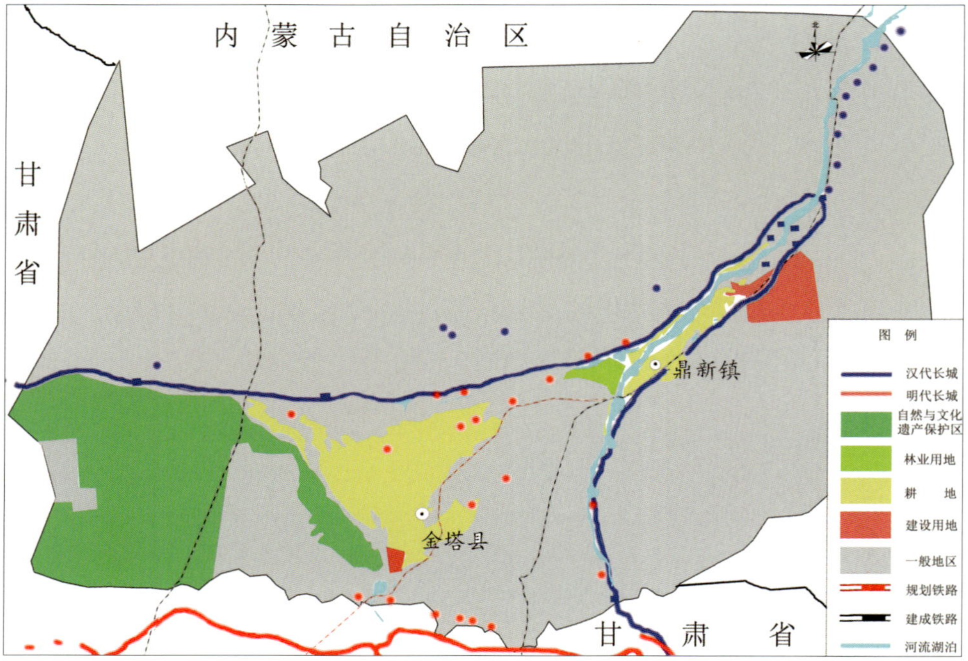


图 6-4
长城与甘肃省金塔县土地利用类型重叠示意图[79]

Fig. 6-4
Overlapping of the Great Wall and a type of land use of Jinta County, Gansu Province[79]

## 二、长城保护有待融入社会

长城是超大规模的文化遗产，分布地域广泛，与农田、厂矿、交通道路、能源管线、水利设施、通讯设施、城镇村庄等存在密切交集。作为旅游资源的长城，其所带来的经济和社会效益很高。但目前看来，长城保护与沿线社会经济发展关系并不密切，旅游活动也并没有对长城保护管理工作形成支撑。相反，长城沿线的生产建设和旅游开发活动对长城的保护管理形成了威胁。

比如，2008 年 1 月 1 日《中华人民共和国城乡规划法》实施以来，长城沿线各省市县积极开展土地利用总体规划和城乡规划编制工作，部分地区的规划已经开始实施。已有地区城乡规划，对于包括长城在内的文化遗产保护措施不足。以甘肃省金塔县为例，在《金塔县城市总体规划（2011-2030）》所规定的县区土地利用类型中，有一类被称为“自然与文化遗产保护区”。对照图纸我们看到，县域内大部分长城遗存都被排除在保护区的范围之外。部分段落甚至位于新规划的建设区之内。（图 6-4）又如部分长城景区，以文物保护的名义实现一些展示性较强的工程，以便开发利用。（图 6-5）这些案例都表明长城的保护管理工作亟待融入当地社会经济发展。

[79] 底图为金塔县土地利用类型图，由金塔县城乡建设局提供。

## II. Great Wall conservation needs to be integrated into local social economic development

The Great Wall, an enormous cultural heritage site, is widely distributed, and frequently passes through farmlands, factories and mines, roads, energy pipelines, water conservation facilities, communication facilities, towns and villages and others. As a tourist resource, the Great Wall brings great economic and social benefits. However, currently, Great Wall conservation is not closely associated with the social and economic development of the areas along the Great Wall, and tourist activities do not support Great Wall conservation and management. On the contrary, production, construction and tourism development activities in the areas along the Great Wall have been threatening Great Wall conservation and management.

For example, since the implementation of the *Law of the People's Republic of China on Urban and Rural Planning* on January 1, 2008, provinces, cities and counties that the Great Wall passes through have been proactively developing master plans for land use and urban and rural plans, and the implementation of the plans of some regions have begun. Some urban and rural plans do not provide sufficient measures for the conservation of cultural heritage sites, including the Great Wall. Taking Jinta County, Gansu Province for example, one of the types of county land use defined in *Master Urban Plan for Jinta County (2011-2030)* is "natural and cultural heritage reserve". As seen from the drawing, most of the Great Wall remains in the county are not included in the reserves, and some Great Wall sections are even located in the newly planned construction area (Fig. 6-4). Also, some Great Wall scenic areas, in the name of cultural heritage conservation, implemented some projects for enhanced presentation purposes to facilitate development and utilization (Fig. 6-5). All these cases show that integrating Great Wall conservation and management into local social economic development is urgently needed.

图 6-5
雁门关原貌与修缮后效果对比（左：沙畹，1906；右：张依萌，2017）

Fig. 6-5
Comparison of original and closed Yanmen after the renovation effect (Left: Chavannes, 1906; right: Zhang Yimeng, 2017)

[79] The background map, showing the types of land use of Jinta County, is provided by Jinta County Bureau of Urban-Rural Development.

## 三、政府保护责任亟待落实

从长城保护身份的多重性、自然与人文环境的多样性以及保护管理理念的复杂性角度来说，正确的认知、明晰的管理权责、优化的保护管理资源配置，对于实现长城的科学保护至关重要。较之一般的文物而言，作为超大型线性文化遗产，长城保护工作需要文物部门更好的统筹规划，逐步推进，在夯实基础研究工作和日常维护保养的基础上，加强与《长城保护条例》配套的地方立法，针对不同长城段落采取有针对性的保护措施。此外，长城还具有跨行政区域分布的特点。这些都要求各级地方政府在更高层次更宏观政策上进行统筹协调，建立及时有效的决策机制和管理体制。而目前长城保护管理主要局限在文物部门内部，重大规划和建设决策参与度低，资源配置层级低，信息管理效率低，国家意志与执行能力脱节。

长城分布范围广泛，与沿线居民生产生活关系密切。随着我国社会经济的迅猛发展和城镇化的推进，长城保护遭到了前所未有的压力，需要在政府主导之下，各级管理部门、各行业管理部门和居民有效协调才能顺利开展工作。然而目前的情况是，文物部门在整个政府部门中处于弱势地位，缺失话语权，缺乏沟通协调能力，所以在长城保护工作中，需要协调实施的工作推动起来往往十分困难。

在长城保护工作中，政府责任缺失所导致的另一个问题是，长城保护管理资源配置存在严重结构性矛盾。基层长城保护管理队伍匮乏。长城保护管理中人员缺少，业务能力不高，保护管理信息不对称、日常管理经费缺乏的问题依然非常突出。基层保护工作跟不上，直接制约和影响长城依法监管工作，很多破坏长城的事情和问题不能及时发现和处理。长城沿线 404 个县市区共 485 处保护管理机构中，仅有 43 处为长城保护管理专门机构，大量地方文物保管机构兼任行政管理、不可移动文物和可移动文物等工作，长城点多线长，无暇顾及。特别是长城沿线 404 个县市区中，有 111 个属于国家级贫困县，工作条件极为艰苦。以内

## III. Fulfilment of governments' conservation responsibilities is urgently needed

In view of the multiple identifies of the Great Wall in conservation, the diversity of its natural and cultural environments and the complexity of the conservation and management philosophies, correct perception of the Great Wall, clear management power and responsibilities and optimized allocation of conservation and management resources are crucial for scientific Great Wall conservation. Compared with that of a common cultural heritage site, the conservation of the Great Wall, an enormous linear cultural heritage site, requires cultural heritage administrations to plan more properly, and gradually promote progress; and to strengthen local legislation supporting *Regulation on the Conservation of Great Wall,* and use pertinent conservation measures for different Great Wall sections on the basis of strengthening basic studies and routine maintenance. In addition, some Great Wall sections span several administrative regions. These require governments at all levels to plan and coordinate using higher level and more macroscopic policies and establish time-saving, effective decision-making mechanisms and management systems. However, currently, Great Wall conservation and management are largely limited within cultural heritage administrations, are not sufficiently taken into account when making major plans and construction decisions, are not deemed important when allocating resources, are inefficient in terms of information management, and see a gap between the national will and the executive capacity.

The Great Wall passes through a very large area and is closely associated with the inhabitants along it. With China's rapid social and economic development and urbanization, Great Wall conservation is facing unprecedented pressure, and requires coordinated efforts by administrations at all levels, industrial authorities and inhabitants under government direction. However, currently, cultural heritage administrations are weak among government departments, have no say, and are not very able to communicate and coordinate. Therefore, it is often very difficult to promote Great Wall conservation when coordinated efforts are needed.

In Great Wall conservation, another problem caused by the absence of the role of governments is a severe structural imbalance in the allocation of Great Wall conservation and management resources. There are not enough grassroots Great Wall conservation and management teams. Great Wall conservation and management personnel are few, not very professional, not equally well informed, and not provided with sufficient administrative expenses. The insufficiency of grassroots conservation efforts directly restricts and affects legal

蒙包头固阳县为例，其境内有秦汉和明代共约 700 千米，固阳文管所人员 10 人，聘用长城保护员 5 人。除长城保护工程专项经费外和地方财政的人头费外，无日常保护经费，固阳长城巡查一遍就需要 3-4 天时间，费用起码 2 万元（越野车汽油费、人员食宿费），这部分费用难以得到保障。而这些重要的长城日常管理工作经费都需要得到地方财政的支持。

专业人员话语权缺失，力量不足，加之长城执法督察和相关监管工作在各地往往不是文物部门的责任，各级政府如果不能发挥应有作用，有效整合人力资源，也会导致长城保护工程施工过程中难以实现有效监管，最终影响工程质量和效果，长城破坏的责任追究困难。

## 四、公众保护意识有待提高

为了对公众认知长城的情况进行了解，报告编写者制作并发放了一份调查问卷，通过“调查宝”网站（http://www.surveyportal.cn）发放及现场发放两种渠道进行（后者在中国教育学会培训中心的协助下完成）。自 2013 年 8 月 1 日至 2014 年 8 月 31 日的一年间，共回收问卷 313 份，其中 297 份为有效答卷，调查对象遍及中国各省（自治区、直辖市），以及美国、英国、法国、意大利、保加利亚、埃及、墨西哥、马耳他、日本、韩国、菲律宾等 11 个国家，其中 180 名受访者来自长城沿线的 15 省。

调查结果显示，社会公众普遍对长城，以及长城的保护管理工作缺乏了解。

Great Wall supervision, so that many cases of damaging the Great Wall were not promptly identified and addressed. Of the 485 conservation and management administrations in the 404 counties, cities and districts that the Great Wall passes through, only 43 are Great Wall conservation and management administrations; many local cultural heritage preservation agencies are concurrently engaged in administration and work relating to movable and immovable cultural relics, and are too busy to take the Great Wall into account. In particular, of the 404 counties, cities and districts, 111 are national poor counties where working conditions are very tough. For example, in Guyang County, Baotou, Inner Mongolia there are Qin, Han and Ming Great Wall sections totalling a length of around 700 km; Guyang Cultural Heritage Administration has 10 workers, and has employed five Great Wall conservators. Except for funds for Great Wall Conservation Projects and financial allocations to each worker, there are no funds for routine conservation. However, inspecting the Great Wall section in Guyang takes 3-4 days and costs at least RMB 20,000 (fuel cost for an off-road vehicle, and accommodation expenses), while these expenses are not ensured. Funds for such important routine Great Wall management should be paid by local finances.

Professionals have no say, and are not powerful enough, and cultural heritage administrations are often not responsible for Great Wall related oversight of compliance with the law and relevant supervisory work. Therefore, if governments at all levels fail to play their due roles and effectively integrate human resources, the construction of Great Wall Conservation Projects will not be effectively supervised, eventually undermining project quality and outcome, and making it difficult to find out who is to blame in a case of damaging the Great Wall.

## IV. Conservation awareness of the public needs to be improved

To ascertain the public's knowledge about the Great Wall, the writers of this report prepared and distributed a questionnaire at www.surveyportal.cn, and on-site with the assistance of the Training Centre of the Chinese Society of Education. In the year from August 1, 2013 to August 31, 2014, 313 copies of

来自长城沿线 15 省的 180 人中，有 78 人（44.3%）认为本省无长城。全部 297 人中，仅 173 人（58.2%）知道《长城保护条例》，认知比例与学历关联不大；人文社会科学专业学生与从业人员对《长城保护条例》的认知度明显高于其他行业，但也仅有 68% 知道该条例的存在；文博行业和非文博行业认知度差距并不明显。此外，中小学在校生对《长城保护条例》的认知度也达到一半以上，而其他行业的受访者平均只有三分之一左右听说过《长城保护条例》。（表 6-1）

公众了解长城信息的渠道较为广泛，但仍以报纸、电视等传统媒体为主，通过专业渠道获取长城知识及相关信息的比例较低。（图 6-6）

**表 6-1：《长城保护条例》认知度调查统计表**

Table 6-1: A survey on awareness of *Regulation on the Conservation of Great Wall*

| 行业 \ 认知情况<br>Industry \ awareness | 听说过<br>Heard of it | 确切知道<br>Know it exactly | 没听说过<br>Never heard of it | 合计<br>Subtotal |
|---|---|---|---|---|
| 文博行业<br>Cultural heritage and musicology | 9(56.3%) | 1（6.2%） | 6（37.5%） | 16 |
| 人文社科（非文博行业）<br>Cultural and social sciences (other than cultural heritage and musicology) | 54（64.3%） | 4（4.8%） | 26（30.9%） | 84 |
| 理工类<br>Science and engineering | 17（32.7%） | 2（3.8%） | 33（63.5%） | 52 |
| 金融商贸<br>Finance, commerce and trade | 9（33.3%） | 0（0%） | 18（66.7） | 27 |
| 医疗 / 保健 / 卫生<br>Medical / health | 4（80%） | 0（0%） | 1（20%） | 5 |
| 其他行业<br>Other industries | 35（45.5%） | 9（11.7%） | 33（42.8%） | 64 |
| 中小学在校学生<br>Middle and elementary school students | 26（53.1） | 3（6.1%） | 20（40.8%） | 49 |
| 合计<br>Total | 154（51.9） | 19（6.4%） | 124（41.7%） | 297 |

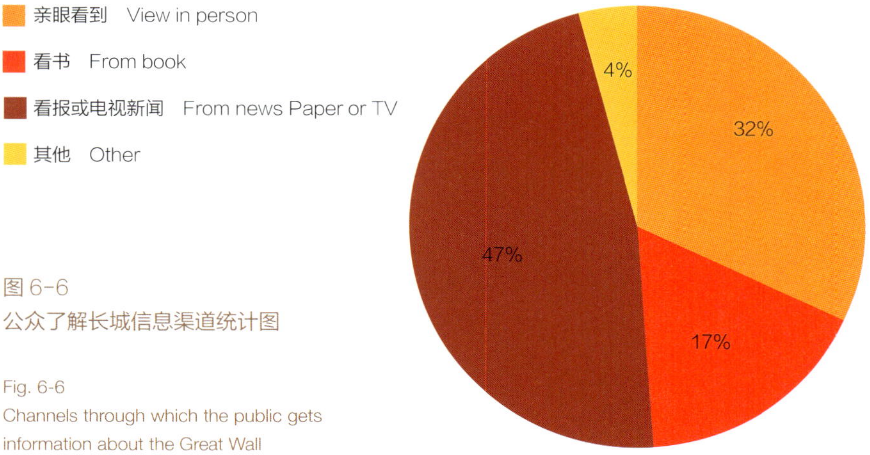


图 6-6
公众了解长城信息渠道统计图

Fig. 6-6
Channels through which the public gets information about the Great Wall

the questionnaire were returned. Validly answered copies total 297. The respondents came from all across China and 11 other countries, namely, the US, the UK, France, Italy, Bulgaria, Egypt, Mexico, Malta, Japan, South Korea, and the Philippines. 180 of the respondents came from the 15 provinces that the Great Wall passes through.

The results of the survey show that the public does not have sufficient knowledge about the Great Wall and Great Wall conservation and management.

Of the 180 respondents coming from the 15 provinces that the Great Wall passes through, 78 (44.3%) believed that there is no Great Wall section in his/her province. Of all the 297 persons, only 173 (58.2%) knew *Regulation on the Conservation of Great Wall,* and this has little to do with their educational backgrounds; much more, yet still only 68% of the students majoring in and practitioners in cultural and social sciences knew the *Regulations* than those engaged in other industries did; not much more people engaged in cultural heritage and musicology knew the *Regulations* than people not engaged in it did. In addition, more than half of the elementary and middle school students knew *Regulations*, while only around one third of the respondents engaged in other industries heard of the *Regulations*. (Table 6-1)

The public gets information about the Great Wall from diverse channels, yet still primarily from newspapers, television and other traditional media; few people get knowledge about the Great Wall and other relevant information through professional channels (Fig. 6-6).

In addition, as to the national Great Wall resource survey, 97, or less than one third of all the 297 respondents, said that they knew it; and only 52, or less than one fifth of all the respondents, said that they knew the two press conferences and the latest data about the length of the Great Wall.

此外，对于国家长城资源调查项目，受访者表示知情的有 97 人，在全部 297 人中不到三分之一；而表示对两次新闻发布会和长城长度最新统计数据有了解的人则仅有 52 人，不足全部受访者的五分之一。

问卷调查结果说明两个问题，一是社会公众对于长城的认知水平整体仍然偏低。社会上对长城保护管理体制的认知程度较低，民间长城爱好者与管理机构的交流存在一定障碍。比如，一些基层政府和文物部门及民间研究者对于长城保护管理的主管机构并不清楚，甚至还将民间社团中国长城学会视为“国家最高长城管理机构”。二是专业人员对长城保护宣传教育的参与度偏低，社会公众对长城的全面认识不足，专业知识普及不广，除北京市八达岭、河北省山海关和甘肃省嘉峪关等个别几处著名景点外，对长城的分布、构成、现状等缺乏基本了解。

## 专栏：长城的想象与真容

位于北京附近的八达岭长城是保存较为完整的段落，也是中国长城的精华部分之一，19 世纪之后，长城的形象开始大量出现在邮票、明信片等印刷品上。由于位于中国的首都附近，交通相对便利，八达岭长城成为当时各国在华人员，包括传教士、驻华公使、军人、探险家等最多踏足和留下影像资料的段落。八达岭长城带有整齐垛口和高大敌台的砖石结构建筑则被视为长城的代表。然而长城真的都是八达岭那样的吗？有心的人也会提出这样的疑问。当我们来到大西北的草原、戈壁和沙漠中，我们会看到土和石块构筑的墙体蜿蜒其间。其实不用去甘肃和陕西，在北京、河北、天津、辽宁，当你走出八达岭、慕田峪这样的长城旅游景区，你同样会看到苍凉的断壁残垣，没有砖砌的垛口，没有高大雄伟的敌台、烽火台。实际上，它们从建造之初，就没有包砖。

中国古人用各种材料建造长城，而在全国范围内，像八达岭那样的长城，比例也是极少的。长城历史悠久，因为朝代更迭、国力兴衰，多数长城仅在当时使用，并很快因为功能丧失而被废弃，加之自然和人为损毁，保存至今的历代长城，呈现出以遗址为主的整体面貌，仅存少量雄伟的地面建筑。这是长城的历史形态，也是客观形态。

The results of the questionnaire survey show that 1) generally, the public still knows little about the Great Wall; the public still knows little about the Great Wall conservation and management system, and nongovernmental Great Wall enthusiasts cannot properly communicate with administrations; for example, some governments and cultural heritage administrations at the grassroots level and nongovernmental researchers do not know Great Wall conservation and management authorities clearly, and even deem the China Great Wall Society, a nongovernmental organization, the "state administration of the Great Wall"; and 2) professionals are not much involved in the promotion of and education in Great Wall conservation awareness, and the public does not have sufficient comprehensive knowledge about the Great Wall; professional knowledge is not widely popularized; the public does not have basic knowledge about the distribution, components, existing conditions and other aspects of Great Wall sections except for famous Great Wall scenic spots such as Badaling in Beijing City, Shanhai Pass in Hebei Province and Jiayu Pass in Gansu Province.

With the improvement of their livelihood, the Chinese want to improve their cultural lives and enjoy leisure time. The Great Wall has become a destination of many tourists. On the one hand, more and more tourists go to those Great Wall scenic areas opened as sightseeing areas, especially on holidays, when these Great Wall scenic areas are overcrowded, undermining the Great Wall and its

## The Great Wall: imagination and reality

The Badaling Great Wall located near the downtown of Beijing is a well conserved section of the Great Wall, and one of the most eye-catching Great Wall sections. After the end of the 19th century, the image of the Great Wall frequently appeared on stamps, postcards and other printed matter. Located near the capital of China and easily accessible, the Badaling Great Wall was then the Great Wall section most visited and photographed by foreign missionaries, envoys, military men, explorers and other foreigners in China. The Badaling Great Wall's brick masonry structure with orderly crenels and tall watchtowers is deemed a model of the Great Wall. However, are all Great Wall sections like the Badaling section? If we go to the grasslands and deserts in Northwest China, we will see earth and stone walls winding through them. You do not need to go as far as Gansu and Shaanxi. Just in Beijing, Hebei, Tianjin and Liaoning, when you go further away from Badaling, Mutianyu and other Great Wall scenic areas, you will also see dilapidated walls without brick crenels and tall watchtowers and beacon towers. In fact, even originally they were not brick enclosed.

The ancient Chinese used diverse materials to build the Great Wall, and there are few Great Wall sections resembling Badaling. The Great Wall has a long history. As dynasties rose and fell, most Great Wall sections were only used for a time and then fell into disuse. This is worsened by natural and man-made damage. Therefore, most surviving Great Wall sections appear as archaeological sites, and only few of them appear as imposing aboveground structures. This is the historic and actual condition of the Great Wall.

随着国人经济水平和生活水平的提高，对精神层面的追求增强，文化休闲成为其中重要的组成内容。长城成为很多人的旅游目的地，一方面已经开辟为参观游览区的长城景区的游客人数增加，尤其在节假日，长城景区人满为患，严重超出合理荷载量，对长城本体和环境造成负面影响；另一方面长城的雄美壮观和沧桑古朴吸引了大量游客前往未开放地区攀爬，不但人身安全得不到保障，而且随意和无序的攀爬破坏了本就久经风霜，年迈苍苍的长城。正确和有效宣传长城价值、保护理念工作不足。

## 五、保护研究与智库作用薄弱

实践正确的长城保护理念，实现长城保护管理科学决策，需要专业研究与咨询机构的智力支持。

目前长城研究的力量分散在不同机构，研究工作多是随性进行，课题缺乏整体设计，国家层面没有有计划有步骤地引导和推进长城保护研究的进展。长期以来的基础研究局限在对长城遗迹属性、分布、历史等方面进行研究，保护研究较少，更重要的是，综合保护能力欠缺，只能将如此复杂的长城遗产分割为一个个的文物点对待，对数以万计的长城遗存进行有限的局部保护。

目前从事长研究的科研人员基本集中于大专院校，以个人兴趣和专长申请科研课题，开展相关研究工作，缺乏能够持续进行长城研究的环境。项目结束后，就曲终人散，他们培养的研究生毕业之后很难有机会再次从事长城研究，难以培养起相对固定的长城专业研究人才。

在当前长城保护工程迅猛增长的情况下，长城保护研究与智库作用薄弱，致使长城保护工作缺乏有针对性的科学方案和引导，这是导致一些长城保护工程质量不高、效果不佳的重要原因。

environment; on the other hand, unopened Great Wall sections, old and impressive, attract many tourists to climb them, posing risks to their personal safety and damaging these weather-beaten Great Wall sections. Efforts in correctly and effectively communicating the value of the Great Wall and Great Wall conservation philosophies are insufficient.

## V. Conservation studies and think tanks did not play sufficient roles

Practising a correct Great Wall conservation philosophy and conducting scientific decision-making in Great Wall conservation and management require intellectual support from specialised studies and advisory bodies.

Currently, those people conducting Great Wall studies are distributed in different organs, and most of them conduct such studies as they wish; an overall plan of their research subjects is absent, and there are no planned, step-by-step national guidance and promotion of the progress of Great Wall conservation studies. For a long time, basic studies of the Great Wall have been limited to the nature, distribution, history and other aspects of Great Wall remains, without paying sufficient attention to Great Wall conservation research. Even worse, these researchers do not know comprehensive conservation well, and just divide the Great Wall, a complex heritage site, into individual cultural heritage sites, resulting in partial and individual conservation of tens of thousands of Great Wall remains.

Currently, most of the long-term researchers work at universities and colleges; they apply for research subjects and conduct relevant studies based on their personal interests and specialties, without an environment supporting continuous Great Wall studies. When a Great Wall related research project is completed, nothing will be continued, and the postgraduates trained in the project have few opportunities to conduct Great Wall studies again, making it difficult to train relatively full-time professional researchers in the Great Wall.

As Great Wall Conservation Projects are multiplying, while Great Wall conservation studies and think tanks do not play sufficient roles, resulting in Great Wall conservation not being provided with pertinent scientific schemes and guidance, which is an important reason why some Great Wall Conservation Projects are not of high quality and are not effective.

# 第三节 长城保护工作的展望

长城保护是一项庞大的系统工程，由于长城在我国政治社会精神文化生活中的特殊地位，长城保护事关民族感情、文化传承和国家形象。国家发展和文化遗产保护事业的新形势，对长城保护管理工作提出了更高的要求。

以“长城保护工程”十年工作为基础，我们应当不断思考和努力实践，针对长城自身特色和社会发展水平，制定科学合理的保护策略和目标，不断扩大长城保护的社会基础，促进长城保护管理工作更加科学、高效的开展。

## 一、积极开展战略研究

进一步加强基础研究，明确长城的概念和构成，深入研究长城的价值，夯实保护的理论基础；

加强长城的保护利用研究，探索多种长城展示利用方式，使长城保护、展示利用有机结合；

从更加宏观的角度审视长城，进一步拓展研究思路和领域。开展大型线性文化遗产保护理论研究，从区域发展的角度考察长城，引入“长城文化带”“长城经济带”等概念，积极探索长城保护管理对地区经济与社会发展的积极作用。

文物部门应当积极参与区域发展规划的编制工作，使长城保护管理融入其中，成为经济与社会发展的有机组成部分。

# Section 3
# Prospects for Great Wall Conservation

Great Wall conservation is an enormous systematic project. Due to the special position of the Great Wall in the political, social, spiritual and cultural lives of the Chinese nation, Great Wall conservation is associated with national sentiment, cultural inheritance and the image of the country. The new situations of national development and cultural heritage conservation pose higher requirements for Great Wall conservation and management.

Based on ten years of efforts in the "Great Wall Conservation Project", we should continue to improve our thinking and practice, develop scientific, reasonable conservation strategies and goals pertinent to the characteristics of the Great Wall and the level of social development, continuously strengthen the social foundation for Great Wall conservation, and promote more scientific and efficient Great Wall conservation and management.

## I. Proactively conducting strategic studies

Further strengthen basic studies to identify the concept and components of the Great Wall, further study the value of the Great Wall, consolidate conservation theories;

Strengthen studies of the conservation and use of the Great Wall, and explore ways to present and use the Great Wall, so as to properly integrate Great Wall conservation, presentation and use;

Look at the Great Wall from a more macroscopic perspective, and further diversify Great Wall studies. Conduct studies of large scale linear cultural heritage conservation theories, look at the Great Wall from the perspective of regional development, introduce the "Great Wall cultural belt", the "Great Wall economic belt" and other concepts, and proactively explore the positive effects of Great Wall conservation and management on regional economic and social development.

Cultural heritage administrations should be proactively involved in the development of regional development plans and include Great Wall conservation and management in them as elements of economic and social development.

## 二、切实落实政府责任

长城熔铸着中华民族勤劳勇敢、自强不息的民族精神，积淀着中华文明博大精深、灿烂辉煌的文化内涵，凝聚着中华儿女同仇敌忾、共御外侮的爱国情怀，涵养着沿线各地发展经济、改善民生的重要资源。加强对长城的保护和管理，对于展示中华民族灿烂文明，增强民族自豪感、凝聚社会共识，开展爱国主义教育、弘扬社会主义核心价值观，促进经济社会发展、提升国家文化软实力，都具有十分重要的意义。保护好长城使命光荣，责任重大，既是党中央、国务院的要求和全国人民的期盼，也是对中华民族、对子孙后代负责任的表现，更是各级政府义不容辞的责任。

按照《中华人民共和国文物保护法》和《长城保护条例》要求，要进一步落实属地管理责任，明确保护职责。编制实施国家长城保护总体规划、省级长城保护规划和重要点段长城保护详细规划，纳入区域社会经济发展规划、城乡规划和土地利用规划，科学划定公布长城保护范围和建设控制地带。长城沿线各级人民政府要结合实际情况和需求，出台地方性法规或政策性文件，落实长城保护机构和队伍建设，确保经费投入，优化支出结构，落实长城日常保护管理经费，切实把长城保护管理的各项制度责任落到实处。加大执法督察力度，严格责任追究，让“有责必问，违法必究”成为长城保护管理的新常态。

## II. Getting governments' responsibilities fulfilled

The Great Wall symbolises the national spirit of the Chinese people, who are industrious and courageous and strive continuously to make new progress, is a product of the extensive, sophisticated and splendid Chinese civilization, represents the patriotism of the Chinese people, who share a bitter hatred and rise in a united resistance again foreign aggressors, and provides important resources for the economic development and livelihood improvement of the areas along it. Strengthening Great Wall conservation and management is significant for presenting the Chinese civilization, improving national pride, achieving social consensus, educating in patriotism, promoting socialist core values, promoting economic and social development, and improving China's cultural soft power. Proper conservation of the Great Wall is an honourable mission and a grave responsibility. It is what the Party Central Committee and the State Council require and what all the Chinese people expect, and is a responsibility to the Chinese nation and our future generations that governments at all levels should take on.

As the *Law of the People's Republic of China on the Conservation of Cultural Relics and Regulation on the Conservation of Great Wall* require, localized management responsibilities should be further fulfilled, and conservation responsibilities should be specified. A national master plan of Great Wall conservation, provincial plans for Great Wall conservation and detailed plans for the conservation of major Great Wall sites and sections should be developed and implemented, Great Wall conservation should be included in regional social and economic development plans, urban and rural plans and land use plans, and Great Wall conservation boundaries and buffer zones should be scientifically demarcated and announced. People's governments in areas along the Great Wall should, based on actual conditions and needs, release local laws and regulations or policies, establish Great Wall conservation agencies and teams, provide sufficient funds, optimizethe expenditure structure, ensure funds for Great Wall routine conservation and management, and put Great Wall conservation and management systems into effect. Oversight of compliance with the law and accountability should be strengthened, so that "people are held accountable for what they did and violators are brought to justice" in Great Wall conservation and management.

## 三、继续加大保护力度

强化日常养护，及时消除自然和人为因素可能造成的安全隐患。严格遵守“不改变原状”和“最小干预”的原则，优先实施一批长城抢险加固工程，消除长城安全隐患。重点推进长城重要点段保护示范工程，保护长城的真实性，完整性和延续性。加强长城考古调查和基础研究，加大专业人才培养力度。积极支持保护条件好的长城段落向公众开放，发挥长城的社会教育作用。实施长城监测预警，加强预防性保护，提升长城资源信息化管理水平。结合工程实施加强长城保护、展示、监测等技术研究，切实改善长城保护状况，确保长城安全。

## 四、促进社会广泛参与

进一步完善社会参与政策与措施，促进社会力量积极参与长城保护。不断拓宽长城保护经费渠道，支持相关各地设立长城保护公益基金，探索 PPP、众筹等新模式，吸引社会力量投入长城保护与展示领域，引导社会公众依法、有序、科学地参与长城保护。培育社会公益组织，开展长城志愿服务行动。发挥有关高等院校、科研院所等专业机构的优势，提高长城保护研究水平。广泛宣传普及长城保护相关法律法规，营造全社会共同参与的良好氛围，不断夯实长城保护的社会基础。

## 五、大力弘扬长城精神

深入挖掘长城精神与文化内涵，加强长城重要点段的现场展示，着力长城专题博物馆、陈列馆现有展览水平的提升，建设爱国主义教育基地；运用互联网 +、全媒体传播、制作科普宣传片、出版通俗读物等多种手段，利用长城文化进校园、进课堂等多种方式，加强对全社会特别是青少年长城精神的宣传教育，充分发挥长城在开展国防教育、爱国主义教育、传承弘扬中华优秀传统文化中的作用。

## III. Further strengthening conservation efforts

Strengthen routine maintenance and promptly eliminate potential safety hazards that can be caused by natural and man-made factors. Strictly follow the principles of "preserving the historic condition" and "minimal intervention", and preferentially implement a number of emergency Great Wall strengthening projects to eliminate potential safety hazards to the Great Wall. Preferentially advance demonstration projects to conserve major Great Wall sites and sections to preserve the authenticity, integrity and continuity of the Great Wall. Strengthen archaeological investigations and basic studies of the Great Wall, andpress ahead with the training of professionals. Support well conserved Great Wall sections to be opened to the public to play their roles in social education. Conduct Great Wall monitoring and prewarning, strengthen preventive conservation, and improve IT-based management of Great Wall resources. Strengthen technical studies of the conservation, presentation, monitoring and other aspects of the Great Wall based on project implementation to improve Great Wall conservation and secure the safety of the Great Wall.

## IV. Promoting wide social involvement

Further improve policies and measures to promote the involvement of social forces in Great Wall conservation. Expand funding sources for Great Wall conservation, support relevant regions to establish Great Wall conservation foundations, and explore PPP, crowd funding and other new models to attract social forces to be involved in Great Wall conservation and presentation, guide the public to be involved in Great Wall conservation in a lawful, orderly and scientific way. Foster public service organizations to provide Great Wall related voluntary services. Give full play to the roles of relevant colleges, universities, research institutes and other professional organizations to improve Great Wall conservation studies. Popularize Great Wall conservation related laws and regulations to encourage social involvement in Great Wall conservation and consolidate the social foundation for Great Wall conservation.

## V. Vigorously promoting the spirit associated with the Great Wall

Explore the spirit associated with the Great Wall and its cultural significance, strengthen the presentation of major Great Wall sites and sections, strive to improve the services of Great Wall themed museums and exhibition halls, and establish patriotism education bases; better communicate the spirit associated with the Great Wall to the public, especially adolescents, by using Internet+ and omnimedia, producing popular science films, publishing popular books and other measures, and by introducing Great Wall culture into campuses and classrooms and other means, so as to give full play to the role of the Great Wall in education in national defence, patriotism and the inheritance and promotion of outstanding traditional Chinese culture.

# 后记

改革开放以来，中国的文化遗产保护工作，尤其是长城保护工作不断与世界接轨，理念不断进步、管理制度不断完善。与此同时，社会对长城的认知依然存在偏差，人民对长城保护工作的流程与现状普遍不了解，也对专业长城保护工作者提出了很多质疑。

长城保护十年，是落实国务院《“长城保护工程（2005-2014）”总体工作方案》和《长城保护条例》的十年。“长城保护工程”的开展，是中国长城保护管理史上一件具有里程碑意义的大事。我们第一次从国家层面，对长城的分布、构成、自然与人文环境、保存状况、保护管理状况等数据有了全面、系统的了解。

回首十年工作，国家在长城保护领域取得很多成就，也提出很多的问题与思考。我们希望通过这部报告，能够把十年长城保护工作的过程和成就向社会进行全面的汇报，对社会的关注与质疑进行回应。

中国文化遗产研究院长期致力于长城保护与研究工作，从 2006 年的“长城保护工程”项目管理小组到 2007 年的长城资源调查项目组，再到 2017 年的长城保护研究室，虽然名称不同，但十年筚路蓝缕，薪火相传，完成了大量基础工作。组织协调“长城资源调查”，建设“长城资源保护管理信息系统”，开展长城保护管理标准规范和长城世界遗产监测研究等等。承担了国家文物局《长城保护维修工作指导意见》和《长城四有工作指导意见》编制、《长城保护条例》长城执法实地督察等多项工作，日益成为长城保护与研究领域不可或缺的力量。

本报告是由中国文化遗产研究院文物研究所长城保护研究室集体执笔完成。文物研究所于冰主持了长城十年总结工作，指导并参与评估框架和技术路线设计，数据调研和分析。其中第一章长城调查与资源概况由张依萌、刘文艳执笔；第二章长城立法与管理体制由李大伟、张依萌、许慧君执笔；第三章长城保护维修工作由李大伟执笔；第四章长城研究与成果展示、第六章长城保护挑战与展望由张依萌执笔；第五章长城旅游与宣传教育由许慧君执笔。报告全文由张依萌、

# Epilogue

Since the inception of the reform and opening-up policy, China has been geared to international practice in cultural heritage conservation, especially Great Wall conservation, whose philosophies and management systems have been improving. Meanwhile, the public does not know the Great Wall and its conservation well, and raised many questions about professional Great Wall conservators.

The ten years of efforts in Great Wall conservation were efforts in implementing *Master Plan on the Great Wall Conservation Projects (2005-2014)* and *Regulation on the Conservation of Great Wall* approved by the State Council. The implementation of the "Great Wall Proctection Project" was a milestone in the history of Great Wall conservation and management. For the first time we gained a comprehensive, systematic knowledge about the distribution, components, natural and cultural environments, state of preservation, conservation and management and other aspects of the Great Wall.

In the last decade, the state has made a lot of achievements in, and raised many questions and got many ideas about Great Wall conservation. We hope that this report can review Great Wall conservation efforts in the last decade and address the public's concerns and questions.

The Chinese Academy of Cultural Heritage (CACH) has long been engaged in Great Wall conservation and studies. We worked as members of the "Great Wall Conservation Project" management team from 2006 on, as members of the Great Wall resource survey team from 2007 on, and as members of the Great Wall Conservation Research Office in 2017. Though the name of our organization has been changing in the last decade, we have done a lot of work, which is pioneering and continuous. We organized and coordinated the "Great Wall Resource Survey", established the "Great Wall Resource Conservation and Management Information System", and conducted studies of Great Wall conservation and management standards and Great Wall monitoring. We developed *Guidance on Conservation and Maintenance Work of the Great Wall Conservation and Maintenance* and *Work Constructive Opinion for Great Wall "Four Basic Works,* undertook "oversight of compliance with *Regulation on the Conservation of Great Wall*" commissioned by the State Administration of Cultural Heritage (SACH), and did a lot of other work.

This report was written by the Great Wall Conservation Research Office of the CACH. Research fellow Yu Bing, has presided over the summary and evaluation of the Great Wall for ten years, directed and attended the design of evaluation framework and sci-tech route, data investigation and analysis. *Chapter 1: Great Wall Survey and Resource Summary* was written by Zhang Yimeng and Liu Wenyan; *Chapter 2: Great Wall Lawmaking and Management System* was written by Li Dawei, Zhang Yimeng and Xu Huijun; *Chapter 3: Conservation and Maintenance of the Great Wall* was written by Li Dawei; *Chapter 4: The Great Wall Research and Achievements* and *Chapter 6: Great Wall Conservation: Challenges and Prospects* were written by Zhang Yimeng; and *Chapter 5: Great Wall Tourism and the Promotion of and Education in Great Wall*

刘文艳完成统稿，刘文艳组织专家评审、英文稿件翻译和出版等相关事宜。国家文物局黄晓帆同志对本书框架结构、文字内容提供了宝贵的意见和建议，在此表示特别感谢！

本报告内容以政府工作为主，也会涉及社会长城保护利用工作。报告中的数据，主要来源于长城沿线各级文物部门。也有部分数据由编写组独立收集。一些由民间团体、志愿者也为报告提供了数据，特此说明。

报告在编写过程中得到了国家文物局、中国文化遗产研究院领导的支持，得到了很多专家的专业指导，特别是刘曙光、吴加安、乔云飞、乔梁、张之平、杨新、张克贵、李永革、兰立志、汤羽扬、段清波、田林、朱宇华、陈平、次立新、刘剑等参加了现场评估工作。长城沿线各级文物局、文管所为报告编写组的调研工作予以大力协助；国家基础地理信息中心、国信司南（北京）地理信息技术有限公司依托长城信息系统专门开发了十年评估数据采集系统，协助进行了大量数据校核工作，并为报告制作了部分图件；天津大学、北京建筑大学、中国建筑设计研究院有限公司、北京市文物研究所，部分长城保护规划编制机构、长城保护维修方案设计和施工、监理单位，中国长城学会、国际长城之友协会、长城小站、凤凰出版传媒集团等科研机构、民间长城保护组织和热心长城公益事业的企业，以及积极参与长城研究与保护的民间志愿者为报告的出版提供了大量珍贵的数据。在此，我们对他们的支持一并表示感谢，同时向长期支持、参与长城保护的各方人士致敬。长城保护意义重大，任务艰巨。面对挑战，我们必须采取更加有力的行动，全面提高长城保护水平，实现长城文化遗产的永续保护和长城精神的传承弘扬，发挥文化遗产保护在坚定文化自信、推进“五位一体”建设中的重要作用，为实现“两个一百年”奋斗目标和中华民族伟大复兴中国梦而奋斗！

中国文化遗产研究院

2017 年 7 月

*Conservation Awareness* was written by Xu Huijun. This report was finalised by Zhang Yimeng and Liu Wenyan. Liu organized experts to review it, and handled its translation into English and publication and other relevant matters. We also extend our special gratitude to Huang Xiaofan from SACH who contributed valuable opinions and suggestions to the framework and contents of the report.

The report mainly focuses on the governmental work and involves the society's conservation and utilization of the Great Wall. The data in this report primarily came from cultural heritage administrations at all levels in the areas along the Great Wall. And some data were independently collected by the report compilation group. Some data provided by nongovernmental organizations and volunteers are also included in this report.

This report was written with the support from leaders of the SACH and the CACH and professional guidance from many experts, especially Liu Shuguang, Wu Jia'an, Qiao Yunfei, Qiao Liang, Zhang Zhiping, Yang Xin, Zhang Kegui, Li Yongge, Lan Lizhi, Tang Yuyang, Duan Qingbo, Tian Lin, Zhu Yuhua, Chen Ping, Ci Lixin and Liu Jian etc. attended the field evaluation. Cultural heritage administrations at all levels in the areas along the Great Wall helped a lot with the investigations carried out by the writing group for this report. The National Geomatics Centre of China and Geo-Compass (Beijing) Information Technology Co., Ltd. developed the ten-year data collection system based on the Great Wall Information System, offered assistance in verification of considerable data and drew part of the figures in this report.Tianjin University, Beijing University of Civil Engineering and Architecture, China Institute of Architectural Design, Beijing Municipal Institute of Cultural Heritage, some organs involved in Great Wall conservation planning, entities undertaking the development of Great Wall conservation and maintenance plans and subsequent construction and supervision, the Great Wall Society of China, the International Friends of the Great Wall, the Great Wall Station, Phoenix Publishing & Media Group and other research institutions, nongovernmental Great Wall conservation organizations, enterprises helping conserve the Great Wall and nongovernmental volunteers proactively involved in Great Wall studies and conservation provided a great deal of valuable data for the publication of this report. We thank them for their support, and pay homage to all those who have long been supporting and being involved in Great Wall conservation, which is a significant, arduous task. In face of challenges, we must take more forceful measures to fully improve Great Wall conservation, achieve the sustainable conservation of the Great Wall and the inheritance and promotion of the spirit associated with the Great Wall, and give play to the important role of cultural heritage conservation in deepening our confidence in Chinese culture and "promoting economic, political, cultural, social and ecological progress", and must strive for achieving the "Two Centenary Goals" and realizing the Chinese Dream of the great rejuvenation of the Chinese nation.

Chinese Academy of Cultural Heritage

July 2017